The Road to Spindletop

THE ROAD TO SPINDLETOP

Economic Change in Texas, 1875–1901

by John Stricklin Spratt

Drawings by Ed Bearden

Published in Cooperation with
The Texas State Historical Association

UNIVERSITY OF TEXAS PRESS, AUSTIN

HOUSTON PUBLIC LIBRARY

International Standard Book Number 0-292-70030-X
Library of Congress Catalog Card Number 55-8782
Copyright 1955 by Southern Methodist University Press
All rights reserved
Original hardcover edition published by
Southern Methodist University Press, 1955
Texas History Paperback, 1970
Reprinted by special arrangement with
Southern Methodist University Press
Printed in the United States of America

Second Paperback Printing, 1983

Requests for permission to reproduce material from this work
should be sent to Permissions, University of Texas Press,
Box 7819, Austin, Texas 78712.

To
Nan, John, and Tom

Preface

What has happened in history constitutes the only intelligent basis by which the bent of the unknown future may be judged. As I write there lies before me a pamphlet from a Federal Reserve Bank entitled *Selected Economic Indicators*. The text and the accompanying diagrams treat of nothing but trends. In some charts the trend lines originate in the 1920's; others begin in the thirties, and some start as late as the forties. Every line points to the future in a most positive manner — up, down, or horizontal. Many government reports are not reports at all; they are projections or forecasts.

The average businessman may be somewhat contemptuous of history — social, political, or economic. Few people, however, make a more consistent use of history than do successful businessmen. With a view of determining future policy they examine their books and records carefully in conjunction with prevailing economic conditions. As their barometer of history plus current conditions indicates the trend of the economic weather of tomorrow — fair, foul, or unchanged — they set future courses for their business. Leaders of organized labor resort to the same devices in determining the nature of demands to be incorporated in new labor contracts.

Certainly the future may not unfold as anticipated. But if all factors have been carefully analyzed, the chances of failure are fewer than if decisions are made by rule of thumb. A familiarity with and use of economic history should enable society to steer a course that will avoid repetition of some of the worst mistakes of the past.

The purpose of this book is to detect and explore discernible economic trends in the development of Texas during the last quarter of the nineteenth century, and to determine the significance of these long-range indicators. The trends reveal a large degree of metamorphosis in the economic system of the state. Such rapid changes in an economy — whether created by depressions, inflations, or a transition from an independent agricultural live-at-home society to a dependent industrialized commercialized one — always generate economic problems. Consequently, attention is given to the efforts of the people of Texas during this period to work their way out of their dilemmas.

The writer of state or local history has not assigned himself an easy task. A state is not an isolated culture. It is part of a region, a unit of the nation. Thus it is progressive, average, or backward depending on the rate and stage of progress of the region or of the nation.

Texas pioneers brought cultures from Northwest Europe and the Iberian Peninsula. The immense sweep of history enmeshes each generation in yesterday's culture pattern. Texas immigrants faced a strange environment, and bits of their culture made obsolete by the new surroundings were discarded or altered and a few new tools and ideas were added. Texas ranching differed considerably from eastern practices. Dry-land farming was unknown east of the Mississippi. Oil well production was thought of in terms of hundreds of barrels until Spindletop. Industrial know-how increased as new tools and drilling techniques followed in the wake of "big oil" in Texas. Texans borrowed heavily from the old; they made some contributions of their own.

Why delimit this study to the last quarter of the nineteenth century? From 1836 to 1875 Texans had gone through a series of wars and their aftermaths. The year 1875 opens a quarter-century of development uninterrupted by war. Texas at that time stood about where the nation had stood a hundred years earlier; approximately 95 per cent of the population was agrarian. Three-fifths of the state was still a wilderness occupied by Indian and buffalo.

Within a short generation the wilderness had become an empire. Ten thousand miles of railroad spanned the state. Agriculture had moved far along the road from live-at-home to commercialization. Percentagewise, urban population was increasing much faster than rural. Industry was in a position to challenge the economic leadership of agriculture. Then came the Spindletop "gusher," an event of sufficient magnitude to change petroleum from an industry of illuminating oil to an industry of fuels, and to alter materially the course of economic growth in Texas.

This volume does not by any means represent an attempt at a definitive history of the economic growth of Texas during the period considered — or an anecdotal one. To be sure, it contains both narrative and anecdotes, but it is hoped that both, whenever they are used, may emphasize some trend, throw light on some problem, or suggest the nature of the approach to its solution.

JOHN S. SPRATT

Dallas, Texas
April 2, 1955

Foreword

IN a large measure historical writing consists of putting together the author's gleanings of a lifetime; hence any list of acknowledgments is only partial. The cataloguing is usually confined to those works and persons contributing to or aiding in the last stages of the writing. Thanks are here extended in the customary manner. In the preparation of this work the library staffs of the University of Texas and Southern Methodist University have been most co-operative. Rare indeed has been the student who ever studied under either Professor Walter Prescott Webb or Professor J. Frank Dobie at the University of Texas who has not carried with him through life an undying interest in the history of the Southwest. I am greatly indebted to Professor C. A. Wiley of the University of Texas for his gift of a refreshing perspective on agriculture and its problems. My deepest gratitude goes to Professor Ruth A. Allen, also of the University of Texas, who endured the tedium of reading and revising the manuscript. Any merit the study may have stems from her timely criticisms and suggestions. And Mrs. Margaret L. Hartley of the SMU Press has smoothed out many passages and contributed numerous suggestions for clarifying the text. My son, Dr. John S. Spratt, Jr., read the whole of the manuscript and criticized it from the standpoint of the lay reader. Any and all faults and weaknesses of the study are mine and mine alone. In the following paragraphs, I have undertaken a brief and partial analysis of the merits of some of the printed sources used in the preparation of this study.

For comparative measurement of economic development one must rely on statistical material compiled by agencies of the United States government, none of which — not even the decennial reports of the Bureau of the Census — can be used with complete satisfaction. In the census report for 1870 prices were quoted in paper money, thereby distorting comparisons with 1880 when deflation had followed passage of the Resumption Act. Not until 1890 did the bureau enter salaries and salaried officials separately from wages and wage earners. In 1900 plantation gins were finally enumerated in the count of cotton gins, and for the first time the census incorporated adequate data on cottonseed. Data from government reports are not used in this volume with the intent to show exactitude; rather, they are employed to depict trends and as measuring rods for comparative purposes. Since most of the data are confined to Texas, the comparisons based on them are probably more accurate than would have been the case had they been used for interstate analyses. In order that the picture may be more nearly complete, government reports have been supplemented by data from other sources.

In the mid-nineties the United States Department of Agriculture began publishing its *Yearbook*. These annual reports furnish crop data for most of the years of the nineteenth century and are perhaps the best source of material on improved acreage, acreage harvested, crop production, and farm prices. Reports given for early years of the century are undoubtedly based on estimate. The wisdom of the departmental policy of using December farm prices in the *Yearbook* is questionable. When December prices are employed as the basis for reckoning farmer income, the estimated income is greater than the realized return. Farmers usually marketed at the peak of the harvest and received lower prices for the bulk of their corn, wheat, oats, cotton, and livestock. By December, commodity prices had climbed above those early season lows.

In 1896 the United States Department of Agriculture published *The Cotton Plant*, which included a summary of findings on insects, pests, and diseases detrimental to the plant, along with the best-known methods for the control of insects and diseases, and descriptions of the most advanced practices of cultivation. The bulletin devoted little attention to cottonseed, but the omission is understandable since the real worth of the seed and its by-products was not fully realized until World War I. At the time of its appearance,

The Cotton Plant was probably the most nearly definitive work on cotton culture. *The Laws of Texas 1822-1897* (10 volumes), edited by H. P. N. Gammel, was useful in tracing the development of railroad and other legislation having a direct bearing on economic conditions. The carefully and well prepared index volume is a saver of time and effort.

The first eleven *Annual Reports of the Railroad Commission of the State of Texas* (1893-1903) include a wealth of material on the growth of the structure of Texas freight rates during the period antedating the existence of the commission, and detailing the work of the commission in its early years in regulating freight rates and passenger fares. The reports summarize court battles in which railroads challenged the constitutionality of the agency and its right to function. Though biased in favor of the commission, the reports are rich in source material relative to problems of railroad development and regulation. *Reagan v. Farmer's Loan and Trust Company, United States Supreme Court Reports 154,* is a necessary supplement to the commission's account of its struggle with the railroads on the question of its constitutionality.

The annual *Report of the Secretary of State of the State of Texas* for 1881 and 1882 and the *Biennial Report* for 1884, 1890, 1892, 1898, 1900, and 1904 contain summaries of data on corporate charters issued by the secretary during the course of the year or the biennium, and all save one list the amount of capital stock authorized in each charter. The reports serve as a barometer of industrial development. The *Texas Legislative Manual for the Forty-fifth Legislature* was helpful in tracing the evolution of the state constitution by amendment, especially those amendments relating to the public schools and to the Railroad Commission.

The Texas State Grange of the Patrons of Husbandry was functioning in 1873. Through it the farmers sought to solve agrarian problems. *Minutes* or *Proceedings of the Annual Sessions of the Texas State Grange, Patrons of Husbandry,* as also *Minutes of the Annual Meetings of the Texas Co-operative Association, Patrons of Husbandry,* and *Minutes of the Texas Mutual Insurance Association* have faults and merits common to such records. They usually contain the annual address by the principal officer of the organization and comments by the secretary, but restrict to a minimum details of the proceedings of the annual sessions of the state assemblies. From their records it is impossible to determine with any degree of accuracy the size of the Grange membership, the amount of capital funds invested in the co-operative ventures, or the volume of business transacted by the co-operative associations. *Platforms of Political Parties in Texas,* compiled by E. W. Winkler, includes statements of policies and purposes of the Texas State Grange and was helpful in rounding out the picture of official Grange objectives.

A number of specialized secondary works which confine their interest to Texas exclusively or to the Southwest with considerable emphasis on Texas have been carefully examined. The rise of organized labor, long a forgotten chapter in the history of the state, has been treated in a scholarly manner by Ruth A. Allen in her *Chapters in the History of Organized Labor in Texas* and *The Great Southwest Strike.* The writer has drawn heavily from material in these two monographs and from contemporary newspapers in preparing his labor chapter. *Making the Constitution of Texas of 1876* and *Texas During the Regime of E. J. Davis,* by S. S. McKay, stand alone as microscopic studies of political unrest generated by economic conditions at the close of Reconstruction.

In 1875 millions of acres of Texas land were still owned by the state. The intriguing story of the disposal of public lands has been the theme of more than one intensive study. A. S. Lang, in his *Financial History of the Public Lands in Texas,* centers his attention on monetary returns to state, to public education, and to eleemosynary institutions from sale of the lands. Reuben McKitrick, in *The Public Land System of Texas, 1823-1910,* emphasizes the land laws and makes critical comparisons between the Texas and federal public land programs. Since no financial history of the state for the last quarter of the nineteenth century could ignore the land question, E. T. Miller gave considerable attention to public land policy in his *Financial History of Texas.* The thoroughness of the authors of these studies makes it unlikely that any significant aspect of the Texas public land policy has been overlooked.

Railroad Transportation in Texas, by C. S. Potts, is brief but is perhaps the most scholarly work on the development of Texas railroads and the consequent conflict between the roads and the populace. A later study by S. G. Reed, *A History of Texas Railroads,* a more comprehensive study but less carefully documented than Potts's, offers valuable contributions, including statistics on commodity tonnages hauled by railroads, and emphasizes the role of the railroads in the settlement of the state and the aid they extended to the development of industry. T. A. Fetter in his *Southwestern Freight Rates* clarifies the intricacies of the early structure of Texas freight rates. *The Building of the Texas and Pacific Railway* by S. B. McAlister is a scholarly contribution which not only depicts the tasks involved in building a frontier railroad but also evaluates the importance of the road to the economic development of its trade territory. *Boll Weevil: Recollections of the Trinity & Brazos Valley Railroad,* by J. L. Allhands, although postdating the period covered by this study, throws some light on early day railroading in Texas.

Grievances of the farmer and his efforts to solve them by political action through his own party constitute the core of Roscoe C. Martin's *The People's Party in Texas,* which is probably the best work on unrest of Texas farmers in the closing decades of the nineteenth century. A rough draft of a dissertation by Herbert Rock Edwards on the "Texas State Grange" is filed in the archives of the University of Texas. Much of his material was taken from the *Waco Examiner,* for a number of years the official newspaper of the State Grange. The raw stage in which the study was left makes it cumbersome to use, but the factual data seem well chosen, although verification is difficult because of indefinite references. Two widely recognized works by Solon J. Buck, *The Agrarian Crusade* and *The Granger Movement 1870-1880,* are valuable aids in visualizing the broad aspects of agrarian problems in the last half of the century. *The Populist Revolt* by John D. Hicks is widely accepted as an excellent treatise on farmer efforts to cope with economic problems through the People's party. Since the party evolved from the Farmers' Alliance, which originated in Texas, Hicks devotes a portion of his book to the early history of the Alliance. Robert Lee Hunt's *A History of Farmer Movements in the Southwest 1873-1925* is a brief but usable summary of regional agrarian unrest.

As a study of a leader of a farmer movement, A. J. *Rose, Agrarian Crusader of Texas,* by Ralph Adam Smith, stands virtually alone in a field which historians and biographers have neglected. For almost twenty years Rose was the leading spirit of the Texas Grange, and much of its policy was undoubtedly formulated by him. At that time the Texas State Grange exerted a powerful influence on questions of public policy. The contributions of A. J. Rose merit further study. In the archives of the University of Texas is a brief manuscript entitled "The Farmers Alliance," written in 1920 by C. W. Macune, leading figure in the meteoric rise and fall of the Texas Alliance. With the passage of time Macune had mellowed, and he wrote the paper in a fairly objective manner. Since he probably relied to a large extent on memory, the manuscript possesses the virtues and faults common to memoirs.

Two works devoted exclusively to cotton were extremely helpful. M. B. Hammond, author of *The Cotton Industry,* seems to have been the outstanding authority on cotton as the nineteenth century drew to a close. His work on cotton was exhaustive, and his conclusions must, therefore, share the responsibility for perpetuating the legend that cotton beggared and impoverished the South. The second work, a study by James A. B. Scherer, *Cotton As a World Power,* emphasizes the political and economic importance of cotton in world trade. Scherer traces the historical significance of the plant in the Orient and among the American aborigines and analyzes its broad economic impact on the economy of the South.

Alkali Trails or Social and Economic Movements of the Texas Frontier, 1846-1900, by W. C. Holden, is a scholarly study (delightful to read) of the western and Panhandle areas of the state. The work, emphasizing both farming and livestock raising, centers on the development and problems of agriculture. B. B. Paddock writes largely of the same period and regions in his *A Twentieth Century Historical and Biographical Record of North and West Texas.* Paddock was an editor in the early days of Fort Worth, serving for years with the *Democrat.* He was particularly interested in railroad building and the growth of the livestock industry, and devotes most of the historical portion of his work to these topics. Even though the author preserved much worth-while material, his work is poorly organized. Much of the writing resembles a memoir, bolstered by frequent quotations from the *Democrat*.

Rudolf Alexander Clemen, in his *The American Livestock and Meat Industry*, covers all phases of the livestock and meat processing industries, including the role of Texas cattle and horses in seeding the western ranges and in developing the Chicago market. He also describes the impact of the expansion of railroads and the perfecting of the refrigerator car on meat producing and processing industries. Edward Everett Dale's *Cow Country* and Ernest Staple Osgood's *The Day of the Cattleman* are restricted to narrower fields; primarily they treat of the range and ranch industry. Osgood centers his attention on the northern ranges but turns to Texas as the source of the herds first driven to northern grazing lands. Dale and Osgood emphasize aspects of the cattle kingdom only lightly touched by Clemen.

Although the majority of local and county histories are poorly done and leave the reader with a feeling of frustration, there are brilliant exceptions. A gem among the better local histories is *The History of Bell County*, by George W. Tyler. Tyler, a Bell County pioneer, relates in an interesting, factual, analytical, and interpretative fashion his rich story of the development of the county. In the field of local history the volume has few peers and no superiors. *The Red River Valley Then and Now* is a worth-while work on the development of northeast Texas by A. W. Neville, who, like Paddock, served many years as a newspaperman in the region about which he wrote. From the nature of the title one would expect sharp contrasts to be drawn between early days and recent times. Neville wrote a readable story, but one feels that the "Then and Now" portion of the title was somewhat neglected.

A good cataloguing of industries located in early German settlements was found in Moritz Philipp Georg Tiling's *History of the German Element in Texas from 1820-1850, and Historical Sketches of the German Singers' League and Houston Turnverein from 1853-1913*. Even though the Tiling catalogue of German industry antedates the period of this study, it has been employed since the nature of shops and industries in Texas underwent little change between 1850 and 1870. In *Dallas County, A Record of Its Pioneers and Progress,* by John H. Cochran, is found a good description of the migratory character of pioneer industry. Carrie J. Crouch, in her *Young County History and Biography,* has done some creditable work in unearthing material on the drought period of 1885-87.

In *Boom Town, the Story of Thurber,* by Weldon Hardman, there are gems from forgotten pages of the history of the development of the coal fields in Palo Pinto and Erath counties, including episodes from the early period of organized labor in Texas. Hardman's material probably came from pioneer mine workers and mining officials with whom he and his family were well acquainted. One regrets that he was not interested in doing a more thorough job. Thomas L. Nugent, twice the People's party candidate for governor of Texas, is the subject of a volume entitled *Life Work of Thomas L. Nugent.* The book, edited and published by his wife, is a mixture of his own political speeches and writings and of eulogies by friends and colleagues. Its chief value lies in the portrayal of the aims and objectives of the Populists as interpreted by Nugent, who was the party leader and principal spokesman in Texas.

When tens of thousands of people are on the move in search of new homes in wilderness regions, almanacs and immigrant guide books play important roles. As was characteristic of this type of publication, those boosting Texas included every morsel of information that might attract another settler. None was published with regularity; most appeared only once or twice. During the quarter-century the *Galveston Daily News* did not publish an issue of its almanac. Editors of the pamphlets relied to some extent on census reports, but most of the material and data were drawn from real or alleged experiences of residents of the state. The almanacs and guides were well salted with success stories of men engaged in agriculture and industry. There were articles on the qualities of the mesquite as a leather tanning agent; on the phenomenal rise of the impoverished shepherd to the status of a wealthy sheepman; on the possibility that hemp might be replaced by yucca (provided, of course, the necessary capital could be raised to finance the project); on how a farmer and his wife by their own labor exclusively raised $900 worth of produce on a small Texas farm.

The publications repeatedly reminded the immigrant of the availability of free land and emphasized the cheapness of land in or near settlements. All emphatically claimed that any crop successfully grown in the temperate zone could be raised profitably in Texas, and some also included plants of the tropics. Almanac editors were never hesitant to reprint letters and articles which were lifted from newspapers wherein the writers developed or repeated ideas on agriculture, industry, soils, climate, and successful crop or industrial experiments. Since the primary purpose of the early almanacs was to induce immigration, they were prone to overstate the good and understate the bad features of Texas. Among those available to the author were: *Texas Almanac for 1870, and Emigrant's Guide to Texas;* Homer S. Thrall's *The People's Illustrated Almanac, Texas Hand-book and Immigrants' Guide for 1880;* and *Burke's Texas Almanac and Immigrant's Handbook for 1882.*

At the close of the seventies, for the purpose of inducing a larger flow of immigration into the state, a number of Texas railroads formed the Southwestern Immigration Company. In 1880 the company issued, under the supervision of W. W. Lang, a handbook entitled *The State of Texas.* The pamphlet was not radically different from its contemporaries, except that it especially emphasized features of the counties served by railroads sustaining the project.

C. W. Raines compiled a *Year Book for Texas, 1901,* followed a year later by a second volume. He had served as state librarian and drew heavily from data compiled in reports by state agencies. Raines also included some census material. In addition, the editor published a number of articles which had been prepared at his request by those well versed in the affairs of certain industries; for example, the secretary of the Lumbermen's Association supplied an essay on the lumber industry. Raines devoted more attention to industry than did editors of earlier almanacs. This may be regarded as evidence that, over the course of twenty-five years, the importance of industry had greatly increased as compared to that of agriculture. The Raines books are good sources on economic conditions at the turn of the century. In 1904 A. H. Belo & Company once again began publication of the *Texas Almanac and State Industrial Guide.* In volume of material the Belo almanacs are second only to official government reports, and they often include data not readily found elsewhere.

The Texas Business Directory for 1878-79 was probably the fruit of an advertising promotional scheme. It definitely does not enumerate all business establishments operating in the state at that time; however, it has some worth in that light is shed on the number, kind, and dispersion of commercial enterprises, shops, industries, and professional men. Likewise, it is difficult to determine whether the *Directory of the City of Dallas for 1878-79* was all-inclusive or whether its listings were restricted to the names of subscribers only. Listings in the Dallas directory were more nearly complete than in the state directory. The city directory undoubtedly gives a fairly complete idea of the number and types of business enterprises to be found in the larger Texas towns at the close of the seventies. Its duplications, e.g., the enumerating of a general store and then the naming of its hat, shoe, saddle, grocery, and dry goods departments as separate establishments, are troublesome to anyone attempting to count or classify distinct business units.

A number of histories have been helpful. Some of those relied on treated the whole of the West or the Southwest; others were confined almost entirely to Texas; and some were limited to specific industries or social or political topics on a regional or national scale. One of the more scholarly histories of the state, edited and brought down to 1914 by Eugene C. Barker and Ernest W. Winkler, is *History of Texas and Texans, 1799-1884*, by F. W. Johnson. This work, published in five volumes, presents a balanced treatment of social, political, and economic conditions. From *A Comprehensive History of Texas, 1685-1897*, edited by D. G. Wooten, the section contributed by O. M. Roberts, "The Political, Legislative and Judicial History of Texas for Its Fifty Years of Statehood, 1845-1895," concentrates almost exclusively on political history. But Roberts, a governor of the state during the eighties, speaks authoritatively, and his discussion of the political battles over the enactment of regulatory legislation for railroads is very good. *A History of Texas from Wilderness to Commonwealth*, by Louis J. Wortham, is slanted almost entirely toward the romantic and heroic phases and has little to offer the economic historian. In *The Greater Southwest,* by Rupert N. Richardson and Carl Coke Rister, and *The South-western Frontier 1865-1881*, by Carl Coke Rister, the concentration of interest is primarily on the development of the livestock industry.

In *East Texas, Its History and Its Makers*, T. C. Richardson follows the history of East Texas in much the same fashion as does Paddock in his history of the western and Panhandle regions. The niggardliness in the use of references makes a check on accuracy needlessly difficult. Carl Coke Rister's *Oil! Titan of the Southwest*, a very readable book, is probably the most comprehensive volume on the petroleum industry of the region. The author did a fine bit of work in piecing together the story of the search for oil from the time of the early known sipes and accidental discoveries to the day of serious exploration and development. Rister was primarily concerned with relating a story — the story of oil. Chapters on fences, water, and cattle from that pioneer study of the Great Plains and their impact on social and economic structures, *The Great Plains*, by Walter Prescott Webb, were most helpful.

This study relies on *A History of the Presidency* by E. Stanwood for platforms of the People's party for the presidential campaigns of 1892 and 1896. This work by Stanwood has long been recognized as a classic, and his story of the influence of the Populists in the last two presidential elections of the century help round out the finale of the Farmers' Alliance. Marcus L. Hansen's *The Immigrant in American History* is an excellent little volume from the pen of one who spent years seeking answers to the question: Why did the immigrant emigrate?

The volumes of the *Southwestern Historical Quarterly* are indispensable to the serious scholar of Texas history. Many of the highly specialized studies were done by authors who have had access to sources and records not available to scholars in general. They have spent countless hours digging in their little crannies and turning out brilliant pieces of work which become accessible to the scholar working in broader areas. Some of the articles were written by men who played lead or minor roles in fashioning the political and economic courses now dominant in Texas.

Material or ideas have been borrowed from several articles in the *Quarterly*. Edwin P. Arneson's "Early Irrigation in Texas" is an excellent study on one of the oldest phases of agriculture transported by Europeans to Texas. Texas Indians apparently made no use of irrigation. Harley True Burton's "A History of the J A Ranch" analyzes the problems encountered in converting from range to ranch, the significance of transportation, the rancher's fear of the farmer, and the struggle between rancher and farmer for control of the grazing lands. The legislative fights over setting up a state railroad commission are reviewed by M. M. Crane in his "Recollections of the Establishment of the Texas Railroad Commission." Crane was one of the leaders of the procommission forces. He wrote the article some forty-five years after the commission was created, when time had long since soothed any rancor he might have held toward political opponents.

The fence-cutting wars constitute one of the nastier pages in Texas history, and Wayne Gard's "The Fence-Cutters" is probably one of the best studies ever made on this episode. "Texas Fever," by T. R. Havins, represents thorough research on a disease of cattle which had much to do with changing the nature of the livestock industry in the state.

State law set aside alternate sections of the range as public school lands, an action which precipitated a conflict between large cattle outfits who wanted to enclose pastures of thousands of contiguous acres and settlers who desired quarter or half sections for farms. The ensuing struggle, or at least a phase of it, is the subject of W. C. Holden's "The Problem of Maintaining the Solid Range on the Spur Ranch." Holden, like Burton, had access to ranch records.

Boyce House, in "Spindletop," unearths useful and interesting material on the discovery of the oil field which made Texas petroleum-conscious. A much broader treatment of oil is found in C. A. Warner's "Texas and the Oil Industry," a brief history of oil in Texas from the date when it was first encountered by the white man.

From his research for his doctoral dissertation on A. J. Rose, Ralph Adam Smith contributed three articles to the *Quarterly:* "The Cooperative Movement in Texas, 1870-1900," "The Farmers' Alliance in Texas, 1875-1900," and "The Grange Movement in

Texas, 1873-1900." Each article is filled with significant contributions to a better understanding of agricultural problems of the
period. His story of the Alliance is probably the best brief history
of that organization. Smith's analyses of reasons for the failure of
the co-operative movement are excellent.

Legislation creating the Railroad Commission did not authorize
the agency to control the issuance of railroad securities. Without
this power the commission could not effectively regulate railroad
rates. To round out fully the regulatory powers of the agency, the
legislature enacted a stock and bond law. Charles S. Potts made a
study of the background of the law and its ultimate effect on the
enforcement powers of the commission, which he published as
"Texas Stock and Bond Law" in *Annals of the American Academy
of Political and Social Science*. Here Potts gave a full treatment
to a topic with which he had dealt only partially in his *Railroad
Transportation in Texas,* and he maintained the same high level
of scholarship shown in the earlier work. S. G. Reed, in "Land
Grants and Other Aids to Texas Railroads," in the *Southwestern
Historical Quarterly,* elaborates on topics given some consideration
in his *A History of the Texas Railroads.*

Also from the *Quarterly* came Clara M. Love's "History of the
Cattle Industry in the Southwest" and Paul S. Taylor's "Historical
Note on Dimmitt County, Texas." The article by Love is especially
good in the treatment of the early history of the cattle industry
and the origin of the longhorns. Taylor's historical note includes
an excellent brief analysis of the causes for the decline of sheep
raising in Dimmit County.

My own article, "The Cotton Miner, 1865-1910," in the *American Quarterly* develops a theme relative to the cotton farmer and
his problems which diverges from what is probably the more common point of view.

Few sources possess as much power to revitalize the past as do
contemporary newspapers. As one scans consecutive issues of old
newspapers, their pages brown, brittle, and exuding the pungent
odor of age, he finds it easy to slip from the present to the past.
In reliving the unfolding past the reader experiences to some degree
the fears, hopes, aspirations, and disillusionments of a yester-gen-

eration. As editors described the events of daily life, their towns and their industries, the information they incorporated was probably no more and no less accurate than that found in old letters, diaries, or memoirs. As a matter of fact, newspapers of the period did print a large number of letters from their readers. Most of these letters described crop conditions and usually included production estimates. Others wrote of experiences with crops and animals, thus passing on to fellow-farmers valuable tips on control of stomach worms and other parasites, or prescribing remedies for diseases of livestock; and some dwelt on personal experiences in industry which resulted in success or failure. All provide details necessary to a complete picture of their day and age.

Because of the general practice of reprinting stories from other papers, any one paper ultimately published every significant or unusual story. This sort of editing enhances the possibility of perpetuating erroneous stories – a possibility which is more than offset by the fact that time is saved in research, since careful selection of a few papers can be relied on to present every important happening. It is clearly understood that errors do creep into newspaper reporting. In a study primarily concerned with an analysis of trends, however, an occasional error regarding some detail does not distort the general picture. Moreover, if editors considered a story of sufficient importance to be run through a series of issues, mistakes occurring in early accounts were usually detected and corrected in later reports.

Over a decade G. W. Robson published his paper in three frontier towns. First it appeared as the *Frontier Echo* at Jacksboro in 1875. Then late in 1878 Robson moved west and resumed publication of his paper as the *Fort Griffin Echo*. By 1882 departure of the military detachment and disappearance of the buffalo hunters left Fort Griffin pretty much a ghost town, and Robson moved south fifteen miles, giving the paper the name of the *Albany Echo*. In February, 1884, poor health forced him to sell the *Echo* and retire from frontier journalism. He had served as a one-man chamber of commerce for each of the towns in which he located. Files of his papers unfold the development of many features of frontier counties. Robson was interested in the livestock industry and was instrumental in founding the Texas Cattle Raisers' Association. He often rode over vast areas of the unsettled western wilderness, and he wrote some of the best descriptions of that country ever penned. Few writers have surpassed Robson's colorful portrayals of frontier regions and communities.

In March, 1885, not long after the Texas & Pacific railroad was pushed through that section of the state, the *Taylor County News* began publication in Abilene. In the territory served by the *News* farming followed hard on the heels of the railroad, and this paper showed considerably more interest in the farmer than did the *Echo*. Like Robson, the publisher of the *News* was an enthusiastic booster of western Texas. Few industries were launched in Abilene or the surrounding towns and counties that were not fully reported in the columns of the *News*. The preserved files of this paper probably contain the most complete contemporary picture of the drought of 1885-87.

Until October, 1885, the *Galveston Daily News* carried a complete news coverage of the state and served as a combination of daily paper and several types of agricultural journal. It regularly reprinted one to four columns of items selected from other state papers. Its "State Press" was a daily commentary on editorial opinion of the day. The Galveston paper ran an unusually large number of letters from subscribers and others who had opinions or information to pass along. It was a clearinghouse for information on every phase of the growth and development of Texas. Stories in the *News* constitute the best account of the period of railroad construction outside of company records, many of which are not available. For many years its September 1 edition gave a résumé of the volume of business transacted in the state during the preceding twelve months. In this annual report the *News* included crop records, railroad freight moved (either by tonnage or by carloads), statements of railroad earnings and expenses, rail mileage laid, volume of imports and exports, number of ship sailings, volume of sales for the larger towns, number of cattle moved to market, and numerous other data, all of which are invaluable to the historian. If errors occurred in data collected by the *News*, they were of the same sort that would be found in census and other government reports. Data incorrectly reported to the *News* were incorrect when published, which is also true of information inaccurately furnished to government agencies.

In October, 1885, the *Galveston Daily News* ceased its efforts to make a complete news coverage of Texas. At that time it founded the *Dallas Morning News,* after which the two papers divided the state on something of a geographical basis and neither attempted responsibility for reporting all happenings. The Galveston paper confined its interests more to the southern part of the state, while the Dallas paper emphasized more the events of northern and western Texas. One valuable feature of the *Dallas Morning News* was its daily market page. From its first edition daily market prices were quoted for groceries, dry goods, farm produce, and livestock, and also for certain manufactured items. The market page was quite helpful in that its composition was not materially changed throughout the remainder of the century.

All papers of the period make occasional reference to wages currently being paid or offered farm labor, cotton pickers, craftsmen of one type or another, and railroad employees. An exasperating practice common to all was publication of the initial phase of a continuing story without a follow-up on the ultimate outcome. This characteristic makes it next to impossible to follow the course of labor disputes. A labor walkout might be reported, then never mentioned again. One is left to wonder whether the strike failed, ended in success for the workers, or was anything more than a flare of tempers between workers and foreman with all contentedly back on the job next day. For the piecing together of cohesive social, political, and economic patterns of the past, invaluable if not indispensable sources are intact files of newspapers published under the supervision of editors whose minds were alert, discerning, and penetrating.

I wish to thank the following publishers, authors, and journals for permission to quote from published works: University of Texas Press, *The Great Southwest Strike* by Ruth A. Allen; Harvard University Press, *The Immigrant in American History* by Marcus Lee Hansen, edited by Arthur M. Schlesinger; University of Minnesota Press, *The Populist Revolt* by John D. Hicks; Yale University Press,

The Agrarian Crusade by Solon J. Buck in the "Chronicles of America" series; Agricultural and Mechanical College of Texas Press, *A History of Farmer Movements in the Southwest 1873-1925* by Robert Lee Hunt; University of Wisconsin Press, *The Public Land System of Texas 1823-1910* by Reuben McKitrick; J. B. Lippincott Company, *Cotton as a World Power* by James A. B. Scherer; *Annals of the American Academy of Political and Social Science,* "Texas Stock and Bond Law," by Charles S. Potts, May 1, 1914; Eliot Jones, *Principles of Railway Transportation;* Clair M. Reed and his mother Mrs. S. G. Reed, *A History of Texas Railroads* by S. G. Reed; and *Southwestern Historical Quarterly:* "Recollections of the Establishment of the Texas Railroad Commission" by M. M. Crane, Vol. L; "A History of the J A Ranch" by Harley True Burton, Vol. XXXI; "The Farmers' Movement in Texas, 1873-1900" by Ralph A. Smith, Vol. XLII.

I also wish to express my gratitude to the *American Quarterly* which published, in Vol. IV, my article "The Cotton Miner, 1865-1910," from which I have drawn heavily for ideas in Chapter IV, "Cotton, 'Big Money Crop.'"

Contents

The Road to Spindletop

I

A Frontier Economy

WHEN streams of economic development suddenly alter their courses, turbulence and perplexity prevail where once were serenity and certainty. For the United States as a whole the last half of the nineteenth century was one of these tumultuous transitory phases, but in Texas the period of change was concentrated in the last quarter of the century. For generations progenitors of Texans had practiced the simple economy of independent self-containment. The economic pattern was understood by all. Economic well-being depended on bountiful harvests. The humble farmer prayed that rains be adequate, that plagues and pests be restrained; and at the end of the season he gave thanks to the Bountiful Giver. Money and the market were conveniences, but not essentials, to the way of life. With the co-operation of the elements the industrious family maintained a full larder, while the lot of the sluggard was penury. A shoat or two beyond the family needs, a few surplus bushels of corn, an excess of sweet potatoes, a small quantity of tobacco, or an occasional bale of cotton went to market, at times to provide a little cash but more often to be exchanged for salt, sugar, coffee, ginghams, calicoes, or possibly a plowshare.

Suddenly, Texans found themselves swept into a maelstrom of economic change caused by the conflicting countercurrents of economic self-sufficiency and dependent commercialization. The force of circumstances posed a problem for the diversified self-contained farmer; either he could continue along the old ways or he could move in the direction of specialized-commercialized farming. Each of the routes presented hazards to the individual farmer. To live as he had lived meant to exist in, but not as a part of, the new world. In the new system money and markets were indispensable elements. A bountiful harvest, formerly the assurance of plenty, now placed the farmer in a paradoxical situation of producing more and more but realizing fewer and fewer goods. The prayer that his arable acres be blessed with heavy yields became ironic. Credit, previously no great necessity, became increasingly important. A system of cheap and reliable transportation was now essential. In the market, in the banks, and in the railroads the farmer encountered that invisible, intangible legal personage, the corporation, to him the essence of greed functioning without soul or feeling. He viewed this ghostly personage as an enemy bent on his destruction. He knew how to deal with physical beings but was puzzled and perplexed at having to shadow-box this ghostlike creature. As a member of successive farmers' movements he puzzled to no avail over possible solutions to the new problems.

Likewise, during the closing decades of the century the state underwent a phenomenal degree of industrial development. Small community service shops yielded to factories of greater output. Local lumber mills were merged into giant organizations supplying world markets. The cypress belt was gutted to roof the buildings of the world. Some farmers forsook the plow in search of mineral wealth, successfully discovering commercial veins of coal and tapping pools of oil. By 1901 the output of Texas industry had increased to such an extent that its value was more than half that of the agricultural produce of the state; thus industry was presenting an ominous challenge to the continued dominance of the economy by agriculture.

As late as the close of the Civil War, however, it was difficult to detect any evidence of the pending sharp increase in industrial growth or the mushrooming of commercialized agriculture. In fact, the War Between the States had been responsible for a phenomenon unique in American history: the Texas frontier had receded eastward temporarily, reversing the usual westward movement. In the late sixties the term "wagon road" meant in most instances nothing more than that some wagons had been driven along trails blazed in earlier centuries by wild animals and Indians. Such a system of roads was wholly unsuited to the needs of either commercial agriculture or industry. In addition, the four years of hostilities had left the mileage of the state's embryonic railroad system considerably shrunken. In 1861 there had been eleven operating railroads in the state, but by 1865 four of them had been either destroyed or abandoned, and properties of the remaining seven were badly deteriorated.

Possible plans for the use of intricate labor-saving farm machinery or for the erection of great factories seemed to be checkmated by the costliness of transportation in Texas. Hence in the absence of a system of cheap transportation the practice of general farming is restricted to small units with a strong implication that agriculture is being operated on a self-contained basis. Surplus farm produce, if present at all, is available in only small quantities, which are normally disposed of on something like a barter basis to the doctor in exchange for medical services, to the merchant in exchange for his wares, or to the local editor in exchange for a subscription to his paper, or else surrendered as payment on past due accounts. During the seventies the basic feature of agriculture in Texas was production for home consumption. Because of the Civil War and the problems of the Reconstruction period, the number of improved acres per farm in the state had declined in the previous decade from 61.6 to 48.5.[1] Since improved acreage is greater than plowed acreage, which in turn exceeds the harvested acreage, the harvested area for Texas farms in 1870 probably averaged thirty acres. The produce from thirty harvested acres of a general farm provided a meager living for the farm family, regardless of the type of farming — whether the farm produced diversified crops contributing to the realization of a live-at-home ideal, or was restricted to a staple money or commercial crop.

In an agricultural economy based on production for home consumption, money prices of agricultural products are not overly important, and a drop in prices of farm products does not cause a degree of distress in rural areas comparable to the hardships engendered by declining prices in a system of commercialized agriculture. During the seventies farm produce was as acceptable as cash in purchase of local merchandise. The *Frontier Echo* (Jacksboro) pursued a common newspaper practice of repeatedly giving notice that corn, eggs, chickens, pecans, and stovewood were items acceptable in payment of subscriptions.[2] Almost every issue of weekly papers carried at least one plea to subscribers to send produce in settlement of overdue accounts. In an economy operating in this fashion money was not a necessity.

Newspaper stories often emphasized the self-contained nature of communities of the seventies. When an editor noted with pride that Jack County corn was about gathered and it was thought enough had been grown "to supply the home demand,"[3] he was rejoicing with the neighborhood that the community would no longer suffer from a dearth of corn, or that the county had become independent of other corn-producing areas. But even in a self-contained society "man does not live by bread alone." Almost everyone raised gourds in a wide variety of sizes and shapes, the largest being used as jugs or cut in half to serve as canisters. Small ones with long stems were fashioned into cups or dippers by slicing off a segment of the bulb parallel to the stem which served as a handle. Beds were crude homemade frames laced with ropes or rawhide thongs or with slats laid across them. Over the slats, ropes, or thongs was thrown a bag made of "ticking" (a thick coarse cotton cloth) cut to fit the bedframe and filled with corn shucks or straw. Over all was placed a second "tick" filled with duck or goose down or, if down was not available, with chicken or duck feathers.[4] For months or years the down or feathers had been accumulated from the plucking of domestic birds or wild ones killed by family huntsmen. Other household furnishings — tables, chairs, benches, and cupboards — usually matched the homemade bedsteads.

During the seventies, according to Sam Woody, a Wise County pioneer, making a living was easy. Farmers then, he said, regularly reaped three hundred bushels of wheat from not more than six acres. Then the grain was cradled and winnowed and hauled by ox-wagon to Dallas for milling. Flour from the wheat supplied the household of the producer and the surplus was sold or exchanged for sugar, coffee, salt, and calico. Hogs were plentiful. After having been given an identification mark by the owner, they were allowed to roam at large until "hog-killing" time, when they were driven home for butchering. The hog was on his own in foraging for food. A beef was slaughtered from time to time in order to break the monotony of a pork diet. Infrequent overland trips to Houston or Shreveport supplied coffee, some sugar (though not much because molasses was the common "sweetening"), and other staples in groceries and dry goods.[5]

An 1876 crop production and consumption estimate for Young County also suggests economic independence:

Estimated production — Wheat, 180,000 bushels; corn, 420,000 bushels; barley, 3,000 bushels; rye, 2,000 bushels. Home consumption — Wheat, 175,000 bushels; corn, 420,000 bushels; barley, 3,000 bushels; rye, 2,000 bushels. Surplus for export — Wheat, 5,000 bushels.[6]

Since the foregoing data were published in the spring of 1877, the figures probably represented known quantities of production; however, the real significance of the data lies in the revelation of a home consumption of 720,000 bushels of grain from an aggregate production of 725,000 bushels.

In analyzing conditions, contemporaries sometimes attributed the self-sufficing nature of the economy to a lack of an adequate system of cheap transportation. In an article purportedly expressing the views of producers in western Texas, the *San Antonio Express* said farmers were convinced that agricultural surpluses represented a waste of time and effort because freight charges tended to equal or exceed market prices of farm commodities.[7] If agricultural produce could not be profitably marketed, farmers were in no position to purchase goods of manufacturers. Before the coming of railroads, the inland farmers of Texas devoted their land primarily to the production of breadstuffs; after railroads reached the hinterlands freight charges declined and farmers found it advantageous to import low-priced foods, gradually shifting from a self-contained to a commercialized economy.[8]

In the seventies efforts to maintain the community as an independent economic unit were second in importance only to the operation of the individual farm on a basis of economic independence. Distance plus prohibitive transportation costs tended to encourage local diversification to the point where community output could satisfy most neighborhood needs. A local newspaper might inform its public that Mr. Watt had grown five acres of fine broom corn which could not be sold because of the distance from a broom factory. The editor probably closed his story with a proposal that the town erect a broom factory, manufacture its own brooms, and save freight charges both ways.[9] No editor recommended construction of a factory ranked lower than "first class." Texas communities did, of necessity, patronize local shops and mills. Contemporary impressions were that any industry should operate at a profit when so located that two-way freight charges — from farm to factory then from factory back to farm — were eliminated. Some historians have characterized the seventies as a decade of small-scale operators, individual or community, who produced primarily for their own consumption.[10]

In the initial issue of the *Frontier Echo*, June 30, 1875, a feature story boosted a "flouring" mill for Jacksboro. G. W. Robson, the editor, quoted prices local farmers were receiving per bushel for wheat as being $0.60 to $0.75, while the price they paid for 100 pounds of flour ranged from $4.00 to $4.50. He invited capitalists to sharpen their pencils and figure potential profits. Robson continued for a year his campaign for a local flour mill, finally reporting that Mr. Adamson had returned from the East where he had bought full mill equipment which the owner hoped to have in operation during the course of the summer. Installation difficulties of one sort or another delayed milling operations for another nine months; this gave the editor a continuing story made up of weekly progress reports. Ultimately, the *Echo* announced that flour ground at the Jacksboro mill was the basic ingredient in bread and pastries being baked by local housewives.

At the dawn of the seventies Texas was busily engaged in repairing physical damages caused by the war and its aftermath, with many of her citizens, especially among the Democrats, convinced that efforts to rebuild were being hampered by the Reconstruction government. On the eve of the Civil War trains were operating over the 451 miles of Texas railroad. During the four war years 110 miles of track were either destroyed or allowed to deteriorate because of the inability of the owners to procure new rails. Dust had scarcely settled from the last battle of the war when railroad construction in Texas was resumed. By the time the Panic of '73 again halted building activities, the railroad system had been extended to 1,578 miles. More than 500 miles of track had been laid in the early part of 1873 before the financial crash.[11] When the crisis struck, Texas & Pacific Railway construction crews working west of Dallas were scheduled to complete the road to Fort Worth by November;[12] but the panic halted the project eight miles out of Dallas, and Fort Worth was compelled to wait another three years before it became a railroad town.[13]

Since Texas mileage was so small the major effect of the Civil War on railroads was to postpone development, but the hostilities were responsible for destruction and heavy losses in other property values. Over the war decade aggregate farm values for Texas, including land, buildings, domestic animals, implements, and machinery declined from $137,186,219 to $88,777,550. Value of farm lands and buildings slumped from $88,101,320 to $48,119,960; value of domestic animals, poultry, and bees declined from $42,825,447 to $29,-940,155; and commercialized farming became extremely difficult because the value of farm implements and machinery fell from $6,259,452 to $2,717,435.[14] During this decade of decline in Texas farm values, the aggregate farm values for the nation increased by approximately a billion dollars.[15] As the national economy improved, economic conditions in Texas worsened. Thus, because of the war, the state was in a retarded economic position relative to the nation. Farmers were probably not concerned over what happened to aggregates — their problems involved wresting a living from the family farms. Within the ten years the average value of individual farm units dropped from $3,198 to $1,322, while the value of the implements and machinery declined from $146 to $44.[16] With so little machinery and so small a farm, farm families faced real hardships. And since the census of 1870 reported dollar values in terms of inflated paper money, losses in values were actually much greater than indicated by the foregoing data.

There was, however, a brighter side: some facets of the economy did not endure losses as a result of the war. By virtually every measurable index the manufacturing and mechanical industries appear to have grown. In the decade of the sixties industrial establishments grew in number from 983 to 2,399, with invested capital rising from $3,000,000 to $5,000,000, while the value of output almost doubled.[17] From the standpoint of the owner-operator conditions were not so good, because the investment per shop had declined, as had the returns. The war was responsible for a sharp increase in the number of industrial units. Because the state was relatively free from the threat of invading armies, Texans had been encouraged to launch small manufacturing enterprises for fabrication of war material. When peace came many of the shops converted to the production of civilian goods for local markets. With the collapse of the southern cause an iron foundry at Jefferson, for example, turned its manufacturing energies from guns to stoves and plowshares.[18]

Presumably banking facilities were ample for a self-contained society, but they had never been adequate to satisfy the needs of a commercial economy. In 1860, Texas had one chartered bank with a capital of $100,000, while ten years later there were four such banks whose capital and surplus aggregated $575,000.[19] In 1870, the banking capital averaged 70 cents per capita. The number of chartered banks does not present an accurate picture of credit facilities. Other credit agencies included the state (sale of public lands on credit), insurance companies, and loan associations. A relatively high percentage of loans were made by individuals. S. S. McKay viewed the low ratio of banks as a blessing in disguise. He argues that because of the small number of banks the depression of the seventies brought less financial distress to Texas than to the rest of the nation.[20]

By 1870 the population of the state had reached 818,479, an increase of 35 per cent in ten years. The greater portion of the increase came after the war as people migrated from other southern states. Rather than remain in devastated regions of the Old South and undertake the task of rebuilding the war-torn areas, many emigrated to Texas. Fear that the backwash of anti-Rebel bitterness might result in harm to their families caused southern sympathizers and former Confederate soldiers to leave the border states. The more populous eastern half of Texas suffered the heaviest economic losses from the war and its aftermath. The unsettled, or sparsely settled, western half underwent little economic distress. Molestation by Indians and other bands of marauding brigands along the tier of "frontier counties" caused the line of westernmost settlements to recede eastward to the protection of more populous communities. Otherwise, the west of Texas suffered no ill effects from the war.

In the sixties twenty counties, selected from the eastern and southern half of the state on the bases of geographic dispersion and their current economic importance,[21] suffered a decline in aggregate farm value from $29,170,818[22] to $16,652,882.[23] Twenty counties, chosen on the same bases from the western half of the state,[24] endured a relatively small loss in farm value from $481,926 to $411,-259. Value of the average farm in the eastern counties decreased from $4,398 to $1,414, while in the western counties it rose from $600 to $613. Increase in the number of farms from 6,630 to 11,778 partially accounts for the great decrease in average farm values in the eastern area. Western farms decreased in number from 804 to 671, so that their average value was left virtually unchanged. War and Reconstruction tended to reduce eastern plantations to the level of self-contained farms, while western farms simply remained at the subsistence level.

As a result of the over-all decrease in the size and value of the Texas farm, average production per unit was much less in 1870 than in 1860. Almost the only crop registering an increased output for all sections of the state was corn. Increases in either value or quantity for crops or livestock in certain sections were more than offset by decreases in value or quantity or both in other localities. The swine population rose in the western counties from 14,676 to 17,466, but declined in the eastern counties from 252,385 to 221,000, leaving a net loss of 28,765 in the hog tally. The number of milch cows decreased in every section of the state.

Cotton production increased during the war decade by a total of 5,458 bales, but the sharp rise in the number of farms reduced the average per farm output from 8 to 5.7 bales; and in spite of a rise in the price of lint, the majority of cotton farmers probably faced a serious financial plight. A survey of the effects of the sixties on economic conditions in Texas leads to one conclusion: in 1870, the average Texan possessed less wealth and enjoyed fewer consumer goods than he had in the forties and fifties. In his task of making an economic comeback he was further handicapped in that he possessed a smaller farm or owned a smaller shop, and toiled in either farm or shop with fewer tools.

Many contemporaries realized that they were in the process of economic change, and a few might have characterized it as a revolutionary displacement of the old system. Some perceived the trend away from the prevailing agricultural economy of production for home consumption toward a production of staples for the market. At no time during the last twenty-five or thirty years of the nineteenth century did either type of agriculture prevail to the exclusion of the other. The overlapping of dissimilar economic systems creates economic problems. Agricultural systems as diverse as production for consumption and production for the market operate from divergent standards and with different objectives; each requires its distinct tools and techniques. When the two systems operate within a given economy, irreconcilable conflicts ensue and questions of economic policy become acute.

The economic development of Texas has been hampered by provisions of the constitution drafted in 1875 by a convention which was dominated by proponents of a self-contained agricultural economy. Immediately following the Civil War the Democrats adopted a constitution designed to satisfy postwar conditions, an instrument which in 1869 was replaced by what is popularly known as the Radical Republican constitution. Many provisions of the Republican constitution would today be pronounced good. Among other things, they outlined an ambitious plan for a system of public education with centralized responsibility. From the day the Radical Republican constitution became effective, however, it was bitterly denounced by Democrats who never made the reasons for their dislike very clear.[25] That the constitution was of Republican origin was probably deemed sufficient reason to place it among the damned.

Had the Republican constitution been prepared under divine guidance, it still would not have been pleasing in the eyes of the Democrats. "Our constitution is very defective; it ought to be amended," became the most effective argument against the fundamental law. Later, Democrats levied the more specific charge that the constitution permitted the carpetbag governor, E. J. Davis, to inaugurate his obnoxious (in Democratic eyes) policies. As has been the case under similar circumstances, ousting the radical (Republican) party brought to power the conservative wing of the Democratic party, who were abetted by members of the Patrons of Husbandry. Democrats and Grangers dominated the convention which drafted the Constitution of 1876.

Responsibility for numerous articles of the new instrument which bore directly on economic matters has been charged to the Grangers. At the time of the constituent convention, the State Grange was at its peak in membership and influence; and, although it insisted that it was nonpolitical, for a few years the agrarian organization exerted a powerful influence on Texas politics. Under the heading of fraternal business Patrons of Husbandry always included for discussion questions on public policy considered important to farmers. McKay estimates that fully half the delegates to the constitutional convention were Grangers.[26] On the convention floor their views often prevailed. The farmer organization and its members were bitterly opposed to monopoly, and constitutional provisions restraining corporate actions, railroads, and railroad practices were incorporated at their insistence. Since Grangers considered banks as part of the superstructure of monopoly, the new constitution denied state agencies the power to charter banks. The Patrons apparently considered all taxes oppressive, and virtually every government expenditure an extravagance, and stubbornly insisted on reductions in both. Granger delegates who had been schooled in the money-scarce economy of self-sufficiency were responsible for constitutional provisions stipulating low salaries for public officials and biennial, rather than annual, legislative sessions.

Constitutional restrictions which barred tax levies for the support of public education were the work of Grangers, and for ten years the absence of funds made a farce of free public schools. Schools suffered from financial malnutrition, and the educational structure was permanently stunted. Most of Article VII, devoted exclusively to public education, spelled out detailed provisions regarding the allocation and disposal of public school lands. The article provided for a state available school fund but made no arrangement for permanent school districts, without which no bonds could be voted and no taxes collected for erection and maintenance of local schools. Under the Radical Republican constitution the established public school system was probably on too ambitious a scale for a frontier society; if so, the Constitution of 1876 went to the other extreme and virtually destroyed the public schools.

In the eyes of the convention the railroad problem was of sufficient importance to merit special treatment. Article X was restricted to railroads, declaring them to be public highways and common carriers. The companies were forbidden to buy or control competing lines, and the legislature was authorized to fix reasonable freight rates and passenger fares. Indirectly Article III, Section 52, denying the right of political corporations to extend credit to, grant public funds to, or become stockholders in corporations was applicable to railroads. The provision stopped the custom employed by cities and counties of voting bonds to foster the construction of railroads. Legislative issuance of special charters to railroads and other groups was prohibited by Article XII, which required that henceforth all private corporations be created under general laws. By Article XIV railroad land grants were limited to not more than sixteen sections for each mile of main line constructed, equipped, and in operation.

These provisions of the Constitution of 1876 established a basis for regulation and control of railroads, and in addition offered some inducement to future development of the rail system. Railroads, railroad policies and practices, and railroad freight rates were fundamental to the transition of agriculture from self-sufficiency to commercialization. Grangers were cognizant of the importance of rail transportation to the development of agriculture in the hinterlands of the state. According to Ralph Smith, Grangers were the spokesmen for agriculture throughout the convention:

The Grangers performed their master work in the constitutional convention of 1875, one-half of whose members were Grangers. Their demands for "retrenchment" found expression in the provision setting small salaries for public officials. The homestead article, a provision instructing the legislature to protect from forced sale a certain portion of the property of all heads of families was the work of the Grangers. The restrictions that they placed on levying education taxes has necessitated the continuous amending of the Constitution in order to provide a system of free public education for the state.

The influence of the Grangers in the convention is also very noticeable in those articles relating to the railroads. The railroad problem had not become as serious for the farmers of Texas as in other western states, but foreseeing the possibility that it might become serious, the Grange delegates placed ample power in the legislative body to regulate railroads.[27]

"The railroad problem had not become as serious" because in Texas agriculture had not become as highly commercialized as in other western states.

The antimonopoly provisions of the Constitution of 1876 and the subsequent enabling acts probably had one salutary effect, at a later moment in Texas history. For a time after the discovery of the Spindletop oil field at Beaumont, they delayed entrance of the Standard Oil Company into Texas. The interim gave a number of new companies time enough to become firmly entrenched in the petroleum industry. This, with the magnitude of the Spindletop field, broke the Standard Oil monopoly more effectively than the combined decisions and orders of state supreme courts and the Supreme Court of the United States.

Also in the year 1875, Texans were introduced to a new type of fencing, barbed wire. Even for well-timbered regions of the state, fencing posed a troublesome problem; and it became still more serious in the treeless western plains. Board, split rail, and rock fences common to the east were just not to be had in the west. On the plains hedges were substituted for fences, and the bois d'arc was in great demand as a hedge bush. A bois d'arc seed industry sprang up, with seed selling in 1870 at $4.00 to $6.00 per bushel.[28] In years of peak demand it sold at $8.00 to $50.00 per bushel.[29] Barbed wire destroyed the hedge seed industry.

In 1874, J. F. Glidden of Illinois patented a barbed wire. Shortly afterward he signed a two-year contract with Henry B. Sanborn and Judson P. Warner making them exclusive agents for the product of the Glidden barbed wire factory. The partners met with only mediocre success when they opened their sales campaign in Illinois. The two men then decided to transfer their operations to Texas, which appeared to be a better potential market. They ordered a carload of wire delivered in small lots to a number of widely scattered Texas communities. As a result their product was well advertised at practically no cost to them. At Gainesville in the fall of 1875, the partners made their first Texas sale.[30] Wherever or whenever a strand of barbed wire appeared it provoked an argument. In Harrison County residents debated the question: Would it be less costly to "fence the stock in and farm the land out," or would it be cheaper to fence the farms and graze cattle over the unfenced ranges?[31] Others doubted whether the wire was sufficiently strong to serve as a barricade for half-wild cattle, horses, or mules. Some admitted, for the sake of argument, that the wire might restrain the livestock, but claimed that it would be at the expense of badly mangled herds suffering from barb wounds inflicted when animals ran into the wire. Demonstration proved barbed wire to be a cheap and effective fencing for livestock, and showed that the animals quickly learned to avoid the sharp barbs. As the arguments waxed and waned sales of barbed wire skyrocketed, soon reaching astronomical figures; and in less than half a decade barbed wire changed the entire system of western agriculture. The open range disappeared as cattlemen resorted to barbed-wire barricades for protection of their grass and cattle against all comers.

The opening skirmishes of the buffalo slaughter rank as a third major episode of the mid-seventies. The Santa Fe, Oregon, and California trails and the transcontinental railroads separated the American bison into two massive herds — northern and southern. The southern herd, whose range extended deep into Texas, made first contact with the army of killers bent on extermination. For decades Indians had steadily increased the size of their annual kill of buffalo — not for the meat, but for the hides which were fashioned into buffalo robes for trading purposes. Left to their own devices, the Indians would eventually have destroyed the herds without the intervention of the white killer. But the westward extension of railroads stepped up the tempo of the slaughter. Railroads brought the buffalo country within easy reach of sportsmen (including foreign kings and potentates) who appeared in hordes to slake their thirst to kill. Furthermore, cheaper freight rates increased the profits on shipments of buffalo meat and thus stimulated the professional hunter to renewed activity. Nevertheless, buffalo herds would probably have survived for decades had it not been for the appearance of a fourth type of killer.

As a result of the shipment of fifty-seven flint hides by J. Wright Mooar, a woodcutter and professional buffalo hunter of Kansas, to his brother in New York with the hope that they could be sold, the hard flinty buffalo hides, which the white hunter considered worthless, came to have a commercial value. As the hides were being removed to a New York warehouse they were seen by a Philadelphia tanner. He became intrigued with the possibility of tanning them and purchased the lot for $200. When tanning tests proved successful an order for two thousand flint hides was placed with the Mooar brothers.

The order received by the Mooars revolutionized buffalo hunting. Where white men had previously hunted bison for sport, they now organized highly efficient crews to slaughter en masse. John Mooar deserted New York for Kansas to hunt buffalo. The Mooar brothers hired a hunting crew and moved to Texas, establishing their headquarters at Fort Griffin. For the season 1874-75 their range hunting camp was located near the present site of Haskell. After a successful hunting season their buffalo hides were marketed at Denison, the nearest railroad shipping point.[32]

The Mooar party was the vanguard of an army of hunters whose sole objective was to slaughter and skin the buffalo herd as quickly as possible. They accomplished their task in less than five years. Within a few months 1,500 hunters filled the territory west of Fort Griffin, while additional hundreds poured into other hunting areas. The ruthless process of transforming a wilderness into an empire was under way.

Extermination of the buffalo removed two major barriers to settlement of the West. First was the buffalo herd itself. As long as the bison roamed at large, fields, fences, domestic livestock, railroads, and immigrants themselves faced possible destruction, annihilation, or irreparable damage from trampling hoofs of countless buffalo in stampede. Hunters wiped out this danger. Once the buffalo slaughter started it became apparent that extermination of the herd was imminent, and bills designed to protect the bison were introduced in the Texas legislature. While the state lawmakers had one of these measures under consideration a joint session of the two houses was addressed by General Phil Sheridan, who spoke in opposition to the bill. Sheridan bluntly told the legislators that instead of concerning themselves with legislation protecting the buffalo they should give the hunters a unanimous vote of thanks and provide funds for awarding bronze medals to each of them, the medals to be struck with a dead buffalo on one side and a despondent Indian on the other. The General continued:

> These men have done more in the last two years and will do more in the next year to settle the vexed Indian question than the entire regular army has done in the last 30 years. They are destroying the Indian's commissary; and it is a well known fact that an army losing its base of supplies is placed at a great disadvantage. Send them powder and lead, if you will, and for the sake of lasting peace, let them kill, skin, and sell until they have exterminated the buffalo. Then your prairies will be covered with speckled cattle and the festive cowboy, who follows the hunter as the second forerunner of civilization.[33]

As General Sheridan predicted, the second menace to settlement, the Indian, disappeared from the plains with the buffalo.

Extermination of the buffalo and forcing the Indian to settle permanently on the reservation were not the only contributions made by the hunters to settlement of the West. In roaming for several seasons over the vast buffalo domain, hunters learned a great deal about its climate, topography, grasses, and soils, and something of the potentialities of the territory. This information they passed on to casual acquaintances, friends, and relatives back east, while some of them settled permanently on choice sites they had discovered on their hunts. The stories told about the buffalo country by returning hunters were probably responsible for the westward trek of many an immigrant. Since marauding Indians no longer endangered construction crews, railroad companies quickly extended their lines into the western plains.

II

The Railroad Comes to Texas

F ROM a casual glance at the map of Texas, a stranger might assume that the state was blessed with navigable streams. Such, of course, is not the case. Even though a number of southerly flowing rivers virtually span the state, none are navigable, except for short distances. According to Paddock, the streams of North Texas have never influenced either transportation or development, nor have these watercourses been followed by immigrants or settlers.[1] In comparison to the eastern United States, Texas is unique in that none of its major cities can credit either origin or growth to a navigable river. Furthermore, the long coast line of the state lacks a good natural harbor. Galveston and other towns were located along coastal waters too shallow to accommodate ocean-going vessels until vast sums were spent for the dredging of channels and removal of sand bars. Even then most ports served local territories only.

In 1870, Jefferson, the largest and most important trading and shipping center of northern Texas, functioned as a river or bayou port. Waters impounded behind a raft stretched across the Red River made Cypress Bayou navigable for several months each year. Boats plied regularly between Jefferson and New Orleans. In 1870, according to estimate, seventy thousand bales of cotton and relatively large quantities of wool, hides, beef, tallow, and finished merchandise cleared through the bayou port.[2] Jefferson trade territory extended westward as far as Dallas and Fort Worth, and memoirs of northeast Texas pioneers are dotted with references to and descriptions of overland trade with East Texas. Frame houses replaced log cabins as Dallas milled flour was offered in exchange for East Texas lumber.[3] In the bayou port's heyday, freight moved to and from West Texas by means of ox-wagons. During the 1870's United States Army Engineers destroyed the Red River raft, causing the bayou waters to recede and become too shallow for navigation so that Jefferson lost its importance as a shipping point. After the Texas & Pacific Railway established connections between Dallas, Texarkana, and the Northeast, freight from the western territory formerly served by Jefferson moved by rail.

Except for water contact with the outside world through Jefferson and the Gulf ports, Texas in 1870 was an isolated landlocked region. S. B. McAlister notes that as late as 1871, interstate rail connections were limited to a road from Texas to Shreveport, Louisiana.[4] With this exception, interstate and intrastate traffic moved overland by wagon and by stage. Since bull trains seldom traveled more than ten to twenty miles per day, movement of freight was time-consuming. The uniformly high freight charges averaged $1.00 per 100 pounds per 100 miles, or 20 cents per ton-mile. These exorbitant rates proved to be a detriment to the profitable movement of staple crops, except for short distances, and tended to retard the development of commercial agriculture. As a matter of fact, full economic development of the state awaited construction of a system of inland transportation which insured a more rapid movement of goods at relatively low rates.

In the course of the evolution of transportation in Texas, stagecoaches, ox-wagons, and trains operated simultaneously. As the railroad system expanded, freight wagons and stage lines shortened their runs. But they prolonged their operations well into the twentieth century before succumbing to a combination of railroads, trucks, busses, automobiles, and airplanes. As railroads entered a territory stage lines and freighters made adjustments so as to link railroad and nonrailroad communities. As late as 1878, the Butterfield line inaugurated service between Fort Worth and Yuma, Arizona.[5] Other stage lines operating for considerable distances were the El Paso Stage Company, the Overland Stage Company, and the Fort Griffin and Fort Concho Stage and Express Line. Local companies operating over short distances served innumerable towns. When railroad competition forced abandonment of a stage run, local newspapers broke the news somewhat as follows: "The stage line between Ballinger and San Angelo has been discontinued and travel between those two places will hereafter be by rail."[6]

Many lines were ephemeral, opening new routes without fanfare and terminating old runs without warning, leaving to editors the task of informing the public that the line no longer operated. Discontinuance stories were tersely worded: "The El Paso Stage Company have [sic] thrown up the sponge on the Fort Griffin Mail route and sent the stock to Concho. Colonel Steele of Griffin has been employed temporarily to carry the mail from here to Fort Griffin."[7] Changes in coach service were more or less continuous, usually from bad to worse, and Robson of the *Frontier Echo* was no man to mince words when criticizing their accommodations: "The El Paso Stage Company have [sic] taken off their four mule stages from here to Weatherford and substituted a grasshopper sort of go-cart. Two mules are now doing the work."[8] With rates high, money scarce, and population sparse, operating a stage company was none too profitable.

For many communities the stage line constituted the only regular contact with other settlements, and residents eagerly anticipated the daily or biweekly arrival of the coach. When, because of unforeseen circumstances, it failed to appear with the mail, the locality sensed something of the completeness of its isolation.[9] Since mail carrying was an important function of stage lines, considerable local interest was manifested in Congressional action creating or abolishing routes, and the *Echo,* among other papers, printed full summaries of what happened in Washington:

Act of Congress approved March 3rd, 1879, provided for new postal routes from and through Griffin as follows:
From Fort Sill via Camp Augur, Buffalo Creek, Red River, Indian Territory, Fort Griffin, Texas, to Fort Concho.
From Fort Griffin via Simpson's Ranch to Buffalo Gap.
From Fort Griffin via Williamsburg to Oregon.
From Fort Griffin to Blanco Canyon.

From Fort Griffin via California Ranch, Reynold's, Tepee's Store, and Indian Creek to Fort Elliott.

From Fort Griffin via Fort Elliott, Camp Supply, and Fort Dodge, Kansas to Leadville, Colorado.

From Fort Chadbourne to Fort Griffin.[10]

At one time a network of thirty-one stage lines connected all regions of Texas,[11] but stagecoaches established no permanent ties between communities. Galloping hoofbeats heralded the arrival of the stage; its stop was brief, allowing the driver time to toss down a bag of mail, to make secure a pouch pitched up to him, probably to discharge one passenger as another scrambled aboard, and to be gone again. Departing coaches left no bond save a memory, and service might terminate with the leave-taking of any stage. The high fares limited travel to those who had money; the passenger with a small parcel of luggage traveled at the rate of ten cents per mile.

In the economic development of Texas, the freight wagon was much more significant than the stagecoach. Since arrival and departure of freighters served as a sort of barometer of economic activity, editors kept careful tab on the stream of freighters in much the same manner in which freight car loadings are tabulated by the present generation. When boasting of a town's prosperity, newspapers cited freighter figures as irrefutable proof. The *Echo* reported: "Five wagons loaded with lumber, each drawn by five yoke of oxen, came in Monday for Conrad."[12] Some months earlier the paper had declared:

It is an indisputable fact the largest and most complete stocks of goods to be found anywhere west of Fort Worth are in Fort Griffin. . . . When it is known that *seventy-four* wagons loaded with goods for our merchants recently arrived here in *one week*, and that in the dull season — an idea of the business of this place may be formed.[13]

At that time (1880), Griffin was already on the road to becoming a ghost town, with the arriving lumber and merchandise destined for other towns — communities soon to absorb Griffin merchants, Griffin residents, even the *Echo* itself.

Because of inadequate transportation facilities, merchants who located at great distances from railroads wrestled with a continuing problem of shortages. From Mobeetie, a Panhandle community, one correspondent, in describing these merchants' plight, wrote:

Freighters is [sic] the scarcest article in the Panhandle. It is impossible to get goods and building material here to supply the demand. Hamburg & Company keep a bull train on the road that hauls 140,000 pounds at a load to Dodge [Kansas] and return every twenty-four days, and this does not keep their house supplied with necessary goods. Truly Mobeetie is booming.[14]

If these isolated communities were fortunate enough to become railroad towns, they sometimes survived as moderately prosperous centers; but if they were by-passed they usually faded away.

As military headquarters for Texas, San Antonio was the central supply depot for frontier posts, and consequently the city became an important freighting center. A rate war among freighters operating from the city in 1877 ended when wagon train operators agreed on uniform freight charges. Under terms of the compact, the rates per 100 pounds on freight from San Antonio were: $3.50 to Fort Davis, $3.00 to Fort Stockton, $1.40 to Fort Concho, $1.25 to Laredo, and 30 cents to Cuero, but 75 cents from Cuero to San Antonio. The newspaper which reported the agreement charged that it was the outgrowth of a combination formed among freighters to stifle competition, and stated that San Antonio businessmen predicted a speedy disintegration of the understanding.[15] It is to be noted that the rates agreed to were less than the customary $1.00 per 100 pounds per 100 miles.

The slow movement and high rates of bull trains restricted shipments to nonperishable essentials. When merchandise moved hundreds of miles overland by wagon, freight costs boosted the prices to fantastic heights. The J A (Goodnight) Ranch purchased Colorado lumber at $225 per thousand feet delivered because the delivery price was lower than that of South Texas lumber, which could be bought at $9 to $12 per thousand in Orange.[16] With prices of lumber so high, a large percentage of frontier settlers could not afford the luxury of frame homes — sod houses were more in keeping with their financial circumstances. Until the Texas & Pacific Railway offered nearer trading points, the J A Ranch did its buying in Kansas, paying ranch prices of $7 per 100 pounds for flour and 10 cents for 25 matches.[17]

One might assume that the great need for stage and wagon routes would have generated some concern over the poor quality of the roads, but it did not. Early day freight and stage route surveys were the responsibilities of concerns expecting to use the routes. Maintenance and upkeep of the routes depended entirely on the discretion of the counties through which they passed — and when it came to the matter of roads, county discretion lay dormant. In timbered regions roads were classified according to the height of stumps, and where none were taller than six inches, the road was first class. A logical assumption would hold that for second, third, and fourth class roads stumps became progressively taller until the traveler found it most difficult to distinguish between road and forest. Until the 1880's bridges, especially iron ones, were virtually unknown to Texans.

As settlers poured into counties and fenced homesteads or carefully demarked property lines, a growing demand for clearly defined highways compelled local officials to provide permanent roads.[18] By 1874 the old trails of Tarrant County were in the process of being closed by an influx of farmers, a problem the commissioners' court met by ordering a system of public roads surveyed for the county. Previously it had been possible for any traveler who knew the general whereabouts of his destination to cross the prairies in any direction without benefit of clearly defined trails or roads.

For years county commissioners did little toward establishing a highway system other than "lay out regular and permanent roads." Many sources attest to the poor quality of the roads. During long rainy spells town merchants complained that trade had been dull for some time,[19] or they rejoiced over the revival of wagon trade after a two-week suspension because of rains and impassable roads.[20] In some communities businessmen attributed loss of trade to a lack of bridges, insisting that farm folk either remained at home when rains brought streams to flood level and fording was impossible, or traded in towns where high water presented no hazard to travel.[21]

When offering excuses for poor roads and bridges, the state of Texas found it convenient to take refuge behind its cloak of poverty.

Yet many Texans realized that the growing number of new settlements and the increasing importance of commercial crops made imperative the improvement of roads and bridges. In the absence of all-weather roads, surplus crops could not be profitably marketed; thus the vicious circle — because of poverty, no roads; because of no roads, poverty. A road work law which required every able-bodied man either to devote a number of days each year to work on roads or to pay a dollar penalty for each day missed was responsible for most of the road labor. Counties hired road overseers to supervise the work. All bridges, except small wooden culverts, were erected by construction crews of bridge companies. Since structural iron for bridges was fabricated in the North, iron bridges were rare until railroads connected Texas with northern states. In 1886, four or five years after railroads arrived, the iron bridge appeared in Bell County.[22]

Under the existing laws an adequate road system uniform in quality could not be maintained, and some newspapers, no doubt expressing popular feeling, were quite critical of the compulsory labor requirement. The *Denton Chronicle* complained that a law requiring labor on the public roads of every able-bodied man between the ages of eighteen and forty-five was unfair and unjust. The editor contended that the law created a type of slave labor and that those who performed the work received no direct benefits from the roads, and he insisted that the fair way to maintain a system of public roads was through ad valorem taxes levied on properties adjacent to the roads whose owners benefited directly from their upkeep.[23] Criticism proved to be of little avail; neither the road system nor the system of road labor changed materially until well into the twentieth century. In the closing decades of the nineteenth century, Texans relied on railway companies to furnish all-weather roads and a cheaper means of transportation.

As the national economy slowly recovered from the Panic of '73, railroad companies resumed construction and Texas entered a decade of great railway development. In 1875 the state had only 1,650 miles of railroad,[24] all of which lay east of a line extending from Denison to the Gulf Coast through Dallas, Waco, Austin, and Corpus Christi. More than half of the state lacked any sort of rail service. The Houston & Texas Central, spanning Texas from Denison to Houston, in conjunction with the Missouri, Kansas & Texas gave a rail outlet to the North and East.[25] And the Texas & Pacific, by way of Texarkana, offered a second railroad contact with the North-east.[26] The two railroad systems diverted incoming and outbound Texas freight from Galveston to St. Louis and played important roles in making the Missouri city a great marketing center for the Southwest. St. Louis, a formidable competitor, deprived Galveston of many North Texas markets, and the "St. Louis drummer" with his inevitable cigar became as much a part of Texas passenger trains as a baggage coach.

More than half the railroad mileage constructed in Texas during the nineteenth century was built between 1875 and 1885. The latter half of the 1870's was characterized by a vigorous resurgence in railway building and by a widespread movement to standardize the width of all track. In the United States all railroads employed one of three track gauges — broad, standard, or narrow. Originally constructed as a broad-gauge road, the Houston & Texas Central, in 1876, changed to the 4 ft. 8½ in. standard width.[27] The Tyler Tap, predecessor to the St. Louis & Southwestern, was an early-day narrow-gauge line. A majority of the railroads conformed to the standard gauge, and by the close of the seventies all roads had either converted to standard or formulated conversion plans.

In the great era of railroad construction, lines were extended into almost all sections of the state. However, the roads moving westward seemed to grip the public imagination most firmly and to attract the greatest attention. In the West, tens of millions of acres of unoccupied lands beckoned as bonuses to railroad promoters, as ranges to livestock men, and as homes to settlers. In the late seventies the buffalo and Indian barriers still persisted, but the buffalo hunters were busy at the task of extermination. By the time the railroads pushed into the range country, the great southern herd of buffalo had been annihilated. As previously noted, the Mooar brothers, probably the only commercial hunters on the range in 1874-75, competed a year later with 1,500 hunters in the buffalo country west of Fort Griffin,[28] the butchery reaching its climax in the season 1876-77 with the slaughter of a million animals. In the twentieth century, statistics on buffalo hunting seem fantastic. Robson of the *Echo* reported a kill of 9,352 buffalo during the season 1876-77 by a hunter employed by W. N. McKay.[29]

The work of the hunter was a boon to railroads. With the buffalo herds destroyed and Indians removed from the range, construction and maintenance costs of railways dropped. The Texas & Pacific, pushing its railhead toward El Paso in 1880-81, was probably the last Texas railroad to request troops for the protection of its construction crews. In addition to removing the buffalo-Indian menace, the hunter supplied a considerable volume of freight for railroads at a time when they needed it badly. For some five or six years shipments of buffalo hides totaled hundreds of cars annually, while each year the hunter demanded return shipments of scores of carloads of merchandise, including food, clothing, and hunting paraphernalia. Holden says it was not unusual to see, strung out across the plains at one time, as many as twenty-five freighter outfits laden with buffalo hides; and frequently processions of more than one hundred wagons passed through Weatherford daily en route to a railroad shipping point.[30] Traders and hide buyers advertised: "Teams Wanted, to haul two hundred thousand pounds of buffalo hides to Dallas, T. E. Jackson & Co., Griffin, Texas."[31] At that period, two hundred thousand pounds of hides loaded no fewer than ten railroad cars. From the hunting season of 1876-77 alone, more than one million hides were said to have been marketed through Fort Worth.[32] During the last quarter of the nineteenth century Texas railroads serviced a sparsely settled country, and, according to their stories, the smallness of the volume of available freight perpetuated their financial distress. The hundreds of thousands of buffalo hides shipped by rail to eastern factories tended to reduce the operating losses.

Some evidence serves to belie, or refute, railroad complaints that inadequate returns were consequences of a dearth of tonnage. At one time during 1876, because it had more freight than it could handle, the Texas & Pacific switched 250 carloads of freight to sidetracks between Fort Worth and Marshall to sit until some future time when they could be conveniently moved.[33] Later that same year, a freight car shortage caused a considerable quantity of cotton to be accumulated at the Mexia depot and held in storage by the railroad. Merchants grew disturbed over the pyramiding storage charges.[34] At approximately the same time, the *Palestine Advocate* reported grumbling among sawmill operators and lumber dealers because of car shortages. One owner of two mills, the paper stated, had over a period of fourteen days been supplied with only four cars, and for other mills the lack of rolling stock caused unfilled orders to accumulate until some of them were more than a month old.[35]

At one time in 1878, the *Beaumont Lumberman* reported a shipment of eighty-four cars of lumber for the week when 180 carloads would have been moved if cars had been available.[36] Eighteen months later a Houston news item claimed a shortage of rolling equipment as the reason why the Texas & New Orleans Railway could not move milled lumber.[37] Prolonged delays in cattle shipments caused by chronic shortages of cattle cars became a continuing irritant to western stockmen. Over and over again the evidence points to an insufficiency of equipment as the primary cause of delay in the movement of freight and of congestions of cattle, lumber, and cotton at shipping points. One is led to wonder whether the low return on railroad investment resulted from the sparseness of population and scarcity of freight, as claimed by the companies, or whether the financial stringency was a consequence of the failure to provide adequate rolling stock. Some roads were probably in financial distress because the original construction was so flimsy that train service could be maintained only at the expense of rebuilding the system. Instead of getting two railroads for the price of one, the state sometimes got one for the price of two.

In spite of the uncertain and inadequate service, communities were eager to procure railroads, for, after all, they were a considerable improvement over stagecoaches and bull trains. Villages hung on threads of hope and fear — hope that the approaching railroad would not pass them by; fear that it would. The railroad dream of every town, from hamlet to metropolis, was reflected in the pages of its newspapers; the press gave a "spike by spike account" of construction, and every paper crammed its columns with railroad news and gossip — the one often indistinguishable from the other. As it suited their purposes to enlighten or to confuse the press and the public, railroad promoters poured out volumes of factual information or supplied the substance for baseless rumors. As the Santa Fe moved northward from Galveston, it first headed north, then veered to the west; and at one time or another it crossed the Texas & Pacific at every town between Fort Worth and El Paso. Over the prospects of a railroad, community enthusiasms flared and waned. By the close of the century public interest in railroad construction had cooled considerably. Factors that contributed to the sagging of enthusiasm included virtual completion of the rail network; a growing realization that gossip and editorials had little to do with the determination of routes; and a feeling of disappointment on the part of communities because of the seemingly small economic returns they derived from funds which they expended to help build railroads.

During the building era, railroads were recipients of considerable aid from public and private sources. From its public domain the state of Texas granted millions of acres as railroad bonuses. To dispose of public lands in a manner leading to the most rapid growth and settlement of the state was the basic intent. Land grants to railroads were part of this policy.

C. S. Potts divides the land grant era into five periods, the fifth of which (1876-82)[38] falls within the scope of this study. During this period, a general law authorized bonuses of sixteen sections for every mile of main line completed. Under this law forty railroads received land, while three other roads drew grants of twenty sections per mile by authority of earlier special laws. In bonuses Texas railroads received 32,153,878 acres of land[39] in return for 2,928 miles of track.[40] The Texas & Pacific collected the largest bonus, a total of 5,167,360 acres. Each of four other roads received grants of more than a million but less than five million acres, while thirty-eight additional companies had to content themselves with bonuses of less than a million acres each.[41] During 1881, state officials made the startling discovery that the supply of public land had been exhausted and that outstanding land commitments exceeded by 8,000,000 acres the quantity available for distribution.

The era of railroad land bonuses finally came to an end in 1882 when a special session of the legislature repealed the Land Grant Law of 1876.[42]

In addition to the state land grants, every railroad received some sort of aid from communities through which it passed. In spite of a constitutional prohibition, two cities and three counties floated a total of $915,000 in public bonds in payment for railroad services.[43] After 1879 local government units no longer attempted to circumvent the constitutional provision which denied them the right to award public funds to railroads; instead they resorted to raising funds through private subscriptions.

Long before railroad construction became active in Texas, promoters had perfected practices for milking — even stripping — communities financially in return for assurances of rail facilities. All known money-raising techniques were applied in Texas. In order to secure railroads, towns were induced to pay cash bonuses in addition to providing rights of way, depot sites, and switching yards. If a community refused to meet the demands, it was bypassed. At times railroads succeeded in maneuvering two or more neighboring settlements into bidding against each other. This usually brought a substantially larger bonus than the road might otherwise have collected. A railroad terminal siphoned trade from an extensive area, and anticipation of the large volume of business that would accrue to such a trade center caused towns to seek the privilege of becoming railroad terminals. By assuring a town that it would be made a terminal point for a year, or possibly two, many promoters fully exploited the terminal lure to extract generous financial contributions. Once terminal money was in hand, promises may or may not have been respected. After assurances, at least by implication, that, in return for a sizable contribution in cash and a free right of way through the county, their town would be made an important division point on the railroad, Belton citizens met every demand only to have the promoters accept the cash and right of way and then found Temple as a competing town and designate it the division point.[44]

In some instances localities took the initiative and chartered companies for the purpose of throwing up an embankment, or constructing a few miles of road along the route of a major railroad, then leasing or selling the project to the larger company. Stock in these local companies could be subscribed in cash, labor, or farm produce.[45] The embankment of the Texas & Pacific between Weatherford and Fort Worth was graded through the efforts of Parker County residents who chartered a company and raised $65,000 to see the project through. Those who subscribed to stock in the Parker County company were promised 8 per cent interest and repayment of their investment within three years.[46] Since more than three years elapsed between completion of the embankment and the time when it was put to use by the railroad, promises made to stockholders were probably never fulfilled.

Now and then a town made a generous contribution to secure railroad facilities without entertaining hopes that it would soon outstrip St. Louis. Sometimes a community regarded the bonus it paid as nothing more than an investment, and hoped that lower freight rates would make the investment profitable. When the Gulf, Colorado, & Santa Fe demanded of Brenham $150,000 in cash, plus a right of way through the county, the businessmen considered the request reasonable and were certain they could convince the people that through lower freight charges the road would be worth at least $150,000 per year to the county.[47] The business group estimated that county residents would be able to purchase merchandise at lower prices, and at the same time receive higher prices for farm produce. During the nineteenth century, Fort Worth, ambitious to develop into an important railroad center, paid bonuses to all railroads entering the city. Its smallest bonus, $78,000, went to the Santa Fe.[48]

No satisfactory measure can be devised for determining the effectiveness of state and local aid as a stimulus to railroad construction. When compared with funds subscribed by easterners and Europeans, financial help proffered by Texans may have been insignificant. Irrespective of sources, funds were obtained for weaving a network of rails over the state excepting only portions of the Panhandle and the Lower Rio Grande Valley. After a late start, railroad construction in Texas, once begun, was pushed with great energy. In 1877 Texas led all states in railroad construction,[49] while the following year Texas construction exceeded the aggregate for all other states and territories.[50]

During the period (1876-82) in which the interest of Texans in railroad building ran highest, the state chartered 126 railroad companies, only nineteen of which ever engaged in actual construction.[51] In the decade 1875-85 the companies laid 4,548 miles of rail. During the last five years of the eighties they added another 2,288 miles, bringing the state total to 8,486.[52] In 1880, the three longest roads were the Houston & Texas Central, 587 miles; the International & Great Northern, 530 miles; and the Texas & Pacific, 504 miles. At that date the Missouri, Kansas & Texas had penetrated the state 53 miles. At the end of two years the Texas & Pacific occupied first place with 1,062 miles; into second place had moved the International & Great Northern with 770 miles; while the Houston & Texas Central dropped to third place with 700 miles. Meanwhile the Missouri, Kansas & Texas increased its mileage from 53 to 301.[53] For Texas, only in the second and third years of the eighties did annual rail construction exceed 1,000 miles.[54] In 1883 only 66 miles of rails were laid. Repeal of the land grant law in 1882 may have precipitated the drop in construction. But this sort of reasoning presumes a shortage of investment funds, which may be largely disregarded since shrewd promoters have never encountered too much difficulty in procuring capital funds for their ventures. It is suggested that moguls paused for reappraisal before continuing with the projects. In any event, by the close of the nineteenth century Texas enjoyed numerous rail outlets to eastern and western seaboards and to all parts of the nation. No master plan had guided the railroad builders, and no government agency stood by with authority to approve or reject proposed routes. The result was that railroads overbuilt in some regions of the state and underbuilt in others.

During the last quarter of the century Texas made considerable gains in railroad facilities in comparison with other states. In 1870 the state ranked nineteenth in population and twenty-eighth in railroad mileage; for 1880 the respective ranks were eleventh and twelfth; and by 1890 they shifted to seventh and third. Before the twentieth century was four years old, Texas ranked first in railroad mileage.[55] On the basis of area, Texas was not as well equipped as a number of other states; but its per capita rail mileage was higher than that of most other states.

During the great era of construction, railroads generated a substantial impetus in secondary industries. Railroad expansion encouraged growth and greater activity in the lumber industry. In 1880 the Texas & Pacific placed an order for 500,000 crossties,[56] and other companies ordered ties in accordance with construction schedules. In addition to crossties, railroads consumed hundreds of thousands of board feet of timber in bridges, stations, cattle pens, and freight and cotton platforms. Other items purchased by the Texas & Pacific while it was building its Western Division included 10,000 tons of rails and fastenings for track on 190 miles of grade, all necessary bridging in the first 100 miles, 20 locomotives, and 350 cars.[57] In its heyday of construction, the T. & P. employed 8,000 laborers[58] and hired thousands of horses and mules. The men and teams consumed vast quantities of agricultural produce, the daily requirements for livestock feed alone running into hundreds of tons of hay and hundreds of bushels of corn and oats. The aggregate of generated industrial activity was a multiple of the number of railroad construction projects in progress at a given time.

Chronologically, the origin of many towns dates from the moment railroad construction camps located on their sites. As a road pushed on beyond an old camp, it was abandoned for a location nearer the railhead. Frequently a few itinerant merchants and a handful of workers remained at the forsaken camp site, forming the nucleus of a permanent town. A number of towns along the Texas & Pacific between Weatherford and Sierra Blanca are of construction camp origin. In 1880 camps along the road gave birth to Gordon,[59] Abilene, Eastland, and Baird, and the next year construction camp sites were responsible for embryonic Sweetwater, Colorado City, and Big Spring.[60] Within forty-eight hours Gordon became a full-blown town. As late as midsummer of 1880 the locale of modern Abilene was a Taylor County prairie. It was transformed by the following January into a thriving settlement only because a construction crew had camped there. As the T. & P. built west of Abilene, every thirty to sixty days it gave birth to a new town. The road averaged laying a mile of track per day and re-located its camps every month or two.[61]

As the growing transportation network approached maturity, criticism of railroad practices intensified. The same complaints made against the railroad companies by citizens of other states were repeated in Texas. Roads were accused of discriminating between persons or places, of granting rebates and drawbacks, of making pooling agreements among themselves, of establishing monopolistic rate associations, of charging more for short than for long hauls, of maintaining poor and inadequate service, and of exerting pressure to procure legislation and judicial action favorable to their interests. At one time it appeared that every man of influence, or suspected of being of influence, carried one or more free railroad passes. Jay Gould and Collis P. Huntington, through the railroad combinations they headed, controlled more than half the mileage in the state. By 1882, the Gould syndicate had established control over the Missouri Pacific, the Texas & Pacific, the International & Great Northern, and the East Line & Red River.[62] Some properties Gould had acquired by purchase, while others he controlled through lease arrangements. The Southern Pacific System constituted the core of the Huntington combination. During the eighties a third major system appeared when the Gulf, Colorado, & Santa Fe, in an exchange of stock procedure, became a member of the Atchison, Topeka, & Santa Fe family.[63]

In 1882 Huntington and Gould, by agreement, virtually apportioned the state of Texas between their systems. By compact the northern half of the state became Gould territory, while the southern half was reserved to the Huntington interests.[64] The understanding — "treaty of alliance," Charles S. Potts called it — grew out of a construction race won by Huntington. Gould instigated action for damages. He contended Huntington had built the Southern Pacific along the right of way granted by Congress to the Texas & Pacific, thereby violating rights of the Gould road. The act by which Congress incorporated the Texas & Pacific provided, for every mile of railroad built through three western states, a land bonus of twenty sections for mileage in California and forty sections for mileage through New Mexico and Arizona. To recover the land bonuses for the T. & P. was the intent of the Gould suits. Huntington filed cross actions.

Possible years of costly litigation were avoided when Huntington and Gould resolved their differences in the "Agreement of 1882."[65] By the terms of the "treaty of alliance" the two sovereigns agreed that henceforth neither would extend the lines of his system farther into trade territory served by the other. The understanding further provided a pooling arrangement whereby the two systems consented to share, on a stipulated basis, through freight between New Orleans and El Paso. The two moguls also included a plan for the joint purchase of competing railroads. It was further agreed that the T. & P. and the Southern Pacific would use jointly the Southern Pacific tracks between El Paso and Sierra Blanca. It is possible that the Huntington-Gould understanding was the factor primarily responsible for the decline in rail construction after 1882. For more than ten years state officials were in ignorance of the agreement. Finally in 1893 a copy fell into the hands of the Texas Railroad Commission.[66] In the course of time the contracting parties violated portions of the agreement; but after a lapse of seventy-three years at least part of it is still operative — e.g., the provision for joint use of the Sierra Blanca-El Paso line. For a time, the Huntington-Gould agreement materially lessened competition between the two railroad systems.

In 1885 a number of trunk line railroads, operating wholly or partially within the state, formed the Texas Traffic Association. The objective was "to establish equitable and uniform rates upon traffic having origin and destination within the State of Texas."[67] Unlike the Huntington-Gould combine, the association made no effort to function in secrecy; in fact, its work was widely publicized. The public was informed that "the lines of this association have allied themselves for the purpose of increasing their revenues and doing away with certain abuses and losses incident thereto."[68] State officials were quick to attack the association for having violated the antitrust law, and in 1888 court decree dissolved the Texas Traffic Association. The railroads countered by forming the International Association, which was shortly replaced by the Southern Interstate Association with headquarters in St. Louis. From the city in Missouri, officers of the Southern Association fashioned a structure of freight tariffs which controlled Texas rates. The various associations fabricated a system of freight charges to which Texas railroads adhered for more than forty years. For twenty-five years the association rates thwarted efforts of the Texas Railroad Commission to act independently in setting intrastate freight charges.[69]

During the course of the last twenty-five years of the nineteenth century, railroads divided Texas into two rate territories. The partitioning line extended roughly from Amarillo to Corpus Christi. The area east of the line was designated as Common Point Territory, and that to the west was known as Differential Territory. In the Common Point Territory rates up to distances of 177, and in some instances 187, miles were based on the length of the haul, while all blanket charges, or postage rates, applied to greater distances. On all freight originating in, or billed to, the area west of the Amarillo-Corpus Christi line was added a supplemental charge — thus the title of Differential Territory. This discrimination was generally referred to as the East-West Texas differential. In addition, the railway companies originated the Houston-Galveston differential whereby Houston enjoyed lower railroad freight rates than Galveston. The roads contended that the differential was necessary in order to counteract the cheaper water rate enjoyed by Galveston.[70]

In spite of a crescendo of discontent over freight charges and railroad practices, and in spite of constitutional mandates which called for strong legislative control over railroad operations, not until the 1890's was a regulatory body established. Farmer organizations had been persistent in demands for establishment of a permanent agency whose sole function would be to police the railroads. But farmers seemed incapable of applying sustained pressure on the legislature, and they were opposed by a rail lobby of great power — hence the long delay. Ultimately, strong political urging on the part of the Farmers' Alliance, plus sturdy support from Governor James S. Hogg, overcame legislative inertia and a railroad commission was established. In the meantime, the state railway system gave momentum to the transition from a self-sufficing to a commercial system of agriculture.

III

Breaking New Ground

"TAKING the word agriculture in its widest signification as including the rearing of livestock as well as the products of the earth, Texas is pre-eminently an agricultural country. With her rich and inexhaustible soils and her genial climate, inviting the farmer to labor the year round in moderation, and not compelling him to hibernate, as it were for many months, where is there a field which offers so many attractions to the man who expects to earn his bread by the sweat of his brow?"[1]

In this persuasive manner, a handbook for the Southwestern Immigration Company baited an appeal designed to attract the potential immigrant-farmer. Texas was "pre-eminently an agricultural country," and for a number of decades it so remained. Nonetheless, agricultural change characterized the last quarter of the nineteenth century. Extensive land usage yielded to a more intensive usage. In the West, as buffalo range became open range, and open range became enclosed pasture, and pastures became farms, the evolution was vividly discernible. Transformation within the livestock industry saw the omnipresent longhorn slowly succumb to the Durham and Hereford; and "native" sheep, slick of belly, head, and legs, gave way to the Rambouillet and other breeds bearing full coats of wool. Improvement in the quality of livestock was in itself a step toward more intensive land utilization. High grade livestock increased per acre returns. The Durham or Hereford consumed little if any more feed than the longhorn, but beef per carcass increased in quantity with improved breeds; blooded sheep required precious little more care and feed than the scrub, yet Rambouillet and Merino fleeces were heavier and of finer quality. And when plows turned pastures into fields, per acre yields were even greater. Although the western type of farming, when compared with the eastern, is classed as extensive, the land is still used more intensively than when devoted to grazing.

Thus, as early as the seventies, a more intensive land utilization persistently encroached on the more extensive system, and throughout the state self-contained production pursued a definite trend toward commercialized agriculture. Also during the seventies, because of subsistence requirements, Texans consumed the major portion of their produce and heavy capital investments came mainly from out-of-state sources. The Southwestern Immigration Company would have liked to further industrial development of the state. It realized, however, that little could be done along the line of industrialization until the public domain had been settled; hence it directed its primary appeal to the immigrant in search of a farm. Those responsible for company policy probably considered that the route to rapid industrial growth lay in placing energetic homesteaders on the millions of unsettled acres. Emigrating farmers, coming largely from the Old South, with scattered clusters from Kansas, Missouri, Illinois, and Pennsylvania, entered Texas by the tens of thousands.

Fascinated by the agricultural evolution in Bell County during the last quarter of the nineteenth century, George W. Tyler became an able chronicler of the changes he witnessed. From his observations, he concluded that greater returns realized from farming made land too valuable for grazing; that is, land prices became so high as to preclude further use on an extensive scale. For this reason, owners of livestock in Bell County either sold their herds and became farmers, or disposed of their pastures to farmers, then moved farther west in search of open range or cheap grazing land. With the coming of barbed wire Bell County was quickly placed under fence, and its free range disappeared.[2] The changes observed by Tyler were not confined to Bell County; they characterized the period. Population growth, railroad development, and the increase in commercialized agriculture tended to cause a rise in land values, and economic well-being demanded an intensive rather than an extensive land utilization. In the eastern half of the state livestock raising became stock farming, and stock farmers cultivated fields of feed as supplements to pastures, thereby making it possible to maintain larger herds on given acreages.

Along much the same line of reasoning, Captain Paddock infers that railroad development and growth of towns placed western farming on a permanent basis, or further stimulated the pasture-to-farm transition. He described the prerail period as an era in which

The range cattle industry was still the occupation that offered the greatest money-making possibilities and to which the unsettled country was best adapted. Farming on a fixed permanent basis was restricted to the area within reach of railroad facilities and the larger towns.[3]

While agricultural practices in the closing quarter of the nineteenth century ranged from self-sufficing to commercial, production for the market characterized the later years, as the phenomenal increase in cotton acreage graphically demonstrates.

That Texas was blessed with any pattern of topography, any type of soil, any degree of rainfall, and any sort of climate to be found anywhere else in temperate or tropical zones was the boast of every newspaper, almanac, and immigrants' handbook published in the state. Contemporary writers apparently believed that the average immigrant sought no unfamiliar soil in a strange world, but rather that he wished a homesite in new surroundings bearing some resemblance to the region he had quitted; and to convince him that in Texas such a "homey" spot awaited him was the purpose of these boosters. The appeal was not without merit. In the absence of scientific soil analysis, physical similarity is the next best assurance that soils of different geographic regions, if not identical, possess some common characteristics. For the settler who established a homestead on strange soils and who was faced with the necessity of applying what were, to him at least, novel methods of cultivation to unfamiliar crops, too frequently the reward was crop failures and privation. Since the average newcomer was a poor man, he lacked the means of subsistence necessary to carry him through months or years of orientation to new crops and methods of cultivation.

Hoping to dispel the haunting fear of want resulting from crop failure, immigration promoters made a practice of enumerating a large variety of crops as having been successfully cultivated in Texas. In one handbook for immigrants, cotton, corn, oats, sugar cane, wheat, amber cane, potatoes (both sweet and Irish), tobacco, apples, plums, pears, peaches, grapes, blackberries, raspberries, and figs were listed among the products well adapted to the state. In addition, the guidebook vouched that nearly all vegetables did well, especially root varieties such as beets, parsnips, carrots, turnips, radishes, and onions, and that melons of all sorts grew to perfection. It also assured the potential immigrant that he would find for his consumption a large variety of wild fruits and berries, among them the "mustang" grape, native to all river bottoms, from which could be vintaged an excellent red wine. Among the nuts which grew in profusion were walnut and hickory, as well as the native pecan, the "toothsomeness" of which had become world famous. Any type of livestock including dairy and range cattle, sheep, goats, horses, mules, and hogs, so the migrant was assured, thrived in Texas. All types of poultry, according to the handbook, multiplied with virtually no care.[4] After the unfortunate experience of the United States Army with its camel corps, contemporary promoters probably assumed that no immigrant would be interested in a camel ranch. Immigrant guides seldom failed to note that citrus fruits of Galveston and Cameron counties were "just as good if not better" than those grown in Florida. Seldom was the phrase, "just as good if not better," omitted by Texas writers when describing soils, crops, fowls, animals, timber, or mineral resources of the state.

In their eagerness to enlarge their populations, counties made extravagant claims of the possibilities they offered the newcomer. Boosters of many counties, likewise, insisted that all crops, fruits, vegetables, nuts, livestock, timber, and poultry did "just as good if not better" in their respective counties as in any other part of the state or nation.

With the expansion of agriculture, land values tended to increase. In the seventies, land prices ranged from nothing to $5.00 per acre with choicest improved land sometimes quoted at $10.00, but seldom at a higher figure. At the close of the century, however, prices ran from something less than $1.00 per acre for the poorest grazing land to $500.00 for the best irrigated land.[5] A phenomenal growth in population and railroad expansion plus a remarkable advance in the development of commercialized agriculture were primary causes for the rise in land prices.

During the first quarter of the twentieth century the changes in market values of agricultural lands pursued a pattern different from that which prevailed in the last twenty-five years of the nineteenth century. After 1900 land values tended to increase with rising prices of agricultural products and to decline with falling prices, whereas from 1870 to 1897 prices of farm produce followed a persistent downward trend while the general trend in land values was upward (see Appendix, Tables I and II). Probably the national depression of the nineties was the fundamental cause of the fall in land prices in that decade. Undoubtedly at the heart of the widespread agrarian unrest in the late nineteenth century was the gnawing depressive force of steadily declining agricultural prices. Here again is a variance in the pattern of price changes between the late nineteenth and early twentieth centuries. In the former, farm and nonfarm price indexes generally moved in the same direction with the farm indexes always the lower. In the twentieth century the two indexes still tended to move in the same direction, but with significant differences. Year after year fewer percentage points separated the two indexes, and for some years farm rose above nonfarm indexes. All of this tends to indicate that, from the standpoint of prices he received for farm produce and prices he paid for finished goods, the nineteenth-century farmer had more justification for complaint than his twentieth-century cousin. Being more nearly self-contained, however, the nineteenth-century tiller was less dependent on manufactured goods than later generations of farmers.

After 1875, as indicated above, although some fluctuations occurred in the prices of corn, wheat, and oats, the general trend was downward (see Appendix, Table III). Between 1874 and

1897 price averages for certain farm staples declined as follows: wheat from 94.4 to 63.3 cents per bushel; corn from 40.9 to 29.7 cents per bushel; and cotton from 11.1 to 5.8 cents per pound. Since these were average prices received by farmers as of December 1 of the respective years, they only portray something of the general decline in prices and do not reflect the extremely low figures at which farmers actually disposed of their produce. Because of straitened circumstances, most farmers marketed their commodities during the summer and early fall when harvests were at their peaks and commodity prices at the lowest ebb of the year; hence average prices actually received by farmers were well below the December prices.[6] During this twenty-five-year period some farmers disposed of wheat and corn for as little as fifteen cents per bushel and cotton for less than four cents per pound.

As an offsetting factor, between 1870 and 1897, the relative rate of increase in farm output was much greater than the rate of decline in commodity prices; in consequence, from decade to decade aggregate values of farm products grew larger and larger. In thirty years cotton production increased sixfold while the price declined by 50 per cent; the result was a threefold rise in the value of the crop. Over the same period wheat production jumped thirtyfold as the price dropped one-third, bringing about a twentyfold increase in aggregate value. And corn output quintupled while the price fell 25 per cent. Considerable improvement in the quality of herds and flocks partially accounted for a sixfold increase in the value of livestock. Because of the terrific increase in the number of farms, the average per farm income remained low, and in spite of enormous increases in aggregate values of farm products, the degree of improvement in the economic well-being of the family engaged in agriculture was not as great as might have been expected. In terms of current dollars, per farm value reached the low in 1880, then began a slow rise which continued through the remaining years of the century (see Appendix, Table IV). However, based on contemporary dollars, the trend continued downward.

Despite all trends to the contrary, yet in keeping with agricultural tradition, advisers persistently urged farmers to preserve and nurture the practice of diversified farming. With the apparent hope of persuading immigrants that in Texas they could live at home, and live well, Texas promoters emphasized as a primary selling point that any family could, on any Texas farm, produce all the essentials of life and happiness. As proof of the bounty of Texas soils, one immigrant guide and handbook summarized the fruits of the labor of a man and his wife on a small farm near Palestine:

10 acres of cotton, which will give 5 bales, $250; 10 acres of corn, 108 bushels, $90; 1 acre of sweet potatoes, 300 bushels, $150; ¼ acre of gubers, 50 bushels, $100; ¾ acre of grass nuts, 12 bushels, $36; ¼ acre of onions, 30 bushels, $60; 1 acre of sugar cane, 100 gallons, $50. His wife raised 150 chickens, $30; 50 pounds of butter, $12.50; saved 20 pounds of feathers worth $10. He sheared 140 pounds of wool, $28; sold four beeves, $48, watermelons $5.00, and will make 3,000 pounds of pork, worth $180, he also made 40 bushels of wheat for his own use besides vegetables, etc.[7]

It is apparent that the farmer and his good wife operated a diversified live-at-home farm on which they produced a small amount of cotton for "clear profit." From the handbook's estimates, the value of the year's output from the farm totaled $999.50, almost three times the average per farm value of commodities for the year 1880 (see Appendix, Table IV). Most of the foregoing figures were estimates rather than data, estimates of both yield and value, and the guesses were in true Texas tradition – high rather than low. The farmer picked three bales of cotton instead of five; value of his corn was likely nearer $50.00 than $90.00; besides, it was counted twice, once as corn and once as chicken, pork, or beef. If the estimated values of the output of the farm were reduced one-half, the resulting total would still be well above the average for that year. However, the story was offered as proof to prospective Texans that, from hog to hominy, their every need could be supplied from a small Texas farm.

Contemporary editors, as a group, were disciples of the doctrine of diversification, and as more and more farmers succumbed to the lure of specialized commercialization, they preached louder and louder against the spreading sin. G. W. Robson of the *Echo* summarized the advantages claimed for diversification:

Diversity in farming has so many advantages that it should find favor in the practice of every sensible agriculturalist. It puts on the home table a great variety and prevents the necessity of many purchases; distributes both the labor and cash receipts pretty evenly throughout the year; prevents the overstocking in any single department, and so tends to keep up prices; is favorable to the rotation of crops, the advantages of which all appreciate; and finally is an insurance against heavy loss by distributing among many products the risks of failure of one.[8]

Clearly the heart of the argument by the proponents of diversified farming was the implied warning, "Don't put all your eggs in one basket." That the point had little validity seemed never to make it less attractive to those who advanced it in condemnation of specialized agriculture. Grasshoppers and locusts, when making their irregular pilgrimages, never seemed to heed the argument. As their hordes swept on, they devoured all crops; destruction was as complete on the diversified farm as on the specialized farm. Furthermore, droughts, floods, and hail never evidenced any great respect for diversity; to all crops in their path, whether specialized or diversified, they gave the same treatment — total ruin. The program advocated by Robson and the fraternity for which he spoke was little more than a plan for living at home, which, if perpetuated, would have bound the farmer to the subsistence level. The reasoning that diversity did away with the necessity of making many purchases was a blow at the very roots of an industrial society.

The publisher of the Mason County *News-Item* was pleased to learn that farmers were awakening to the evils of specialization. "Nearly every farmer in Mason County," he said, "is opening his eyes to the fact that it pays better to raise a diversity of crops than to put all his land in one cereal."[9] Subsequently, the *Albany News* gave as its studied opinion the statement that failure would at some time overtake the man who devoted all of his land to cotton. "Plant cotton," it advised, "not all cotton, but some cotton."[10] And the *Texas Farm and Ranch* painted a beautiful picture of happiness and contentment as the reward for diversified farming:

When a farmer has a good smokehouse with plenty of bacon and things in it, a lock on the door, and the key in his wife's pocket, and has enough corn, oats, potatoes, turnips, and collards, and his taxes paid, he is really more independent than one who has $1,000 cash in hand, which he has borrowed from a loan association at 10 per cent and trimmings, secured by a chattel mortgage.[11]

And, as late as 1895, the *Taylor County News* vowed: "The 'man with the hoe' can make as much and live as well as he ever could provided he don't want to sell everything he makes and buy everything he uses. That system will knock all the profits out of almost any business."[12] These quotations illustrate the confusion in editors' minds, the consequence of a failure to comprehend the trend of the economy in which they lived. They appear to have had no clear concept of the functioning of the essential elements of a commercial economy; and they attempted to brand as a dunce, or at least as a foolish sort of soul, any farmer who attempted to synchronize his operations with the new order.

According to W. C. Holden, the low cotton prices which prevailed during the decade of the nineties were primarily responsible for the firing of a barrage of diversification propaganda directed at farmers;[13] yet, in the face of all contrary advice, these same farmers persistently moved toward a system of commercialized agriculture. However, from the above quotations it would appear that the barrage of diversification propaganda had begun much earlier than 1890.

In making the transition from independent self-sufficiency to dependent specialization, agriculture tended to move through a period of barter to a monetary economy. Merchants of 1875 used somewhat the following type of advertising:

Those in want of choice groceries, cigars, tobacco, dry goods, boots, bridles, and in short anything you can call for, should see Major Horton before purchasing elsewhere, as he takes country produce for goods as willingly as cash.[14]

As the century drew to a close and the use of money became more common, this sort of advertising was seen less frequently.

As a source for determining the rate of economic change during the last quarter of the nineteenth century, contemporary newspapers stand unchallenged. In one instance the New Orleans *Picayune* noted, "Farmers are pouring into western Texas so fast that ranchmen have just time enough to move their cattle out and prevent their tails being chopped off by the advancing hoe."[15] Though the *Picayune* spoke figuratively, it was not far from the literal truth, for settlers were flooding the state. In June, 1875,

G. W. Robson, desirous of publishing a newspaper for cattlemen, founded the *Frontier Echo* at Jacksboro, then considered to be the heart of the cattle country. After three and one-half years, because the center of the industry had shifted farther west, Robson moved the *Echo* to Fort Griffin, sixty miles west of Jacksboro. Ironically, in an early issue of the *Echo* after its removal to Fort Griffin, Robson observed: "We notice quite a number of plows going to the country. Farmers are making preparations for spring work."[16] The publisher probably resigned himself to the fact that he would have to live with both cattlemen and farmers. Although cattle remained Robson's first love, he sprinkled advice to both groups throughout the columns of his paper. In one issue he recommended restraint in the planting of cotton:

The subject of raising cotton is being agitated by a number of our farmers. We believe the staple has never been tried in this county, and it would be well for those who do engage in it to place their reliance on other crops until they can thoroughly test the adaptability of our soil for this crop.[17]

In previous years Jack and Shackelford had been livestock counties exclusively, but after its removal to Fort Griffin, the *Echo* regularly carried plow and seed advertisements.

Hordes of hoe-equipped farmers marched doggedly into the cattle empire. In 1885, a news item from Sweetwater gave warning to livestock interests that a "colony of over a dozen families [has] made arrangements to settle in Fisher County not far from Sweetwater. The men are intelligent, industrious farmers."[18] This colony was undoubtedly the vanguard of farm families who subsequently settled in communities throughout Fisher County. After the lapse of three years another correspondent wrote that in spite of the fact that Fisher was considered a livestock county, value of farm produce for the previous year totaled $15,000 and would exceed $30,000 for the current year.[19] Also during the eighties a story under a Sweetwater dateline reported that large numbers of local cattlemen had moved their livestock to pastures farther west, and that owners of other herds were considering plans to follow them. In closing, the writer observed that the glory of the cattlemen had departed, leaving the fertile soil to await the coming of the "man with the hoe," and that according to local opinion the future success of the stockman depended on his reducing the size and improving the quality of his herd and cultivating some feed for his livestock.[20] At approximately the same date, press dispatches from Wichita Falls revealed the fact that large pasture men were giving serious consideration to cutting up their ranches because of a prevalent feeling that the future welfare of livestock interests would depend more on smaller herds of thoroughbred cattle[21] than on larger herds of longhorns.

Following successful experimentation with the cultivation of cane on a thirty-acre field in a J A Ranch pasture, Charles Goodnight warned his foreman, "Let this be the last thing planted on this ranch. If the nesters see this they will fill up this country in sixty days." Goodnight's statement attested the excellent quality of the cane. In spite of his precautions, the nesters were moving to the Panhandle in considerable numbers by 1887, and within another five years farmers had squatted on lands claimed by the J A Ranch interests.[22]

An important stimulus to a change in usage patterns of western lands was the steady rise in land values. When the free open range served as the grazing grounds for longhorn cattle, remuneration to owners of the cattle was comparable to an annual find, or an annual gift, of twenty-five cents per acre grazed. But as land fell under private ownership and its per acre value increased from $2.62 in 1870 to $7.78 twenty years later,[23] owners became interested in more lucrative returns than those offered by a crop of longhorns. Any grain or row crop, if rainfall were sufficient for it to grow at all, offered a greater monetary reward per acre (see Appendix, Table III). Hence, farmers kept encroaching on the livestock ranges; however, the relatively low value of Texas land ($2.62 per acre when the national average stood at $18.26)[24] did not require that farmers make a very intensive utilization of their land.

During the last half of the nineteenth century, the extensive economic adjustments and readjustments being made in Texas did not bring the state economy abreast of national development. Adequate supplies of modern farm implements and machinery are essential for the change-over to commercial farming, and in this respect destruction of farm machinery and equipment during the Civil War decade (see Chapter I) placed Texas agriculture at a disadvantage for the remainder of the century. In 1870 the average value of implements and machinery per Texas farm reached a low of forty-four dollars. Over succeeding decades equipment values per farm crept slowly upward to fifty-two, to sixty, and ultimately to eighty-five dollars (see Appendix, Table II). By way of contrast, per farm value of implements for the state stood, in 1860, approximately twenty-four dollars above the national average; but for the remainder of the century Texas farm machinery averaged fifty to sixty dollars below that of the nation. During the war the state had been deprived of tools essential to the maintenance of its relative position among other states in the national trend toward commercialized agriculture. As a result, states of the Midwest moved well ahead of Texas. After 1870, the impoverished condition of Texas farmers, who possessed neither funds nor credit, made the purchase of farm implements extremely difficult. Not only were Texans too poor to replace or add to the farm equipment, but immigrants from other southern states were even poorer. Undoubtedly the inability to provide adequate farm machinery prolonged the period of self-contained farming, which was "poor man" farming — the unit restricted to family size, and the work done entirely by the farm family, a single team, and a few simple tools without additional help other than perhaps a little at harvest time.

For some reason contemporary newspapers failed to develop a graphic and continuous story of the introduction of newer and more efficient farm machinery. Discerning pioneers, among them George Tyler, were cognizant of the significance of the impact of improved machinery on the size of the farm. By use of census data Tyler shows that the improved acreage per farm in Bell County rose from 43.66 in 1869 to 89.66 in 1879. He credited the increase to the introduction of "labor-saving machinery, such as riding plows, cultivators, and threshers."[25] Almanacs and guides sometimes made reference to the introduction of late developments in farm equipment: "Expensive agricultural implements are being bought, fencing put up, excellent dwelling houses and superior farm out-buildings erected, fine stock bred and cared for, and the general material wealth of the state increased on every hand."[26]

By 1878 (and probably at a much earlier date), steam threshers were operating in the grain fields of the state; two were reported that year in Comanche County.[27] The machines were not common, however, and that after the lapse of some years they were still oddities is emphasized by correspondents, one of whom wrote, "The steam thresher received by T. & B. Gardner last week was a considerable source of amusement and curiosity while it remained in town."[28] Now and then some person wrote to a newspaper relating his experience with some new type of farm machinery; John McClane wrote from Corpus Christi that "he [sic] had been on a trip up the Nueces 30 miles. He [sic] went to see a sulky plow at work — the first one in the country."[29] That is to say, by the close of the seventies Nueces County farmers were being introduced to the riding plow.

At Kelleyville, in Marion County, one of the state's oldest foundries manufactured stoves and plows. It was claimed that its iron plow outlasted those produced elsewhere of steel. For 1877, the production quota for the foundry was in excess of 15,000 plows,[30] an increase over the output of the previous year of something above 50 per cent. This was an instance in which Texas industry and agriculture complemented each other.

The more fortunate farmers, those who had acquired the latest improved farm machinery and who applied the more scientific agricultural processes, produced larger crops than their less modern brethren. By expressing their satisfaction with the new implements and methods, farmers made the idea of technological change more acceptable to their fellows. That is to say, when dirt farmers pronounced new machinery and agricultural methods worthy, other farmers regarded the innovations more favorably. The press gave experience letters a wide circulation, including some, such as this one, written by residents of other states:

It is my candid opinion that a great deal is gained by drilling wheat. In the first place the saving in seed, where a large area is sown, will pay the cost of a drill in one or two years, a bushel to a bushel and a half more with the hand. Then I know from experience that drilled wheat bears the winter much better than that broadcast; and lastly, as drilled wheat can be cultivated, the yield is greater and the quality of the grain finer than where the seed is sown broadcast. The price of the drill is from $90 to $100.[31]

When a farmer spoke from "experience" his words carried great weight among his colleagues.

According to Holden, the West Texas farmer quickly acquired an aversion to any kind of walking plow. Fundamental to this allergy was the greater acreage which could be cultivated with a riding plow as compared to a walking plow. Walking plows, planters, and cultivators were quickly discarded, and westerners chose instead sulky plows, riding planters, and riding cultivators.[32] The riding plows — which included binders, threshers, gang-plows, two-row planters, and two-row cultivators — so readily accepted by western farmers tended to increase the volume of their surplus products and to lead to a more permanent establishment of commercial, or market, farming.

In economic significance, the spread of agricultural education parallels the introduction of farm machinery. Throughout the closing decades of the century, the average Texas farmer held "book farming" in profound contempt; but he profited from his own trials, and to a lesser extent from what was learned when neighbors compared experiences.[33] Agricultural associations served as forums for the exchange of information; in fact, they might be classed as the forerunners of the agricultural college. In 1879 a number of these associations were functioning in Texas, and some of them had assumed sponsorship of experiments designed to test the adaptability of certain plants to soils and climate. Agrarian societies reported that under proper cultivation tobacco, rice, sorghum, broom corn, the ramie plant, and the castor bean were profitable in almost every county. (Now, in the mid-twentieth century, the castor bean again looms as a crop of great potential importance.) The agricultural associations emphasized to their members the economic importance of improving the quality of crops and livestock. According to studied judgments of farm societies, there were few fruits, either tropical or temperate, which could not be produced in the state to the great profit of the grower. And as a means toward increased production, the agricultural associations encouraged the introduction of labor-saving machinery and equipment.[34]

That there were differences in the tempo of development of East and West Texas in the last quarter of the century may be determined by a comparison of population and production data. Let us use for comparative purposes the forty counties previously enumerated (see Notes 21 and 24 for Chapter I). In thirty years the twenty eastern counties increased in population from 221,176 to 756,855, while for the twenty western counties the increase was from 13,674 to 172,243.[35] With regard to comparative outputs, gains in the west were relatively greater than in the east. While the value of farm products for the eastern counties rose from $10,526,810 to $39,980,915, the western increase was from $574,866 to $8,403,341.[36] On a per capita basis, farm produce values for East Texas increased from forty-seven to fifty-three dollars, and for West Texas from forty-two to forty-nine dollars. When considered from the standpoint of a possible increase in anticipated monetary gain, comparative data on per capita incomes fail to prove that a westward move brought about any improvement in the economic status of the settler. If prospective monetary gain stimulated the urge to go west, the reward was not forthcoming through income. As a matter of record, fewer than one out of four newcomers actually sought homes in the western part of the state. Probably those who went on into the West were attracted more by the cheap land. The possibility that cheap land held some magnetic attraction is indicated by a temporary lull in migrations to Texas following the opening of Indian Territory to settlement — for a short period even Texas lost population to Oklahoma.

By the close of the century residents of both East and West Texas consumed smaller quantities of home-slaughtered meats than in earlier days. Aggregate value of meat butchered on farms in eastern counties increased from $925,371 to $1,571,489, but per capita consumption decreased from four to two dollars. Value of home-butchered meat in the western counties rose from $67,745 to $441,228,[37] but per capita consumption decreased from five dollars to two dollars and a half. Livestock prices were higher in 1900 than in 1870; consequently the decline in dollar value of per capita consumption of home-butchered meats is indicative of the degree of change from the older independent, self-contained order to the newer interdependent commercialized system — farmers were relying more and more on Swift and Armour to do the butchering.

In all sections of the state the ratio of milch cows to persons decreased. The eastern county ratio dropped from two cows to every five persons to one cow to six persons, while the western decrease was relatively sharper, changing from two cows to one person to a one to four ratio.[38] The great improvement in the quality of dairy breeds resulted, however, in a per animal increase in milk production which more than compensated for the lower ratio of cows to persons. During the nineties alone, the decline in dairy herds amounted to 140,000 animals, but milk production rose from 118,475,320 to 251,342,205 gallons per annum; and milk sales, which in 1870 totaled 62,771 gallons, had by 1900 skyrocketed to 8,091,205 gallons. Even though the volume of milk sold in 1900 was small, relative to mid-twentieth-century sales, it did represent a tremendous expansion in commercial dairying. In thirty years butter production jumped from 3,712,747 to 47,991,492 pounds, a gain which also meant a possible threefold increase in consumption per person. Statistics on dairy herds and dairy products point to an intensified utilization of land by owners of milch cows.

For the most part, through the closing decades of the nineteenth century, the production of specialty crops paralleled the remarkable gains made in the dairy industry. In almost every instance production increases were modest until the nineties, when sharp rises occurred. When the honey crop rose from 275,169 to 4,780,204 pounds, Texas became the leading state in honey production. The chicken population grew in twenty years from 3,127,770 to 13,562,-300, also quadrupling egg output. The rice crop spurted from an 1890 crop of 100,000 pounds to a 1900 crop of 7,186,863 pounds grown on 8,711 acres in 84 farms.[39] Virtually the entire increase in production occurred during the last six years of the century, after Dr. Seaman Knapp introduced in 1894 a method of irrigation suitable for rice culture along the Gulf Coast.[40] The Southern Pacific

Railroad undertook an advertising campaign designed to increase the consumption of rice and manifested a great interest in developing the rice region of Texas. By 1901 the company had distributed 60,000 copies of a rice recipe booklet and had made plans to open a Chicago bureau to solicit settlers for Texas rice lands.[41]

As cities and towns grew in size and numbers, production of fruits and vegetables became more profitable. Before the Civil War truck gardening was confined largely to German settlements, but this type of agriculture became more widespread during the seventies. Thrall's *Almanac* for 1880 stated that farmers in the vicinity of populous centers found truck farming very remunerative. Thrall entertained a hope that the earlier Texas season would eventually place Texas vegetables on northern markets weeks ahead of northern produce. He expressed the opinion that from one acre in truck a farmer could market produce equivalent in value to the product from ten acres of corn or cotton. What prevented the development of the truck farm as a major branch of Texas agriculture? High freight rates.[42]

N. A. Taylor, who wrote extensively of conditions in Texas at the close of the century, gave a vivid description of the impact of a thriving town on the surrounding agricultural community. Thurber, a mining camp of 1,550 employees, he said, was a Godsend to farmers who brought all manner of farm produce to camp, selling at full prices and paying nothing to commission men or transportation companies.[43] From a radius of fifty or sixty miles Thurber attracted farmers who drove beeves to the mining company slaughter pens, or came in wagons laden with melons, fruits, vegetables, hay, corn, oats, fresh meat, homemade lard, and sausage. Except for cotton, they brought to Thurber everything produced on the farm, and for a few years in the twentieth century the company gin processed their cotton. The writer, as a boy, well remembers the streets filled with wagons of farm peddlers who canvassed from house to house, sending a "young'un" down either side of the street with display samples, or crying their wares as they used the reins to swish molesting flies from the backs of the slowly moving teams. A successful trip to Thurber sent the farmer home with change in his pocket, plus clothing, dry goods, groceries, and perchance a bottle of whiskey from company stores. Until sometime after the mines were closed in 1922, farmers continued to peddle to the residents of Thurber.

Even though Thurber and other prosperous communities provided attractive markets for farm specialties, farmers in specialty market territories did not turn hastily from staple crops. In the marketing radius of Thurber, cotton continued to be the most important money crop. While the production of vegetables had steadily increased, value of the output remained small, totaling, as late as 1899, only $2,368,346 or slightly more than 1 per cent of the aggregate value of all farm produce. The average vegetable plot covered approximately four-tenths of an acre.[44] Commercial production of vegetables was largely confined to the eastern half of the state. Throughout the closing quarter of the century, newspapers and farm journals emphasized the importance of fruit culture; but orchards remained small, and in 1900 their crops aggregated in value $1,345,423, which represented only one-half of one per cent of all farm produce (see Appendix, Table IV). By 1900 per capita value of Texas-grown fruits and vegetables averaged forty and seventy-five cents respectively.[45]

In the production of sugar cane, another minor crop, commercial growers gradually took over. As the source of syrup, a self-contained farmer's substitute for sugar, sugar cane had for decades been widely grown over the state. As late as 1900, cane patches were still planted for syrup; however, 18,000 acres in commercial fields then produced 54,758 tons of cane from which was refined a total of 2,789,250 pounds of sugar with a residue of 888,637 gallons of syrup. Practically the whole commercial crop came from three counties: Fort Bend, Brazoria, and Cameron.[46]

Irrigated farming has a long history in Texas, dating from systems inaugurated by Spanish settlers. In his essay on early irrigation, Edwin P. Arneson says that many present-day irrigation projects come by direct descent from Bagdad, through knowledge transmitted by Arabs to Spaniards and by Spaniards to Texans.[47] Irrigation tends toward specialty crops and commercial farming. Despite its long history in Texas, irrigation, through the nineteenth century, remained a small scale operation. In 1900 a total of 581 irrigation systems supplied 1,325 irrigators with water for 49,652 acres. When placed beside comparative data which number farmers by the hundreds of thousands and cultivated acres by tens of millions, statistics on irrigation seem puny (see Appendix, Table V). The 581 projects represented an investment of $1,027,608 for an average capital outlay of $20.70 per irrigated acre. Irrigation was concentrated in ten counties: El Paso, Menard, Pecos, Presidio, Reeves, Tom Green, Val Verde, Ward, Jefferson, and Orange, with a combined total of 40,000 acres, which constituted four-fifths of the irrigated acreage in the state. Eight of the counties were located in the western portion, usually described as the semiarid region; the remaining two, located in the extreme southeastern corner, were on the Gulf Coast in the most humid section of Texas. With a per capita outlay of $2.81 per irrigated acre, Reeves County watered at the lowest construction cost, while Jefferson County, with an average outlay of $45.23, operated the most costly project.[48] Only a fraction of 1 per cent of the land in the counties was irrigated, but hopes were high that the projects represented only a beginning, which in certain instances proved to be true. Practically all water used for irrigation was drawn from springs or living streams. By 1900, irrigation in the Lower Rio Grande Valley had scarcely begun, and the great irrigation wells of the South Plains were undreamed of.

Sometimes specialty crops, such as rice in Jefferson and Orange counties, were responsible for the development of irrigation. In Reeves County irrigation was applied to a wide variety of crops; a number were mentioned in a news paragraph from Pecos: "Vegetables, cereals, cotton and fruits, almost perfect in quality, were displayed at the pavillion today, raised on irrigated farms in this valley."[49] An irrigated farm in San Saba County was said to have produced a crop of El Paso onions valued in excess of $1,000 per acre, while another irrigated farm in the same vicinity was reported to have been leased for gardening at a rental of twenty-four dollars per acre. Although devoted to a large number of different crops, most of the irrigated land, except that in the coastal counties, was planted in hay and corn. Three crops of hay were harvested annually; the corn yield averaged 125 bushels per acre.[50] The location of the land largely determined whether it would be planted in feed or in fruits and vegetables. In the western counties, lying in the heart of the livestock country, production of feeds was very profitable. Sometimes irrigated soils contained chemical compositions not found elsewhere, compounds which endowed certain plants, e.g., the "Pecos" cantaloupe, with rare quality or unusually fine flavors. Produce of this sort usually commanded premium prices, and much of the land responsible for the distinctive feature was given over to the crop.

A land agent, advertising in the *Texas Almanac* for 1904, offered for sale 30,000 acres of irrigated Cameron County lands, available in tracts of fifty acres and up. He claimed them to be "the finest rice and truck garden lands in the world." Irrigation systems invariably cost several times the value of the lands watered, were built with borrowed funds, and were, consequently, a boon to commercial farming. Repayment of the loans and meeting of interest payments on the investments called for cash crops. Or, if the projects were constructed by promoters, land prices were boosted severalfold in order to pay for the system and yield a profit to the promoters. The usual sale was a small tract, on credit, at a high price and with a high rate of interest, a transaction which bound the purchaser-operator to commercial crops.

A great increase in the number of tenant farmers relative to the number of owner-operators characterized the last two decades of the century, and is frequently offered as evidence that the status of farmers underwent a considerable change, all of it for the worse. While, over the 1880-1900 period, the number of farms doubled (see Appendix, Table V), farm tenancy trebled. Why this sudden upsurge in tenancy? Standardized explanations are plentiful. All of them merit consideration, but none presents reasons wholly satisfactory. For the Turner school, the answer is simple: the state was fresh out of free land. Since all land was now privately owned, all newcomers to the agricultural fraternity must enter through the ignoble status of tenancy. At least some landowners might have been induced to sell all, or a portion, of their land to the newcomers.

Nor does foreclosure on farm mortgages as a consequence of

the depression of the nineties appear to be the real reason. Why? Because the census of 1890 showed only 7,221 mortgaged farms in the state (see Appendix, Tables VI and VII). Had foreclosures been executed on all seven thousand mortgages, relegating all owner-operators to tenant status, scarcely 10 per cent of the increase in tenancy would have been accounted for. Extremely low prices received for farm produce could have caused some owners to dispose of their property while they remained as tenants; however, it is unlikely that any great increase in the tenant population came from this source. Severe depressions in this country have a tendency to reverse the migratory trend from farm to city. A depression-inspired back-to-the-farm movement offers a possible explanation for some increase in the number of share tenants. A person with no funds, no credit, and no implements, returning from city to farm and finding the doors closed to him as owner-operator, could still function as a share tenant. Enumerations dealt only with the number of tenants, not the source of tenancy.

Fluctuations in land prices were undoubtedly responsible for some of the growth in the number of farm-renters. A sharp rise in land prices during the eighties was followed by a precipitate decline during the nineties. Periods of fluctuating prices are field days for speculators. The cheap land of the nineties presented attractive speculative possibilities. A nonfarming group of landowners began to assume an important role. This group, composed largely of professional men, bankers, and businessmen, bought cheap improved land with the intent to hold until rewarded through an increment in value. This group derived their livelihood from sources other than land; and if the farms were cultivated at all, tenants, not owners, did the tilling. If prices rose as anticipated, those holding land for speculative purposes made profitable returns on investments. In the opening decade of the twentieth century, Texas land prices trebled. This insured an average return, with no income from crops, of 20 per cent or more on investments in land. If owners leased the land to farm tenants, any rentals derived from cultivation were supplements to the 20 per cent. The increase in numbers of nonfarming landowners was partially responsible for the growth of tenancy.

In the course of a score of years beginning with 1890, the rise in volume of farm mortgage indebtedness caused considerable alarm in the ranks of agricultural experts. The mortgage debt has been classed regularly among the evil forces operating to repress the farm class. Hence, any increase in farm debt was viewed as another incumbrance for the overburdened farmer. That is to say, as a sympathy-evoking device, farm mortgage data proved very effective. For the state of Texas, in 1890, the aggregate farm-home mortgage debt totaled $6,494,633. By 1910, this had increased to $76,098,272 (see Appendix, Table VI). The major portion of the increase occurred after 1900. If a greater indebtedness is irrefutable evidence of deterioration of the farmer's economic well-being, the financial plight of the twentieth-century farmer was indeed grave. However, when all data are compared and carefully analyzed, the $76,000,000 debt proves to be less burdensome to the individual farmer. The 1910 farmer held a 74.5 per cent equity in his home in a period of rising commodity prices, while the 1890 owner-equity was 58.3 per cent in a period of falling prices. Irrespective of the size of the farm unit, the owner-operator should find it less difficult to retire a mortgage debt equivalent to 25 per cent of the value of his investment from the returns of a 75 per cent equity and rising prices, than to retire a 42 per cent mortgage from a 58 per cent equity and falling prices.

For the census years 1890, 1900, and 1910, it is significant that the number of mortgaged farms very nearly equals the increase in the number of owner-operated farms (see Appendix, Table VI). One could draw the erroneous conclusion that all new farm homes were mortgaged. Although this is not true, undoubtedly a high percentage of the new owners did operate mortgaged farms. In twenty years the ratio of mortgaged to nonmortgaged farm homes increased from one out of sixteen to three out of every ten. For this analysis, reasons for the growth of farm indebtedness are secondary to the consequences. Regardless of cause, the farm lien, once incurred, compelled the owner-operator to direct his efforts more and more toward commercial farming. Interest and principal were payable only in money, and cash returns were realized from commercial crops. No longer was it possible for the farm family to live at home, planting "a little cotton" for ready cash. Annual monetary needs demanded sizable sums which could be realized by turning more and more land over to market crops.

Too, during the last twenty years of the century, the growth of farm tenancy must be considered as a factor in the trend toward greater productivity of marketable crops. For the tenant who paid a money rent, there was no recourse other than to produce, as a bare minimum, cash crops sufficient to provide adequate funds for rental payments. All families found it increasingly desirable to have some cash income over and above rental requirements; hence the acreage devoted to money crops, always more than enough to pay the rent, grew ever larger. The landowner applied pressure to the share tenant — a tenant who furnished his own seed and equipment, paying as rent one-fourth of his cotton and one-third of all other crops — to plant more and more of the land in cash crops. The sharecropper, who furnished nothing save his own labor, taking half of the crop for his share — the other half going to the landowner — exercised no control whatever over the crops he cultivated. Usually the cropper's share was mortgaged at the beginning of the year, either to the landowner or to a merchant, and he drew no return until the crop-lien had been satisfied. As the system of sharecropping operated, the landowner customarily decreed that all acreage be planted in cash crops. In many regions the sharecropper was not even permitted to cultivate a small garden lot for his own use, the owner demanding that every square foot of tillable land be planted in a commercial crop. In 1900, half of the farms in Texas were tenant operated; in twenty years their numbers had increased by 110,000 (see Appendix, Tables V and VII). This gave a vigorous boost to commercialized agriculture.

Thus the closing decades of the nineteenth century were characterized by a pronounced shift from self-contained to commercialized agriculture, with a marked acceleration in the tempo of change during the nineties. While not highly satisfactory, statistics on staple crops do offer a basis for comparing the degree of change. Corn production, with 85 or 90 per cent of the crop being consumed by the producer, increased 400 per cent while its acreage doubled (see Appendix, Table VIII). But wheat and oat production

increased thirtyfold on triple the acreage. As further evidence of
the new order, there was a decrease of more than 40 per cent in
the number of flour mills, but a fourfold increase in the aggregate
value of the output of flour and its by-products. No longer were
mills restricted to local markets in self-contained communities; no
longer did they operate as custom-mills; rather, they operated as
strictly commercial mills serving large markets. What is more, at
the close of the century, the wheat crop was marketed, not consumed, by growers. However, cotton must be credited with leadership of the movement toward commercial agriculture. It was a 100
per cent market crop whose output in Texas alone increased by
1,700,000 bales in twenty years. Cotton dealt to self-contained agriculture a death blow.

IV

Cotton, "Big Money Crop"

IN the closing quarter of the nineteenth century cotton was both a cause and a result of considerable economic development. Historically, the plant has accommodated itself perfectly to self-contained and interdependent economies. Prior to the invention of the cotton gin a major portion of the lint was spun and woven on the premises of the grower for consumption by members of his household, including servants. The hand method of removing seed from the fiber was time consuming, a day, or often longer, being required for a slave to free a pound of lint. As long as hand linting prevailed, upland cotton never became a crop of great commercial significance; but when, in 1793, the gin appeared, cotton assumed a status entirely new, becoming, in the words of James Scherer,

the only crop of importance all of which is sold by those who produce it. Only seventeen per cent of the corn crop, for instance, leaves the farms; the rest is consumed or fed to the stock by those who produce it. Cotton, therefore, generates an enormous commerce and provides a medium of exchange that almost entirely takes the place of gold in the settlement of interstate and international balances.[1]

Cotton was a prime consideration in the development of southern railroads, and, in turn, railroad development contributed to the expansion of the Cotton Kingdom. Scherer, speaking in general terms, gave cotton credit for generating "an enormous commerce"; but, in citing a specific example, S. G. Reed pointed out that:

Cotton inspired the building of the first railroad in Texas — the Buffalo Bayou, Brazos and Colorado. General Sidney Sherman counted on 50,000 bales along the route to furnish the bulk of the revenue for the road. When he reached Richmond on the Brazos in 1855, he had only 24 cars "capable of loading 16 bales each," but in them or on them he moved 8,000 bales of Brazos Valley cotton at 75 cents a bale — about one third of what it cost the farmers to get it to market by ox team. Cotton from that good day has caused the building of many other railroads, the extension of many others.[2]

From the point of origin to the Richmond terminus, the Buffalo Bayou, Brazos and Colorado covered a distance of only thirty-two miles,[3] but for cotton shipped from Richmond it reduced freight costs an average of $1.50 per bale. This saving in freight, approximately one-third cent per pound, might well be regarded as a price increase to the farmer.

S. B. McAlister compiled convincing evidence that there existed a close relationship between extensions of railroad systems and growth of cotton acreage. From the day it first moved a car of freight cotton was one of the principal sources of revenue for the Texas & Pacific Railway. Cotton shipments began with the construction of the road; and as the line nosed its way westward, substantial cotton loading platforms were erected at each small town. In 1874 the Texas & Pacific, extending from Dallas east, moved 102,414 bales; four years later it hauled 350,951 bales.[4] Since in the four-year period Texas & Pacific lines were extended only twenty-five or thirty miles, the tripling of tonnage must be attributed to an increase in the number of acres of cotton planted along the railroad.

Prerailroad freight charges were high, and oxen-powered units moved goods at snaillike pace. In general, charges for overland freight averaged twenty cents per ton mile or a dollar per hundred pounds per hundred miles.[5] A farmer, moving cotton from the interior at prevailing bull-train rates, encountered an added cost of a penny per pound for every hundred miles traveled to navigable water; for example, an overland haul of five hundred miles added five cents per pound to the farmer's costs of producing cotton. With the coming of railroads, freight rates began to decline, and in a number of states the legislatures fixed maximum rates applicable to railroad freight charges. In 1879 the legislature of Texas prescribed a maximum intrastate rate of fifty cents per hundred pounds per hundred miles,[6] the maximum rail tariff being set at approximately half the prevailing ox-wagon rate. However, the trend in railroad freight charges was downward from the fifty-cent maximum, declining over a period of thirty years to a penny per ton mile, which, according to the estimates of C. S. Potts, represented a 95 per cent reduction in freight charges from the old ox-wagon level.[7]

Actually, railroads gave farmers in the hinterlands a greater reduction in shipping costs than the afore-mentioned 95 per cent. This they did by applying postage rates on all freight traveling a greater distance than 187 miles. Under the postage rates a farmer who shipped cotton 400 or 500 miles was charged no more than if it had been transported only 187 miles. As early as 1879, the Houston & Texas Central established a mileage-postage rate on cotton. Between Galveston and Mexia the rate was based on mileage; that is, the farther from Galveston the higher the charges, reaching the maximum of $4.50 per bale at Mexia. On all cotton billed to Galveston from any point between Mexia and Denison, freight charges were only $4.50 (postage rate) per bale.[8]

Even in the prerailroad period, cotton could be transported for greater distances more profitably than other staple agricultural commodities. Livestock, moving to markets in herds and flocks by walking on their own feet, were a possible exception. The same wagon that hauled to market sixty bushels of wheat valued at forty-five to sixty dollars could have carried five to seven bales of cotton marketable at $200 to $350. Dollar wheat and ten-cent cotton had respective monetary values of $1.67 and ten dollars per 100 pounds. At these prices, when his crop was moved at ox-wagon rates to markets one hundred miles distant, the farmer had left as remuneration for his year of toil sixty-seven cents for wheat or nine dollars for cotton. A two-hundred-mile market meant a thirty-three cent loss on wheat but a return of eight dollars on cotton. Without railroads neither perishable nor low per unit value farm products could compete on a commercial basis with cotton. With railroads low per unit value products, perishable or nonperishable, unless they were crops of phenomenal yields, still gave cotton no formidable competition in commerce.

In general, Americans seem to encounter great difficulty in comprehending one of the primary reasons for their rise to industrial pre-eminence, which is nothing more than the abandonment of self-contained agriculture. A nation of self-sufficient farmers, by its very nature, could never have produced raw materials or markets in necessary volume to build and maintain the gigantic industrial empire now functioning. A school of thought prevailed, and still prevails, which held that a self-contained agricultural economy offered the greatest rewards in goods and happiness. M. B. Hammond blamed the railroads and cotton for the destruction of self-contained agriculture in the South, saying:

> By cheapening the transportation of corn and bacon to the cotton lands, and cheapening the carriage of cotton to the seaboard, an unaccustomed adjustment of prices came about, which led the farmers into the vicious semblance of economy of which the evil effects are still seen and felt throughout the states, whereby the independence and the substantial comforts of farm life are sacrificed to the pursuit of money returns from a large cotton crop.[9]

In effect, Hammond has said that only a system of monotonous, primitive, independent, self-contained agriculture offers adequate rewards in comforts and happiness. Hammond apparently overlooked, among other things, the fact that "a large cotton crop" encouraged large corn and hog crops, and that the big crops were produced on lands to which they were best adapted, thereby bringing about a more efficient land usage. Land used more efficiently produces in greater abundance, thus providing more comforts and greater happiness — that is, supposing that comforts and happiness are dependent upon goods.

George W. Tyler, a Bell County pioneer, described the transition in agriculture as he saw it unfold in his home county. He witnessed the rise in cotton and decline in wheat production, a change which he also attributed to the coming of railroads. By the use of census material he showed that wheat production, in ten years beginning with 1879, fell from 84,267 to 20,936 bushels, while the cotton output increased from 9,217 to 37,473 bales. Tyler then analyzed the reasons for the change:

The rise and decline of wheat growing, as well as the rapid growth of cotton production, calls for a brief comment. Before the railroads reached into central Texas, Bell County people had grown all their own breadstuffs, as well as feed for such stock as did not run on the open range, and were able to sell most of the surplus to immigrants. They did not grow much cotton, for the expense of hauling it by wagon to far-off markets of Houston and Galveston was too great. During the seventies numerous small flour mills in the county enabled them to convert wheat into flour, which was hauled to the counties below and sold there. When the railroads reached the county in the early eighties, they began to bring in cheaper flour from the great northern mills and the growing of local wheat declined. The same railroads furnished a cheaper outlet for the more profitable cotton, which rapidly became the "money crop."[10]

Two things are emphasized in the Tyler analysis: the importance of low transportation costs to commercial agriculture, and the fact that an increase in cotton production was advantageous to the farmer. By lowering freight tariffs, railroads gave the cotton farmer a two-way price increase: they delivered merchandise to him at lower prices, and they saved him money on cotton freight charges. As a result, the Bell County farmer did the rational thing; he devoted his land to "the more profitable cotton."

An example of the influence of the approaching railroad on the introduction and expansion of cotton may be seen by reviewing a phase of agricultural development in Jack County. Until the mid-seventies, the railroad nearest to Jacksboro was approximately eighty miles distant, and the county grew no cotton. In 1876 a railroad reached Fort Worth and half of Jack County fell within the fifty-mile radius of the rail terminus. That fall the *Echo* informed its readers: "Two and a quarter cents is what our [Jacksboro] merchants are paying for cotton."[11] The quoted price was for seed, or unginned, cotton. With an average of three pounds of seed cotton required to gin one pound of lint, Jacksboro merchants were paying 6.75 cents for lint cotton. That year cotton prices averaged 11.73 cents per pound on the New York exchange,[12] and 9.9 cents to the farmer.[13] Evidently, with a railroad less than fifty miles away, Jack County farmers found 6.75 cents a profitable price for cotton; however, costs of ginning and ox-wagon freight rates account for the differences between the Jack County price and the New York exchange, or price to farmer, averages. At that time, a railroad through Jacksboro would probably have increased the cotton price to Jack County farmers to more than eight cents per pound.

That 6.75 cents was considered a satisfactory price for Jack County cotton is proved by a fourfold increase in cotton acreage for the next season. In the fall of 1876, a gin began operations; but it broke down after processing five bales. The following year two gins were kept busy by the Jack County cotton crop.[14] Through the columns of the *Frontier Echo*, Robson described the opening of Jack County to cotton; then two years later in his *Fort Griffin Echo* he narrated the account of the arrival of cotton in the more westerly Shackelford County. Cotton culture moved westward with the Texas & Pacific and northwestward along railroads through Wichita Falls and into the Panhandle until halted by aridity.

Following the Bell County example, many communities in the southeastern portion of the state substituted cotton for other crops. From a crop of 350,628 bales in 1870, Texas cotton production grew to more than 3,000,000 bales in the late nineties, and the century closed with a 2,506,212 bale crop (see Appendix, Table VIII). The last crop of the century came from 7,000,000 acres, or three and one-half times the acreage devoted to the 1880 crop. In three decades the value of the cotton crop rose from $21,212,994 to $107,-510,010, the latter sum exceeding the value of all other farm products (see Appendix, Tables IV and IX). During this period ginnings, in the afore-mentioned twenty representative eastern counties, increased from 152,000 to 451,000 bales, while cotton production for the western counties jumped from 193 to 47,799 bales.[15]

In Texas, wherever it was grown, cotton assumed commercial leadership among agricultural products, frequently equaling or exceeding the aggregate home-consumption and commercial value of all other agricultural output. For the 1870's Denton may be regarded as a typical county in which, for livelihood, the people relied on general farming. The estimated value of its cotton, corn, wheat, oats, barley, rye, pork, wool, beef, mutton, horse, and mule output for 1876 totaled $1,345,000, of which cotton contributed

$750,000, corn $210,000, and wheat $150,000; then, in descending order of importance, came horses, mules, and hogs. Beef, with a product valued at $50,000, occupied the niche below hogs.[16] For the succeeding year, major crops for the entire state were valued at $67,266,330, with $37,054,000 credited to cotton and $21,070,000 to corn.[17] Thrall, in his *Almanac,* estimated the value of farm, ranch, and timber products for 1878 at $57,820,141. Cotton led with $38,043,720, and in second place with sales estimated at $8,241,903 were cattle;[18] for some unknown reason Thrall failed to include an estimate of the corn crop. As late as 1941 statistical studies revealed that "cotton is still the largest contributor to Texans' livelihood, as measured by the number of persons making all or a major part of their living from a single industry."[19]

Cotton was planted in the bottoms and on the uplands, on the plains and prairies, along the "big roads" and the byroads. Cotton encroached on acreage formerly allocated to other crops, and in an effort to get "new ground" for more of it, forests were uprooted. It drove livestock from the range. For mile after countless mile, railroads were paralleled by fleecy fields of cotton. During the last twenty years of the century, approximately a quarter-million acres were added annually to cotton fields. Wherever its seed would germinate, cotton was planted; yet the cotton acreage for 1900 was only half the twentieth-century maximum.

Why did cotton move on with unchecked persistence, uprooting the established order and mode of life, destroying the self-contained farm, and replacing all with a relatively new system — commercial agriculture? It is doubtful whether any other crop throughout the course of history has faced attacks so bitter and violent as those made on cotton. Producers of no other crop ever suffered the degree of condemnation that was heaped on cotton farmers. Writers, journalists, editors, agricultural colleges, farm journals, farm leaders, and farmer organizations, contemporary and twentieth-century, have dealt none too kindly with the cotton farmer. To them his worst offense was specialization — he would not diversify. To contemporary critics diversification meant primarily self-containment — they allowed for a very small cotton patch for "clear profit." Whether proponents of diversification actually advocated a self-sufficient economy, or whether they were proposing cultivation of a number of different crops as a sort of insurance, since in case some failed others would mature, they prescribed an inefficient utilization of land. Under either system excessive allocations of lands were made to poorly adapted crops, while deficient allocations were set aside for well adapted crops. Either proposal denied the use of land to its fullest productive possibilities.

At the first annual session of the Texas State Grange, W. W. Lang directed a portion of his address as Worthy Master to a criticism of cotton farmers:

That the planters of the State generally are in debt, is a truth that needs no argument to establish. Cotton planting for several years has been attended with actual loss of money. The effort of the Southern agriculturalists to produce cotton to the exclusion of all other crops, has brought distress upon the country.[20]

Lang charged cotton with the sole responsibility for farm debt, which, the Worthy Master seemed by implication to believe, could be abolished only by a return to diversified farming.

The views of R. L. Hunt, who saw the situation in retrospect from a twentieth-century vantage point, coincided with the Lang analysis; namely, that cotton culture had created and perpetuated the agricultural problem. Hunt wrote:

Another subject mentioned in the State Grange of Texas Worthy Master's first annual address that always incited a good deal of talk and writings was the one-crop system of cotton growing. The same things the Worthy Master said in 1874 have been repeated hundreds of times ever since, and his words do not sound unlike those of some of our present day Directors of Extension Service Deans of the Schools of Agriculture in the Southern states. It is one of the strangest things of Southern Agriculture that almost all agricultural teachers and leaders, and various kinds of newspapers, have consistently advocated one thing [diversification] for over 50 years, while the farmers have elected to practice the contrary.[21]

At the turn of the century the *Dallas Morning News* was conducting a contest for the best essay on diversified farming, and at times devoting as much as a full page to the publication of essays received. The cotton farmer kept right on planting cotton.

Throughout its history the Texas State Grange carried on a

fairly persistent fight for diversification. One student of Grange history summarized its position on cotton:

Viewed from the standpoint of the Grange the life of the farmer ought to have been the happiest and most independent of all occupations. He could have his wheat, corn, cotton, and pastures well stocked with horses, cattle, and other domestic animals. His table could be well supplied with fruits and vegetables from his own orchard and garden. In spite of these possibilities there was the constant complaint that farming did not pay. The Committee on Agriculture of 1882 suggested several reasons for this condition of affairs. One of them was that the farmer planted too much cotton and not enough cereals and foodstuffs. Another was that the farmers had their smokehouse and corn cribs in the North. The grangers did not raise their own meat and corn and had to buy them every spring from the local merchants at heavy expense.[22]

The tenets of the National Grange, as expressed in its declaration of purposes, strongly commended diversified or self-contained farming:

3. We shall endeavor to advance our cause by laboring to accomplish the following objects:
. . . . To buy less and produce more, in order to make our farms self-sustaining. To diversify our crops and crop no more than we can cultivate.[23]

In the foregoing Grange objective is found the key to the failure of the organization. Decisively the national economy moved in the direction of buying more and more. Members of any organization taking a position diametrically opposed to the trend by pledging "to advance our cause by laboring. . . . To buy less" condemned their fraternity to economic failure.

To keep the farmer in the cotton field in the face of abusive, persuasive, and persistent criticism must have required something more compelling than railroad extensions and declining freight rates. In answer to the question: Why did cotton remain the leading southern staple? John D. Hicks finds a simple answer. To him,

The ignorance of the southern farmer was indeed so complete that most of the propaganda for diversification, so common in the South from Granger times on, was utterly unintelligible to him, if it reached him at all, and doubtless he would have been incapable of acting on such advice even if he had known what it was all about.[24]

There is no denying that illiteracy in the post-bellum South was widespread, but the establishing of ignorance as the primary cause for the prevalence of cotton culture poses a problem of considerable difficulty.

Contrary to what has so often been implied, Texas was not converted into one big cotton field. In 1900 the harvested cotton acreage constituted approximately one-third of the state's improved acreage (see Appendix, Tables V and VIII). For 1880 the area planted in corn, wheat, and oats exceeded the cotton allocation by almost one million acres. At the close of the century, however, cotton acreage was slightly more than the grain aggregate. In value, cotton regularly surpassed by 50 to 100 per cent, or more, the grain aggregates. On a regional basis there was a considerable diversity in agricultural crops, but so long as horses and mules remained the power units of the farm, the farmer, when he planted some corn, was not practicing diversification. He did not raise corn as insurance against a cotton failure. He was a cotton specialist, and so remained; but as long as he could raise corn for his teams cheaper than he could buy it, yet not restrict his cotton acreage to less than he could otherwise have cultivated, he was reducing cotton production costs and increasing profits.[25]

In the main, cotton retained its position at the fore of agricultural crops because of its high per acre value. For the last thirty-five years of the century, comparisons in per acre value of wheat, oats, corn, and cotton may be made from Tables II and X in the Appendix. It will be noted that almost invariably cotton showed a higher value than any of the grains; frequently the cotton value more than doubled that of its nearest competitor among the grains. Only twice did a grain exceed the value of cotton: in 1894 the monetary worth of oats averaged $1.71 per acre more than cotton (though the succeeding year the monetary value of an acre of cotton was more than three times that of corn); and for 1897 wheat exceeded cotton values by $3.83 per acre. Never did the per acre value of corn rise above cotton. A closer scrutiny of the two tables reveals less fluctuation in cotton than in grain values, meaning, of course, that the cotton farmer could depend on a more stable money income. Moreover, it may be safely assumed that, even though the nineteenth-century farmer was no cost accountant, he was pretty fair in mental arithmetic. If, over a period of years, he planted twenty acres in cotton and twenty in wheat, and his harvest values averaged $34.12 per acre for cotton but only $17.66 for wheat, his mental arithmetic valued his crops at $682.40 for cotton and $353.20 for wheat. His calculations convinced him that he would have benefited financially had he planted all forty acres in cotton. Critics and well-intentioned advisers might argue against cotton, but by the farmer's arithmetic $682.40 was still almost twice $353.20; he therefore assumed that wisdom dictated the planting of more cotton and less wheat. As a general rule, cotton and grain prices rose and fell together. Therefore, over the thirty-year period of falling agricultural prices, there was little to induce the farmer to turn his back on cotton, high in per acre value, in favor of grain crops of lower per acre values; at least, to him there was no sound reason why he should jump from the cotton field into the corn, oat, or wheat field.[26] So, he stayed with cotton.

Of all southern farm crops, cotton was the most dependable. According to the *Texas Almanac*, "It [cotton] is practically a sure crop. There is never a total failure even under very unfavorable circumstances."[27] During the eighties, Texas suffered from drought conditions more severe than those experienced at any other period in the last quarter of the century. George Tyler described the tragic results of the dry years on Bell County crops:

All the old-timers will remember the droughts of 1886 and 1887. In the winter and spring of the former year there was no rain. The early summer passed without relief and corn failed completely. Late in the summer scattered showers saved some of the cotton, but the crop was very short. The drought continued. . . . The first copious rain, on June 4, 1887, was too late for corn but ensured a better cotton crop than in the previous year.[28]

Over two successive years, there was virtually complete failure of the corn crops, but not of the cotton crop. In those years, newspapers of the drought-stricken regions were filled with advice to farmers. Cotton was recommended as an economic savior:

We appeal to the farmers to plow up every foot of land that has not the appearance of making a good crop and put it in cotton. You have two or three weeks to go on yet for this crop and if the rains come, as we believe they will, you will yet make good crops of cotton.[29]

After the passage of some years, another drought appeared imminent and the *Taylor County News* again became concerned over the welfare of the farmers, advising "that if they [farmers] have a single acre that does not promise to make a good crop, they should at once plow it up and plant cotton."[30] From generations of experience with a great variety of crops, southerners had long known that a cotton failure was practically unheard of, whereas success with other crops posed a much higher degree of risk. That farmers elected to rely more and more on a crop almost certain to mature rather than to face the hazards of crops of more doubtful nature does not make a very strong case for the "ignorance of the southern farmers."

There are still other reasons why farmers clung to cotton. Cotton was known to deplete the soil less than any other major staple. When cottonseed were returned to the field as fertilizer, the soil lost practically none of its vitality.[31] Almost every dirt farmer, from his own experience, had made that elementary discovery. In spite of the small amount of sustenance cotton drew from the soil, the farmer was accused of "mining" his land. Suppose he did mine his farm? It was a period when users of natural resources pursued a general policy of land mining. A large percentage of producers, agricultural and nonagricultural, before becoming concerned with restorative measures, habitually exhausted the soil as long as it was profitable to do so. If the cotton farmer followed a like program, his policy, in every respect, should have been considered strictly modern and up-to-date. Demonstrations have proved, however, that cotton can be grown in deep fertile soil for as long as seven successive years without any perceptible difference in production between crops on manured and nonmanured lands.[32] Instances have been recorded in which as many as forty consecutive cotton crops have been harvested from the same field.

Plant composition is not an infallible guide to fertilization requirements essential to maintain soils at a given richness; however, a chemical analysis does indicate something of the degree of withdrawal of certain important elements from the soil. A chemical breakdown of cotton lint, cottonseed, and cotton stalks reveals, in pounds, quantities of three major elements contained in them to be as follows:

	Nitrogen	Phosphorus	Potassium
Cotton lint (500 lbs.)	1.5	.2	2.0
Cottonseed (1,000 lbs.)	31.5	5.5	9.5
Cotton stalks (2,000 lbs.)	51.0	9.0	29.5

On the basis of one-third bale to the acre, the above weights are divided by three to arrive at the annual per acre depletion. When all lint, seed, and stalks were removed from fields, and in terms of 1926 prices, nitrogen, phosphorus, and potassium to the value of $20.89 were withdrawn from the soil per bale of cotton. If lint alone was removed, as was often the case during the last quarter of the century, each bale consumed only forty-one cents' worth of the three elements, an average of fourteen cents per acre. It is estimated that rains wash and leach as much chemical matter from the soil as is consumed by cotton. Any other type of row crop would cause an erosive depletion equivalent to the loss from a cotton field. Moreover, in the production of corn, a hundred bushels of grain consumed a hundred pounds of nitrogen, seventeen pounds of phosphorus, and nineteen pounds of potassium, worth, in 1926 prices, $23.93.[33] These data are not presented with any intent to argue that the use of fertilizer was unnecessary in cotton farming, but rather to emphasize the fact that cotton did not exhaust the land in comparison wih other crops, so that it could be planted over a relatively long period of consecutive years without causing appreciable diminution in productivity. And when prolonged periods of planting did exhaust the chemical properties of the cotton field, permitting the land to lie fallow for a short time quickly restored its fertility.

Finally, the world in which the nineteenth-century farmer lived was becoming more and more specialized and dependent. His happiness, his comfort, and his peace of mind were relative to his living as nearly as possible in the mode of the people about him. If his friends and neighbors regularly used granulated cane sugar, he too developed a strong desire for cane sugar as sweetening for his coffee in lieu of "bee tree" honey or "black strap" molasses. If his neighbors wore "store bought pants," he felt conspicuous in homemade jeans. If his friends brewed coffee from the best grade of Rio beans, he developed a taste for Rio coffee. Breaking the monotonous diet of "hog and hominy" with a can of Columbia River salmon was a gustatory event. Before 1880, ice, ice cream, lemons, oranges, and other exotic foods had crept into the frontier outposts of civilization. These and many other items of like nature were articles of specialization and commerce; they could not be "cropped" on a Texas farm. They were available to the farmer who produced for the market; and cotton, in addition to being the most certain, was by far the most rewarding commercial crop. The farmer clung to cotton, the crop most likely to insure a money income. With a cash income he could more conveniently purchase goods and devices similar to those being consumed by his neighbors. He wanted to feel that he was a part of the world in which he lived.

An argument hallowed by decades of authoritative repetition insists that the crop lien, universally applied to sharecropping and sometimes used also by nonsharecroppers, forced southern farmers to cultivate cotton to the exclusion of all other crops. Under the system, the holder of the lien dictated to farmers what to plant, when to plant, how much to plant, when to harvest, and when to market.[34] By means of the crop lien farmers had obligated themselves to debts which had to be cleared before they were again free agents. Worthy Master Lang, in an annual address to the Texas State Grange, held cotton to be the primary cause for indebtedness and poverty which saddled the farmers:

We were left poor after the war. Cotton was the most marketable product by which we could raise money. Its high value induced us to devote our attention to its production to the exclusion of all other crops, thus neglecting home supplies. We could, at 20 cents per pound, with a disorganized labor, realize some money in its production, but by paying a high rate of interest for money to defray the current expenses of the farm, we became involved, and have continued to raise cotton, with the hope of meeting our obligations, but find ourselves sinking deeper and deeper in our embarrassments, with each revolving year. The price has gone below the usual cost of production. We are left with our farms going to dilapidation — our homes are without supplies — and we are growing poorer from year to year.[35]

No contention is made that liens, mortgages, and sharecropping debts were of little consequence. They were significant. Facts marshalled by the author, however, convince him that liens, mortgages, and sharecropping obligations did not originate on the cotton farm. Furthermore, had the Worthy Master of the Grange taken the time to analyze production figures and produce prices over a period of years, he would have discovered (presumably to his amazement) that had cotton been abandoned in favor of other crops, Texas farmers would have sunk even deeper in their "embarrassments," their homes would have become more dilapidated, and the families would have been poorer than they were. For some strange reason, this facet of the cotton picture never seems worthy of study.

To the author, the evidence clearly refutes the old contention that cotton was the cause of debt; the increase in farm indebtedness was the consequence of a changing agricultural economy. Rising land prices required more funds for the purchase of any given acreage; hence increasing prices were contributory to the growth of farmer indebtedness. The more widespread use of farm machinery demanded, if the equipment was to be used efficiently, larger and larger fields. With increasing land values, the need for high-priced farm machinery, and larger acreage requirements per farm, the farmer encountered greater difficulty in purchasing for cash, and his credit requirements grew larger and larger. In order to obtain credit, he was compelled to shift from self-contained to commercial agriculture. Neither individuals, banks, nor other loan agencies would extend credit to a farmer whose entire farm output was consumed by the household. Cotton, the crop with the highest per acre value and the one most certain to mature, became the choice commercial crop; consequently, it became associated with, and was held responsible for, farmer indebtedness. Invariably the cart has been placed before the horse by those who class cotton farming and farm debt as concomitant; they present cotton as the cause, when it is in reality the result, of debt.

Gradually declining production costs tended to encourage the expansion of the Cotton Kingdom. In addition to railroads, a number of other industries contributed to increases in cotton profits by way of lower production costs. When Galveston cotton compresses reduced charges from sixty to thirty-five cents per bale, the *Galveston Daily News* inferred that the action had been taken to attract more cotton to the Galveston market.[36] The reduction in compress charges should have added twenty-five cents per bale to the cotton farmer's receipts. Among the major reasons for locating the Grange wholesale agency at Galveston was the possibility of saving on cotton commission charges.[37] About 1880 manufacturers began attaching to gin machinery a blower which created an air current used to lift cotton from farm wagon to gin. The new attachment greatly reduced the time and labor required to unload a bale of unginned cotton. Savings in labor resulting from addition of the blower and from other improvements throughout the gin brought about a reduction of two dollars per bale in ginning charges. Any diminution of cost to the cotton farmer in cultivation, transportation, compressing, or marketing was tantamount to an increase in the price of cotton. Because of the many reductions in production costs, the ill effects of three decades of falling cotton prices are partially offset.

Throughout this discussion, all considerations of prices, costs, and per acre values have been confined exclusively to cotton lint. Not always, however, did lint have "to bear its burdens alone." Prior to 1860 disposal of cottonseed posed a major problem and extra cost to the ginner or the farmer; after that date the seed came to have a commercial value which increased the returns from the crop while reducing costs. Thus cottonseed became a significant factor in offsetting declining lint prices. Hammond summarized the importance of the discovery of a commercial use for cottonseed:

There is another way in which the loss to the farmer through lower prices of cotton has been partly offset, and that is through the sales of the cotton seed, a product whose uses were scarcely known previous to the war, and which was not highly valued for many years afterwards.[38]

More than half a century of effort to develop a method for extracting the oil from cottonseed was climaxed by discovery of a satisfactory process, and by 1860 a cottonseed oil mill operated at Hempstead.[39] But not until the census of 1900 did the Bureau of the Census consider cottonseed of sufficient commercial importance to be included in census data.

In an analysis of a quarter-century of national development, the bureau analyst observed that no other economic development of the period had attracted more attention than the manufacture of cottonseed products. The report also pointed out that prior to 1860 disposing of cottonseed gave ginners considerable difficulty. Two of the more common methods of ridding the premises of seed were to dump them into running streams and to stack them in out-of-the-way places to rot. The cottonseed oil industry developed slowly, and its history before 1870 was harassed by failures that outnumbered its successes. Until more profitable uses were discovered, cottonseed hulls were burned as boiler fuel. Experiments demonstrated them to be suited to the manufacture of paper stock, but Texans discovered them to be more profitable as cattle feed. A mixture of cottonseed hulls and meal became one of the choice feeds in the stock-raising and dairy industries.[40]

In 1870 the cottonseed industry of the United States consisted of only twenty-six mills; but the number doubled within a decade, with six located in Texas.[41] In 1894 the oil mill industry's bill for cottonseed totaled $18,000,000,[42] and if cottonseed purchases were allocated among the states in proportion to their cotton production, Texas farmers collected something like $6,000,000 for their seed. At the opening of the twentieth century, the cottonseed oil mill industry numbered 357 plants; and by 1904 Texas alone reported 158 mills with a capacity for processing 11,000 tons of cottonseed daily.[43] Through the period 1870-1900, cottonseed prices ranged from six to twelve cents per bushel, which was the equivalent of five to ten dollars per ton, or an additional two dollars and fifty cents to five dollars per bale for the cotton farmer. Once the possibilities of cattle feed from the by-products of cottonseed had been fully realized, some Texans were quick to visualize profits running into sums of eight or nine figures. For example:

The oil-cake and hulls from the cleaned seed ground up together, for fattening stock, are worth to stock-raisers fully five dollars per head, over and above its cost at $40 per ton, and the surplus from 200,000 bales will fatten 4,000,000 head of beeves feeding two months, which, at a profit of $5 each is $20,000,000. . . . Every cotton planter who has a gin can now hull his own seed and sell it to stock-raisers or to oil factories, and use the hulls for manure or to feed his own work horses or mules, for either of which it is very valuable.[44]

No accurate determination of the aggregate investment in cottonseed oil mills is possible. The report of the Texas secretary of state for 1881 names three cottonseed oil companies as the recipients of charters with a total of $130,000 in authorized capital stock. According to the secretary's biennial reports for 1884, 1890, 1892, 1898, and 1900, in ten years charters authorizing $8,222,-000 capital were granted to 123 oil mill companies. The Twelfth Census reported 103 mills with a capitalization of $7,986,962 in actual operation in the state. The previous census reported only 13 mills capitalized at $2,358,615.[45]

Industries other than the oil mills received some stimulus from the expansion of the cotton empire. While a few industries deriving direct benefits from cotton were as highly specialized as the oil mills, general industries, too, drew aid directly or indirectly from cotton. Cotton contributed materially to railroad freight tonnage, which, in turn, required additional equipment and the movement of extra trains. In the mid-seventies cotton tonnage was outranked only by lumber in the volume of freight moved over the Texas & Pacific Railway.[46] The first Report of the Texas Railroad Commission ranked cotton fourth in tonnage of freight handled by Texas railroads; however, if the tonnage of cottonseed products was also included, the rank became third. Through the first thirty-five years of the twentieth century the combined tonnage of cotton and cottonseed products remained among the ten major contributors to railroad freight.[47] By 1885 railroad tank cars had been introduced as special equipment for transporting cottonseed oil.[48]

Cotton ginning, another secondary industry created by cotton, antedates by decades the cottonseed oil industry and the impetus it gave to railroads, but reliable gin data are relatively scarce. Not until 1890 did census tabulations include data on gins, and then only custom gins — those available to the public — were counted; excluded from the census tabulations were gins owned and operated by plantations for the ginning of their cotton exclusively. The census count for 1900 showed 3,222 gins operating in Texas with an aggregate value of $9,282,101, whereas the previous report counted 572 gins with a capital value of $1,568,902.[49]

A majority of all gins were operated as individual proprietorships, or as partnerships. For this reason corporate data in reports of the secretary of state are not very helpful in determining the number of gins in Texas or arriving at an estimate of their value. In the first four years of the eighties only four gin companies were chartered by the state. In five out of the last six biennial reports of the century, however, sixty-six gin company charters are listed with an authorized capital of $779,000, averaging almost $12,000 per gin. Since these charters were for large establishments, with ginning capacities of twenty-five bales or more per day, they by no means include all gins constructed in the twelve-year period. Smaller gins erected at lower costs were seldom incorporated. Small gins, common to most communities, appear to have had a uniform plant value; at least, when one was destroyed by fire, the universally quoted loss was $2,500.

Shortly after railroads opened up a new cotton territory, cotton compresses appeared. For the last two decades of the century, incomplete files of reports of the secretary of state enumerate charter grants to seventy cotton compress companies which were authorized to issue $7,802,000 in stock. Undoubtedly the figures do not give a true picture of the number of compresses or their capital value. Most of the compresses were constructed at a figure below the authorized capital, and likely a few were never built at all. A goodly number of compresses were erected as individual proprietorship or partnership establishments. In the ante-bellum days, Thrall says, the state's only compress was located in Galveston; but by 1880 every important railroad shipping point boasted one or more.[50] After railroads came to Bell County in the early eighties, a group of businessmen organized the Belton Compress Company, operating it for twenty years before allowing it to fall into the hands of a compress trust which terminated its further use except as a warehouse.[51] At Paris a compress had been built some years earlier than the one at Belton.[52]

Brief consideration may be given two other industries whose development is attributed directly to cotton. In 1880 an item in the *Galveston Daily News* gave a brief summary of two gin factories, Hussey Gin Works and Barnes Gin Works, located at Daingerfield. Although the story gave no information concerning the investment or number of employees, it did say that the plants were manufacturing eighty-saw gins, machinery with the capacity for ginning a bale of cotton an hour.[53] Finally, there were the cotton textile mills. Undoubtedly Texans expended more effort on the endeavor to attract capital for textile mills than on any other manufacturing industry, and always with disappointing results. In the course of the last twenty years of the century, the secretary of state issued more than thirty corporate charters to texile companies, both cotton and woolen, authorizing capital stock in excess of five and one-half million dollars. Most of the companies must have encountered great difficulty in raising capital funds, a fact borne out by the Twelfth Census (1900) which estimates a total investment of $2,227,184 in Texas cotton mills.[54]

Thrall says, in his *Almanac* for 1880, that a number of cotton mills had been built in the state but none had proved very successful.[55] In fact, the most profitable textile mill venture was not in cotton at all; rather it was the New Braunfels woolen mill, which in 1878 netted $81,000.[56] In a review of the state industries for 1870, the *Texas Almanac* said:

The Concordian Manufacturing Company, of Hempstead, has this year received additional machinery, and is now turning out about 2,000 yards per day of heavy brown goods. Eight hundred spindles have also been added to this factory, and a gin-house is attached for the purpose of enabling the company to buy the cotton in the seed. About forty hands are steadily employed.[57]

The apparent prosperity of the Concordian Manufacturing Company evidently did not continue for long. After nine years the *Galveston Daily News* reported that the Concordian machinery had been purchased by an Alabamian and was being boxed for shipment to its new home in Blakely, Alabama.[58] Many, though by no means all, cotton mills of the period suffered a fate somewhat similar to that of Concordian. Farmer organizations maintained a continuing interest in the development of a textile industry. At one time the State Grange memorialized the legislature to appropriate funds for the purchase of at least one Clement attachment for each penitentiary.[59] The attachment appears to have been a device for spinning unginned cotton, and, for a period, it created considerable excitement among cotton farmers who visualized mills in their own fields. However, the legislature gave no heed to the Grange petition.

Although data on investments are none too accurate, probably as much as one-fourth of the state's $90,000,000 industrial structure for 1900[60] was invested in establishments having something to do with the processing of cotton. The secondary influences of cotton on investments in such industries as lumbering, railroad construction, railroad rolling stock, and credit institutions is not measurable, but the aggregate likely accounted for more than 50 per cent of all industrial investments.

When the cotton crop began to "move," all economic activity throughout the South became highly animated. When Scherer wrote his classic description of the impact of the cotton harvest on the southern economy, his remarks could have been restricted to Texas:

Cotton was and is the Southern "money crop." From autumn to autumn the banker and the merchant "carry" the South on their ledgers, and scant is the interchange of coin; but when the "first bale of cotton" rolls into town behind a jangling team of trotting mules, their grinning driver cracking out resounding triumph with his whip, money makes its anniversary appearance, accounts are settled, and the whole shining South "feels flush." The gin houses drive a roaring business, and the air is heavy in them and the light is thick with downy lint, and their atmosphere pungent with the oily odor of crushed wooly seeds. Steam or hydraulic presses, with irresistible power then pack towering heaps of seedless fleece into coarse casings of flimsy jute wrapping, metal-bound. These bales, weighing roughly to the tale of five hundred pounds, pass the appraisement of the broker, swarm the platforms of the railway warehouses and overflow to the hospitable ground; then they are laden laboriously into freight cars, and, after being squeezed to the irreducible minimum of size by some giant compress, are hauled to the corners of the earth.[61]

The domain of the "King" continued to spread, ultimately encompassing 238 of the 254 Texas counties within the realm of cotton culture.

Droughts, floods, locusts, grasshoppers, and low prices, separately or in unison, seem to have exercised no serious retarding effect on the expansion of the cotton industry. When the boll weevil, in 1893, crossed the river from Mexico and launched a devastating attack on Texas fields in the Lower Rio Grande Valley, cotton encountered its first major setback. After entering the state near Brownsville, the weevil within two years infested cotton fields as far east as Cuero and as far north as San Antonio.[62] The U.S. De-

partment of Agriculture, when advised of the destructive effects of
the insect, sent an expert to Brownsville to investigate conditions.
Following two years of intensive study in the field, the Department
of Agriculture suggested that the legislature enact certain regulatory laws. Among the measures recommended was one requiring
farmers to destroy cotton stalks as soon as the cotton was picked.
The legislature of Texas refused to become excited, however, and
the proposals of the Division of Entomology, U.S. Department of
Agriculture, were not acted upon.[63] Had the legislature enacted the
legislation recommended by the department, the destructive advance of the boll weevil might have been curbed. In the absence
of any effective efforts at control, the weevil spread over Texas and
throughout the South. Because their climatic conditions were unfavorable to his existence, certain areas of the state, more especially
the high plains and the Panhandle, suffered no ill effects from the
weevil.

For a specialized economy cotton was an ideal crop; hence the
plant played a leading role in the transition of agriculture toward
specialized commercialization. The invective heaped on the cotton
farmer should have been directed at the credit system and the
small size of the economic unit. The Department of Agriculture
estimated that thirty-four and one-half acres constituted the maximum cotton field for man and team. The unit could normally be
depended on to produce a crop of ten to fifteen bales, worth on the
basis of ten-cent cotton $500 to $750 in cash. In reality, the average
production per farm was slightly more than eight bales; therefore,
cotton acreage allocations on a majority of farm units were much
smaller than the estimated maximum of the Department of Agriculture. There were tens of thousands of cotton farms that produced
no more than two or three bales of cotton, and on these farms cash
incomes from cotton ranged proportionately below the $500 to $700
maximums. In pursuing its analysis further, the Department of
Agriculture estimated that out-of-pocket costs of raising cotton were
very low, whereas the implicit costs ran very high.[64] The average
cotton farmer was not at all concerned with implicit costs — he was
strictly an out-of-pocket cost operator. Consequently, to him, cotton
profits seemed large.

During the last quarter of the nineteenth century the cotton plant and the lowly cotton farmer were prime contributors to the phenomenal progress made in the economic development of the state. Early in the period, the annual cotton crop's value averaged approximately $20,000,000; but it climbed to $100,000,000 or more for the closing years of the century. Merchants, banks, and towns thrived and grew wealthy on cotton. However, glamour and romance, children of fiction and mythology, splashed and bathed the Cattle — not the Cotton — Kingdom. The author grew up on tales and wondrous stories of the contributions of cattle to the welfare of the state; especially pungent were the yarns of the cattle drives and how they insulated Texans against the degree of poverty endured by other southerners in the Reconstruction era. But in contributing to the development of commercialized agriculture, cattle ran a distant second to cotton. In dollar value of the product, in number of persons employed, and in industrial activity generated, cotton stood alone — far, far in advance of all competitors.

V

Fencing the Range

OVER the virgin semiarid lands of the great Southwest Spanish dons strewed seed from which sprang the western livestock industry. And for many decades the progeny of the droves and flocks, without benefit of ranchman, herder, or cowpoke, flourished in a half-wild state. That is to say, in Texas the raising of cattle, horses, mules, sheep, and goats is an occupation transmitted through Spain in direct lineage from the nomadic herdsmen of the Levant. The swine also appeared in the droves of the friars and dons. As the history of the region unfolded, scions of early Spanish masters sometimes sank to the role of herdsmen, and the long-legged, flat-sided steers from Andalusia gave way to short-legged, straight-backed, round-sided, broad-hipped, white-faced cattle of English descent. The original sheep of the Southwest were from the scrub flocks of Spain. In those days, it was virtually impossible to circumvent government regulations which prohibited the exportation of better breeds of sheep. After the passage of generations, and by a circuitous route through France, Rambouillets, Merinos, and other descendants of top quality Spanish breeds appeared in Texas. Spanish animals constituted the base and bedrock from which the modern western livestock industry sprang.

When the Anglo-American finally reached Texas, he was spared both the pain and the trouble requisite to building a livestock industry — already it was there awaiting his coming. Fresh beef was to be had for the butchering. To become a cattleman, one rounded up mavericks in numbers limited only by one's energy and ability to herd and hold them on the open range. The wild mustang was the property of the man who captured him. When "broke" to the saddle, the pony became part of a rider's remuda, serving his turn at rounding up longhorns, as a trail driver's mount, or in holding herds on the range.

In the early days, the livestock industry might be considered as a sort of placer mining operation — a surface-scratching process with low operating cost in which a small investment brought high returns. That is to say, when the longhorn and the open range dominated the cattle industry, ranching procedure was analogous to that of placer mining — where the gold miner panned and re-panned the sand in search of nuggets, the cattleman rode and rerode the range in search of longhorns. Those were the days when men staked out claims and began to mine: gold, iron ore, timber, coal, or cattle. Gold mining and livestock mining were, however, somewhat different. The gold miner might exhaust his sand or his ore, but the cattle miner's "vein" had the power of reproduction, by which the size of his herd was maintained or increased — that is, as long as each animal had a grazing plot of at least ten acres. Hence, "striking it rich" in cattle came ultimately to depend on laying claim to as many ten-acre tracts as possible. Gentlemen's agreements parceled claims while the range was open. But many livestock men began to establish land titles in fee simple, laying claim to all ten-acre plots within reach; for well they knew that the greater the number of claims that could be established, the greater the flood of riches that would accrue to them from the "mines." With the appearance of barbed wire, potential landowners gained a formidable ally to aid in proving title to thousands, tens of thousands, and even hundreds of thousands of "ten-acre" plots.

In romantic appeal, the Cattle Kingdom surpasses the Cotton Kingdom as far as the Cotton Kingdom, during the last quarter of the nineteenth century, surpassed the Cattle Kingdom in economic importance. The continuing deluge of fiction, folklore, and mythology about the cattle country tends to shroud factual material in a fog of obscurity. A moot question: Why has the loneliest person on earth, the cowhand of the late nineteenth century, been clothed in heroic glamour, while the cotton farmer, who contributed so much to the economic development of the state, has in Hicksian fashion been dubbed an "ignoramus"? Reasons for the differentiation are elusive. Perhaps it is heroic to live a lonesome, Godforsaken life. Or again, cotton may be associated with the servile condition of slavery or the poverty of sharecropping. Whatever the explanation, the fact remains that cotton ranked first in economic importance but very low in romantic appeal.

Many persons have, at one time or another, undertaken to trace the family tree of Texas cattle. In a brief paragraph a correspondent for the *Chicago Tribune* summarized the course of their lineage:

That the cattle of Mexico and Texas descended from the herds of old Spain is almost universally believed. It is thought that when those gentle and pious worthies, the Spanish invaders, brought their swords to America to help make the introduction of saving grace and sweet charitable teachings of the church militant, they also brought cattle of the herds of Andalusia. Some of them it is supposed, escaped, or were abandoned to roam and breed at freedom on the sunny plains of the Rio Bravo del Norte. The resemblance there between the picturesquely gothic Andalusian bullock and the slabsided cathammed racer of the southwest is considered good evidence, if not proof positive, that they had a common remote origin.[1]

That the first Spaniards moving into or across New Mexico drove before them their commissary of sheep and cattle is a matter of historical record; and as early as 1714 cattle ranches were reported in Spanish East Texas. Although settlers of the Austin colony brought with them cattle of British origin, and descendants of French herds drifted in from Louisiana, in 1830 fully 80 per cent of the estimated cattle population of Texas (100,000 head) were of Spanish extraction.[2] For the following thirty years, the increase in cattle was by geometric progression. Not until the post-bellum period were there distinguishable differences between the story of the cattle industry in Texas and its history in states east of the Mississippi.

Exodus of Indians and buffalo from the Great Plains made that whole region accessible for a quick blanketing by cattle outfits. Never before in the history of the country had an area so vast, so free of brush, trees, Indians, buffalo, and farmers suddenly opened its doors to grazing interests. Cattlemen made the most of their opportunity — they engulfed the region.

Folklore suggests that the war decade left Texas cattle free and unmolested, to do nothing but propagate; census data present a contrary picture. With the exception of horses, the war period checked increases in all livestock populations. The 1860 census enumerated the cattle population at 3,535,768, while the next census showed a decrease of 40,000 head. Actually, the range cattle population increased more than 100,000 head, but losses in the ranks of working oxen and milch cows totaling perhaps 140,000 animals more than offset the increase. There was an increase of 100,000 in the horse population. Through the war decade the decline in the aggregate value of all livestock approximated $15,000,000.[3]

By 1870 the eastern section of the state appeared to be well stocked with cattle. In the last thirty years of the century cattle in the representative eastern counties showed a gain of 140,000 head. It was, however, the western half of the state where the phenomenal increase in cattle numbers really occurred. In the twenty key western counties, the cattle total rose from 154,433 to 906,424. Cattle in the eight Panhandle counties of the group increased from zero to 256,673 head.[4] Within thirty years the Panhandle came to typify the cattle country, and over its grassy undulating surface sprawled some of the world's largest ranches.

As late as the mid-seventies, as we have seen, the plains were still overrun with Indians and buffalo; and this accounts for the fact that no cattle were to be found in the Panhandle in 1870. It has also been noted that the Texas herd of buffalo was destroyed in a matter of months. After the hunting season of 1876-77, virtually no buffalo remained, and hunters who overestimated the size of the herd remnant bankrupted themselves outfitting and financing crews to slaughter a buffalo herd already nonexistent. Returning hunters of the season 1877-78 reported no buffalo on the range.[5] As bison and Indians became scarcer, the influx of settlers increased sharply, and freighters who carried buffalo hides east returned with heavily laden wagons bearing merchandise and lumber.[6] Robson mused, through the columns of the *Fort Griffin Echo*, that in 1872 only two persons in Shackelford County owned their homes, but that in the brief span of seven years population had increased sufficiently to organize the county, which then boasted two towns, a steam mill, a jail, several churches, and a Masonic lodge.[7]

The rapidity with which settlers filled the adjoining counties, Shackelford and Throckmorton, can only be attributed to the clearing of the buffalo range. Some of the more eager nesters even moved out on the range while the buffalo slaughter was yet in progress. One enterprising fellow, sensing, on the eve of the big season (1876-77), an opportunity to fatten hogs on buffalo carcasses, moved out into the hunting territory with 400 shoats.[8] In the course of the season his drove probably salvaged more buffalo meat than the hunters did. With the passage of another year, 150,-000 head of cattle were said to be pastured within a fifty-mile radius of Fort Griffin.[9] The Mooar brothers, while engaged in hunting buffalo, staked a ranch in Fisher County, which at the time was near the heart of the buffalo country.[10]

Nostalgia prompts some to bemoan the extermination of the buffalo herds. But as long as the buffalo occupied the Great Plains, farmers and ranchers could not. Neither farm nor ranch could endure the destructive pounding from millions of stampeding hoofs. Under farmer and rancher the plains became far more productive than ever they did under buffalo and Indian. And with the demolition of his hunting preserve, his chief source of food, the Indian was compelled, as a requisite for drawing government rations, to remain within the confines of the reservation.[11] Since beef was a major item in the rations, government purchases of sizable herds gave some stimulus to the cattle market.

In the fall of 1877, Colonel Charles Goodnight established along Palo Duro Canyon what is said to be the first ranch in the Panhandle. This was the beginning of a big cattle outfit, spreading at first over five and later over seven counties, and a herd which eventually numbered 70,000, including 9,000 high-grade Herefords.[12] Men worked with feverish energy to seed the range, and contemporary newspapers teem with accounts of cattlemen on the move, driving herds to the open range in the North and West. The method of establishing occupancy of open grassland, according to Rudolf A. Clemen, followed a fairly consistent pattern. When a cattleman moved into virgin territory he laid claim to all land in sight. The arrival of a second outfit necessitated a division of the range, with each cattleman obligated to restrict the grazing of his herd to one side of an agreed boundary line. As others came, the range was further subdivided until its estimated grazing capacity had been reached. Often there was an underestimate of the number of acres necessary to graze one animal, and the range was overstocked, a tragic situation when dry years came. Often the range was considered well stocked when headquarters of cattle outfits were located within fifteen to thirty miles of each other. By priority of occupation and through the continuity of possession "range rights" became established.[13] The cattle boom was on, and high and rising cattle prices tended more and more to cause outfits to crowd the range beyond the widely accepted rule of thumb limit of one animal to ten acres of grass.

An immigrant handbook for 1880 described the rapidity with which conditions on the range tended to change:

The rapid increase of population in the State and consequent enhanced value of land, have to some extent interfered with the operations of the old time "cattle men," who, perhaps without possessing an acre of the soil, owned thousands of head of fat cattle and could boast of enormous wealth. They have either been compelled of late years to limit the increase of their stock by free sales, to buy and fence in large tracts of land, or to move their stock farther west.[14]

Sponsors of the handbook were a group of railroad companies, the recipients of land bonuses totaling millions of acres. Quite naturally the pamphlet did not fail to mention that in the West vast tracts of land could be leased from railroad companies at a rental of about two cents an acre or $12.80 per section.[15]

For the benefit of prospective settlers, immigrant handbooks made estimates which proved, on paper, that phenomenal increases could be anticipated from a herd of cattle. With cattle, it was no trick at all to grow fabulously wealthy overnight. By means of a propagation table, one writer graphically illustrated how an immigrant starting with 100 cows, two bulls, and 100 calves could in twelve years increase his herd to 14,368. If, at the end of the period, he wished to retire, the lowest possible sale price would bring him $64,160 in cash. Included among the illustrative material was a reprint from the Henrietta *Journal* in which the paper had undertaken to analyze costs and profits in the cattle industry:

The cost of keeping cattle is about $1.50 per head, or $1,500 per thousand. Four men, with twelve to sixteen horses, will tend a herd of 1,500. The profits are as follows: Beeves per head, cost $15; running expenses, $1.50; sell at $22, with a profit of 32 per cent. Profit on cows costing $13.50 per head; cost of keeping, $1.50-$15. Increase of calves, 75 per cent, worth $5 per head. Net profit, 23 per cent. On a mixed herd the beeves sold will pay expenses, and the increase will double itself in three years. A discount is made on a herd of 10 per cent, for losses. The profit on a mixed herd is about 20 per cent.[16]

Seldom did estimates like the above include land as a cost factor. Richardson and Rister cite a *Texas Guide* for 1878 as the source of an itemized list of needs for launching a ranching venture with no more than $1,000 in funds. According to the pamphlet, this sum of money would provide three hundred acres of land (the reader is allowed to use his own imagination as to whether the land was leased or purchased), twenty cows, one hundred ewes, eight mares, all necessary farm implements, a comfortable and adequately furnished place of abode, and a surplus of $250 for current expenses. In their text, Richardson and Rister also incorporate an estimate of investment requirements for establishing a successful ranch which was taken from the census report for 1880. Census calculations called for a cash outlay of $12,350 for stocking and equipping a ranch of thirty thousand acres, but the calculations made no allowance for either purchase or lease of the land.[17] Needless to say, the operator of a thirty-thousand-acre ranch, well stocked, was more likely to succeed than the operator of the $1,000 venture. The larger ranch was an economic unit of sufficient size to make possible accumulations against adversity. But not many people found it possible either to save or to borrow $12,000 or $15,000 for launching a thirty-thousand-acre ranch enterprise.

It is unlikely that migrations to the range country were greatly affected by either guidebooks or census reports; nonetheless, cattle outfits soon swarmed over the free grasslands. As late as 1879, by

Osgood's reckonings, the range cattleman was a frontier figure whose capital was in his herd. He lacked funds for, and was not particularly interested in, the purchase of land. When his herd depleted a range, or when he learned of a more desirable supply of grass and water elsewhere, he migrated.[18] In Texas, when railroad land grants were surveyed, alternate sections were reserved for the public schools, and many a cattle outfit leased grass rights on railroad land but grazed school land free.

For a time, from 1867 to 1875, the chief interest of cattlemen seemed to center on drives to northern markets — not on occupying the western ranges. They were probably none too keen on challenging the Indian and buffalo for possession of the western grass. In the first successful driving season an estimated 260,000 cattle were marketed in Sedalia, Missouri. Within a few years drives became well-organized processions, under the direction of experienced hands and moving along well-marked trails. Contemporaries seem to have been prone to overestimate and overstate the economic value of the drives. For example, Thrall, in 1880, reckoned drives and shipments for the year at 502,196 head valued at $8,241,903.[19] This estimate exceeds the Bureau of the Census figure by about 100,000 head. Thrall was quite probably, and no doubt unintentionally, a victim of the error of counting cattle twice, once as a drove herd and once as a rail shipment. He also overvalued the cattle. If 400,000 were actually marketed at the average per farm value for the year (see Appendix, Table XI), receipts would have totaled $6,452,000. Texas cattle on northern markets were invariably quoted, however, at three to five dollars per head less than cattle from other regions. With this price differential counted in, actual receipts for the year's drives were closer to five or six million dollars.

Texas cattle drives for 1875-85 inclusive totaled 3,123,976 head,[20] averaging approximately 284,000 annually. A number of old-time drovers, in reviewing events of the last quarter of the century, seem to agree that 10,000,000 is approximately correct for the number of Texas cattle sold on northern markets during that period. If the estimate is correct, sales for the final fifteen years averaged 500,000 per annum, an annual increase of 200,000 over the first ten years.

Because of railroad expansion which expedited the movement of cattle, yearly sales of half a million appear to be a reasonable estimate.

For the twenty-five-year period, average prices received by Texas cattlemen have been reckoned as high as twenty dollars per head, a figure which is definitely excessive. Primarily because the "slab-sided, cat-hammed" longhorn was not choice beef, Texas cattle prices invariably ranged below the national average. Furthermore, immature stock rushed to market in excessive numbers from Texas ranges never commanded the premium prices paid for prime cattle. Too, northern fear of Texas fever had a depressing effect on the price of Texas cattle. Local newspapers frequently commented on the low price of Texas cattle as compared to animals from other states; for example, the *Echo*, in 1878, quoted $9.24 as the average price for a Texas steer, whereas contemporary prices for beeves in New York and Massachusetts averaged $33.50 and $40.81 respectively.[21] Some years later steer prices were quoted for Central Texas at seven dollars for yearlings and eleven dollars for two-year-olds, while West Texas animals brought $8.50 for yearlings and $12.50 for two-year-olds. Because of the absence of Texas fever in the Panhandle and the much higher percentage of improved stock in western herds, West Texas cattle commanded premium prices over Central Texas animals.

In 1884 the *Albany Echo*, making calculations of the trail drives for the seventeen years immediately preceding, concluded that drovers had moved 4,707,973 cattle valued at more than $50,000,-000.[22] George W. Saunders, one-time president of the Old Time Trail Drivers Association, is credited by Richardson and Rister as having estimated a twenty-eight-year movement by drovers of 9,800,000 cattle valued at ten dollars per head, a total of $98,000,-000.[23] Annual drives, according to Mr. Saunders' calculations, averaged 350,000 cattle valued at $3,500,000. The number of cattle shipped by rail and by boat for the twenty-eight years was probably not sufficient to increase the value of annual sales to a $5,000,-000 average. Throughout the last three decades of the century both cotton and corn crops annually exceeded in value the total cattle sales, and for the last year of the century cotton farmers received for their crop more money than had been paid cattlemen in the course of twenty-eight years of cattle driving.

Until 1875, as we have seen, northern cattle drives served primarily to supply the beef market; afterward emphasis shifted to seeding the northern range, and some additional sales were made to northern feeders. Within ten years after the buffalo slaughter had driven the Indian from the range, a great percentage of the western plains and the Rocky Mountain regions was being used to pasture hundreds of thousands of cattle. The earlier arrivals succeeded in establishing and maintaining a priority to grass rights in the regions they settled. The plains of Texas were quickly occupied by cattle outfits, large and small, and large land and cattle corporations came into their own. In 1881 the state granted only two corporate charters to cattle companies authorizing a capitalization of $200,000 in aggregate; but for the biennium ending with 1884, no fewer than 104 land and cattle companies received charters which authorized $37,190,000 in capital. While a number of the companies were permitted capital stock issues in excess of $1,000,000, the over-all average of $350,000 was approximately thirty times larger than the estimate by the 1880 census report for funds necessary to establish a thirty-thousand-acre ranch. With the exception of railroads and dredging companies, land and cattle companies were possibly the largest corporations chartered by the state of Texas during the nineteenth century. In the biennium 1883-84, capital authorizations for cattle companies alone exceeded by $9,000,000 the stock allowed in new railroad charters; and the total for land and cattle companies was greater by $16,500,-000 than the capital stock totals allowed the railroad companies.

Organization of cattle companies continued to set a brisk pace through 1885; once during the year seventeen new companies were incorporated within a week. Out of the seventeen, eight were capitalized at $100,000 or more, and five were capitalized at $1,000,-000, $800,000, $500,000, $300,000, and $200,000, respectively.[24] During the eighties big cattle companies were formed throughout the range country of the western United States. Rudolf Clemen names twelve large cattle companies, all of which were flourishing in 1883; four years later none declared a dividend, and after the passage of forty years only two remained in existence. In Clemen's judgment the number of cattle actually on the range was never greater than two-thirds of the count shown in ranch tally books,[25] evidently an unwise bit of "stock watering" on the part of cattle outfits, many of whom soon faced bankruptcy. Although some of the big Texas ranches were financed by local capital, capital funds for financing the largest ones came from foreign countries, particularly Scotland and England, or from the eastern states.

For a period of fifteen years following the Civil War, prices of livestock, with the exception of sheep and hogs, followed a downward trend in keeping with the price pattern of other agricultural products (see Appendix, Tables II, XI, and XII). But by 1880 a divergence was to be noted in the movement of agricultural prices: while the prices of produce of the fields continued downward, prices of cattle, milch cows, horses, and mules began to rise, moving upward rapidly until the mid-eighties. For half a decade cattlemen truly enjoyed a bonanza. They seemed determined on filling, in one stampede of great magnitude, the void created when Indians and buffalo were driven from the Great Plains — a condition which created an apparently insatiable demand for cattle, and in turn caused livestock prices to skyrocket with the result that speculative and venture capital from the world over was attracted to the range country. This was capital in search of quick profits on a "wild bull" market. During the time when the fever of speculation ran highest, the money market was easy and livestock outfits encountered little or no difficulty in raising hundreds of thousands (even millions) of dollars for cattle companies. At the same time, farmers found it well-nigh impossible to raise a few hundred dollars for launching a Grange store. Farmers thought in terms of small forty-acre farms; cattle barons visualized empires of thousands of cattle roaming over tens of thousands of acres of pasture lands. Farmers worried, fretted, and organized the Grange and the Alliance because of declining incomes resulting from falling prices of farm produce; cattlemen basked in the comfortable security of rising cattle prices and growing fortunes. While farmers dwelt in an atmosphere of poverty, cattlemen might swagger among others of the new-rich.

The fantastic growth in the number of cattle outfits resulted in a sharp increase in demand for ponies with a consequent boost in the price of horses averaging twenty-two dollars per head. The market price for milch cows was always higher than that of range stock; consequently the increase in demand for and rise in price of beef cattle tended to cause a rise in the price of milch cows. However, the price differential between the two types of cattle narrowed appreciably. As livestock outfits filled in the range country, farmers, too, poured into the arable regions west of the Mississippi, with the intent of placing millions of acres under cultivation. This created a demand for mules sufficient to cause the price to rise an average of twenty-eight dollars per head. Some contemporaries were convinced that rising cattle prices tended to retard the sheep industry, and a paragraph in the *Echo* gives substance to the conviction:

Many sheep men in the country tributary to Corpus Christi are disposing of their flocks as fast as possible and going into the business of raising cattle. This is owing, says the Corpus Christi Free Press, to extensive Kansas drives, which have made cattle scarce and valuable.[26]

The cattle bonanza was of short duration, the boom bursting as suddenly as it had begun. When the bubble burst, livestock prices tumbled toward the low levels other agricultural prices had already reached.

Through the whole of 1883 and most of the following year, cattle prices remained high and held steady. Following a tendency to show considerable weakness the previous fall, by mid-year of 1885 cattle prices wholly deteriorated and the boom collapsed completely. A Texas cattleman, who in 1883 refused an offer of $1,500,000 for his cattle and range rights, three years later sacrificed them for $245,000.[27] The insecurity of heavy cattle loans, which had been made on the basis of padded tally sheets, created an inevitable crash situation. Had cattle prices continued to rise, loans would have been relatively secure. But as the range tended to become well stocked, demand for seed cattle eased and prices tended to weaken. Weather conditions conspired to topple the tottery price structure. Two successive winters of unusual severity literally froze out thousands of northern cattlemen, while the drought of

1885-87, one of the driest in the state's history, bankrupted many Texas cattlemen. Cattle, which in April, 1883, brought $4.25 per hundredweight on the Chicago market, did well in 1887 to command a dollar per hundred.[28] Texas cows, selling on the eve of the drought for as much as thirty-five dollars, could scarcely be disposed of a year later for as little as five dollars per head.[29] As range sustenance became exhausted, cattlemen sent herds scurrying hither and yon in search of grass and water — especially water. Losses suffered as a result of either drought or blizzard brought to a sudden end any show of ranch profit, and cattle companies suspended dividend payments and defaulted on mortgages and bonds. Cattle company stock issues became worthless, and mortgage foreclosures became common, often revealing the mortgage to be practically worthless.

Following the crash, cattle prices remained at a low level for quite some time, and in 1887 the Chicago *Drovers' Journal* made an analysis of conditions which it considered responsible for perpetuating the dull market:

There are many good reasons why the producer does not get more for his cattle.
1. By badly over-stocked ranges.
2. Quarantines by all the northern sections.
3. Railway and general labor strikes.
4. Glut, and demoralized foreign meat market.
5. The heaviest marketing of beef cattle ever known in a like period.
6. The general depression of trades and industries all over the country.
7. The pool of railroads running east from Chicago on the 1st of last March raised their rate 40 per cent. on dressed beef. This took $1.25 per head off from every head of beef cattle.
8. The oleomargarine bill took off from $2 to $2.50 more, aggregating over $7,500,000 in this market alone, to say nothing about the numerous markets of the west; and this vast amount of money goes into the United States Treasury, which is already full to overflowing, and into the pockets of the railway magnates, and it all comes out of the producers and consumers.[30]

Although the analysis was made while the Texas drought was at its very worst, except for an indirect reference no part of the low prices was attributed to the poor and underweight range cattle being thrown on the market. The freight increase in dressed beef was in keeping with the railroads' intent to discourage the shipment of frozen meat. In July, 1887, the *Taylor County News* reported, "A large number of cattle on the drive to northern markets have been turned back to Texas. There was no market for them." Another paragraph in the same issue re-emphasized the financial distress caused by the drought, saying, "Several prominent cattlemen at Henrietta had attachments levied on their stock Saturday by the Merchant's National Bank of Fort Worth."[31]

Even before the bubble burst some evidence suggested pending changes in the nature of the cattle industry. Year by year cattle drives grew smaller. The ranch interests themselves became powerful factors in halting the drives. Once a cattle outfit succeeded in establishing a permanent claim to a portion of the range, it sought to close that part of the range to trail herds. As established ranches grew more numerous, drovers found it increasingly difficult to move herds. The appearance of barbed wire was a great aid to farmers and ranchers in restricting the movements of migratory herds. Each additional fence post shut off another bit of the open range. Furthermore, as railroads penetrated additional western territories cattle drives became more difficult and less necessary. A fear of Texas, Mexican, or splenetic fever on the part of northern cattle interests caused numerous legal restrictions to be placed on the movement of cattle. Northern cattlemen, aware of infections of fever among their herds following the passage of Texas cattle, suspected that "slobber" from mouths of Texas cattle contaminated the grass along the trail. In consequence, a number of states enacted quarantine laws designed to prevent the movement of Texas cattle. When cattlemen of the Panhandle learned that their own herds were free of Texas fever except when infected by South Texas animals, they too became hostile and undertook to prevent the passage of southern herds across Panhandle ranges. Some Panhandle outfits resorted to extralegal "Winchester quarantines" to block drives of South Texas cattle.

In 1885 certain Panhandle ranchmen agreed among themselves to establish a blockade against the movement of any and all southern cattle.[32] Also in that year the Texas Livestock Association deemed it advisable to warn South Texas cattlemen:

The only safe and practicable trail for southern cattle to be driven out of

Texas is the old Fort Griffin and Fort Dodge trail, crossing the Texas and Pacific railway near Baird, thence by way of Albany and Doan, crossing Red River near the latter place, and thence on the present trail to Caldwell.[33]

Probably the route was safe because it avoided contact with most of the largest outfits in North Texas. The following spring managers of cattle companies controlling no fewer than 5,000,000 acres, at a meeting called to consider ways and means of discouraging southern drives, formally resolved that they would not permit herds to be driven across their ranges, and warned would-be offenders that every legal means would be resorted to in preventing the crossings.[34] After 1888 no cattle were driven up the trial from the J A Ranch — they were either marketed locally or shipped by rail.[35] Seemingly a combination of circumstances was responsible for bringing to a halt the incessant movement of cattle and confining operations of the industry within the fixed boundaries of ranches.

In addition to being a contributory factor to the collapse of the cattle boom, the drought of 1885-87 generated a great interest throughout the stricken region in the erection of windmills and the construction of earthen tanks. When drinking water disappeared, cattle losses became appalling. Practically every ranch outfit financially able to do so undertook to prepare surface tanks which would impound a portion of the runoff water from future rains. In the summer of 1887 the Anson *Voice* commented on the number of tanks in the county:

We notice in several parts of the county, some nice tanks of water, and those who have made them already feel paid for their work on them. We ought to have many more and larger ones—they will be of great benefit to those who have them, and a blessing to the whole county.[36]

Surface tanks were formed either by scooping depressions in the surface or by throwing earthen dams across ravines. However, nature in the West seems to have a habit of storing more water below the surface than above the ground. Consequently the drilling of water wells was pushed with energy and windmills were erected all over the country; frequently scores of windmills could be seen for one residence. The mills were allowed to run day and night, continuously pouring a small stream into an earthen tank. In a land where, supposedly, the wind never ceased blowing, a week of calm could create serious water problems — stock water disappeared and animals suffered from thirst. The major problem confronting the livestock man was in reality a double-barreled one of water and grass: to keep an abundance of stock water within grazing distance of an ample supply of grass. In part, hardships suffered by the rancher during the drought did not spring from a complete lack of either grass or water, but rather from the fact that grass was so far from watering places that it could not be pastured.

Drought conditions undoubtedly expedited the sale of barbed wire, thereby contributing to a speedier disappearance of the open range. Fencing the range offered a simple means of preventing overgrazing and blocking poachers. By means of cross fencing a cattleman could control grazing conditions; that is, pastures could be grazed in a pattern of rotation designed to insure a greater supply of grass. Furthermore, on the open range it was next to impossible to improve the quality of a herd. With pastures fenced, reducing to a minimum the mixing of herds and the appearance of bothersome estrays, the cattleman could control breeding and build up the quality of his herd; consequently, an improvement in beef breeds followed in the wake of the barbed-wire fence. Dale insists that barbed wire all but revolutionized the Texas cattle industry.[37]

Cattle drives and census reports suggest that the quality of Texas livestock was low compared with that of animals in other states. The press of the state persistently spoke out for improvement in the breeds of livestock. Comparing values of Texas cattle with those of high-grade breeds of another state appears to have been a favorite pastime for some editors. The *Planter & Stockman*, from census data of 1880, presented a contrast in livestock values between Texas and Iowa:

It is remarked that according to the census of 1880, Texas had more horses than Iowa, nearly twice as many cattle, three times as many mules, and four times as many sheep, while Iowa, outranked Texas only in the number of swine. Yet the total value of livestock of Texas is placed at $60,000,000, while that of Iowa with a less number is placed at $124,000,000. There is an important lesson in these figures for the individual farmer. Values are not determined by numbers, but by quality. It is the quality of Iowa stock which makes it worth more than twice as much per head as that of Texas.[38]

Some years later a West Texas paper made use of data from the Eleventh Census (1890) in making another comparison of livestock values between Texas and Iowa:

In round numbers Iowa has 4,000,000 cattle while Texas owns 7,000,000. At the same time Iowa has almost twice as much money invested in cattle as has Texas. The increased valuation of Iowa cattle over those of Texas is due alone to "breed and feed."[39]

Texans labored to improve "breed and feed," but the process was time-consuming. To convert from several million lank long-horns to the sleek beef breeds was no small undertaking. It is prob-able that there had been intermittent introductions of high-grade cattle over a period of several decades, but Paddock insists: "The first attempts to introduce better blood into the rough range stock were made in Texas about 1875."[40] The process of experimentation with various breeds consumed a good ten years, and had little or no effect on the grade of range cattle. Blooded animals had to over-come the prejudice held against them by large numbers of cattle-men who believed that they could not endure the rigorous winters of the plains and would not thrive on the range.

Apparently "quality" or "high-bred" stock survived the cold and the drought of 1885-87, faring about as well as rough range stock; and thereafter allocations for purchases of pure-bred and regis-tered bulls tended to grow larger and larger in the budgets of all first-class cattle outfits.[41] Many big cattle concerns had fenced their pastures early in the eighties, and were in position to improve the quality of their herds. Better grades of livestock served partially to offset the decline in cattle prices.

Among the first breeds of blooded cattle introduced was the Durham, and as early as 1876 some of the bulls ranged with the herds of a few North Texas cattlemen. The *Echo* briefly contrasted the size and value of Durhams and natives:

T. J. Atkinson, one of Jack county's progressive men has a thorough-bred Durham bull from which he has raised a few good grades this season. He sold a six months old bull calf which is as large if not larger than the average native yearling, to W. A. Benson for $30.[42]

In the late seventies and early eighties, papers frequently reported that this or that rancher had purchased either a single bull or a small herd of Durhams. The breed appears to have been rather widely dispersed over the state; among others, the counties of Dallas, Frio, Williamson, Brown, Limestone, Tom Green, Shackelford, and some in the Panhandle included Durhams among their cattle. Until the eighties, when some of the larger ranches began to introduce the Hereford, no other quality breed seems to have given the Durham very much competition. Among the earlier notices to the effect that the Hereford had arrived was one which read:

Messrs. Towers & Gudgell of West Las Animas, Colorado, have imported and now have on their Cimarron ranch, Texas Panhandle, twenty-five Hereford bulls. They are all young, smooth, round-bodied, and from some of the best English herds.[43]

In the mid-eighties forty Hereford bulls, imported directly from England, were located in the vicinity of Wichita Falls. And as the decade closed, a Fred Proyser of Fisher County purchased twenty-nine Hereford bulls from the Seven Rivers Cattle Company and moved them to his VXV pastures.[44]

Why did the Hereford largely supplant the Durham? The question is still debated. One side contends that the Durham did not endure the rigors of the range any too well, and that consequently an animal better adapted to conditions in the West was sought. The Hereford, it is argued, met these conditions and thus became the popular beef animal. The other group insists that the Durham did thrive on the range, but that a few big cattle concerns began to import Herefords, widely advertising and publicizing the merits of the breed. Many small ranchers, emulating their larger neighbors, also turned to Herefords. The Durham, however, still retains some loyal supporters. His partisans argue that a person who intends to remain in the business of raising beef cattle should be interested in producing the largest animal possible, and the Durham is the larger animal of the two. Nonetheless, the Hereford has for many years ranked high among the peerage of Texas cattle.

To improve the quality of several million cattle required a great deal of time and patience. The author recalls that as a lad in the decade of 1910-20, he crossed and recrossed the western half of Texas, seeing tens of thousands of cattle, the quality somewhat improved over the longhorn but still falling far short of meeting the requirements of prize-winning Herefords. From the outset of his ranch career, Charles Goodnight is said to have worked steadily at the task of improving the quality of his cattle. His first blooded stock were principally Durham, which he claimed did not thrive in the Panhandle. Hence he shifted to Hereford. Goodnight maintained separately a high-grade herd and a low-grade herd; until he fenced his pastures, he employed herd riders to see that the two groups did not intermingle.[45] Ultimately the low-grade herd came to number sixty thousand head, while the high-grade Hereford group approximated nine thousand animals.[46] When, under controlled and ideal conditions, forty years were necessary to convert 14 per cent of the Goodnight herd into high-grade animals, it should be understandable why the improvement of the quality of the average herd by less efficient methods required a much longer period.

The milch cow in Texas, facing competition from longhorn, Durham, and Hereford, found the role of glamour girl denied her. But with a rising interest in the improvement of all breeds of cattle, she was not forgotten, and the *Echo* informed the people of Shackelford County that certain of the county's citizens had taken steps toward improving the breed of dairy cattle:

Judge C. K. Stribling received three thoroughbred Jersey cows a few weeks ago, and although they were thin in flesh, looking almost like the last remains of an ill spent life, they showed up such good qualities that he ordered two more, one heifer and one bull for himself and one heifer each for Messrs. F. E. Conrad, Sheriff D. G. Simpson and Treasurer L. N. Keener. This is the opening wedge we judge for the introduction of this, one of the best breeds of cattle known for milk and butter.[47]

Other cattlemen manifested some interest in a dual-purpose animal, one combining features of both milk and beef breeds; a Taylor County rancher purchased Holstein bulls:

Capt. C. M. Pearce of Southwest Taylor county while east a few days ago purchased two registered thoroughbred Holstein bulls, and they were shipped to Abilene and from here driven to his ranch. They are magnificent animals, and we believe will be the best cattle to be had for this section. They are a very hardy cattle and combine, in a happy degree the two essentials in cattle raising — beef and milk, and unlike most other breeds of large cattle the Holsteins are excellent milkers.[48]

Since during the last decade of the century milk production more than doubled while dairy cattle decreased in numbers, improvement in the quality of dairy herds must have been pursued more expeditiously than was that of beef breeds. Until after 1900, however, the bulk of all milk produced was consumed on the premises of the producer; for that reason the milch cow is more closely related to the self-contained past, while longhorns, Durhams, and Herefords were valued chiefly as market products, and therefore form a part of the movement shifting the whole of agriculture toward a dependent commercialized economy. Even the higher quality milch cow became a part of the trend toward commercialization; when milk production increased beyond home consumption, the family sought to peddle the surplus.

The fact that milch cows always commanded higher prices on a per head basis than beef cattle, plus the additional fact that the great majority of milch cattle were congregated east of the ninety-eighth meridian, kept aggregate values of East and West Texas cattle far more nearly even than is commonly suspected — and this in spite of the fact that the western half of the state was identified as the cattle country.

The horse has often been considered as a tool or a by-product of the cattle industry:

It was not till the occurrence of the Boer War that the importance of Texas as a horse and mule producing territory was fully realized. British remount officers were dispatched to the United States at the outbreak of hostilities in the fall of 1899. Purchases, more especially of horses, were confined at first to the larger middle-western markets; it was found, however, that for unlimited supplies of animals best suited to the needs of campaigning in South Africa, constitution, size and price considered, they must come to the Southwest. Purchasing agents were accordingly sent to Texas, whence they were very soon drawing by far the larger supply of mules and big per cent of their horses . . . out of a total of about 85,000 mules obtained from the United States, it was found that forty odd thousand had been purchased from Texas dealers, besides ten thousand bought in Texas and Indian territory, and disposed of at other points as natives, and out of a total of a hundred thousand horses purchased, some thirty thousand were bought in Texas.[49]

S. G. Reed estimated that "from 1874 to 1892 the country around San Antonio produced and shipped more horses and mules than any other locality, state or nation in the world."[50] For the last three decades of the century, horse sales averaged, in dollar value, approximately 10 per cent of the cattle sales.

During those decades, although the herds involved were smaller, horse drives were as common as cattle drives. The *Democrat* estimated that for the year 1878 not fewer than 40,000 horses had passed through Fort Worth as they were driven up the trail;[51] in the same year more than 250,000 cattle passed through the town on their way north. A number of months earlier it had been said that a "large and rapid increase" in the number of horses in western Texas was creating a grave problem — one which, the source continued, a number of persons hoped to solve by rounding up and driving several herds of horses to Kansas. The correspondent for the *Galveston News* said one herd of 800 was in readiness to move.[52] In the late seventies, droves of wild horses roamed Concho County, the property of anyone who could capture them; and in that county, said the *News*, a party was corralling a herd for a drive to Iowa.[53] Horse drives were terminated by the same forces that put a stop to cattle drives.

Henry B. Sanborn, who made a fortune selling barbed wire to Texans, was an early pioneer in improving the blood of Texas horses. A year after his arrival in the state, he bought in Grayson County a tract of two thousand (later increased to ten thousand) acres of land which he stocked with cattle and horses. For breeding purposes he maintained fine-blooded Percheron and French coach stallions. After operating the Grayson County stock farm for a number of years, Sanborn transferred his livestock to ranch lands he had obtained near present-day Amarillo. Captain B. B. Paddock said that Mr. Sanborn derived special satisfaction from proving that Texas prairies were as well suited to raising high-grade horses as any grazing region in the Union.[54] But in spite of the interest manifested in better breeds of horses by Sanborn and others, the cow pony remained predominantly a mustang.

For a number of years sheep gave some indication of seriously challenging cattle for the number one position in the Texas livestock industry. Until the eighties fortune hunters appear to have found success as quickly with sheep as with cattle. But when flocks were not moved onto the range as it was vacated by Indian and buffalo, sheep began to lose ground. Then the cattle boom of the early eighties dealt sheepmen another retarding blow. As a result the sheep industry went into a decline which ultimately reduced the sheep population to one-third its former size.

In Texas George W. Kendall, whose memory is perpetuated in the sheep country by a county which bears his name, is generally acknowledged as the founder of the sheep industry in its modern form. Prior to 1856 when he became a resident, he had established his flocks in the state. Before Kendall became interested in Texas sheep, the animals had been maintained primarily for mutton; he shifted the emphasis to wool. Within a very few years his flocks had increased from hundreds to thousands, and his success "demonstrated the adaptability of the country to sheep-raising and wool-growing on an extensive scale."[55] Soon hundreds of other persons were following the trail blazed by Kendall in hopes that they might meet with equal success as sheepmen. For the *Texas Almanac* of 1859 Mr. Kendall wrote an article describing the steps he considered essential to success in the sheep industry:

We all know how delusive profits on paper ordinarily turn out; yet I think if a person will follow, in the main, the plan I have suggested, he may hope to realize handsomely from an investment. I will here give a statement, and allow a wide margin for losses:

Cost of 1,000 American ewes, at $2.50 each	$2,500
Cost of 15 merino bucks, at $50 each	750
Total capital invested	$3,250
Interest on above at 10 per cent	$ 325
Cost of hiring and feeding shepherd	275
Cost of salting sheep	50
Expenses at shearing time, and other extras	50
Total cost of keeping	$ 700
Value of 2,000 lbs. of wool from ewes, at 20 cents per lb.	$ 400
Value of 150 lbs. of wool from bucks, at 30 cents per lb.	45
Value of increase in the flock, say 700, at $3 each	$2,100
Total receipts	$2,545
Deduct from this cost of keep, &c.	700
And we have a clear profit of	$1,845

This is a tolerably fair business, as any one will say, and I think that I have allowed liberally for losses. With such luck or success as I have had during the last two lambing seasons, the increase should be nearer 900 than 700. I have put down the amount and value of the wool at low figures, as well as the value of the increase; for it should be borne in mind that at least 350 of the lambs should be ewes, which I should esteem cheap at $4 each when one year old, while fat wethers, after being shorn in the fall, readily command $2.50 and $3 each in San Antonio, for mutton. But as the increase, all half merinoes, should average 4 lb. of wool each, it would be more profitable to keep the wethers until aged — at least, such is my impression. I have neglected to take into account that in one sense a man's capital is to an extent compounding; for it is to be presumed that any one entering the business should keep all his ewe lambs for breeding.

In concluding an article, perhaps already too long for your valuable annual, I would again impress upon all the necessity of first finding a suitable range for their sheep before they purchase a flock, and to make suitable preparations to see their animals safely through the first winter.[56]

The master sheepman had drawn the blueprint of a road to wealth, with all the clarity his long years of experience as a New Orleans journalist could command. Although the article had been published originally in 1859, range conditions had changed so little in Texas that when the *Almanac* resumed publication in 1870 it was reprinted *in toto*. The primary requirements for success appear to have been access to a few sections of free range land and the ability to borrow $3,250, the latter a difficult condition for most people to meet. Kendall's estimate of cost of Merino rams was high for the seventies; they could then be bought for about fifteen dollars a head. Also, allowance for herders during the seventies included twelve dollars for wages and six dollars for board, a total of $216 for the year. Kendall undoubtedly spoke from experience when he estimated a wool clip of four pounds from a half-breed offspring, twice the clip from its native ewe mother. This meant that by holding the flock at a thousand head, selling the old native ewes, and retaining the half-breed offspring, in approximately three years one could increase the wool clip from two thousand to four thousand pounds. Although he did not say so specifically, Kendall certainly implied that the wool yield per animal would increase as the ratio of Merino blood became greater.

Whether they had access to or followed Kendall's advice or not, many persons appear to have done well with sheep. The *News* tells the story of "an Italian boy named Laly who came to this country eight years ago a poor organ-grinder. His monkeys died and he hired as a sheep-herder near Laredo, and by hard work got a herd of his own. He is now independently rich."[57] Bee County, by broadcasting success stories of local residents, offered fortunes in sheep to all who might be interested. One appeal, which was evidently designed to attract newcomers, said:

Immigrants who desire to raise sheep and hogs, and raise small cereal crops, would do well in the County of Bee. Men who were poor in 1865, by turning their attention to sheep, have made fortunes. Some who had but just enough money to buy a few head of fine bucks, have bred them to the coarse Mexican sheep, and have in a few years so increased the value of the wool as well as the sheep, that the same flock will sell for three or four times as much as before.[58]

Most of the wool crop of the state seems to have moved through Corpus Christi during the seventies; and Nueces, with 700,000 sheep, clipped more wool than any other county in the state. Bee and Webb were also important sheep counties. The heart of the sheep range tended, however, to shift to the north. Mr. Robson, of the *Echo*, became enthusiastic over the potential fortunes to be made in sheep, and in his columns wrote of advantages that would accrue to farmers and livestock men who added sheep to their operations. But by 1881 Robson had become disillusioned; having convinced himself that sheep prices were highly inflated, he then began a series of warnings to sheepmen, arguing that financial losses in sheep were inevitable because prices always became abnormally high on the very eve of a reaction.[59]

Efforts to improve the quality of sheep appear to have antedated a general interest in better breeds of cattle. As we have seen, the original Kendall flock was a mixture of blooded Merino bucks and American ewes. In 1878 a correspondent analyzed for the *News* the good and bad features of each of the five leading breeds of sheep in the state (Merino, Leicester, Lincolnshire, Southdown, and Coltswold or Gloucester), and concluded that the Coltswold was the most desirable.[60] The name of the Rambouillet, widely popular in a later period, did not appear at all; however, Rambouillet bucks were in the Kendall flocks. During the sheep boom flocks from California and New Mexico were driven to Texas, which quickly became the third ranking state in number of sheep; but when the interest in sheep subsided their numbers declined sharply, and at the close of the century Texas ranked no higher than tenth as a sheep state.

Booming cattle prices of the seventies and eighties were not wholly responsible for the loss of interest in sheep; the decline of wool prices was also a significant contributory factor. The drop in the price of wool is pointed to by Paul S. Taylor as the primary cause for the reduction of the sheep population in Dimmit County. Sheep, Taylor said, outnumbered cattle throughout the eighties, but by 1892 from a former sheep population of 131,000 only 5,000 were left in the county.[61] Actually, there were a number of reasons for the decline in sheep numbers. The wool prices of twenty cents per pound for ewe and thirty cents for Merino buck, which Kendall thought were conservatively low estimates, proved, in later years, to be overoptimistic. Throughout the seventies wool prices remained high, reaching ultimately thirty-five cents per pound,[62] but the eighties were characterized by low prices. Reported wool sales for the mid-eighties followed somewhat the following pattern: "One of the largest individual wool transactions of the season was that of R. W. Wylie's clip of 250,000 pounds, sold last week to T. W. Scollard. The proceeds of the sale aggregated $27,000."[63] In this particular sale the price averaged ten and eight-tenths cents per pound. Throughout the decade ten cents per pound was a frequent St. Louis quotation for Texas wool; consequently the price to the grower was ten cents less the freight charges on wool from Texas to St. Louis. In 1880 one flock of high-grade Merinos was sold at a low price which averaged $3.33 per head;[64] but after the middle of the decade prices were even lower, commonly ranging between one and two dollars per head, and the sale price for a flock of 300, made in the fall of 1885, averaged sixty cents per sheep.[65]

Sheepmen frequently suffered heavy losses because of adverse weather conditions. The death toll from excessive cold weather — and the death rate did run high if freezing temperatures came hard on the heels of the shearing season — tended to depress the industry. Within a very few hours a Texas blue norther could put any sheepman out of business. Spells of exceedingly cold weather were usually followed by the appearance in papers from all parts of the state of news items detailing stories of heavy losses among the sheep:

> The recent cold weather has made sad havoc with the sheep in this vicinity. Messrs. Jacobs and Poe lost 600 out of a herd of 1,500. Mr. Seymour lost nearly his entire herd of 1300 head. Curtis and Robinson have lost about half of their herd of 2200 head. Eagle and Holstein owning about the same number lost one half. They also lost nearly all of their fine bucks. Dr. Culver and Mr. Goodman are among the fortunate ones; out of a herd of 2300 sheep, the doctor lost but 47 while Mr. Goodman lost only 24 out of 800.[66]

One of these heavy blows, striking suddenly, was oftentimes sufficient to bring a sheep owner to financial ruin. Fence wars, fights over grazing rights, droughts, and a prevalence of diseases among the flocks were other forces contributory to a temporary decline in the sheep industry. Also, sheepmen tended to come from northern, cattlemen from southern states — the Civil War again.

Although horses, hogs, and mules continued to increase in numbers for another decade, by 1890 the livestock population of the state appears to have reached its peak. Beginning with 1880 the sheep industry entered a period of financial decline followed by a numerical loss during the nineties. The sheep industry had apparently thrived on a free range and under a highly protective tariff. Judging by the low prices of wool and sheep which prevailed during the eighties, however, the tariff did not insure prosperity. During the latter half of the nineteenth century the livestock industry, operating under a protective tariff, partially on a free range, and with a segment aided by a tax on oleomargarine, was the recipient of government aid and protection far beyond that accorded the farmer — especially the cotton farmer.

As the century closed, horses and mules were selling below their 1890 prices; but cattle prices had risen almost 66 per cent in the decade, and sheep and hog prices had risen too, although the percentage increases were not as great as for cattle (see Appendix, Tables XI and XII). If we may take the average national price, less five dollars, times the number of head of cattle in the state as an acceptable method for figuring up the aggregate value of Texas cattle, then for 1900 we arrive at a figure of $150,000,000 instead of the $95,000,000 estimate made by the *Texas Almanac* (see Appendix, Table XIII). The $150,000,000 is more in keeping with the value of livestock as estimated by the Bureau of the Census, and, in spite of a sharp rise in cattle prices, seems to represent a considerable improvement in the quality of the animals for the ten-year period.

In East Texas the livestock industry began as a part of the system of self-contained agriculture; in the western part of the state it began on a strictly commercial basis, lending its support to cotton to swing the whole of agriculture toward the commercial system. Expansion of the livestock industry during the last quarter of the century brought the remaining open lands of the state under man's control. In the period of rapid expansion and development many problems and grievances appeared to hex and vex those engaged in agriculture. Henceforth production and well-being would be determined more and more by the efforts and planning of man and less and less by the whims of nature.

VI

An Era of Bewilderment

FOR the agriculturalist, more particularly the farmer, the second half of the nineteenth century was an age of bewilderment. The dawn of the era of specialized-industrialized commercialization revealed to him that agriculture no longer accounted for the major portion of national income. This was something new in the experience of Americans. The rural resident was confronted with the necessity of readjusting his way of life. The task was not easy. He sought to adjust himself to the present in accordance with patterns that had governed the past. He continued to pray the prayers of a self-contained farmer, asking the Lord to bless him with a plentiful harvest and thanking Him for the bounty which His munificent goodness had so graciously bestowed. He then blamed the government, the middleman, the railroad, the banker, or monopolists in general for the resulting low prices of agricultural commodities. Under an economy of self-sufficiency, the more bountiful the harvest, the more affluent the family larder and "the higher the family ate on the hog." The agriculturalist found it extremely difficult to understand and adjust himself to the paradox of a market economy where the more bountiful the harvest, the lower the price of farm products and, oftentimes, the family income.

In a study of political unrest in Texas, Roscoe Martin attributed agrarian discontent to: (1) appreciating debts caused by stationary or, what was worse, falling agricultural prices; (2) a scarcity of

111

labor following the disruption of slavery, and the consequent re-
luctance of the Negro to work either on shares or for wages; (3) a
crop lien system which deprived the farmer of control over his
crops, increased his indebtedness, and resulted ultimately in a foreclosure on his farm. Prevailing market practices also contributed to
agrarian unrest. According to the widely held belief, the merchant
paid ruinously low prices for farm produce but charged exorbitant
prices for his merchandise; thus the farmer received at the hands
of the merchant a two-way fleecing. Just behind the middleman
stood the army of monopolies awaiting their turns to finish robbing,
defrauding, and destroying the farmer. Martin concluded, as did
others before and after him, that the farmer could have saved himself had he produced all of his own foodstuffs and planted just a
little cotton for "ready cash."[1] Most immigrant handbooks contended that the Texas farmer could grow his own tobacco, and then
he would not have to raise cotton to provide cash for his tobacco.
When the farmer turned his back on diversification, so this line of
argument seems to hold, he flung himself to the very bottom of
the pit of economic despair.

Contemporary newspapers frequently attempted to analyze the
then current views on political and economic questions. Thus in
1858 the Fort Worth *Democrat* gave its version of the wants of the
people of Texas:

> The people of Texas are in favor of making greenbacks a full legal
> tender for all debts, public and private.
> They are in favor of retiring national bank notes and substituting green-
> backs therefor as the circulating medium of the country.
> They are in favor of making the volume of greenback currency equal
> to the commercial and industrial needs of the country.
> They are in favor of making a dollar of paper, as well as of metal — the
> paper being most convenient.
> They are in favor of the repeal of the resumption act.
> They are in favor of the free and unlimited coinage of silver.
> They are opposed to any further increase of the bonded indebtedness
> of the country for any purpose whatever.
> They are opposed to any statute that conflicts with the original contract
> entered into between the people and the purchasers of the people's bonds.
> They are opposed to any tariff, except for the purposes of revenue only.[2]

For the times, those were radical views. But in the course of subsequent years, all save three have been incorporated into government economic policy, and one of those presently stands in the twilight zone of indecision. Wants emphasized by the *Democrat* bear a remarkable similarity to the purposes of the State Grange of Texas and to planks in the platform of the Independent Greenback party. The prevailing low prices for agricultural commodities were attributed by virtually all agrarians to a scarcity of money. In part national banks were held responsible for the dearth of money; for monopolistic reasons, it was charged, they restricted the volume of national bank notes. Strongly appealing to farmers was the Greenback party proposal that the federal government alone should issue money,[3] and in quantity "equal to the commercial and industrial needs of the country."

Existing or newly founded agrarian organizations attempted to spell out farmer views on current economic injustices and to formulate programs designed to solve economic problems. Some proposed that farmers act alone, others appealed also to the city worker for aid, and still others suggested government aid and support. When the State Grange sought government action, its grievances were voiced through resolutions addressed either to the legislature or to the Congress. One of the earlier Grange protests called for repeal of the "smokehouse" or "corn crib" tax, a levy on farm commodities still in possession of the farmer who produced them. Actually the case of the "smokehouse tax" should be classified as a minor grievance. The agricultural fraternity seemed convinced that a solution of the economic problems of the individual was to be found, in part at least, in increased productivity. This idea fostered an interest in agricultural education and led to innumerable petitions requesting the establishment of experimental farms in conjunction with the Agricultural and Mechanical College. At other times agrarian resolutions petitioned that there be added to the curriculum of the common schools a course in elementary agriculture.

Repeatedly the Grange and other farmer organizations denounced the protective tariff, demanding a downward revision to the level of a tariff for revenue only. Likewise agrarian fraternities and political groups persistently pressed for the regulation of railroads. More particularly they wanted freight rates regulated and unfair and unjust railroad discrimination between persons and places made unlawful, with severe penalties imposed for violations. Grange delegates incorporated into the Constitution of 1876 a section which prohibited the chartering of state banks. At one time the State Grange itself resolved: "That the creation or allowing of monopolies is in violation of the spirit and genius of free republican government. The National banks are monopolies."[4] The Congress did not, however, see fit to abolish the national banks. As a result of Grange proddings, the legislature sometimes considered bills designed to alleviate grievances. More often, resolutions were ignored. At times the legislature granted relief in form of a "hock" when the Grange had anticipated a "whole ham."

For a time planks in platforms adopted by the Democratic party resembled resolutions approved by the Texas State Grange. The party advocated cheap money, though it never went quite so far as to advocate payment of United States government bonds in greenbacks. The party declared that the legislature was duty bound to enact statutes for regulation of railroad freight charges, and it gave support to the Grange in advocating repeal of the "smoke-house tax."[5] Democrats took cognizance of the fact that gigantic land and cattle companies functioned by virtue of state charters, and that vast acreages within the state were falling into the hands of alien corporations, by formally disapproving the practices: "We declare that the legislature of this State should limit the amount of real estate owned or held by corporations in this State, and that our incorporation laws should be so amended as to prevent rather than encourage land and other monopolies."[6] The political party also sided with the Grange when it called for legislation outlawing unjust railroad discrimination against persons or places. With regularity and without exception, political parties, agrarian movements, and labor organizations demanded lower taxes and reduction in government expenditure.

To the platforms of the Democratic party and the resolutions of the Texas State Grange the Grand State Farmers' Alliance of Texas, in 1886, added its "demands" directed toward ending abuses of "arrogant capitalists and powerful corporations." The Grange had sent polite memorials and resolutions to legislative bodies; but from its very beginning the Alliance assumed the attitude of a "demanding" master. From the state it demanded railroad regulation, and from the federal government currency control, specifying at a later date that currency be maintained on a per capita basis and expanded when necessary to meet the needs of business interests and a growing population. The fraternity re-echoed old cries for lower taxes and "extinguishment" of the national debt. By means of countercombinations made up of farmers, laborers, and consumers, it sought to counteract the growing power of corporations. Specifically the Grand State Farmers' Alliance demanded:

1. The recognition by incorporation of trade unions, co-operative stores, and such other associations as may be organized by the industrial classes to improve their financial condition, or to promote their general welfare.

Vehemently the Alliance denounced the land policy of the state, and advocated that limitations be placed on land holdings. It insisted:

2. That all public school land be held in small bodies, not exceeding three hundred and twenty acres to each purchaser, for actual settlement, on easy terms of payment.
3. That large bodies of land held by private individuals or corporations for speculative purposes, shall be rendered for taxation at such rates as they are offered to purchasers, on credit of one, two, or three years, in bodies of one hundred and sixty acres or less.
4. That measures be taken to prevent aliens from acquiring title to land in the United States of America, and to force titles already acquired by Aliens to be relinquished by sale to actual settlers and citizens of the United States.

6. That all lands, forfeited by railroads or other corporations, immediately revert to the government and be declared open for purchase by actual settlers, on the same terms as other public or school lands.
7. That fences be removed, by force if necessary, from public school lands unlawfully fenced by cattle companies, syndicates, or any other form or name of corporation.

The agrarian organization was firmly convinced that those who speculated in commodity futures were partially responsible for the low levels of agricultural prices. Therefore it demanded:

5. That the lawmaking powers take early action upon such measures as shall effectually prevent the dealing in futures of all agricultural pro-

ducts, prescribing such procedure in trial as shall secure prompt conviction, and imposing such penalties as shall secure the most perfect compliance with the law.

Furthermore, it insisted that the attorney-general rigidly enforce the statutes in so far as they were applicable to the payment of state and county taxes by corporations; moreover it demanded that corporations should be required to pay their employees in lawful money. The Alliance advocated a mechanics lien law and abolition of the infamous practice of contracting prison labor. Classing its membership as laborers, the Grand Alliance proposed "a National labor conference, to which all labor organizations shall be invited to send representative men, to discuss such measures as may be of interest to the laboring classes."[7]

"Demands" enunciated by the Alliance at its Cleburne convention in 1886 constituted its basic proposals for rectifying economic ills suffered by agrarians and other laboring groups. In later sessions of the Texas and Southern Alliances, the "demands" of 1886 were expanded and modified, but never discarded or materially refashioned. Perhaps the subtreasury plan constituted the most significant addition to the "demands." This plan called for direct issuance of money to farmers in the form of crop loans bearing very low interest rates. In addition to spelling out the programs of the Texas and the Southern Alliances, the "demands" became the heart of the platform of the People's party.

After cataloguing his numerous grievances and enunciating many remedial proposals, the farmer learned that much of his program bore a label of radicalism. In identifying two types of nineteenth-century radicalism, Marcus Lee Hansen says:

The American radicalism of the nineteenth century assumed two distinct forms. From 1830 to 1850 it was a reflection of the contemporary European scene. From 1880 to 1900 it was an attempt to preserve the American individualism then threatened by growing monopoly in land and industry.[8]

Viewing the rise of the corporation and the growth of monopoly as common dangers, farmer and laborer of the nineteenth century usually worked as a team, but near the end of the century the farmer withdrew from the partnership. Often the question has been asked: Why? From colonial times through the nineteenth century, the southern farmer has, more than once, faced the accusation that he used his land as though it were a tool, never as an investment to be nurtured and improved. As with other farm equipment, the charge continues, when the land became dull and worn, it was junked. If the indictment be true, then the southern farmer should be classed as a tool user — a laborer. The contemporary literature certainly does not imply that the farmer ever considered himself a capitalist — at least, not in Texas. Newspapers published in agricultural communities extended frequent invitations to capitalists to investigate possibilities of profits in some local enterprise—hoping to find one who actually would invest in the project. As used by the editors, the term capitalist did not refer to the farmer. In the first ten years of the twentieth century land values of the nation doubled, but in Texas they tripled. Probably the phenomenal rise in land prices caused the farmer to realize that he could become wealthy by the mere holding of land; that is, land offered him a reward without labor. The full realization of this fact could have been fundamental to his shifting his viewpoint and sympathy from laborer to capitalist. Whatever the reason, the farmer seems to have been primarily responsible for the break. The cleavage was clean and sharp, and apparently final.

A common fear of and dislike for monopoly inspired a continuous stream of anticorporation or antimonopoly resolutions from agrarian groups of all sorts. In their thinking they made very little effort to distinguish between a corporation and a monopoly. Farmers charged that the government had relinquished its money powers to the national banks; and the banks, because of their restricting the quantity of money, were, in turn, held responsible for the decline of agricultural prices and the appreciation of agrarian indebtedness. Furthermore, the scarcity of money, which banks artificially created, was responsible for the exorbitant rates of interest charged by bankers — or so the farmers contended.

It is difficult to determine whether railroads were considered to be more or less dangerous than banks. Railroads faced perennial indictments for charging monopolistic freight rates on farm produce. Moreover, by acquiring millions of acres of the public domain

in the form of bonuses, and making later disposals of these lands
in large blocks, railroads lent aid to the formation of land monopolies. Also facing indictment from farmers were the large land and
cattle companies whose land holdings, since they deprived settlers
of access to small homesteads, were said to be monopolistic. A common view held that the democracy conceived by Jefferson, a
democracy bulwarked by armies of settlers firmly implanted in their
small homesteads, was threatened and endangered by the tendency
to concentrate the ownership of land in the hands of a few.
Monopolies, through their ability to control government agents and
agencies, many farmers believed, received preferential treatment
in the assessment and collection of taxes. According to agrarian
contentions, corporations reaped the benefits while farmers paid
the taxes. A basically sound indictment charged corporations with
unfair treatment of their workers, alleging that they oftentimes
allowed weeks and sometimes months to elapse between paydays.
Tariffs fostered monopolies by removing the threat of foreign
competition but forced farmers to sell on competitive world markets.
An indifferent government, by permitting monopolists to engage in
futures transactions with farm commodities, contributed to the further detriment of farmers. All merchants and middlemen were
monopolies, or the agents and henchmen of monopolies. In other
words, farmers, more especially during the seventies and eighties,
seemed to hurl the charge of monopoly indiscriminately toward
any person, corporation, circumstance, or condition which did not
appear to work toward their welfare. At least, these viewpoints
were common among agrarian groups.

By the mid-eighties the public had probably arrived at a better
understanding of the functioning and structure of the corporation.
As a result blanket charges of monopoly on the part of agrarians
began to subside. Afterward, more and more, specific industries or
definite practices were pointed to separately as being monopolistic
and requiring remedial treatment. Because the newer organizations
had a broader understanding of the corporate structure, Alliance
and Populist criticisms of corporate practices were far more penetrating than the general accusations of monopoly which had been
hurled by the Grange.

An old philosopher of ancient Greece, more than two thousand years ago, observed that many Greek farmers were in distressed circumstances because their farm units were entirely too small to provide adequate sustenance for their families. Had the old Greek philosopher made a trip through rural America, including Texas, at any period of the nineteenth century, he could have described the gravest problem confronting nineteenth-century American agriculture in terms of his ancient writings. This very evident fact, which has been true of every agricultural community throughout the ages, seems to elude many students of history. In the period 1870-1900, the number of improved acres in the average Texas farm increased from 48.5 to 55.6 (see Appendix, Table II). Naturally, since these were average figures, the improved acreage of some farms was several times larger, but for the majority the number of improved acres fell below the average. But harvested acreage is more important than improved acreage, and harvested acreage is always the smaller. That is to say, harvested acreage on the average Texas farm fell well below the 48.5 to 55.6 improved acre averages. In addition to the small number of harvested acres per farm, one should give consideration to the dearth of farm tools and equipment. When the value of implements averaged eighty-five dollars or less per farm, then the subaverage farmer was indeed poorly equipped to cultivate other than the smallest of fields. With the incursion of farm machinery, the farmer whose principal tool was a hoe became an economic laggard. As repeated efforts were made to discover a solution to the agricultural problem, the simple and evident answer of larger farms, more farm machinery, and fewer farmers appears never to have been seriously considered.

Even had the average nineteenth-century farmer been fully aware of the economic necessity for larger holdings, his chances of acquiring more acreage were lessening as large tracts of the public domain disappeared, legally or illegally, into the possession of big land and cattle companies, many of which were foreign-owned. Since many of these concerns demonstrated outright hostility toward the "nester," or the farmer, the two groups "squared off" for a finish fight. In many communities polite rules of judicial or parliamentary procedure were quickly forgotten, and differences were settled by direct action. Land laws might be important in prescribing *de jure* ownership, but pasture-burning, fence-cutting, and fence-burning became the determinants of who possessed the land *de facto*.

The state of Texas once owned millions of acres of land,

to use as a source of general revenue; to sell or give away in order to encourage other people to settle within its borders; to aid internal improvements; and to reserve from individual occupation and settlement in order to create an endowment for its educational system and thereby secure a greater return at a future time. All of these plans have been tried. In most instances they have been attended with some measure of success, but, generally speaking, lack of good business judgment and a representation of selfish private interests in the legislature have kept the state from realizing the largest possible benefits from its vast heritage.[9]

Much bitterness concerning the public land policy centered around reserves set aside for educational purposes. By 1876 Texas had disposed of 110,000,000 acres of land. There remained in the public domain some 61,000,000 acres, out of which educational reserves were set up in amounts as follows: the permanent school fund, 27,744,850 acres; the University of Texas, more than 2,000,000 acres; and 2,000,000 to be allocated among counties for local schools.[10] Most of the remainder of the 61,000,000 acres went to railroads as construction bonuses. The state made the railroad grants in a checkerboard pattern with the alternate or in between sections reserved as school lands. The railroads either sold or leased millions of acres of their lands to livestock interests, and as barbed wire became obtainable, many land and cattle companies enclosed school lands in their pastures along with acreage previously acquired from railroads.

Certain large ranch interests fenced pastures of hundreds of thousands of acres. A breakdown, according to ownership, of the Adair-Goodnight lands making up the J A Ranch in 1884 included:

Land in fee	333,000 acres
Leased from Railroad	39,686 "
Unleased school land	200,000 "
Private land leased inside pasture	25,000 "
Vacant land	60,000 "
Grand total	668,520 [sic] acres.[11]

And in addition to the lands enumerated above, the Adair-Goodnight interests in 1891 showed their Tule ranch to be made up of acreage as follows:

Owned	163,914	acres
State school land	224,000	"
Leased land	40,000	"
Private land not owned or leased	10,000	"
Grand total	438,068	[sic] acres.[12]

Among the Tule holdings, but not listed, were 70,000 acres of San Jacinto school land, and the source fails to make clear whether or not a rental was paid on any of the school lands included in the Tule ranch. Since an item was entered, "Leased land 40,000 acres," one might safely assume that the school funds received no lease money. If that be true, Adair and Goodnight in the two ranches availed themselves of 494,000 acres of rent-free school land.

Prior to 1879 the state made no effort to collect for the use of school land, but in that year the legislature levied a rental of twenty-five dollars per section on land enclosed to the exclusion of the public.[13] Enforcement provisions of the law were inadequate, and for a number of years thereafter collections were not very effective. In 1886 the county court of Jones County assessed fines of $980 each against Swenson and Dyer, who had been found guilty of fencing lands not their own.[14] If the fines were actually collected, they probably constituted very cheap rentals for the lands involved.

On the surface, state land laws were in perfect agreement with James J. Hill's statement to the effect that "land without population is a wilderness, and population without land is a mob. . . . A prosperous agricultural interest is to a nation what good digestion is to a man."[15] From the tenor of the laws, one gathers that the legislatures wanted no mobs. State laws, at one time or another, made farm lands available, either as a grant or through purchase, in tracts of 40 to 640 acres. The same laws permitted individuals to acquire grazing lands in blocks of 1,920 to 4,480 acres. Until 1899, when the courts ruled that the state no longer possessed a public domain, homesteads were granted, 160 acres to married men or 80 acres to single men, contingent on proof of three years of residence on the land. By law, minimum prices for state lands ranged from one to three dollars per acre, while down payments varied between one-fortieth and one-tenth of the purchase price. Payment periods extended from ten to forty years and interest rates were never less than 5 nor more than 10 per cent on the unpaid balance.[16] Sometimes the law delegated to county officials the authority to classify the public lands of their respective counties either as arable or as grazing. Since livestock interests largely dominated local politics, nearly all western lands were classed as grazing. Where lands were classified as grazing, ranches gained a twofold advantage: the land could be leased or purchased at lower prices than arable land; and grazing land could be obtained in larger blocks.

Conditions did not permit an enclosed possession of land to prevail forever in the absence of an established legal right to it. The steady influx of farmers compelled the holders of large blocks of land, as a measure of precaution, to establish clear legal titles to the land in their possession. In the endeavor to retain their holdings intact, operators of big ranches employed a wide array of ruses and devices. They made every effort to discourage farming ventures in the range country. Farm livestock "disappeared"; fields were overrun and pastured by range cattle; homes, barns, and fences were put to the torch; and Winchesters barked at nesters, either as a warning or worse. Farmers were fenced in and fenced out, but nothing seemed to deter the plodding advance of "the man with a hoe." Loopholes in land laws abetted the large landholders. When title to a portion of the public domain passed from the state to private hands, no legal barriers restricted further transfers. In establishing solid ranges, ranchers took full advantage of the law. They themselves filed claims to every square foot of land to which they were legally entitled, and then caused like claims to be filed on contiguous land by their wives, children, relatives, ranch managers, cowpokes, and now and then a nester. Just as soon as the claims were proved, all titles were transferred to the ranchers or to the cattle companies. The wording of Texas land laws seemed to imply an intent to give little land to little men. The manner in which the law was circumvented is another demonstration of the truth of the maxim that what is important is not what a law says, but how it is interpreted and enforced.

While the range was still open, the clash of interests between livestock men and farmers flared into violence. Newspapers went into considerable detail in descriptions of the extent of damages caused by range or pasture fires, frequently expressing the opinion that the burning had been deliberate, and reminding readers that wilful firing of pastures was a serious criminal offense:

> Cattle men of all others, are deeply interested in preventing the prairie grass from being burned. It would seem this evil cannot be prevented or a stop put to it. There are stringent laws to punish any person who through design or carelessness sets the prairie grass on fire and permits it to go beyond his own premises. Last week nearly the entire country west of the Brazos river and north of Elm Creek was burned over, also all between Red river and Little Wichita, and east of the telegraph line, and the fire was at last accounts still burning along the Wichita. These fires will compel a number of men to move their cattle to a new range.[17]

About four months after the publication of the above paragraph, and undoubtedly because the editor was incensed over the burning of two pastures, the *Echo* printed a story bearing a Jones County date line and containing a veiled threat to the "nestors":

> Jones county, Texas.— There has been quite a burn on Eaton's and Carpenter's ranges. I heard their men fought fire for several days and nights before succeeding in whipping it out.
>
> Some of our "Nestors" are making preparations by building temporary brush fences. I think they are just fooling away their time by trying to farm where cattle range by thousands and hogs by hundreds and nothing but brush to fence with *which is liable to burn up at any time.* Most of them are poor, having nothing to subsist on and in my judgment would be better off had they remained in the settlements where they could rent improved places.[18]

By means of a bath of fire, farmers and livestock men evidently hoped to drive each other from the land as each group applied the torch to any inflammable object or property belonging to the other. It was a fight of "no quarter," and the consequences were feared by even the largest operators. Thus Charles Goodnight had "Hawkins and Hassar plow 200 miles of furrow as fire guard"[19] around his pastures.

By the opening of the eighties, barbed-wire fences were becoming quite common and acts of vandalism shifted from applying the torch to pastures, homes, outbuildings, brush, and rail and plank fences to snipping barbed wire. On a per acre basis, barbed-wire fencing costs were relatively low where large tracts were enclosed, but ran relatively high where only a small acreage was fenced. Construction costs of a three-strand barbed-wire fence, by an 1885 estimate, averaged $100 per mile.[20] Thus, to fence a one-thousand-section ranch (640,000 acres) in a rectangular block forty miles in length by twenty-five miles in breadth required 130 miles of fence which could be erected at a cost of $13,000, or two cents per acre. However, a mile of fence was required to enclose a quarter-section (160 acres) at a cost of $100, or sixty-two and one-half cents per acre; in many instances the costs of fencing for small farms would exceed the value of the land. When fencing pastures under conditions of decreasing costs, some big operators enclosed everything in sight: farms, small ranches, towns, and sometimes counties. As a rule, the larger the enclosed pasture, the fewer the gates; consequently some of the earlier wire-cuttings involved barbed-wire fences which had been thrown across public roads, or places where a nester sought ingress and egress to his enclosed farm. When fences deprived livestock of access to water holes, resentment ran high against the owners of the fences. The drought of 1883 is credited with inspiring well-organized, large-scale fence-cutting operations. Accusations of wire-cutting and pasture-burning flew thick and fast, usually phrased in such words as these: "Thirteen thousand cedar rails, enclosing a pasture near Corsicana, were burned last week, supposed to have been done by wire-cutters."[21] On some occasions the vandals or vigilantes made use of both wire-snippers and torches:

A Waco special to the Galveston *News* says: "Some weeks since Messrs. Bart and Luke Moore purchased a tract of 700 acres of land lying on the Tehuacana river, nine miles south of here, and let a contract out to fence it in with barbed wire. The work was progressing nicely, when, a night or two ago, some country roughs burnt the Sanger and Putnam pastures, in the same neighborhood, cut the fence in many places and dug up several posts, leaving them flat on the ground. Hearing of it, Mr. Bart Moore rode out there, found things as above stated, and found the following note, written with a pencil, stuck upon a gate just put up:

'You are ordered not to fence in the Jones tank, as it is a public tank, and is the only water there is for stock in this range. Until people can have time to build tanks and catch water, this should not be fenced. It is no good man who will undertake to watch the fence, for owls will catch him sure, and there is no more grass on this range than the stock can eat this year.' "[22]

By insinuating that the fence war was a struggle between the few and the many, writers of threatening notes hoped to gain either recruits or widespread public approbation of their actions. A note of warning written by fence-cutters and published in the *Echo* summarized the case of those who posed as champions of the many:

Cutters recently destroyed the wire fence of Mr. C. J. Wise of Hopkins county, and posted a notice, the following being the conclusion of it:

"This pasture business is getting to a nice pass now that a poor man cant by [sic] himself a little home. We dont care to be made serfs of yet like poor old Ireland and the majority of Ingland [sic], we are a free people and if we cant have protection we will protect ourselves and the least you can say the better it will be for your own hide and neck."[23]

Fence-cutting was often the work of well-organized bands, extending in some instances over several counties. Signatures such as "The Owls," and the "Hatchet Co.," which were employed on their warnings, implied group action. Gang work extended a greater degree of protection to the individual and insured more thorough destruction, on a much broader scale, in a shorter period of time. In an issue of the Comanche *Chief* for 1883, the editor estimated that no fewer than seventy-five miles of fence in Comanche, Brown, and Coleman counties had recently been destroyed in a single night. The *Echo*, in reprinting and commenting on the story, charged that a well-organized band of cutters operated in those counties, and further stated that in the opinion of the editor a similar organization functioned in Shackelford County.[24] Every region of the state suffered some damage from the fence war. It was no unusual thing for the cutters to snip every strand of wire between every two posts and then drag the posts out of the ground. The war grew more bitter and violent.

As the struggle raged on, Governor Ireland was compelled to call the legislature into extraordinary session to consider ways and means of bringing the era of violence to an end. In 1884 legislation was enacted which declared a person who fenced land unlawfully (enclosing land not legally in his possession) guilty of a misdemeanor. That is to say, one found guilty and convicted of having unlawfully enclosed half of the state in his pasture suffered no graver penalty than a fine and/or a possible jail sentence. The legislature further declared fence-cutting to be a felony, which, of course, carried a possible penitentiary sentence and loss of rights of citizenship. Thus a person convicted of cutting the fence surrounding an unlawfully enclosed pasture faced a term in the penitentiary. W. C. Holden says that the fight was one of survival, or for "the preservation of the ranching industry."[25] One may wonder how the protection of land grabs in blocks of hundreds of thousands of acres, or at times more than half a million or even a million acres, was in any way connected with the preservation of the ranching industry. Action by the legislature may have checked fence-cutting, but it did not stop it. Through the years the number of wire-cuttings grew smaller and smaller, but the authorities of the twentieth century have had to deal with intermittent cases of fence-cutting. The steady rise in the price of western lands, brought about primarily by the coming of railroads and the steady infiltration of nesters, no doubt had something to do with the gradual dying out of the fence war. The high price of land convinced numerous large holders that bigger profits might be had through the sale of their land than could be realized in ranching operations. As a result many large pastures were broken up and sold as farms, leaving both farmers and ranchers relatively happy.

Definitely the vast majority of residents of the state had no direct personal interest in the disposal of public lands. Landowners of the eastern section held titles in fee simple and displayed no active interest in the fight for control of the western lands. Now and then they may have "fired-up" a bit in election years when reminded by politicians that the "children's grass" was being stolen by big land companies. However, all agricultural interests, east or west, were deeply concerned over the supply of money, market prices of agricultural commodities, and interest rates on agricultural credit. Fence-cutting might temporarily flare into open warfare, and at intervals severe economic distress might be felt throughout the state because of damages suffered from droughts, grasshoppers, and unseasonable freezes, but money, prices, and interest rates seem to have been the eternal problems faced by all who engaged in agriculture. The last quarter of the nineteenth century was conceived in the "Crime of '73" and born in the depression which followed, and throughout its history the money question posed a major issue in every political campaign — state or national. Moreover, reverberating echoes of the voice of an orator who declaimed against the evils of crucifixion on "A Cross of Gold" and the "16 to 1" chant voiced by millions provided the century's swan song.

Farmers were virtually unanimous in demanding more money and higher prices, yet many were bitterly opposed to banks. Why? There persisted among farmers a strong feeling that bankers conspired to restrict the quantity of money, and that this brought about the inevitable results of lower prices and appreciated dollars. Too, banks were havens of mortgages; mortgages were evidences of debts; and as money appreciated, indebtedness grew more burdensome. Hence, the proper method to pursue in ridding farmers of debt was to destroy the fountainhead of debt — the banks. As has been pointed out, Grangers, at the constitutional convention of 1875, did what they could to restrict banking in Texas. The constitution denied the power to charter state banks. Banking operations for the period were thus largely restricted to private and national banks. A state business directory for 1878-79 listed 112 banks serving sixty-four towns: twelve national, three state, and the remainder undoubtedly private. Four were capitalized at $50,000; authorized capital for thirteen ranged between $50,000 and $300,000; all others were capitalized at less than $50,000. Aggregate capital for the 112 banks was less than that of one in the medium category of Dallas banks of today, yet Dallas in 1954 had one-third as many people as had Texas in 1878. Just what authorized bank capital meant is none too clear. Some banks of that period are known to have operated for as long as two or three years with no paid-up capital whatever. Thirty-three of the 112 banks were concentrated in the seven largest towns of the state.[26] Within a decade Texans were served by ten national banks with $1,460,000 in capital and surplus; but within another ten years the number of national banks had grown to 214 with $26,325,000 in capital and surplus.[27] It must be kept in mind that at the close of the Civil War Texas was entirely without banking facilities; and the increase in these services for the period 1870-1900 was much greater than the relative growth in population. The author strongly suspects that the bank structure was adequate to serve the credit needs of an economy largely self-contained; it certainly would not have met the needs of an industrialized state.

The Greenback party attracted many followers with its demand for a more flexible currency. Even then a large number of people subscribed to the belief that a paper currency could be readily adjusted to meet the requirements of industry and agriculture in the expanding economy of a nation with a growing population. On the other hand, many were convinced that the supply of national bank notes was controlled in such manner as to be most profitable to the banks; that the degree of flexibility possessed by the notes was always manipulated inversely to the monetary demands of the farmers. In time of depression, farmers wanted no contracting currency; in fact, farmers wanted *no* contracting currency. Many of them were convinced that monetary expansion would reverse the trend of falling prices. Farmers firmly believed, says J. D. Hicks, that wide fluctuations of commodity prices within the year were the consequences of rigidity in the monetary supply. Dumping crops on the market as they were harvested sharply depressed agricultural prices; yet farmers heavily in debt had little choice other than to dispose of their produce as quickly as possible.[28] During the period of 1873-91, in the face of an expanding economy and growing population, national bank notes in circulation decreased from $339,-000,000 to $168,000,000.

Agricultural regions knew their quantity theory of money. Reduce the quantity of money, increase agricultural and industrial output, add a growing population, and you came out with low prices for farm produce. But increase the supply of money relative to agricultural, industrial, and population growths and prices remained equal; make a further expansion in the monetary supply and farm prices would rise. Hence, all farmer groups persisted with demands that the supply of money be increased. In their contemporary struggles with those who controlled monetary policy, farmers won skirmishes but lost the main battles which embraced free and unlimited coinage of silver and increase of the supply of greenbacks in circulation.

Another problem, just as difficult as agrarian efforts to bring about an expansion of the monetary supply, involved the interest rate. There was no clear-cut understanding among farmer groups of the direct connection between the quantity of money and the rate of interest. They seemed to hold to the theory that the interest rate was determined by law. Therefore Grangers wrote into the constitution a proviso which declared that contractual interest in excess of 10 per cent was usurious. In the absence of an enabling act, the section was less than meaningless. In seeking to procure an enabling act, the State Grange poured into the legislative halls a stream of memorials petitioning the enactment of laws, with severe penalties for violations, making usury unlawful.[29] The rate of interest remained high. Large segments of farmers believed that the Ocala Demands of the Farmers' Alliance provided the answer for more money, stable farm prices, and low interest rates. In brief, the demands proposed that direct government loans in the form of greenbacks be made to farmers, secured by nonperishable farm products, or land, at interest not to exceed 2 per cent per annum.[30] Naturally market value of produce would determine the amount of the loan, and if prices dropped below the loan value, the commodity collateral would be forfeited to the government; if prices remained above the loan value, farmers sold their produce and paid off the government loans. Government land and crop loans at 2 per cent would have compelled private loan agencies to lower their charges on loans — so reasoned farmer groups.

Other schemes devised by the Grange were designed to protect its members against debt and exorbitant rates of interest. One of them, a "pay-as-you-go" plan, encouraged members to buy and sell for cash only. Under this plan the Grange stores appeared. The constitutions and by-laws of these stores stipulated that they should operate on a strictly cash basis; yet, as we shall see, the membership forced the retail associations to extend credit. Violation of the "no credit policy" was a primary cause for failure of local Grange stores, and contributed to the failure of the State Grange wholesale agency located at Galveston. Speaking before a meeting of the State

Grange in 1882, A. J. Rose, Worthy Master, summarized the organization's views on credit and mortgages:

We believe the credit system to be demoralizing, tending to make mankind lose confidence in each other, and also to lessen their opinion in their own ability to do. We are clearly of the opinion that the credit and mortgage system is one of the greatest curses that a people ever permitted fastened upon them, and all just means should be used to eradicate it from us. Who can be sociable with a heavy debt hanging over them? or how can we educate our children without the means?

Co-operation has a code of laws and principles which, if put into practice, will stimulate and arouse to greater action, in each participant, thereby increasing self-confidence. We know of no instance where the laws of co-operation have been complied with, where business has not been a success.[31]

Irrespective of the sincerity with which it was tried, co-operation did not eliminate farmer use of "the credit and mortgage system." Co-operative buying and selling under the Alliance came to a quicker and more disastrous end than it did under the Grange.

Not until late in the nineteenth century did the state press give any great amount of attention to financial news; however, an occasional item or an editorial comment gives an insight into prevailing discount rates, credit terms, or the supply of money:

The reduction to 8 per cent. of the rate of discount of the First National Bank of Galveston, which was announced yesterday, will not surprise those who have been familiar with our money market for some time past. It is not long since the cotton exchange committee on banking made public the fact of a reduction from 12 down to 10 per cent., and this further reduction to 8 per cent., although it does not extend to all the banks as yet, will no doubt be immediately adopted as the maximum figure to be charged on ordinary discount business. This may be inferred from the fact that current rates on the street for some time past on first-class business or good collateral paper have not exceeded 7 @ 8 per cent.[32]

Even though reduction in the rate of discount was only temporary, it may be doubted whether the farmer, since his paper was not generally classed as "good collateral paper," benefited from the lower rate. Interest rates of 12 to 15 per cent, or even higher, were not uncommon, and bulletin boards at county courthouses were filled with notices advertising dates of foreclosure sales.

At one time the *Taylor County News* expressed a rather unusual point of view for papers of that day. It said:

Undoubtedly the farmer has just as much right to borrow money for use in his business as any other man; yet . . . , the farmer ought to go reasonably slow, governing his actions by a due amount of caution. One of the things governing ought to be a certainty that he has an equal use for the money borrowed. It sometimes pays to borrow money, even at a high rate of interest, but in borrowing money, as in other transactions, one must be sure to get from its use more than it cost him. When a farmer receives $700 and pays annually $80, he ought to have it as a settled fact that from its use he gets in every year $100 more than he would get had he not borrowed the money. There must be no supposing in the case — he must absolutely know that he is getting the $100. Unless he can make clear $20 a year on the $700 he had best leave the money to somebody else — it is not worth fooling with and worrying over.[33]

The advice offered by the *News* is applicable to any and all enterprisers. It is wise to borrow at any time when by borrowing one can increase his net income. In spite of this evident fact, historically farm indebtedness has been viewed as bad per se. Those engaged in agriculture have probably been most to blame for perpetuation of this viewpoint; too frequently their borrowings have been for consumption purposes rather than for increasing incomes.

The Grange seems never to have accepted the fact that it was possible to increase farm income through borrowing. Nor did the organization ever relax its hostile attitude toward state banks. However, Hogg Democrats incorporated in their platform for 1892 this plank:

10. We oppose the National banking system. We demand the repeal of the Federal tax on State banks, and favor an amendment to our State Constitution permitting the incorporation of State banks under proper restrictions and control for the protection of depositors and the people.[34]

It is possible that the liberal branch of the Democratic party thought such a plan might serve to break the monopoly of note issue then held by national banks. Perhaps they hoped to increase the monetary supply by once more permitting state bank notes to circulate. The tax was not repealed, and Grange and Alliance opposition prevented, until the twentieth century, the chartering of state banks.

The state constitution did not, however, prohibit the chartering of building and loan companies, and throughout the twenty-five-year period these institutions seem to have thrived. Reports of

Texas' secretary of state reveal that for 1881 eight charters were issued to building and loan companies, authorizing $832,500 in capital; in the biennium 1883-84, forty-six more were chartered, their capital stock totaling $5,509,000; and 193 charters were enumerated in four biennial reports of the nineties which authorized the loan companies to issue $28,553,000 in stock. A few trust and insurance companies received charters, but building and loan companies appear to have been the main source of credit. Furthermore, it is to be noted that loan association facilities increased as agriculture tended to become more highly commercialized.

Newspapers tended to leave the impression that loanable funds were abundant. But when they observed the presence of easy money, most editors could not refrain from warning against the evils of debt:

Texas is overflowing with money-lenders. You cannot pass one block in the business portion of any town or city of any importance without confronting walls placarded, "Money to Loan." The fact of the business seems to be that our unsurpassed agricultural interests and great bodies of valuable lands are being mortgaged to the capital of New England. Our advice is — keep your property out of the grasp of the meanest of all devil-fishes — the mortgage. — TERRELL TIMES.[35]

A few months later the easy money market was mentioned as evidence that times were prosperous: "One of the very best evidences to be found of the solid financial basis of the business of this country is the numerous loan agencies anxious to loan money on both city and country property."[36] An advertiser in the *Taylor County News* promised would-be clients, "If you borrow from John A. Williams and pay it back by installments, you will save $450 on a $1000 loan at 10 per cent for ten years."[37] In the then prevailing practice, the principal of a loan was payable in a lump sum on the maturity date of the note; interest only was payable annually. That is to say, amortization privileges were the exception rather than the rule. Sums loaned to individuals ranged upward from $250, and only rarely did a loan agency claim to have funds in excess of $100,000.

Although, until the last two or three years of the century, prices of agricultural commodities followed a downward trend, from harvest to harvest farm prices fluctuated widely. At the same time, nonfarm prices did not vary greatly within the year; and even though most nonfarm prices also tended to decline, the movement was slower than for farm goods, while prices of some finished goods remained constant for months on end, or even years. The farmer puzzled over differences in the reactions of farm and nonfarm prices. To him, there seemed but one satisfactory explanation — he was the victim of two-way price control monopolies.

Publishers of the *Dallas Morning News*, beginning with the first edition of the paper in 1885, regularly reported current prices on farm and nonfarm commodities. Through 1901 those reports reveal that the price per keg of rifle powder ranged from $3.00 to $6.25. In one period of three years the price did not vary from $5.00 and it held steady at $6.25 for a year. For eighteen months the per keg price remained at $4.50, while for the last three years of the century the price was $4.25. In those sixteen years, rough lumber was quoted anywhere from $13.50 to $20.00 per 1,000 board feet, but most of the time the price range extended between $17.50 and $20.00. Columbia River salmon in lots of twelve two-pound cans were quoted within the price range $1.35 to $2.10. Over one two-year period the price held at $2.00, but a price which approximated $1.75 prevailed for more than half of the sixteen years. Peaberry coffee prices ranged between 10 cents and 25¼ cents per pound. Even though coffee prices for the last four and one-half of the sixteen years varied from 10 cents to 13 cents, for more than nine years they fluctuated between 20 cents and 25¼ cents. In dozen lots, two-pound cans of peaches were quoted at $1.25 to $2.25, while two-pound cans of tomatoes in the same lots sold at 85 cents to $1.20. To the farmer, the relative steadiness of these prices could be explained only in terms of monopolistic control.

The farmer was certain that the prices he received for produce followed a pattern at considerable variance with those quoted for finished goods. During the sixteen years prices of farm commodities ranged for country butter from 8 cents to 25 cents per pound; for wheat, from 40 cents to $1.20 per bushel; and for oats, from 15 cents to 60 cents per bushel. Eggs were practically given away at 4 cents and never sold for more than 25 cents per dozen; market quotations on middling cotton never rose above 10 cents but fell as low as 4.31 cents per pound; and medium good wool brought the producer 10 cents to 18 cents per pound. It will be noted that in price variances of finished goods — merchandise the farmer bought — the high seldom doubled the lowest quotation; but, with the exception of wool, price fluctuations of farm commodities, goods the farmer sold, were much greater, the highest quotations being from three to six times greater than the lower prices. To the farmer, business, transportation, and money monopolies manipulated markets and created these discrepancies between the prices he received and the ones he paid. With produce prices low and money scarce, the editor spoke with more pathos than humor when he jested that the village "was visited by a circus last week, and now small change is scarce." In rural communities, change large or small was usually scarce, with or without a circus visit.

If one undertook to search for the eternal grievance of all agricultural regions, the find would certainly be taxes. Panola County farmers, back in 1877, were grumbling that taxes and courts would surely be their ruination.[38] Since the brunt of taxation was borne by real property, rural communities considered themselves the victims of prodigal state and local governments. Fully two-thirds of the state tax receipts for the eighties and nineties were derived from general property, which as late as 1901 still contributed more than 60 per cent of the tax revenue.[39] State ad valorem taxes do not appear to have been overly high. In 1870 these taxes amounted to less than 2 per cent of the value of the products of farm and industry, and by the close of the century they had fallen to a mere 1 per cent of the value of the output. State expenditures, which in the mid-seventies approximated 3½ per cent of the product, at the close of the century constituted only 1½ per cent of the value of the product of farm and industry.[40] The state constitution placed a ceiling on the state tax rate, but property valuations for state taxing purposes were determined by county tax assessors and commissioners' courts; that is, the value assessed for county taxes automatically became the assessed value for state taxes. Hence, by setting low property valuation local officials were able to reduce the amount of state taxes paid by property owners of their respective counties.

The state tax rate for 1875, and five years thereafter, was fixed at 50 cents on the $100 valuation, after which it was reduced to 40 cents; there it remained for two years before being lowered to 30 cents. Thereafter, until the twentieth century, the rate fluctuated between 22½ and 38 cents. Beginning with 1884 the rate was split, a portion going into the state's general fund and the remainder to the available school fund.[41] At first the state constitution placed a 75-cent ceiling on the county tax rate, which in 1883 was reduced to 65 cents.[42] By constitutional amendment in 1879 the "smokehouse tax," against which farmers had complained so bitterly, was abolished.[43]

In the late seventies, even though taxes were low, property sales made to satisfy delinquent tax bills grew to alarming proportions. The *Galveston News,* disturbed because of the large number of forced sales, commented editorially on reasons for the "multitudinous catalogue of real estate advertised to be sold for taxes." As the editor analyzed conditions, sales were approximately equal between rural and urban properties. He posed a number of questions as to probable causes for the volume of unpaid taxes, questions which he proceeded to answer. The lack of wise statesmanship was the fundamental reason. Why? Wise statesmen would have provided a currency of stable value, but the country enjoyed no such currency. Quite the contrary, Washington politicians had fashioned an atrocious monetary system, "which, by an arbitrary manipulation of the currency, has from year to year contracted values and inflated debts."[44] Here again, high interest rates, inadequate credit, low prices, and the burden of taxes were all charged to a manipulated currency in the hands of a money monopoly.

Seemingly the farmer of the last quarter of the nineteenth century considered himself attached to an industry of permanent depression, under which conditions he became aware of a general depression only because the gloom seemed to thicken. Because of the self-contained nature of the Texas household, the average Texan suffered fewer ills from the depression of the seventies than did the inhabitants of many other parts of the nation. But the Texan then engaged in commercial pursuits suffered more severely than his brother on the farm. For a number of years the panic prostrated business, but the steady flow of immigrants did not abate and the agricultural resources of the state continued to be developed. According to one writer's analysis, a steady growth of agriculture, the state's primary industry, kept the basic economy sound and healthy:

Accordingly, the delay [caused by the depression of 1873] that prevented the railroads from extending their lines to the west and northwest cannot be regarded as an unmixed evil, since with the revival of prosperity progress was more stable and has continued without abatement.[45]

In the decades following the depression of the seventies, Texas became more thoroughly integrated into the national economy and tended to suffer from later depressions the same degree of hardship endured by the rest of the country.

Any sudden reversal of prevailing conditions in agricultural communities caused economic repercussions in urban areas. Captain Paddock has described the impact of the collapse of the cattle boom on the growth of Fort Worth:

The depression in the cattle industry during 1884-85 had its effects on the growth of Fort Worth. The period of stagnation was short, but in comparison with the season of prosperity that had preceded was severely felt. In fact, such rapid progress as was experienced in 1883 was not again duplicated for nearly twenty years. A striking evidence of the business conditions of these years appears in the fact that railroad building, which had been going on at a phenomenal rate during the first half of the decade, was now almost stopped. But beginning with 1887 there was a revival.[46]

Other towns which were dependent on the cattle industry suffered ill effects of equal magnitude.

However, hardships endured by Texans in earlier economic reverses were mild compared to those borne in the depression of the nineties. The period of stagnation suffered by Fort Worth in the nineties has been attributed to the economic depression which gripped its rural trade territory:

From 1892 to the close of the decade Fort Worth suffered its longest and most severe period of financial and industrial depression, and all lines of business, including the livestock market, were at a standstill. The city has always been closely dependent upon the industrial conditions of its tributary West Texas, and during the long time when immigration into the western counties had practically ceased, Fort Worth was unable to advance faster than the region of which it was the business metropolis.[47]

In keeping with the "long wave" theory of prices advanced by

Kondratieff, the thirty-year period of declining prices came to an end in the trough of the depression of the nineties, and the long sweep of rising prices set in. George Tyler described consequences of the price reversal in Bell County:

The depression had run its course by 1899. Cotton prices were better that fall and the next year the crop was unusually large with prices still better. In consequence most farmers in Bell county were able to pay themselves out of debt and business generally was brisk. Even old debts barred by limitations were in many instances paid off by the debtors. With the return of business confidence and prosperity, the political agitations, which had marred the preceding decade, died away. Conditions seemed favorable for new business enterprises.[48]

Tyler's comments concerning the reactions in Bell County might well have been expanded to include the whole state.

As has been true in almost every depression, the theory of underconsumption became the popular explanation of the depression of the nineties. Through the use of statistical data, the *Texas Stockman* proved to its own satisfaction that underconsumption was the sole reason for the depressed condition of prices:

In 1892 the consumption of wheat was 5.91 bushels for every one of our population, while for the year 1893 the consumption fell off to 4.85 bushels for each person. While there are no official statistics on the subject, there is every reason to believe that the consumption of beef for the same years would show a falling off of at least 33 1/3 per cent. These figures show that it is not overproduction, but under consumption that is responsible for prevailing low prices for farm and ranch products.[49]

Certain farm-labor groups and the People's party contended, however, that the fundamental cause of the depression was a scarcity of money. Populist views on the money question were stated in the *Southern Mercury* in an article by Judge Thomas L. Nugent, twice the party's candidate for governor of Texas. Nugent wrote:

Indeed, the money question, as understood by the rank and file of the people's party, is quite distinct from that advocated by the so-called silver or bi-metallic party. With the latter, the free and unlimited coinage of silver is the sole vital issue before the country; while the populists, not under-rating the silver question, have always contended that full monetary relief can only come to the country from a comprehensive financial scheme involving: 1st, the abolition of banks of issue altogether, and their divorcement from the general government; 2d, the practical recognition and enforcement of the doctrine that the money coining and issuing function belongs exclusively to the government; and that government should, upon some proper plan, emit and keep in circulation a sufficient volume of metallic and paper money to supply the demands of trade; 3d, that all the forms of money so issued should be of equal legal tender quality, and that no part of it should consist of convertible, treasury notes. In other words we insist upon a system of true scientific money, maintained permanently by the government without dependence upon intermediary agencies of any kind whatever.[50]

William Jennings Bryan lured the Populists to his crusade for the free and unlimited coinage of silver, thus disrupting their political organization as they followed him to defeat.

The depression of the nineties brought Texas for the first time face to face with unemployed persons in numbers too great to be accommodated on her county poor farms. What to do under such circumstances posed a vexing question. At one time the *Taylor County News* suggested: "If the unemployed could be worked on state and county roads during times of stringency and paid for out of the public treasury a perplexing problem would be solved."[51] Within another few months the *News* had taken South Texas plantation owners to task because they had displaced native with imported foreign labor, thus tending to push the economy "still further along the road to social and financial ruin."[52] On another occasion it remonstrated that if "calamity howlers" would just go to work and turn their money in the right direction the depression would quickly end. Going to work, it continued, would put contented smiles "on their faces and different ideas in their heads."[53] In other words, the *News* was repeating the age-old charge that large-scale unemployment exists only because the unemployed do not want work. In general, there was much talk about what could and should be done to restore prosperity, but the unemployed remained idle until "natural forces" functioning through the channels of "natural law" brought the depression to an end.

George Tyler has vividly described how the depression influenced farm ownership and tenure in Bell County:

The depression lasted until about 1898 or 1899. Strangely enough, the price of farm lands increased throughout the period. Many small farmers lost their land through mortgage foreclosures while others sold them and moved to some part of western Texas where lands were much cheaper. There was a marked tendency for farm lands to be consolidated into the hands of fewer owners, many of them business or professional men who had foreclosed on mortgages or had invested their profits in farm lands. These large owners usually held the lands for a rise in value and rented them to immigrant farmers from the older southern states. Tenantry was increasing and continued to do so. . . . Nearly all these tenants paid their rent with a share of the crop, the customary one-fourth of the cotton and one-third of the grain. But this did not pay the owner as much interest as he thought he was entitled to on the increased value of the land and many landlords began to require an additional money rent. This caused much resentment among the tenant farmers and later became a political issue.[54]

Apparently Tyler attributed the sharp rise in farm tenancy to economic adversities arising from the depression of the nineties. This problem of farmers without land grew in magnitude as the nineteenth century drew to a close. In short, tenancy tended to increase because rising land prices made purchases of farms more difficult for those without funds. Institutionally, tenancy has been placed on a status below that of owner-operator, but economically the tenant's position need not necessarily be bad. Given a just contract, he could be better off financially than many owner-operators. The majority of tenants, however, have not been able to rent with that kind of contract; consequently their economic circumstances have been bad. Everyone seemed to be alarmed over the growth of white tenancy, but no one appeared to know how to check the rise.

There seems to be little evidence to indicate that a scarcity of farm labor caused any grave concern except at harvesttime. As long as an agricultural system of self-sufficiency prevails, there should never develop any great demand for farm labor other than what can be supplied by the family. A self-contained farmer usually offers no wages except in "keep and kind." The fact that while plow hands could be hired during a greater portion of the period at 75 cents per day, harvest hands drew $2.00 or more per day, indicates that there was a greater scarcity of harvest workers. Cotton pickers were paid 75 cents to $1.25 per hundred pounds picked, and farm laborers hired on a twelve-month basis were given room and board and $10.00 to $20.00 per month. In general sharecroppers could be contracted for a cash advance of $50.00 per head per year, while a few large plantation owners worked their cotton fields with convict labor contracted from the state.[55] A rumor, at the close of the seventies, to the effect that Negroes were planning a mass migration to Kansas caused a brief flurry of excitement among land-owners of East Texas. Stories describing the movement of small trains of Negro emigrants were published in a number of newspapers:

San Augustine County.
A train of eight wagons left this week bearing twelve families of negroes and their effects from San Augustine county. It is their intention to rent land and make a crop somewhere in north Texas this year and then onward to Kansas.[56]

The threat of migration seems to have been the outgrowth of a convention at which Negroes resolved to leave the South. Some whites were of the opinion that the whole thing had been promoted by Kansas land agents. When the great exodus failed to materialize, excitement quickly subsided. A Dallas newspaper story of January, 1880, claimed, "The negro exodus has been checked by the gloomy reports from Kansas. Hundreds have located in Dallas and Collin counties."[57]

An ever present threat of drought conditions was faced by all persons who engaged in agriculture, and the more nearly self-contained a region, the more tragic the results of a prolonged drought. Since newcomers were usually not prepared to endure drought-caused crop failures, long dry spells created severe economic distress in recently settled areas. Often people who were familiar with the recurring nature of droughts suffered as much from long rainless periods as did the newly settled immigrant; the "old-timers" had allowed themselves to be lulled into a sense of false security by a succession of rainy seasons and had come to believe that droughts were of historical importance only. Neither the government nor monopolists were ever directly blamed for causing a drought; however, both were accused of intensifying privations of the victims: monopolists because they refused to lower prices as a measure of relief for the drought victims; the government, because of the niggardly monetary policy it pursued.

The year 1879, states Thrall's *Almanac*, was exceptionally dry. From May until August there was no general rain, and only a few widely scattered thundershowers. Thrall, however, did not fail to describe a method for dry-land farming, which was probably intended as reassurance to the immigrant that one need not fear a crop failure because of an extended period of dry weather. Thrall wrote:

In the crop reports which appeared from time to time during this excessive drought, we noticed this observation often repeated: "Farmers who broke up their ground thoroughly and early in the winter, will make fair crops." In a long residence in Texas, we have often heard the same observation. Deep and early plowing will insure crops almost any season, in any part of Texas.[58]

In other words, if a farmer were not lazy, he need have no fear of a crop failure because of a lack of rainfall. For the year 1879, Lampasas County reported a greater scarcity of water than ever before known;[59] Washington County anticipated a very poor cotton crop, making not more than a bale to eight acres;[60] and in Erath County the lack of moisture killed trees and caused entire patches of shrubs to die.[61] Although of great severity, this drought was of short duration.

From early summer in 1885 to late spring in 1887, the counties of Northwest Texas suffered one of the severest droughts of the last half of the nineteenth century. Weather conditions in the early part of 1885 seemed to promise an exceptionally good crop year, and optimistic reports flowed from counties then on the eve of the prolonged dry period. Crop conditions in Palo Pinto County were considered very good:

Mineral Wells, June 4. — The harvest is fully begun and with 10 days more good weather the small grain of this section will be saved. The yield is immense and will not fall short of 25 bushels of wheat to the acre. The oat crop is better than ever known in this section.[62]

Spring rains insured a fair corn crop and late showers saved most of the cotton, but through the following winter and spring no rains fell over the section of Texas north of Williamson County and west of Fort Worth.

Throughout the stricken region the corn and small grain crops for 1886 failed completely. In Young County the grain "merely came up." The county had no grass and no crops, but it had more than its share of dried-up water holes. At the order of the county judge, a $1,700 road and bridge fund was distributed among the needy; in addition, the judge offered to pay a dollar per day for work on the county roads. Cattlemen who were financially able to do so shipped their livestock from the desert-like country, but there were countless thousands of head that died of thirst and starvation.[63]

A correspondent, describing conditions in Wilbarger County, pictures the complete crop failure suffered by practically every county gripped by the drought:

> Vernon, July 17. — There is no cotton raised in this county. All kinds of small grain are almost a total failure. It is now given up by farmers that the corn crop will be the poorest for the past five years. There will hardly be enough corn raised in the county for seed for another year so protracted is the drouth. The acreage is about double that of last year.[64]

Fortunately, some counties in the distressed area, among them Jones, Taylor, and Shackelford, had introduced cotton a short time before the period of dry weather set in. In each of the dry years, those counties produced some cotton, thereby escaping the extreme hardship suffered by Wilbarger and other noncotton counties. Because farmers realized some returns from cotton, while other crops failed completely, it won many new converts; and the breaking of the drought was accompanied by a great expansion of cotton acreage. In the spring of 1888, Shackelford County farmers were reported to have planted an unusually large cotton crop,[65] and that fall Sweetwater, in Nolan County, managed to gin its first bale of cotton.[66]

Small ranchers endured privations and losses equal to those suffered by farmers, while larger outfits strove desperately to protect their livestock against the worst consequences of the dry period. In Ellis County, optimism prevailed among the farmers, who hoped to realize a good price for corn sold to feed the thousands of cattle that had been driven into the county from the drought-stricken area.[67] S. M. Swenson, in 1887, received three cars of well drilling machinery with which he proposed to sink a number of wells on his ranch in Jones County.[68] Still others hoped to save their herds by moving to territory where water was plentiful. A Nolan County ranch partnership, Martin and Milleken, informed a reporter for the *News* that the poor condition of the range was forcing them to move their cattle at once, and that they were in search of a pasture blessed with an abundance of grass and water. The partners were positive they would find such a place somewhere in the vicinity of the Pecos River.[69] No sooner had the drought broken than the Anson *Voice* recommended a program designed to insure an abundance of rain and timber:

... don't let those who have good large tanks fail to plant trees around them — water and timber are what we want. They will mutually produce each other. Try it and see whether we are correct or not? No one who has a section of land should fail to have a large tank of water.[70]

Another drought-prevention theory, advanced by the *Southern Cultivator*, had to do with retaining the greatest possible amount of rain water in the soil on which it fell. The *Cultivator* argued that the greater the amount of moisture that could be stored and held in the subsoil, the more able the country would be to withstand prolonged dry spells. Specifically, the *Cultivator* said:

It is, therefore, of greatest importance that all rainfall should, as much as possible, be detained where it falls, by deep plowing, sub-soiling and running deep and wide hillside ditches on a level, or in other words all obstructions that can be produced to hinder the escape of water on the fields which are being cultivated will tend to effect this object and by this the same effect is produced that is found in the original forest and natural growth by which the escape of water is prevented.[71]

The suggestions were basically sound but appear to have had relatively little effect on the methods of cultivation which were then being employed.

In the course of the drought, a few fortunate communities received an adequate supply of moisture from local showers; some less fortunate settlements lost in population; while the driest areas were entirely depopulated. Fully half the population of the drought region, Holden estimates, sought relief, either temporary or permanent, by emigration.[72]

As described by the Cisco *Round-up,* exodus from the stricken territory was more in the nature of a stampede:

The exodus arising from the drouth-stricken districts is taking the shape of a panic, arising more from demoralization than the prospects of the refugees benefitting their condition. Many are leaving without any defined object or destination, and it is to be feared that some of them, when they get to the end of their row and are forced to stop, will find that they have "jumped from the frying pan into the fire." The feature most to be regretted in this stampede is the breaking up of homes, the exposure of women and children to the deprivations and hardships of camp life while hunting for the means of subsistence, with chances of failing to find it.[73]

The town of Henrietta admitted the loss of a few citizens because of the drought — but only a few.[74] In the opinion of the *Taylor County News*, the drought had paralyzed all industries and brought all local improvements to an end; furthermore, it had stopped immigration, which the *News* considered to be a good thing unless the people who entered Texas had the means of subsistence until conditions changed. Real estate prices, the paper continued, were bottomless because people had been forced to sacrifice their property for funds on which to live; and wages had been reduced to the level of bare subsistence.[75]

When rains began to fall during the summer of 1887, privation and hardship were soon forgotten and many an exile came trooping back to the home whence he had so recently departed. Whereas the editor of the Cisco *Round-up* could write only in the most serious vein when describing the exodus, he could inject a bit of humor into a story of the returning "refugees":

Wagons are daily passing through town from the east, laden with household plunder and children. Most of these wagons bore away the refugees from the drouth and among those that have returned are to be recognized two that were conspicuous by inscriptions on wagon sheets in bold but rude letters — one of them bearing, "In God we trusted, went west and got busted;" the other, with more sentiment: "Last fall came from Rackin Sack, got sorry and now go rackin' back." Each wagon coming from Arkansas is followed by a number of dogs, yearlings, and colts, showing that the trip has been favorable to the increase in livestock, as well as children.[76]

As the rains continued, immigrants began to join returning exiles. Reporting a sale of 57,000 acres to a Pennsylvanian who bought the land for a colony of farmers, a Haskell writer boasted: "These are the finest agricultural lands *and with the seasons we are now having*, will become almost invaluable."[77] No one was supposed to remember that only two months earlier the lands had resembled a parched desert.

In the midst of the drought, communities did what they could to alleviate the distress of their people, but appeals had to be made for outside relief. In the summer of 1886 the state government was petitioned to ease the burden of persons who had purchased state lands located in the drought region by waiving interest payments on the monies still owed the state. The law prescribed forfeiture of the land for a nonpayment of interest. Interest payments were not canceled, but more time was allowed for payment and the state did waive the penalty of forfeiture.[78]

Governor John Ireland issued a proclamation appealing for contributions for the relief of the counties gripped by the drought.[79] Newspapers of the rain-hungered counties requested aid; but, in general, since their circulations were purely local, their appeals probably did little good other than to give the victims a chance to read in print just how pitiful their plight really was. County judges from the drought counties met at Abilene in 1887 and addressed relief pleas to "the State Government, the National Congress, and all Philanthropists, Charitable Societies and charitable persons."[80] Congressman Lanham of Texas introduced a bill in the House of Representatives calling for an appropriation of $50,000 to the commissioner of agriculture to enable him to distribute seed to farmers in the stricken area. Eventually Congress did appropriate the sum of $10,000. Governor Ireland and the legislature went into action and came up with a state-appropriated relief fund of $100,000. They also created a commission to disburse the funds among the needy in the affected counties. Counties sharing in the fund received from $200 to $2,000, Eastland County drawing the largest amount. Sums were doled out in direct relief, each destitute family being allowed fifteen dollars. The relief commission recommended, but to no avail, that the legislature make a supplemental appropriation for the purchase of seed to be distributed free to the hard-hit farmers.[81]

To those in need of help, private agencies made heavy contributions in goods and services. The Grand State Farmers' Alliance allocated some $12,000 from its funds to be expended in the drought region. Through 1886, a total of seven carloads of wheat had been sent to Albany for distribution to needy families. The people of St. Louis shipped a car of miscellaneous goods to the unfortunate and destitute of Palo Pinto County.[82] Newspapers of the stricken communities appealed to the nation's capitalists, begging that they launch new enterprises in the drought region which would serve to end the financial stringency of the people and make money for them. The new ventures need not be large in size — a number of modest-sized ones employing from fifty to one hundred persons would be adequate.[83] The papers of East Texas, however, devoted relatively little space to the drought, and mass meetings called in that territory for the purpose of soliciting relief funds for the people of West Texas were either poorly attended or complete failures. At Paris a meeting called for the purpose of extending help to families in the arid counties was so poorly attended that it did nothing but appoint a committee to solicit contributions from the businessmen.[84]

Institutions in the hard-hit counties did what they could to help people survive the drought. Thus, the First National Bank of Abilene announced its intent to loan to distressed farmers in the vicinity of Abilene up to $10,000 at low rates of interest.[85] Farmers of Callahan County were called together in a mass meeting for the purpose of considering means of self-help. While assembled the farmers adopted a proposal in which they agreed to sign each other's notes for seed loans, the notes not to exceed $100 per farmer. Even though they had received some help, those who remained in the drought area continued to suffer from privation until the "copious" rains of May and June, 1887, gave relief to all, spilling on Taylor County alone, according to calculations made by the editor of the *News*, 5,355,000 tons of water.[86]

Drought conditions recurred in 1893-94. But the dry spell was of much shorter duration than the one of the eighties and, being overshadowed in significance by the depression of 1893, received comparatively little publicity. In the interim, residents of western counties had undertaken to fortify themselves as well as they could against another drought. They had greatly increased the number of surface tanks and water wells, and had made some progress in developing a system of dry-land farming; hence they were probably better able to survive than they had been in the eighties. Not a few pastures had been cross-fenced, thereby insuring a more ample supply of grass. Actually, these developments were nothing more than manifestations that the people of the arid or semiarid West were striving to solve the age-old problem of adaptation. When man migrates to regions where geographic and climatic conditions differ from those of his past experiences, he has two choices: either he must conform to his new environment, or he must withdraw. The people of the West chose to make the necessary adaptations.

During the last twenty-five years of the nineteenth century, stock raisers and farmers alike suffered from the lack of rainfall, shortages of money and credit (at least, there appeared to be a shortage when they wished to borrow), high interest rates, and low prices. Livestock men, too, were victims of depressions and discriminatory freight rates; in addition, they had to meet problems peculiar to the livestock industry. However carefully the open range was policed by range riders, neighboring herds became intermingled. Often relatively large herds of stock were stolen before owners were aware that their animals were gone. In order to simplify the procedure of unscrambling mixed herds, and to devise some scheme to control cattle thefts, a group of livestock men decided that cattle-men should unite in a permanent organization. This decision resulted in the formation in 1877 of the Stock Raisers' Association of North West Texas, at a meeting in Graham. Later in the spring, at a second meeting, the organization scheduled nonconflicting dates and places for spring roundups, it being agreed that each cattle outfit would furnish a sufficient number of hands to help with the work, each being responsible for cutting its own animals from the main herd, holding the estrays in separate herds until the work was finished, and then returning the estrays to their respective home ranges.

At the second meeting steps were also taken designed to make cattle stealing more difficult. It was agreed that stockmen were not to slaughter unbranded cattle or calves unless the animals belonged to them or their employees. Penalties were prescribed for any and all violations of the above rule: owners of butchered cattle were to be paid twice their market value; one guilty of slaughtering an unbranded calf, not his own, was to pay a twenty-five-dollar penalty; in addition, all violators were to be prosecuted to the fullest extent of the law. The association further resolved that each of its members should be required to furnish the secretary with a list of brands, marks, and descriptions of all cattle in his herds which did not belong either to himself or to his neighbors; and, in addition, members were to supply the secretary with lists of estray horses on their ranges.[87] It was intended that these rules should compel the keeping of closer inventories of range herds — in the hope, of course, that even though the information did not prevent cattle-stealing, operations of cattle thieves could be more quickly discovered.

Like organizations were formed in other sections of the state. They were, for the most part, mutual aid associations with small memberships. For several years these associations of cattlemen went their respective ways, largely ignoring each other and often working at cross-purposes. The quarantine which North Texas cattlemen had established to protect their herds against splenetic fever infection from South Texas herds was a source of considerable conflict between northern and southern cattlemen's associations. Wise heads realized, however, that rivalry between the associations was self-defeating, and the executive committee of the Stock Raisers' Association of North West Texas proposed that all organizations send delegations to San Antonio to consider the possibilities of uniting. In response to the proposal, some two hundred men representing the cattlemen's associations met in 1893 and set up a committee to formulate merger plans. From this action the Texas Cattle Raisers' Association was born.[88]

From their beginnings these associations had taken a keen interest in all problems appertaining to livestock and the livestock industry. At a called meeting of the Stock Raisers' Association of North West Texas in 1879 the matter of freight charges was included in the agenda:

Among other questions, the meeting will take into consideration the extraordinary high rates now charged by Texas railroads for transportation of beef cattle to market, and devise some plan by which cheaper rates shall be had; or unite the cattle men in driving to other roads. This is a matter of great importance and it is necessary that every cattle raiser should attend.[89]

In an appraisal of this feature of the organization's work Captain Paddock said:

The Cattle-Raisers' Association of Texas has been foremost in agitating the question of governmental regulation of railroad rates and suppression of rebates and similar practices that now are admittedly the pre-eminent politico-economic questions before the American people for solution.[90]

Because of the slow movement of freight trains (many were scheduled at speeds of twelve miles per hour or less) livestock shipped any great distance suffered terribly from hunger and thirst. In addition, the careless manner in which trains were handled resulted in injury and death to many animals. Thus railroads caused livestock men to suffer heavy financial losses which the associations determined could be prevented. Their protests ultimately brought about legislation which required railroads to extend more humane treatment to livestock in transit.

Because the source of the dread Texas fever was unknown, it struck fear into the heart of every cattleman. All stock raisers' associations were interested in determining the cause of, and finding a remedy for, the fever. Seeking aid in this work, a cattlemen's convention in 1885 petitioned the legislature to establish a livestock sanitary commission. After seven years the legislature got around to creating the commission, but greatly restricted its powers until well into the twentieth century. In 1888 Dr. Theobald Smith made a significant discovery. He found foreign bodies within the red blood cells of cattle that had died of Texas fever. Within the next few years the foreign bodies were found to be protozoa spread by the bite of the tick. With this information, it was apparent to all concerned that control of Texas fever depended on the destruction of the tick. The cattle raisers' associations, the Agricultural and Mechanical College of Texas, and the U.S. Department of Agriculture united in an effort to discover a satisfactory method by which the tick could be destroyed without injury to the cattle. Richard J. Kleberg began a series of experiments with a variety of mixtures in which tick-infested cattle could be dipped.[91] These experiments resulted in the perfecting of a cheap dip which was successfully demonstrated in the Fort Worth stockyards. The effectiveness of the dipping compound had been greatly improved before the end of the century; since it had an oil base, it became very cheap after the vast production of the great Spindletop oil field reduced the price of crude petroleum to a low level.[92]

During the nineteenth century, the livestock associations did not become as powerful politically as the farmer organizations, the Grange and the Alliance. Yet the agrarian fraternities faced so many similar problems that bodies of farmers and livestock men could unite on some issues — for example, the control of railroads and the regulation of rates. Unlike farmer organizations, the Texas Cattle Raisers' Association did not wane and die with the nineteenth century; instead, it grew in both economic and political power.

VII

Grangers Have a Try

THAT satisfactory solutions to post-bellum agrarian problems were not found can in no wise be charged to a lack of interest, or to a failure of farmers to organize in their own behalf. In 1867 a government clerk, Oliver H. Kelley, organized the National Grange, or Patrons of Husbandry, a fraternal order dedicated to enriching the social and intellectual life of agrarian peoples — especially in the South. A trip through the rural regions of the South had convinced Kelley of a need for some organization dedicated to raising farm families from the dull monotony which characterized their isolated, backward existence. The Grange was his answer. Its original purposes, as prescribed by the founder, included an educational program, social gatherings, and the discussion in Grange meetings of political and economic questions having a bearing on agriculture. Although designed to meet southern needs, the fraternity was only reluctantly and belatedly accepted in the South. Southerners, said Robert L. Hunt, were suspicious of the secrecy of its closed meetings, fearing it might be another post-bellum political organization cleverly disguised, the better to subject them to further harassment.[1] It would appear, however, that more plausible reasons explain its slow growth in the South. During the first five or six years of its history, economic problems of agriculture were cast aside while its organizers devoted their time and efforts almost exclusively to rituals and degrees.

Farmers were not particularly interested in ritual or degrees; and, for those who were, the Masonic and other lodges had long existed. In 1872, however, after four or five years of very slow growth, membership in the National Grange began to increase very rapidly. Most of the new members were dirt farmers who shortly removed all government clerks, with the exception of Kelley, from national offices, replacing them with farmers. When Grange policy fell into the hands of farmers, ritual and degree work was shunted aside in favor of an emphasis on interest in agrarian economic conditions, and within a year the number of subordinate granges had more than quadrupled.[2] The vigor of the rejuvenation created a momentum which swept the movement through the midwestern farm belt and into Texas.

At Salado, the approximate geographic center of the state, Bell County farmers in 1873 organized the first Texas chapter of the Patrons of Husbandry. Shortly the subordinate lodge forwarded to officers of the National Grange a request that a lecturer be supplied to assist in organizing additional chapters, and within a month numerous locals were in various stages of the founding process. By fall a sufficient number of local chapters had been organized to meet in Dallas and create the State Grange of Texas.[3] Official minutes of the organizational meeting are brief, and reveal little more than that a meeting was held, that an organization was perfected, that Austin was selected as the site for the next session of the state body, and that the constitution and by-laws of the State Grange of Mississippi were adopted to govern the body until its own constitution and by-laws could be drafted and approved.[4] The meeting received very little publicity in the state press. One Dallas paper reported on the meeting and its work in four brief paragraphs.[5]

Seven years after its birth, the National Grange formalized its objectives in a "Declaration of Purposes," wherein its members pledged themselves "to labor for the good of our Order, our country and mankind," and adopted as their motto: "In essentials, Unity; in non-essentials, liberty; in all things, Charity." By means of the "Declaration of Purposes," members of the fraternity pledged themselves:

To embrace the comforts and attractions of our homes, and strengthen our attachments to our pursuits. To foster mutual understanding and co-operation. To maintain inviolate our laws, and to emulate each other in labor to hasten the good time coming. To reduce our expenses, both individual and corporate. To buy less and produce more, in order to make our farms self-sustaining. To diversify our crops, selling less in the bushel and more on hoof and in the fleece; less in lint, and more in warp and woof. To systematize our work, and calculate intelligently on probabilities. To discontinue the credit system, the mortgage system, the fashion system, and every other system tending to prodigality and bankruptcy.

We propose meeting together, talking together, working together, buying together, selling together, and in general acting together, for our mutual protection and advancement, as association may require. . . . We shall earnestly endeavor to suppress personal, local, sectional, and national prejudices, all unhealthy rivalry, all selfish ambition.[6]

Since the program of the Grange was built around these objectives, one need not look further for a reason for its failure. Virtually every economic intent expressed in the "Declaration" was diametrically opposed to the trend of the economy. A fraternity fostering such objectives was doomed to failure. In the "Declaration" the order claimed to be politically nonpartisan. While it opposed the tyranny of monopoly in business, in high tariffs, or in railroad practices, the Grange claimed to be the enemy of no legitimate business. And for a time, at least, the "Declaration of Purposes" struck a responsive chord among Texas farmers. Within two months after its adoption by the national body, the "Declaration" was ratified by the State Grange of Texas.

After making an intensive study of the Patrons of Husbandry in Texas, H. R. Edwards concluded that the fraternity appealed to farmers for a number of reasons. To farmers who were confronted by low produce prices, the prices of farm implements and supplies appeared to be unduly high. Rumors persisted to the effect that Grange co-operatives of the Northwest had been able to dispose of farm commodities at higher prices while delivering merchandise to members at lower prices. Texans joined the Grange with hopes high that they might achieve similar benefits. The "pay-as-you-go" plan sponsored by the Patrons of Husbandry appealed to farmers as a possible means of escape from debt. Individually farmers were helpless; collectively they might achieve a degree of success in curbing monopolistic practices. Some farmers believed that, even though they constituted a majority of the body politic, they were being pushed around by organized minorities. As an organized majority under Grange leadership, farmers hoped to reverse the shoving tactics. Edwards further pointed out that some newspapers credited the rise of the Grange in Texas to sufferings the people had endured under the radical Republican regime.[7] The latter view might perhaps have been more accurately classified as an opinion of highly partisan editors.

Once the Patrons gained a foothold in Texas, their numbers increased very rapidly. Six months after the first local was chartered, the number of subordinate lodges had grown to fifty-five. Within another three months, the State Grange of Texas consisted of 365 locals and had a membership of between fifteen and twenty thousand. In 1875 the Grange reached its peak with an estimated membership of forty thousand, from which it dropped in four years to a mere 4,352. Five years later, A. J. Rose, dubbed "Agrarian Crusader of Texas," was elected Worthy Master of the State Grange, and under his untiring leadership the fraternity for a few years showed signs of a partial recovery. Over a period of four years, Rose succeeded in building the membership up to 13,500 before a decline again set in, this time a permanent one. When the century closed the membership had dwindled to some six or seven hundred members, and the number of subordinate lodges to fewer than twenty.[8]

Although the above data on subordinate lodges and membership were taken from official Grange records, their accuracy is questionable. In his official address to the 1878 session of the State Grange, the Worthy Master reviewed the status of local chapters and their memberships, and revealed that record-keeping practices were such as to cast doubts on the reliability of the reports on membership. In part, the Master said:

Some of the subordinate Granges of the State have become dormant but are occasionally reorganizing, . . . Others are so far in arrearage with their dues to the State Grange that the debt paralyzes all effort to restore themselves. I would recommend that the dues of such Granges be remitted to a certain date upon condition that they reorganize and report to the Secretary by that time.[9]

In addition, annual reports of the Worthy Secretary indicate that records of many subordinate granges were kept in a most haphazard fashion. In his report to the State Grange in 1879, the Worthy Secretary stated there were left

on the books of the Secretary 1165 granges holding charters, nine hundred and fifteen of which are delinquent, or dormant; four hundred and ninety-five of this number have not reported or paid dues for two years. There are two hundred and fifty (250) paying granges with an aggregate membership of nine thousand five hundred and sixty.[10]

With 499 locals delinquent for two years, the report which claimed 1,184 subordinate granges for the previous year is invalidated. The excessive numbers of dormant or delinquent locals caused Worthy Masters regularly to devote a portion of their annual messages to a discussion of possible ways and means for salvaging them. In an analysis of why so many lodges had become nonoperating, Worthy Master Lang once observed:

The most important subject for your consideration, and to which I respectfully invite attention, is the condition of some of the Subordinate Granges, with regard to their status in the State Grange. Many have become dormant and inactive. This, in many instances, resulted from Granges being organized in thinly settled localities where the entire farming community were received as charter members. Others from receiving into the organization those who had no identity of interest, and felt no pride in the success of our objects. Another class for want of insufficient instruction in the aims and purposes of the Order and its practical teachings.[11]

Up to the time the above remarks were made, the Texas State Grange could point to very few positive accomplishments, and the lack of achievement was undoubtedly a primary reason for the loss of membership. Farmers who joined the organization because of their economic distress hoped for immediate results, but when, as Grangers, their circumstances showed no tendency to improve, many quickly dropped out. A shortage of trained leadership to organize chapters and guide them through their first few tottering months resulted in a heavy mortality among Texas granges. Leadership in the State Grange seemed wanting in initiative to launch Grange projects with dispatch; consequently the order was on the decline before its most ambitious undertaking, the co-operative program, was fully under way.

Accomplishments by the state body were largely determined

by the personality and ability of the Worthy Master. Annual sessions of the State Grange were mainly devoted to a consideration of matters laid before them by the Master. W. W. Lang was chosen Worthy Master in 1874 and held the position until his resignation in 1880 to accept the presidency of the Southwestern Immigration Company.[12] While Lang was an orator of repute and an able man, he does not appear to have had the welfare of the farmer so much at heart as did his successor. With Lang's retirement in 1880, A. J. Rose became Master and held the office for a number of years. Rose may not have been quite as good a speaker as Lang, but in ability and integrity he was a superior man. Furthermore, Rose led the Grange with a crusading zeal unmatched by other Texans. Since early in the Lang regime, membership in the State Grange had been declining, and Rose inherited a sickly organization.

It was probably Lang's feeling of kindliness toward railroads that restrained the Texas Grange, in its early history, from undertaking the immediate attack on them that granges of the Midwest had made. When the Salado chapter was organized, all railroad mileage in the state lay east of Fort Worth. In tempering the attitude of farmers toward railroads, Lang argued that the two were complementary and should co-operate. In his first message as Worthy Master, Lang emphasized Grange-railroad mutual dependency:

I am unable to discover any antagonism to railroads or to transportation companies by the Patrons of Husbandry. The aims, objects and intentions of the order being to elevate and ennoble by educating the mind, to promote the interest of the country, and the purpose of transportation companies being to furnish the means of conveyance, the two are dependent on each other. There can be no opposition; for unless the farmers are successful, there would be but little to transport. Railroads are indispensable auxiliaries to the agricultural prosperity of the country. To correct the ills and evils too frequently incident to monopolies, is not opposition to the monopoly. Let us, my friends, in a spirit of charity, apply the corrective should the necessity arise, without any intention of injury to any of the great industrial interests of the country. Make no war upon railroads. They have been of incalculable benefit to our country, and are indispensable to our prosperity.[13]

The delegates adopted views set forth by the Master as the official position which the State Grange would take toward railroads.[14]

On occasion, while presiding over annual sessions of the Grange, Lang relinquished the chair in order to oppose from the floor approval of resolutions which censured railroad practices. For a number of years before Lang resigned as its Master, however, the State Grange had begun to condemn with monotonous regularity certain railroad practices. Furthermore, it must be remembered that Grange delegates to the constituent convention of 1875 have been credited with the responsibility for writing into the constitution the strongly worded regulatory provisions applicable to railroads. The low railroad mileage (less than 1,600 when the Grange began as an organization) of the state may have tempered to some extent the attitude of the State Grange of Texas toward railroads. The majority of Grangers undoubtedly realized that if agricultural potentialities of the state were ever to be fully developed, thousands of miles of railway must be constructed. This may or may not have caused them to be a little hesitant about jeopardizing the future of agriculture by adopting an official policy toward railroads which would appear to be so belligerent as to endanger their future expansion.

Members of the Grange soon learned that constitutional prohibitions, however strongly written, were not sufficient within themselves to put an end to railroad abuses. In the absence of a permanent regulatory agency, the enforcement of railroad legislation rested in the hands of local authorities and the attorney-general. Enforcement under these conditions was never entirely satisfactory. Railroad legislation was enforced either with extreme laxity or with harsh relentlessness by politicians who sought by this means to further their own political ambitions. By 1877 alleged railroad abuses had become so common that the Grange petitioned for legislation against discriminations in freight or fare. As originally offered, the resolution also called for the outlawing of the practice of charging higher freight rates for short than for long hauls. Lang took the floor in opposition to the long-short haul phrase, and before final approval succeeded in having it stricken from the resolution.[15] In response to pressure from Grangers and others, the legislature, in 1879, prescribed a maximum freight charge of fifty

cents per 100 pounds per 100 miles and declared it unlawful for
any railroad to practice discrimination against any person or
place.[16]

From the date when A. J. Rose became Worthy Master, the
Grange became perceptibly more aggressive in its demands for
effective regulation. Rose never appeared to be any too kindly
disposed toward the roads. Moreover, in the period between the
organization of the Salado Grange and Rose's rise to the Master's
chair, Texas railroad mileage had trebled, and abuses, or at least
complaints of alleged abuses, had more than trebled. In response
to continued agitation for control, the legislature, in 1881, gave
serious consideration to the creation of a railroad commission.
While the bill was pending, and ostensibly for the purpose of inspecting his Texas properties, Jay Gould made a hurried trip to the
Southwest. But while in the state he availed himself of every
opportunity to speak of his great hopes for the future of Texas,
and issued stentorian warnings against jeopardizing that glorious
future by permitting the enactment of hostile legislation which
would drive capital from the state. When interviewed for the
Galveston News, he cautioned:

> There is one peril — injudicious interference by Congresses and State
> Legislatures with business. It was a legislation that precipitated the panic
> of 1873; the Granger legislation of the Northwest some years ago cost this
> country more than it will ever know. The peril is legislation. That is the
> danger always.[17]

Opposition by Gould and other railroad interests killed the commission bill. In 1882 the legislature, in an effort to quiet Grange
clamor against railroads, reduced maximum passenger fares from
five to three cents per mile.[18] Reduction of passenger fares touched
off, however, a reaction the very opposite of what the legislature
had anticipated.

Later in the year, when Rose reviewed the Grange case against
railroads, he reminded the fraternity that even though seven years
had passed since adoption of the constitution, the state still lacked
effective freight rate control. In his address, he ignored the law
of 1879 which had set the maximum freight charge at fifty cents,
but attacked bitterly the reduction in passenger fares and the

practice of charging more for a short haul than for a long one:

> The reduction of fare from five to three cents per mile, which does not materially affect the farmer's interest, who seldom travel on railroads. . . . The railroads have not been more than realizing the three cents per mile, carrying so many at half fare, excursion rates, and free, men of influence, whom they expected to use, do, and will continue to use, when needed; . . . It is of common occurrence for them to charge more for a short haul than for a long one, thereby damaging one section for the benefit of another; and charge one citizen more for the same service rendered than another. In carrying the farmers' produce to market, special rates are given to speculators, which robs the farmers, as they are forced to sell to the speculator. . . . Mills, in his speech in Congress, shows that on a carload of machinery from New York to San Francisco, 3,400 miles, $300 is charged, and on the same road, same kind of freight, 306 miles less, $818 is charged; that from St. Louis to Galveston, 817 miles, at one time $60 was charged per car, by way of Palestine, and at the same time from Palestine, 201 miles from Galveston, $90 was charged; . . . These corporations have already reached the point where they deny the right of the government, State or national, to pass laws that will in any way interfere with them. It has been admitted by their friends that passenger trains in this country don't clear expenses, but at the same time they are carrying men for half fare — at excursion rates — and for nothing, saying that this loss must be made up, if at all, on freight. Now we, as an order, are opposed to any part of the farmers' proceeds being thus appropriated without his knowledge or consent.[19]

The free pass evil so bitterly denounced by Rose continued unabated until well into the twentieth century. Although the curbing of railroads came about slowly, the Grange has been credited by more than one person with having played a major role in bringing about regulatory measures. In acknowledging the importance of the fraternity in this respect, S. G. Reed wrote: "The most powerful and effective influence in moulding public opinion and causing legislative action for the regulation of the railroads in Texas was a farmers' organization called the Patrons of Husbandry, but commonly known as 'The Grange.' "[20] The continuous application of pressure for a more effective railroad control forced the legislature of 1883 to create the office of state engineer, the engineer to be appointed by the governor for a term of two years. His duties, as prescribed, consisted of making semiannual inspections of the roads, filing an annual report with the governor, and preparing a report for the legislature.

The law which created the position also specified that uniform rates should be applied to freight of given classes moving in the same direction; declared all discriminations against persons or places to be unlawful; and required railroads to post in all stations printed schedules of rates. The law stipulated that any change in the posted rates without a five-day notice was illegal, and it required that proposed rate changes be posted in conspicuous places in all stations in order that the public might take advantage of the five-day forewarning period. For failure to post notices as directed, the law provided a penalty of $500 per day per station involved. When the attorney-general was informed, by the engineer or any other person, of violations of the terms of the law, enforcement became his special duty. Moreover, any person who had been the victim of discriminatory freight or passenger charges might sue the offending road in his own name.[21]

Actually the state engineer was given no powers to regulate or to correct real or alleged abuses, nor could he compel the attorney-general to take action on filed complaints. By the terms of the law, the engineer was a sort of glorified inspector, but not a regulator of railroads. The first and only state engineer ever to serve under the law, finding himself frustrated at every turn, resigned in disgust and recommended that the office be abolished. Although the Grange continued to send petitions to the legislature, the waning of its membership weakened Grange influence. The law of 1883 was the last major attempt at railroad regulation until, under proddings of the Farmers' Alliance, the legislature submitted for adoption a proposed constitutional amendment which specifically authorized the creation of a railroad commission.

The regulatory law of 1883 pleased neither the Grange nor its Master. Instead of reducing the number of rate discriminations and abuses, it caused them to increase. Interstate railroads, whose main offices were located in other states, fixed very low interstate rates. In volume their freight tonnage was almost wholly interstate; consequently if these roads reduced intrastate rates in compliance with the law, i.e., charged less for short than for long hauls, they suffered virtually no loss in either tonnage or revenue. But intrastate roads were wholly dependent on intrastate (short-haul) tonnage, and had they lowered their charges, making them proportionate to inter-state (long-haul) charges, the loss in revenue would have bank-rupted the roads. In keeping with the $60.00 Galveston-St. Louis rate mentioned in Rose's message, a short-haul carload rate from Galveston to Palestine would have been $15.00. A relatively high percentage of the cost of moving freight involved switching cars to and from trains, and for this reason Texas officials did not force intrastate roads to reduce their rates in keeping with interstate rates. As a result, short-haul freight charges remained higher than long-haul rates.[22] After 1884 the major Grange contribution to rail-road regulation was to keep the issue alive until James Stephen Hogg, with the aid of others, fully capitalized on its political possibilities.

The Grange did not reserve its accusations of monopoly exclu-sively for railroads; it also levied similar charges against the Galveston Wharf Company. Galveston draymen were willing to remove cotton from railroad cars to shipboard for fifteen cents per bale, but they were not allowed on company wharves. Thus cotton could be placed on shipboard only by the Galveston Wharf Com-pany, whose charges were forty cents per bale. The Grange argued that the overcharge of twenty-five cents came out of pockets of farmers, who, in disgust, sold their cotton at inland points for lower prices rather than be robbed by the wharf company. Part of the reason for the lower inland price was a buyer allowance for the forty-cent loading charge, so when the farmer sold his cotton inland the Galveston Wharf Company still "robbed" him. The Waco *Examiner*, for a time official organ of the State Grange, declared the Galveston Wharf Company and the Houston & Texas Central Railroad to be great monopolies whose exorbitant rates left the farmer but a mite for his year of labor. The paper insisted that these monopolies should be forced to reduce their charges to reasonable figures. It even went so far as to propose two ways whereby the wharf company monopoly might be destroyed: either all funds for harbor improvements could be withheld, or the city of Galveston might purchase the company's franchise and property and conduct it as a municipal enterprise.[23] Grange protests brought no reduction in wharf charges, but the monopoly was eventually destroyed by development of the port of Houston and completion of rail connections to St. Louis and New Orleans.

Throughout its history, the concern of the Grange for the economic well-being of the farmer caused it to manifest an interest in a wide variety of ideas, schemes, and projects. Because they were definitely at cross purposes with the trend of the times, many of its policies and ideas were destined to failure. Among other things, it seemed to have some hopes of checking the movement of rural people to the cities,[24] and often plans were considered which it might employ in an attempt to persuade country boys to remain on the farms. The Master more or less habitually opened his address with an expression of thanks for a bountiful harvest, then devoted the remainder of the message to a review of the reasons why prices of farm produce were so low.[25] No Grange Master ever appeared to learn that under a system of commercial agriculture bountiful harvests and high prices were paradoxical. Rather consistently the fraternity opposed further spread of cotton. A typical committee report on cotton reads:

The life and home of the farmer is or ought to be the most happy, as it is the most independent of all occupations. By his well cultivated fields of wheat, corn, and cotton with his pasture lands stocked with sleek and contented flocks and herds; his table supplied with fruits and vegetables from his own orchard and garden, he ought to every day be thankful for the blessings that surround him; yet how often do we hear him express complaints and exclaim that farming don't pay. A sad expression, yet a true one.

Your committee will attempt to show a few of the reasons why farming does not pay:

1st. We plant too much cotton to the exclusion of cereals and grasses.

2nd. We have established our smoke houses and corn cribs in St. Louis and other cities of the Northwest.

3rd. We, as agriculturalists, depend almost entirely upon the use of muscle to the exclusion of brain, which should be the grand motor and advancer of all enterprises.

Your committee would recommend to the Patrons of Husbandry and farmers in Texas the removal of their smoke houses and corn cribs from the Northwest to their own homes, and the diversification of their crops, so as to raise everything at home that our own soil and climate will produce and that they make the cotton crop a surplus one.[26]

The committee report actually said but one thing: that Grangers should adopt a live-at-home policy. No poorer advice on the allocation of land and labor could ever have been conceived. The Grange invariably sought to turn agriculture in the very opposite direction from the trend of the national economy, which moved toward dependent specialization. Under its third reason, the committee could have developed a sound idea. True, the farmer did "depend almost entirely upon the use of muscle"; but the closing phrase should have been, "while the rest of the nation depends more and more on the use of machinery." The committee could then have concluded accurately: "The lot of the farmer is bad because muscle production cannot keep pace with machine production."

In keeping with its interest in agricultural education, the Grange considered in 1877 a proposal that an experimental farm be established and maintained near Austin. The proposition was referred to a committee instructed to make an investigation and report on the possibilities. The committee found the State Grange financially unable to support the project. The order then petitioned the legislature to establish, at the earliest time practicable, an experimental farm at the Agricultural and Mechanical College.[27] The Grange, fascinated with the prospects of an experimental farm of its own, continued to toy with the idea and ran a notice in its official newspaper requesting interested parties to submit propositions. Two responses were received: one offered for $40,000 a 1,700-acre plantation near Jefferson, terms half cash and the balance in three years; the other tendered as gifts $1,000 in cash and a twenty-five-acre tract for a college campus, plus 500 acres of land rent free for five years. Since the Grange treasury showed no improvement over the previous year, both offers were rejected.[28] But in order to increase educational opportunities for farm boys, the Grange requested that there be set aside by the state agricultural college a five-hundred-acre field which could be cultivated by part-time student workers who would thus obtain partial defrayment of their college expenses.[29]

When possible the State Grange made contracts with manufacturers to sell merchandise to Patrons below normal retail prices. In return for these special discounts the fraternity recommended merchandise of the manufacturers to the membership. Upon findings of its investigating committee the State Grange at one time approved a sewing machine:

> Your Committee on Good of the Order No. 1, have considered the resolution in relation to the American Sewing Machine and being fully satisfied it is a first class machine in all respects, and performs its work equal to any other machine upon the market, while the price is less than one-half of what machines of its class are sold, we would, therefore, recommend the adoption of the resolution.[30]

As a usual thing, manufacturers, in return for the official commendation of their products, guaranteed the merchandise; and when a Granger complained that a guarantee had not been "made good," the Grange resorted to boycott. On one occasion its executive committee presented to the Texas State Grange a report concerning a complaint that a wagon manufacturer had refused to abide by its guarantee. The committee reported:

> Complaint has been made to your committee by Bro. Robert Hanna, of Pleasant Hill Grange No. 473, concerning a wagon purchased from George Devany & Brown, manufacturers at Overton, Texas, who were reported as manufacturers by the State Grange at its last session, of which complaint Devany, Brown & Co. have been informed by the chairman and requested to make their guarantee good by giving satisfaction to Bro. Hanna, &c.
>
> To which said Devany, Brown & Co., have made no reply, nor have they rendered satisfaction to Bro. Hanna, hence the complaint, with all evidence therewith connected, is hereby submitted for the action of this body.[31]

The facts as presented by the executives were referred to a committee on the good of the order who, after further study of the case, recommended that the firm be boycotted:

> Your committee to whom was referred the matter concerning a wagon sold by Devany, Brown & Co., to Bro. Hanna; report that we find from the testimony, that said company did not comply with their contract; and recommend the Patrons of Husbandry do not buy wagons of said firm. Concurred in.[32]

Price arrangements entered into between the Grange and manufacturers never appeared to work very well in either direction. Although Patrons were highly incensed when price discriminations were practiced against them, they do not appear to have found anything objectionable when the practice worked in their favor.

Among other proposals originating with the Patrons of Husbandry and designed to bring financial relief to farmers were petitions to the legislature that fees of physicians, surgeons, and oculists be regulated.[33] At other times they sued for legislation prohibiting speculation in cotton futures.[34] Even at the subordinate level, granges incubated ideas the application of which, they hoped, would insure higher prices for agricultural commodities. The theme of a district Grange meeting in Johnson County, as reported by the Cleburne *Tribune,* was a plan to bring more money for Grangers' wheat:

Delegates from some fifteen or twenty Granges met in Cleburne a few days since for the purpose of taking into consideration the best plan for disposing of the present year's wheat crop. It was recommended that the Grange advance a sufficient sum to enable the farmers to hold for better prices, the Grange to secure the means from those who will lend and take a lien on the wheat. Caddo Grange has already lead off in the matter.[35]

This could have been the germ of the idea which the Farmers' Alliance later developed into their subtreasury plan.

While the Grange officially opposed extending cotton into new areas, or allocating any sizable acreage on a given farm to cotton, it apparently held no scruples against the dissemination of information on more efficient methods of cotton production. Published in full in the proceedings of one state session was a letter in which the writer outlined a plan of sharecropping employed by him with satisfactory results:

In answer to your letter of inquiry concerning the method which I have adopted to manage the negro. I would say that my plan is to contract with them for half of their time, my part of the time always embracing the three first working days of the week. I furnished the land; mules and feed for them and agricultural implements; I allow and set apart about twelve acres to the hand; all the hands I have engaged report on Monday morning, and are worked according to my direction for three days. No excuse is acceptable than the weather. If, for instance, I have engaged twenty hands, I make my calculations to make a crop with a force of ten full hands, and cultivate 150 to 200 acres. During the three days they are at work for me I give them my personal attention.

On Thursday each one repairs to his own crop, which is separate or together as they please. They use my mules and implements, feed all the time in my lot and with my forage. Negroes generally being without means, I contract with them to advance $50 to the head during the year, which is always reimbursed by their crops, kept under my control until the advances are satisfied.

This plan keeps my portion of the crop under my control, also my mules are under my superintendence and not abused as in the system of renting out.

From my experience in the above and other plans, I am satisfied, of its superior adaptability to that particular kind of labor. Truly, W. Warren.[36]

Annually the plantation owner's share of the cotton ran from forty to sixty-five bales. From ten to twelve acres allotted each "cropper" not more than three to six bales could be expected. Irrespective of the price of cotton, this meant for tenants, either white or black, only subsistence incomes at all times. Not mentioned in the letter was another possibility, that the landowner might have set aside the better land for himself and allocated the poorer land to the workers.

Because of the economy-mindedness of Granger delegates, the constitution prohibited use of state funds to aid in soliciting immigrants. Patrons were as eager as anyone else, however, that there be a steady stream of immigration, as they said, "To improve our social condition, to develop our resources and to advance our property." Because of a pro-immigration attitude on the part of individual members, the Grange in 1877 resolved:

> That for information of the people of the state, who are engaged in the development of her resources, and for the purpose of informing the people of other countries of the resources and advantages that Texas offers, the legislature should provide the necessary means for the collection and publication for gratuitous distribution of all statistics, facts and information relating to the resources, growth and development of the State.[37]

At one time the committee on immigration for the State Grange declared that crops were going to waste because of a labor shortage, and that it was also for want of labor that the water power of rivers and the coal and iron deposits of the state remained undeveloped. The committee further declared that sparse settlement denied the people the blessings of a compact society and hampered the proper maintenance of schools and churches. It contended that property taxes were a burden because of millions of acres of unsettled and unproductive land. In order that these conditions might be remedied the committee proposed that the legislature appropriate funds for the encouragement of immigration.[38] As late as

1888 the Grange committee on immigration, still working on ways and means to attract settlers to Texas, proposed that residents, when writing friends back in the old states, inform them of the advantages of the state: its homestead exemption law, the availability of free homesteads, and the recently established system of free public schools. It also suggested that maps giving information on annual rainfall and location of schools and churches be prepared by each county for free distribution.[39] The Grange did not wish reports of the recent drought to leave "foreigners" under the erroneous impression that it never rained in Texas.

During its history, the Texas State Grange engaged in a few co-operative manufacturing ventures. When George A. Kelly offered to sell the Patrons of Husbandry a partnership interest in his Marion County iron foundry, he gave the Texas State Grange its best chance to own and operate a profitable manufacturing establishment. For a number of years Kelly had manufactured plows and stoves. He proposed that the co-operative association be capitalized at $250,000 with shares at $25.00 par value. The Grange and its membership were to subscribe more than 50 per cent of the stock, for a controlling interest, and Kelly was to remain with the organization as plant superintendent. When the offer was made, daily output of the foundry was valued at $300; but plans were ready to step up production to $600.[40] After three years, the Grange having failed to purchase the agreed amount of stock, Kelly requested that the agreement be dissolved. He offered to refund stockholders their money plus interest for the time it had been used by the plant.[41] The fraternity could do nothing but agree to the severance. The Grange, like most of its members, never had very much money. Either it was unable to raise the necessary capital for launching an enterprise, or it doomed ventures to failure by setting them up with too little capital.

The Grange did succeed in establishing a number of miscellaneous co-operative undertakings — gins, warehouses, tanneries, implement stores, and several others. A relatively large number of co-operative gins were organized under its sponsorship, many of which operated with a greater degree of success than was generally true of its co-operative projects. In 1876 the Shiloh

Grange of Titus County erected a tannery in which it planned to produce leather for home consumption and for sale to outsiders.[42] A year later the Kaufman County Grange withdrew from the farm implement business and sold machinery on hand to a private dealer. The Patrons had lost $1,200 in the venture, but by salvaging the grain elevator, which had been erected at a cost of $345, they reduced the over-all loss to $860. They also retained possession of a warehouse built at a cost of $600 and presented to them by the citizens of Terrell.[43] For a time, a mechanical device known as the Clement Attachment attracted considerable attention at annual sessions of the State Grange. The contraption purportedly spun thread directly from raw or seed cotton. Cotton growers could visualize a revolution in the textile industry, which would transfer the mills from New England directly to southern cotton fields.

But the Texas State Grange appears to have given only secondary consideration to co-operative manufacturing ventures and to negotiating agreements with manufacturers whereby Patrons were to make direct purchases at discounts. Its major effort was reserved for an undertaking which appeared to offer the greatest relief to farmers by freeing them from paying high prices for merchandise. Collective, or co-operative, buying and selling, therefore, became the heart of the Grange program. Early in the seventies groups of farmers often agreed to market their produce collectively, and contracted with dealers for discounts on merchandise in return for assurances that all business of the group would be thrown to the contracting merchant or merchants. As the Grange membership grew, businessmen, wholesalers, and manufacturers undertook to monopolize Grange business by supplying members with lists of goods which they could buy at discounts well below customary retail prices. Acting through subordinate lodges, Grange members readily agreed to restrict their purchases to establishments granting discounts. But instead of keeping price discounts confidential, Grange members took a delight in boasting that "they could get it wholesale." Non-Grange customers became highly incensed at the discrimination and discount lists were quickly withdrawn.[44]

Toward the close of the seventies, the Grange launched its own wholesale and retail co-operative stores. At the outset, possibly because it grew so fast, the Texas State Grange gave very little attention to co-operative merchandising. The National Grange, however, approved a co-operative plan, quite similar to the British Rochdale co-operative, which it submitted to state bodies for their consideration. With apparent misgivings Worthy Master Lang laid the plan before the 1877 session of the Texas Patrons:

> To me the scheme which has been denominated "International Co-operation," and proposed by the National Grange at its last session, and which is here submitted for your consideration, is impracticable and unsuited to the wants of American farmers. It has taken fifty years to build up a business of any importance in England upon this plan, and that too among operators in manufactories who receive the wages of their labor each week. The American farmer receives his after the harvest has past.
> Again, it is surely not progress if in this day the farmer has to return to the primitive modes of trade. Certainly the boasted perfection of commerce is not an empty and hollow delusion. In this enlightened age of competition, and subdivision of labor, to which we are indebted for the rapid and easy exchange of commodities, we will not have to return to the antediluvian mode of life, where the producer from the soil was required to perform all the labors and duties of merchants and manufacturers. We are farmers, not merchants.[45]

Lang was correct in warning Texas farmers that they were in no position to maintain co-operative stores operating on a cash basis. The fraternity could have profited materially had it heeded the Master's warning, "We are farmers, not merchants." Instead "farmers" were usually placed in charge of co-operative stores — "not merchants." The placing of inexperienced managers in charge of commercial establishments proved costly. In lieu of the Rochdale plan, Lang recommended employment of a state agent:

> Then an agent at your commercial centers, freed from selfish gains in the business and employed by the producers to especially guard and protect their interest would be of untold benefit in pointing out and aiding in correcting such excesses and extravagant charges as may have grown up in commerce, through a too eager desire for gain and by those who formulated the rules for its government. Such an agent should be fair and impartial in feeling, and of enlarged and comprehensive views, possessing mercantile skill and knowledge. What the results of such agent might be in the way of savings to the producers of the country, would depend upon the amount of patronage, he would receive. If feebly supported, he would have no influence, and if ignorant and prejudiced, he would only excite the scorn and derision of intelligent men, and be more a stigma upon the Order than a benefit to the farmers. But if intelligent, liberal

and just, and strongly supported by members of the Order, he might become a tower of strength in making and shaping the rules of trade to which you are subjected.[46]

The matter of a state agent was referred to a Grange committee whose report recommended that there be employed at Houston and Galveston such persons

whose duty it shall be to make all purchases ordered by Patrons, properly authenticated, including dry goods, groceries, farm implements, machinery, everything needed by Patrons on the farm and in the house.

Resolved, That it is the wish of this State Grange that there be an agent employed at St. Louis, Missouri, for like objects and aims, as set forth in the foregoing resolutions and that Brother, A. J. Child, Missouri State Agent, be recommended as a suitable person to fill said agency.[47]

The State Grange authorized its executive committee to effectuate the resolutions at the earliest practicable time and to notify subordinate lodges when the agency was ready to serve the membership.

The session which authorized the hiring of a state agent also approved plans to govern procedure when Patrons undertook to organize local trade associations. The recommendation did not differ essentially from the one adopted by the National Grange. Stock in local associations was to be offered Patrons at $5.00 to $100.00 per share, each member purchasing according to his ability. Voting could be on an individual basis or by share, as the group decided. Shareholders should elect a board of three or five directors empowered to appoint the business manager, necessary agents, and other employees, and fix salaries. Associations were advised to incorporate and to adhere to a strictly cash basis in purchases and sales, and to sell all merchandise at a fair margin of profit. After all expenses had been met and interest had been paid on the stock, quarterly dividends might be declared, two-thirds being allocated to shareholders and one-third to Patrons who were customers but nonshareholders.[48] George Tyler says that the first local co-operative association was organized at Salado, home of the first subordinate Texas Grange.[49]

Some subordinate lodges, acting independently, had organized merchandising concerns before being authorized to do so by the state assembly. A group of farmers in the vicinity of McCabe formed, in 1875, a joint-stock company capitalized at $1,800 and opened a retail store selling merchandise at a 10 per cent markup. At the end of a year the directors declared a 25 per cent dividend, and after two years the McCabe venture was out of debt and carrying a $5,000 stock of goods.[50] By mid-year, 1878, the executive committee of the State Grange had completed arrangements for the state agent, who was to function under direction of the Texas Co-operative Association incorporated at capitalization of $100,000, divided into 20,000 shares with a par value of $5.00 each. The charter authorized the association to transact business in Galveston and other places designated by its board of directors.[51] Purposes of the co-operative were set forth in the charter:

> This corporation is formed and created for the purpose of establishing and maintaining a general commission business and wholesale and retail cooperative store or stores, of buying and selling real estate and other property, as may be necessary, to promote the objective of its creation; and of transacting any and all kinds of business incident or appertaining thereto, for the mutual profit and benefit of its stockholders and customers, who are members of the Order of Patrons of Husbandry.[52]

In its first two years of operation — which, incidentally, coincided with the last two years of Lang's tenure as Worthy Master — slightly more than $1,000 in Texas Co-Operative Association stock was sold. However, Lang's successor was an enthusiast of the co-operative movement, and during the first two years of his administration Grange members subscribed to more than $13,000 worth of stock in the association.[53] After another five years, books of the association showed its capital to be $51,715; by 1892 capital had increased, on the books at least, to more than $86,000.[54]

An accurate picture of the financial condition of the Texas Co-operative Association can never be determined for any period of its history. In 1883 the association resolved to establish a branch wholesale, retail, and commission agency at Fort Worth or Dallas. This action was taken in an endeavor to lessen the discontent among North Texas Grangers. The association advised that a "meeting of all Granges and Co-operative associations of North Texas be called to meet as soon as practicable for the purpose of raising a sufficient amount of funds to operate and maintain such a business."[55] Even though North Texas Grangers failed to raise the necessary funds, a branch agency was opened in Dallas, its merchandise and operating funds being drawn largely from the Galveston store. How the branch weakened the whole co-operative structure is discussed in a committee report to the T.C.A. board of directors:

> The step taken by this association for the relief and advantage of the farmers and Patrons of North Texas, has not been as favorable as by some anticipated; and the account of having to place at that point about one-half of the stock of the T. C. A. where no profit has accrued, but a continual loss, has prevented the extension of the main business this year. But it is not to the propriety of the establishment of this branch business at Dallas, to which we direct attention, but to the time consumed, the high expense, the stringency and shortage of business, and to the further fact that no crop season has passed to offer the common advantage securing to such a business. Then if we consider that one-half of our means is invested where a loss, ever so light, is falling, and that this loss must be met by the existing profits of the main business, shows very conclusively that not only that loss has to be met, but we lose also the profits in the use of that amount in the principal business. Further, if we had been possessed of the power of this half of means in the main business at Galveston, it would be reasonable to conclude that our net profit would have reached $25,000.[56]

Since the Dallas branch never became profitable or self-sustaining, the Galveston agency might have had a more successful history had the North Texas agency never been established. However, as we shall see, there was enough mismanagement, if not outright dishonesty, in the conduct of the Galveston agency to have bankrupted it even though no branch agency had been opened.

In summarizing the results of its first five years in business, the state secretary of the Texas Co-operative Association reported:

> This association began business with a paid up capital of $265, on the first day of August, 1878; the net profits of the first year was $39. In the five year's business there has been a net profit distributed to the stockholders and customers of forty-four thousand five hundred and eighty-five dollars ($44,585); interest on the capital 10 per cent., $3,362, making a total of $47,947. You should bear in mind that the commission charged on cotton will not amount to 50 cents per bale. Here is a saving from the usual commission charged by commission merchants of 2½ per cent., or 75 cents per bale, which will amount to twenty-seven thousand seven hundred and fifty dollars ($27,750) on cotton sold by the Agent. If we should add 2½ per cent. commission for purchases and sales of other produce shipped by this Agency besides the cotton, we would have forty thousand

dollars more. These amounts saved to the people for whom it has done business, amount to one hundred and fifteen thousand six hundred and ninety-seven dollars ($115,697) less the interest.[57]

The most profitable year for the wholesale house at Galveston appears to have been 1883, when sales aggregated $560,282.16 and 16,045 bales of cotton were handled on a commission basis for members. For the year, its books indicated a net profit of $20,542.00. The following year the agency's volume of sales dropped to $497,618.47,[58] its commission business fell to 13,118 bales of cotton, and profits decreased to $11,644.37. By 1888 the business of the wholesale house had declined to $255,966.64.[59] Sales at the Galveston store for its twentieth year in business (1898) totaled only $40,861.33,[60] it factored a mere 400 bales of cotton, and profits were a trifling $363.45. According to the records of the Texas Co-operative Association, the Galveston store continued to show increases in assets and liabilities until 1890, when the balance-sheet total reached $217,345.04. Of the assets, $113,874.24 were listed under "bills receivable" and "debts due us," while $118,228.17 of the liabilities were found under headings of "bills payable," "Texas Mutual Fire Insurance," and "debts due by us."[61] The accounting entries were indeed strange: credit items made up more than 50 per cent of both assets and liabilities of an institution dedicated to a strict "pay-as-you-go" policy.

In proportion to its limited operating capital, the wholesale agency of the Texas Co-operative Association transacted an enormous volume of business. Never, at any one time, did the Texas Co-operative Association have as many as 725 individual stockholders, nor in any given year did it ever receive the support of as many as 150 retail associations, either as stockholders or as customers. The association's annual report for 1884 said that 119 retail associations had been customers during the year. The next annual report gave the number of stockholders as 497, including subordinate lodges, retail co-operative associations, and individual Grangers.[62] The small amount of capital with the large volume of business created an ever-dangerous situation which could have caused the T.C.A. to fail at any time. Actually, the operating capital was much smaller than indicated by the books of the association.

In his report for 1892, the secretary noted that during the fourteen-year history of the association cash received for stock totaled only $19,108.02, while $81,581.98 in stock certificates had been issued through dividends.

But there is more to the story. The wholesale agency had been launched to operate on a strictly cash basis; but when it extended credit to customers the agency was forced to resort to credit to replenish its depleted inventories. Under the association's accounting system, net profits were shown when there had been no profits. Bad debts were carried as assets; this produced "book profits" when no profits existed. The question arises: Did any part of the $81,581.98 in stock issued as dividends represent profits? Minutes of the board of directors for 1892 state that since its organization $14,325 in stock had been withdrawn from the Texas Co-operative Association, which would leave only $4,782.02 actually subscribed in cash for stock. In these board minutes, the annual statement listed $86,095.00 in capital, and assets totaling $186,085.29, of which $103,324.71 was entered as "bills receivable" and "open accounts," most of which should long since have been written off as bad debts. Liabilities of the association included $72,191.79 as unpaid debts entered as "bills payable" and "open accounts," to which should be added $10,511.96 borrowed without security from the Grange-sponsored Texas Mutual Fire Insurance Association. Additional liabilities, entered under the headings "undrawn dividends," "reserve fund," and "undivided profits," totaled $17,286.96. Realizable assets in possession of the Texas Co-operative Association at the beginning of its fourteenth year in business included $67,478.82 in merchandise on hand, real estate valued at $1,871.77, and $782.27 cash in the bank — against which stood $186,085.29 in liabilities.[63]

With the discovery in 1892 of a shortage of several thousand dollars in the accounts of the manager of the Galveston agency, the Texas Co-operative Association received a blow from which it never recovered. The committee appointed to examine the agency's books found on the ledger $2,500 already barred by the statute of limitations, and it estimated that fully $20,000 had never been entered on the books at all and consequently was not subject to recovery. J. S. Rogers, the agency manager, was discharged and suits totaling

$12,716.16 were filed against him by officers of the association.[64] Within a short time a countersuit was filed with the intent of forcing the association into receivership — an action, according to Texas Co-operative Association records, inspired by the discharged manager in retaliation for the suit filed against him and his bondsmen. Minutes of the board of directors declare embarrassment of the association to have been Rogers' primary object:

Court adjourned until Monday Nov. 14, at 9 o'clock, a. m. At the above date and hour, the Board were present, and the case proceeded with. While progressing the plaintiff's attorney arose and said: Upon consultation with his client, he was instructed by him to withdraw the suit.

Thus ended a case, that was brought through malice, and one which has caused great loss to the business, both in expense and in the confusion of the minds of the friends of the T. C. A., those who were not familiar with the facts in the case. But the T. C. A. has withstood all opposition, and has come out far better than its enemies expected.

The judge rendered the following verdict, in substance:

"That the evidence does not warrant the issuance of a restraining order, and that no good cause is shown for the appointment of a receiver, as the business, from the evidence before the court, appears to be properly conducted."[65]

The association probably came out of the legal tilt "better than its enemies expected," but, judging by its subsequent history, not as well as its friends had hoped. In spite of optimism expressed by the directors, business of the wholesale agency steadily declined.

After uncovering shortages in Rogers' accounts, the association was confronted with the necessity of reducing the indebtedness of the wholesale house as rapidly as possible. A new manager was appointed; within six months after assuming his duties, he succeeded in reducing past due obligations by a total of $31,554.49.[66] Within two years liabilities of the association had been lowered from $186,085.29 to $39,507.86. At that time (1894) the books of the association showed a net value of $24,743.86 against which stood $68,375.00 in stock outstanding,[67] indicating a net worth of 36 per cent of the par value of the stock. Since most local associations had ceased to function, because of either dissolution or bankruptcy, sustaining business of the Texas Co-operative Association during its last years came largely from non-Grangers. Because of fears arising from a threatened suit by the Island City Savings Bank, in 1900 officers of the association closed the wholesale agency and officially terminated the life of the Texas Co-operative Association. Contending that doctored statements had been submitted as evidence of solvency for procuring loans, the bank accused the association of falsifying reports. Without authorization, the agency manager, H. G. Niblo, assigned to the bank a lien on properties of the association, an action which gave the board of directors no alternative other than to order liquidation of the wholesale house. In settlement of obligations due it, the bank accepted notes and accounts totaling $60,000 from the agency, and in addition filed a suit for $16,000 against former manager J. S. Rogers and his bondsmen.[68] The state agency had been the victim of every ruse and practice contrary to sound business principles. However, it was progressive failures among local associations that brought final collapse; as the number of local retail stores grew smaller, sustaining customers became fewer and fewer.

Prosperity and depression of local co-operatives and of the Texas Co-operative Association closely paralleled each other. In 1881 the secretary of the association, with an apparent show of pride, reported: "We have great cause to be encouraged, for we have not a failure to report, nor will we ever have if we closely adhere to our adopted rules and laws. Cash down on all business transactions is the only sure road to success."[69] In response to repeated requests for a set of rules to be used for guidance by those interested in organizing and operating local co-operative stores, Secretary Rose submitted a number of carefully thought out suggestions. He warned that a local enterprise should never be launched with less than $200 in capital. Stockholders were advised to elect seven directors empowered to select a president from their midst. He cautioned directors to invoke rules requiring all officers and employees to be bonded, to adhere strictly to the rule, and to dismiss summarily negligent officers and employees.[70] Later Rose came to realize that meagerness of operating capital was one of the major weaknesses of retail co-operatives. He then raised to $500 the minimum capital requirement suggested for a new retail store.[71]

In reporting to the fourth annual meeting of the Texas Co-operative Association, the secretary gave an optimistic account of progress being made by retail co-operative associations. The report said that three retail stores had temporarily suspended, but all planned to resume business operations shortly.[72] In summarizing the volume of business transacted by twenty-nine local co-operatives, the report read:

Two of these associations began business in 1875, one 1878, seven 1879, ten 1880, nine 1881.

The aggregate capital at beginning	$ 18,078.00
Which gives them an average capital	623.00
These had a capital at beginning this year	69,111.00
Which gives them this year average of	2,393.00
Total purchases made during 1881	295,150.00
Total sales made during 1881	350,000.00
Gross profits	45,000.00
Net profits	22,530.00
Capital in house and fixtures	16,588.00

Several don't give the amount of trade by share-owner, non-shareholding Patrons and non-members of the Order, which prevents our making the report that we wished to. The interest on capital, 10 per cent; profits on trade to share-owners approximate 7 per cent; cumulation, 10 per cent. Fourteen are insured; fifteen are not. Twenty-three are chartered; six are not.

Our business will be over a million dollars in 1883, with over one hundred stores of which eighty-one have taken stock in the Texas Cooperative Association.[73]

There can be little doubt that the twenty-nine retail store reports from which the secretary compiled his summary came from the more progressive and businesslike among local co-operative associations — a fact proved by the average beginning capital of $623, which was unusually high for retail Grange stores. Reports of the secretary of state indicate that retail co-operative associations when filing for charters seldom requested less than $10,000 in capital, but it is very doubtful whether any of them ever raised capital funds closely approximating $10,000. Toward the close of the century, local co-operatives became more modest when filing for charters and limited their requests for authorized capital to amounts between $2,500 and $5,000.

For 1884 the Texas Co-operative Association reported 119 retail co-operatives engaged in business, forty-four having rendered statements of their activities and progress to the secretary. Of the number reporting, thirty-one had been in business for one year or longer, and the remaining thirteen had been organized for less than twelve months. Purchases of merchandise for the year made by the forty-four associations totaled $315,000, while sales aggregated $356,000, slightly more than half the goods being bought by Patrons. The secretary's report listed $2,944 as the aggregate starting capital for the thirty-one oldest stores, something less than $100 each (the $2,944 undoubtedly appeared as a result of a typographical error and probably should have read $12,944, which would have made an average beginning capital of slightly more than $400). At the close of the fiscal year (June, 1884), capital claimed by the thirty-one stores totaled $138,690, or approximately $4,500 each.[74]

In his next annual report, the secretary said there were 132 retail co-operatives, an increase of thirteen for the year, but only twenty-nine had filed progress reports. Capital and merchandise inventories of the reporting associations totaled $138,330, and their sales for the year aggregated $370,000, of which $310,000 represented purchases by members. The increase in the percentage of sales to Patrons marked the most significant difference between the two summaries.

For both years, net profits were the same — $23,000. The secretary concluded his report with the following assumptions:

It will be seen from the above, that if we take these as average of the total 132 stores that are stockholders in the T. C. A. and in business, the following would be approximate:

Total capital in retail stores	$ 629,640.00
Total purchases for one year	1,612,812.00
Total net profits in retail stores for one year	104,630.00
Total profits on purchases from wholesale T. C. A. at 3 per cent	48,384.00
Say the average shipment of cotton, 500 bales from the local agents equals 66,000 bales, saved in commission, $1 per bale	66,000.00
Sample 10 cents on each bale	6,000.00
Other produce	4,000.00

Grand total saved on one year's business ....$ 229,614.00[75]

Other than in his own fertile imagination, the secretary had no grounds on which to base such assumptions. Quite the contrary: at the time he engaged in the game of pretense, he had before him the annual statement of the wholesale agency which reported total sales of $362,931.04 — and some of its customers were not Grange co-operatives. If, as assumed by the secretary, retail associations actually had purchased during the year $1,612,812 worth of merchandise, and if all merchandise sold by the wholesale agency had been purchased by them, approximately 80 per cent of their goods had been purchased elsewhere. Retail Grange stores never gave the Galveston store 100 per cent of their business; but surely, as early as 1883, more than 20 per cent of their purchases were made from their own wholesale store. Instead of receiving the assumed 66,000 bales from Grange members, the Galveston agent factored fewer than 11,000 bales of cotton. More than likely, local associations did not aggregate a volume of business one-half as large as the amount assumed by the secretary.

Early in their history, local co-operatives began to encounter demands for credit. Seemingly, the mandate to operate on a cash basis was a difficult co-operative rule to enforce. By 1882 there had been a few failures among the retail associations, and the secretary attributed them all to one cause — the co-operatives had not adhered to the cash basis.[76] How to prevent credit from creeping into transactions of retail co-operatives was an ever-present item on the agendas of the Texas Co-operative Association and meetings of its board of directors. Repeatedly the association cautioned against the evils of credit. At one time it warned:

> Co-operative stores that buy and sell on time injure their cash customers. They give a premium to their credit customers and their cash customers pay the premium. It is asserted by some that the cash plan can not be successfully carried out. We entertain the opposite view of this matter. It has been clearly proven all over the state that the opposite prevails, for all co-operative stores that have stuck to the cash plan have succeeded. The same cannot be said of the credit plan. The largest co-operative house in England, that has several hundred clerks employed, and which has been a success, the superintendent attributes all to cash payments in buying and selling. We cannot afford to be led astray from our adopted plan of business. Buy and sell for cash. 'Tis true, all will not have ready cash. It is equally true, if you sell on time you will find many never ready to pay.[77]

Poor crop years intensified demands for agricultural credit, and refusals were not easily made by local managers; in fact, had they made a practice of refusing cred: they would not long have remained as managers. Seldom did a retail store have the necessary capital to conduct successfully a credit business. And if we accept a statement entered in the minutes of the board of directors for 1892, capital stock figures for retail co-operatives were highly fictitious:

> Many Patrons of Husbandry were made stockholders who never put a dime of cash in their business, but received from it the profit on their trade. In nearly every instance where stores failed it could be traced to indifference by members, and credit by the agent, he permitting his sympathy to supersede his judgment.[78]

The drought of the eighties forced many Grange stores to sell on credit, and by 1887 the volume of credit posed a threat to the entire co-operative structure. In taking cognizance of the "galloping" departure from the cash system, the Texas Co-operative Association resolved:

> Whereas, Co-operation, financially, if strictly carried out in accordance with our laws, is of great good to our people; and,
> Whereas, a departure from these rules has, and always will result, in disaster to all our co-operative enterprises, as seen in the failure of a number of houses, therefore, be it
> Resolved, That the T. C. A. do most earnestly and fraternally suggest to all of our local houses that they return to cash principles as soon as possible; and then suffer no pressure to lead them astray; knowing that so long as they adhere to these principles, they are safe; but the moment they depart from them, they are at sea without wind or sail.[79]

Through a series of warnings the T.C.A. attempted to advise local associations that they could succeed only if they did not permit themselves to become engulfed in the raging tide of credit. The Texas Co-operative Association and its directors might warn others, but they were never able to heed their own warnings.

When retail stores extended credit, they in turn demanded credit from the wholesale agency. It is not known when the Galveston house departed from the "cash" policy, but by 1887 more than half of its assets were included in "bills receivable" and "sundry accounts due." Operating capital of the wholesale association was so small that goods sold on credit to others could be replenished only by credit purchases. The annual statement for 1887 indicates the extent to which the Galveston store had resorted to credit to maintain its inventories; under "bills payable" and "sundry accounts due others," it admitted an indebtedness of $44,742.[80]

In revising corporate laws, the legislature of 1885 deleted the section under which co-operative associations had been chartered.[81] The action aroused a storm of protest from Grange leaders who contended that repeal "was detrimental to the masses, and especially to the Patrons of Husbandry and farmers of Texas." They urged Patrons to keep the wrong prominently before the people through the press, by means of public lectures, and by private conversation, until the legislature reversed itself and re-enacted the deleted section.[82] At the session of 1887, the legislature again legalized co-operative associations;[83] however, terms of the law were not as favorable to co-operatives as legislation that had been effective prior to 1885. Early laws prescribed a corporation filing fee of $500; raised later to $25.00, it was further increased by the law of 1887. This law, argued the Grange, raised fees so high as to make prohibitive the incorporation of farmer co-operatives. Actually, from 1887 on, a sliding scale determined the corporate filing fee; the larger the amount of capital stock requested, the higher the fee.[84] This sliding scale fee probably explains the sudden drop in the amount of authorized capital requested by retail co-operatives. When the filing fee was a fixed amount, the charters stipulated capital in amounts of $10,000 and up, but with the sliding scale law, capitalization requests were for $5,000 and less. In spite of Grange displeasure, and in spite of objections voiced by secretaries of state who criticized the law as favoring foreign corporations at the expense of domestic ones, the law was not further revised.

Early in T.C.A. history, its secretary proposed that possibilities of establishing a mutual fire insurance association and a co-operative bank be duly considered. The appointment of a committee on insurance and banking followed.[85] The idea of a bank was discarded, and after four years the committee reported:

We, your Committee on Insurance, beg leave to report, that the whole subject was exhausted by argument at our last meeting, and plan perfected and patrons failed to respond in sufficient amount to justify the issuance of policies, and we now recommend that the only way to perfect the same is, that each and every one file his application now with the Association and individuals so as to raise the amount at once, as all insurance companies have advanced their rates recently of insurance, and before the advance eighty per cent. of the amount paid by our Association was profit to the companies. G. A. Hodges for the Committee.

On motion, the Committee on Fire Insurance was ordered to take subscriptions. The motion was carried.[86]

Before the session adjourned the committee reported that policy applications had been filed to the amount of $193,000.00.[87] Policies were issued forthwith. By-laws of the company permitted it to insure merchandise and store buildings, the properties of Grange co-operative associations, and dwellings, barns, and other insurable property of Patrons.[88]

A statement by the company covering its business transactions from date of establishment through July, 1887, showed premiums collected, $10,457.24, and disbursements of $8,549.75, of which $7,811.86 had been paid to claimants. Insurance in force then totaled $136,030.98, but the company's cash balance, $1,907.49, fell below the $2,500 minimum stipulated in the by-laws. In lieu of resorting to assessments, the company secretary asked that premiums for the ensuing year be paid when due.[89] Cash balances of the company gradually increased until they reached their peak of $11,828.33.[90] In 1890 the cash assets of the insurance association appeared among the liabilities of the T.C.A., apparently having gotten there via the route of an unsecured loan.[91] Once insurance funds fell into the hands of the wholesale agency the company was never able to extricate them, and when the Texas Co-operative Association was liquidated, the mutual insurance company was no longer able to continue. When dissolved the Texas Mutual Fire Insurance Association had on hand $385, which A. J. Rose refunded to its twenty-six policy holders.[92]

The Texas Mutual Fire Insurance Association, within itself the most successfully conducted Grange co-operative, was the victim of interlocking directorates. So nearly the same were the officers and directors of the Texas Co-operative Association and the insurance company that, for all practical purposes, they operated as one company. When directors of the co-operative association discovered that Rogers had jeopardized its continued existence, practically the same group, meeting as directors of the insurance company, placed insurance funds at the disposal of the wholesale agency. In an effort to salvage the financially weak wholesale house, the directors sacrificed the insurance company.

One can do little more than guess at the degree of influence exercised by officers and directors of the Texas Co-operative Association in policy matters of local co-operatives. From the looseness of ties holding the structure together, one suspects that local stores conducted their affairs with considerable independence. Actually, they may have followed carefully the pattern set for them by those who directed the wholesale store. For, while the presidents and secretaries of the T.C.A. delivered speeches and drafted resolutions damning credit, their preachments were not practiced by the wholesale agency. These men had advised retail stores to discharge agents who violated the fundamental co-operative law — buy and sell for cash; but they did not discharge the state agent when he resorted to credit. They advised local associations not to set up a store with too little capital; yet they launched the wholesale agency with only $265 in capital funds. Furthermore, they censured retail co-operatives for issuing stock in payment of dividends on merchandise purchases; yet the T.C.A. received less than $20,000 in cash for $138,000 of capital stock. In all things, local stores could have been aping the established practices of the wholesale house.

When it made provision for the establishment of the agency at Galveston, the Grange charged the agent to deal directly with manufacturers. Instead of carrying out these instructions, almost from the very beginning the agent purchased from other wholesale houses for resale to the local co-operatives. This is the major reason for the Galveston wholesale agency's not being able to hold the patronage of retail co-operatives. Local stores quickly learned that they could buy from wholesale stores on terms as favorable as could the Galveston store. It was actually cheaper for a retail co-operative to buy directly from wholesalers than to purchase from the Galveston agency which bought from the same wholesalers and then resold at a marked-up price. When the Lost Creek Association filed a complaint against J. S. Rogers, stating it could buy goods elsewhere cheaper than from him, his defense was a statement to the effect that lower prices prevailed because local stores could save on freight when buying from wholesalers located nearer them than the Galveston store.[93] He dodged the issue neatly. The local had not said it saved on freight; its complaint was to the effect that it could buy from other wholesalers at lower prices.

In almost every instance where principles of co-operation were violated by local stores, violations by the state agency were equally flagrant. The co-operative stores failed because, as Worthy Master Lang told the Grange, Texas farmers were in no position to pay cash. In opposing the use of credit, the Patrons of Husbandry undertook to reverse the trend of the times, which was toward a more extensive use of credit. Nor were members of the Grange by means of collective action able to supply themselves with the credit requirements of commercialized agriculture, which was tending also to become fairly well mechanized. Where the Grange centered its most ambitious efforts — buying and selling collectively — it failed.

In other areas achievements of the Grange have drawn high praise. Tyler said:

> The Grange did much to promote social intercourse among farmers and their families, brought about a more general habit of reading and investigation, especially along economic lines, and induced broader thinking and a more liberal attitude in the minds of a great body of citizens whose outlook had been too much limited by the hard routine of life on the farm. Though now no longer functioning in Texas, the Grange left its imprint, virile and lasting upon the period.[94]

One should bear in mind that, even among farmers, Grange membership was small, as a usual thing its meetings were poorly attended, and members who were shareholders in co-operatives were only a fraction of the whole; all of which is but to say that its activities touched directly only a small percentage of the people. Like many minority groups, Grangers, through their criticisms of monopoly, railroads, middlemen, and monetary policy, and because of their many co-operative ventures, received an unusually large amount of publicity. In other words, indirectly the Grange exerted a considerable influence. Its spadework did much to pave the way for the Farmers' Alliance, the Populist party, and later farmer organizations. Beginning with the mid-eighties, the decadent Grange lost steadily in prestige and membership to the younger and more "virile" Farmers' Alliance. The formal objectives of the

Alliance were plagiarized, without any great effort at concealment, from the Grange Declaration of Purposes.

Much of the Grange's handiwork in the state constitution has been deleted or altered by amendments. Its interest in experimental work helped to bring into being the present system of agricultural experiment stations. And Solon Buck credits the Grange with stimulating the circulation of agricultural journals, thereby causing a great increase in the number of farm publications.[95] By direct methods, both the Grange and the Alliance sought to solve agrarian problems. Each failed in its efforts to bring about a degree of economic relief through co-operative ventures. Each claimed to be nonpolitical; yet both were centers of heated political controversy. After undergoing repeated failures in both fraternities, many farmers concluded the time had come to cast aside the pretense at being nonpolitical and to seek economic redress through their own political party. There was a widespread feeling among farmers that where agricultural interests were at stake neither of the old parties could be trusted. The People's party, whose platform evolved from the "Cleburne Demands" of the Alliance, came into being as a farmers' party. Populist leaders were either farmers or the tried and trusted friends of farmers. By means of the People's party, farmers hoped to gain control of the political machinery and put through a legislative program designed to meet the demands of the American farmer.

VIII

The Farmers' Alliance

THE Grange, brain child of a government clerk, conceived as an uplift fraternity, had been carefully packaged in ritual and degrees and presented to agrarians as an institution for their own betterment. In contrast, the Grand State Alliance of Texas, purloining Grange "purposes" and parading them without embarrassment as its very own, was homespun and farmer-fashioned. It has been said that the Farmers' Alliance "sprang from the soil ... and, ... 'just growed' instead of being deliberately planned and put into operation by a group of founders."[1] The Alliance was more earthy than the Grange in its origin, more versatile in its activities, more direct in its methods, more demanding in its requests, more spectacular in its rise, and more precipitous in its decline. In Texas, the Grange was the older by some two or three years; it had passed its prime and was on the wane before the Alliance burst into full bloom. In fact, the rise of the Alliance hastened the decline of the Grange; but by the mid-nineties the Alliance, too, had become a "ghost" organization.

In a Central Texas community fifteen miles from Lampasas, a number of local farmers and stockmen organized an association and called it the Farmers' Alliance. This group proposed to take vigilante action to halt depredations of bands of livestock thieves, to prevent certain illegal practices of large land and cattle companies, to co-operate in purchasing supplies, and to see that estray stock was returned to the rightful owners. Describing circumstances which caused farmers and small stockmen to form the Alliance, Ralph Smith wrote:

"Cattle kings," who turned herds loose to destroy nesters' crops, fenced up whole counties, and drove farmers' milk cows off in their herds, became as common as southern ante-bellum "colonels." Working independently or in conjunction with these "syndicates," land sharks, under the boon of the law of 1870, arrived with genuine or forged certificates to survey the domain, dispossess squatters, or sell their scrip to settlers to secure their own improved acres. Some, posing as ranchers, settled in peaceful communities, built hideouts, offered to buy out a small rancher or nester neighbor at half price; if he refused to sell, they had his fence riders killed, poisoned his cattle, or hired a crooked lawyer to fake a document and throw him into expensive litigation. Nesters, organized into vigilantes, . . . attempted to deal with these problems.[2]

Members of the association proceeded to warn land sharks and other undesirable characters that any difficulty would be settled with guns. In order that the membership might function more effectively in apprehending thieves, the Alliance ritual incorporated a horse-thief-catching formula. By engaging in a conversation of coded questions and answers, two Alliance men could, without arousing his suspicions, identify a third party as a thief. Furthermore, the Alliance organization set up a system for expeditious identification of ownership of estray livestock. After several local Alliance associations had been formed, a state secretary was named. All members were then instructed to file their personal brands with the secretary, who, when given a list of brands borne by estray or stolen cattle, could quickly determine their ownership by checking his brand rolls.[3] Owners were then notified of the whereabouts of their lost cattle.

In February, 1878, a number of locals met at Pleasant Valley and organized the Lampasas Grand County Alliance. Later in the spring other alliances were formed in Hamilton and Coryell counties. At that time the Greenback party was sweeping the country like a prairie fire. Since the party drew its membership largely from the rural areas, it attracted a large following among the Alliance men. Strongly partisan Greenbackers were able to inject politics into the Alliance, with the result that a rift created by the Greenback-Alliance members killed the farmer movement. By the close of 1878, not a solitary suballiance remained in existence. The following year, Maestro Baggett, a newcomer to the community, learned that Parker County farmers were suffering heavy livestock losses in raids conducted by bands of thieves who operated out of the Indian Territory. Baggett suggested that by co-operative effort farmers might convince the desperadoes that cattle stealing was an unhealthy vocation. His proposal met with an immediate response, and Parker County farmers organized at Poolville, an action which started the Alliance anew. Greenbackers were not permitted to split the revived fraternity over politics. The manner in which the Alliance borrowed freely from Grange ritual and literature indicates a membership drawn largely from the Patrons of Husbandry. Within a short while a second lodge was organized in Parker County and a third in adjoining Jack County. By February, 1881, twenty-two suballiances had been established. Some fifteen months earlier a number of local lodges had united in organizing the Grand State Alliance, which functioned for two and one-half years without a charter. For some time the rejuvenated Alliance seemed to be primarily interested in preventing theft of livestock and apprehending cattle thieves.[4]

In some respects the account of the origin of the Alliance written by C. W. Macune, an outstanding leader of the Alliance when the movement was at its peak, differs from the story as told by others. In relating its early history, Macune wrote:

It is generally conceded that the Farmers Alliance was first started about the year 1876, and that the first organization was in either Wise or Parker county; possibly some of the members lived in each of those counties. The country at that time was largely devoted to stock raising, but many farms were being opened up and farming was making decided encroachments upon the ranch. The country was being infested by many transient characters who seemed to have no employment. At the same time the prevalence of horse-stealing was so common, and the mysterious manner in which the stolen horses were taken completely out of the country with no known man disappearing at the same time, indicated that there was an organized gang of horse thieves working many counties simultaneously. These conditions becoming more and more annoying, a number of farmers met, and, after consultation decided to organize themselves for the purpose of assisting the civil officers to apprehend and prosecute horse thieves. As all the members of this new organization were farmers, they decided to name it the Farmers Alliance. It was a secret organization, with passwords, signs, and grips. There was a formula of questions and answers to be used in the dark. By the use of this code, a man could ride up to a house in the night and call, and an answer would come from within. Then a certain request would be made, and a certain answer given. The form of the dialogue apprised the farmer that the caller was an Alliance man and that he had with him a civil officer, and that they desired to arrest a certain man whom they believed to be stopping for the night with this farmer. Then as the officer was allowed to come into the room where the man was, the farmer's wife would hold the only light in such a way that it would shine upon the man but not upon the officer following him, who would keep in the shadow. This would give the officer a chance to "get the drop" on the man and arrest him in safety.[5]

Macune, writing almost fifty years after the formation of the Alliance, no doubt relied heavily on memory for many of his facts. His date for the first alliance agrees with other records, but it was the founding date of the Lampasas County organization, not the Wise or Parker County lodge of some years later. As we have previously noted, the Lampasas association had more than one objective, but Macune limited the objective solely to the apprehension of horse thieves. Perhaps the Alliance, when reorganized at Poolville, had only the one purpose; if so, others were soon added.

For a number of years the fraternity grew slowly and showed few signs of its later aggressiveness. This may be partially explained by a revival of the Grange and the intensified interest in its cooperative ventures, which paralleled the first few years of Alliance history following its reorganization at Poolville. But when the Grange was entering the stage of permanent decline, the Farmers' Alliance showed signs of increasing vitality. As 1885 drew to a close, the Alliance claimed approximately 50,000 members scattered among 1,200 suballiances. At Cleburne the following year, attending the annual convention were representatives from 2,700 local lodges.[6] One description of the phenomenal growth of the Alliance reads:

Alliance lecturers and papers using bandwagon psychology seemed "determined to kill" and "to annihilate the Grange" by opposing everything it was doing and by accusing it of helping the poor only as long as they had money. In isolated regions they had many Grangers even believing that the Grange was dead. Sweeping through North Central, and West Texas the Alliance "swallowed" Hunt, Parker, Camp, Hopkins, Morris, Rains, Titus, and Wood counties, all once Grange strongholds, and in Van Zandt County left only three Granges. In Hamilton, Blanco, and Gillespie counties the story was the same. In March, 1886, there were in Bell County, the cradle of the Texas Grange, twenty-six sub-alliances and in Texas nearly 1,700 with 70,000 to 80,000 Patrons.[7]

Never, not even in the heyday of its youth when it stood alone and unchallenged as the sole farmer organization, had the State Grange claimed a membership and subordinate organizations comparable to these totals, and the Alliance had "not yet begun to fight."

Macune gave his own explanation for the mushrooming growth of the Alliance:

One reason for the rapid growth of the Alliance was it had such meager literature and such a brief and broad declaration of purposes. The discontent was strong; and the desire for a remedy urgent; an organization was offered, a secret organization of farmers for the purpose of "mental, moral, social, and financial improvement." That was the whole platform. Every man who joined could easily persuade himself that it stood for his own ideas. Every lecturer in the field could on this broad foundation describe his own ideas of the problems and their remedies. They did, and it went like wild-fire. That statement in the "Declaration of Purposes" of the Farmers Alliance, to-wit: — "We united for the purpose of mental, moral, social, and financial improvement" was full and complete and the only declaration made for that purpose in all its literature. It attracted all the discontented, it appealed to all who were not entirely satisfied with existing conditions, and it repelled none because it made no expression upon detail or method about which there might be different opinions.[8]

The promise of "financial improvement" was probably the fundamental clause which attracted farmers to the Alliance. The mental, moral, and social phrases gave the novice a sense of security in the knowledge that he had affiliated with an organization dedicated to his economic improvement, which, at the same time, remained anchored to the bedrock of moral and social respectability. Other factors which contributed to the rapid growth of the Alliance included dues lower than those paid by Grangers; a simple ritual comprising only one degree as compared to seven in the Grange; and "demands" directed by the Alliance to legislatures and the Congress which bespoke a greater determination to see that economic wrongs of the farmer were redressed than was evidenced in the polite Grange memorials.[9] Large numbers of farmers were disgusted with the Grange because its co-operative plan had failed to release them from the credit system and were in the mood to join or become a part of any organization that promised general relief.[10] Then,

Alliance purposes, as noted by Macune, were probably broad and indefinite enough to satisfy all. Significantly, no one in analyzing reasons for the unusual growth of the Alliance included "catching horse thieves" among them.

In the earlier years of the Alliance county trade committees constituted an important part of its structure. By 1885 these committeemen were included among the regular officers of county alliances. Functions of trade committees varied widely from region to region. Duties of committeemen were explained to them in secret by the organizers, each organizer emphasizing his own ideas; hence no uniform policy was established for committee guidance. In a number of counties committees solicited bids from local merchants, guaranteeing to deliver to the successful bidder or bidders the trade of all Alliance members in the county. Occasionally trade committees encountered organized resistance where merchants agreed among themselves not to bid for Alliance trade, in which case the membership took the action of merchants as proof of their opposition to the principles of the farmer organization. By the mid-eighties farmer sentiment had grown very bitter against merchants. In other counties, trade committees established Alliance cotton yards where cotton belonging to the membership could be stored, graded, weighed, and sold.[11]

When the Grand State Alliance met in annual convention at Decatur in the fall of 1885, it attracted the largest gathering of farmers ever assembled in the state up to that time. Equally as significant as the size of the gathering was the appearance of a new corps of farm leaders. The two facts were indicative of widespread interest in the meeting and attracted considerable publicity for the Alliance. Results of publicity growing out of the Decatur session were reflected by a large increase in the number of suballiances and a flood of new members. Within a year the number of local lodges had grown from 660 to 2,750, and within two years there were 3,500 suballiances.[12]

At Decatur delegates to the convention occupied their time in debate and in deciding policy matters for the ensuing year. Because of a growing disparity between farm and nonfarm prices, the Grand Alliance decided that since contracts entered into between county trade committees and local merchants narrowed to some extent the disparity-gap between the two sets of prices, this work of the committees should be continued for another year. The convention also adopted a cotton marketing plan which it hoped would insure higher cotton prices for its members. Briefly stated, the marketing plan proposed direct cotton sales in lots of hundreds of bales. It was hoped that when large quantities of cotton were assembled at central points, representatives would be on hand from cotton buying firms in Dallas, Houston, Sherman, Waco, and Galveston, who through competitive bidding would pay better-than-market prices. Alliance members were to be notified in advance of the time and place to assemble their cotton for sale. Buyers in the large cotton markets would also be supplied with schedules of dates and places where cotton was being assembled. In practice the scheme met with only partial success.

On October 2, 1885, Waxahachie seemed to be flooded with cotton brought to town for an Alliance sale — 1,500 to 1,700 Alliance bales plus 300 to 500 bales belonging to non-Alliance men who hoped to sell at the high prices Alliance cotton was expected to bring. Alliance men were asking 8.75 cents per pound for the lot, but buyers insisted that they were not able to pay that price. The result — no sale. Disappointed members of the Farmers' Alliance threatened to boycott Waxahachie and take their cotton to Ennis.[13] A few days later the Navarro County trade committee refused an offer of 8.40 cents per pound for a lot of 800 bales, but cotton buyers from Dallas, Sherman, and Galveston bought non-Alliance cotton from individuals at prices ranging from 8.40 to 8.63 cents per pound. It was reported that the Alliance feared its members too would bolt and sell individually.[14] In Denton County the trade committee, when notified that North Texas bankers had refused to advance loans of sufficient size to enable local buyers to purchase in lots of 1,000 bales, canceled scheduled dates for bulk sales.[15]

A buyer-seller deadlock over a mutually acceptable price for Alliance cotton at Fort Worth was broken to the satisfaction of both parties. A reporter for the *Dallas News* wrote of the sale:

The deadlock between buyers and sellers of cotton was broken by a compromise between the Farmers' Alliance and H. L. Barnett, by which the latter became possessed of all the cotton at 8.67½, or five cents per hundred higher than the average yesterday, but seven and a half cents lower than the price asked yesterday. It is said that Mr. Barnett immediately sold to Westlow & Co. at 8.70, free on board. The farmers were pleased with their share of the bargain, and the empty wagons returned homeward bearing blue flags and other evidence of rejoicing.[16]

Following a conference between local buyers and merchants at Lewisville, a lot of 50 bales of cotton sold at 8.80, the price asked by farmers.[17] At Jacksboro the Alliance trade committee concluded negotiations by selling to a local merchant 50 bales at 9.10, and two weeks later the committee sold 100 bales at 9.00 cents per pound.[18] When merchants at Farmersville refused to pay the price asked, 75 bales of Alliance cotton were taken to McKinney.[19] After turning down a bulk bid of 8.56 for 150 bales at Bowie, individual members disposed of their cotton at 8.50.[20] In a somewhat similar situation, Alliance members at McKinney, after refusing a bulk offer of 8.35, sold 499 bales in individual transactions at 8.30.[21] It would appear that members of the Farmers' Alliance failed to receive the price they asked more frequently than they were paid the asked price for cotton. Even though the trade committee policy of cotton sales did not work out as satisfactorily as anticipated, it did sustain interest in a growing organization which at least made an effort to procure better prices for cotton.

In a subsequent scheme, the Farmers' Alliance instructed the manager of its State Exchange to lend assistance to members in every section of the state in selling their cotton. Under this plan, county business agents were directed to weigh and store cotton grown by Alliance men, and then to forward samplings of the cotton to the Exchange for grading and classifying. From the samplings, buyers visiting the Exchange would be able to buy in quantity cotton of uniform staple which could be assembled for them from all parts of the state. Or, if members wished to conduct local sales, samplings would still be graded and classified by the Exchange, whose manager would, on the advertised sales date, notify the county agent of current market prices for cotton grades included in the samples. During the first year under this plan a considerable quantity of cotton was sold through the Exchange, and in the second year some sales were made to foreign buyers for export. In one sale for shipment to England, France, and Germany, 1,500 bales were assembled from twenty-two different localities. Macune speaks in high praise of the system; but the results were probably none too satisfactory, because the plan was soon abandoned — or, as he said, "other methods supplanted it."[22] To farmers, efforts of the Farmers' Alliance to market their cotton at good prices were much more appealing than Grange condemnation of cotton specialization and its encouragement of diversification. In fact, the Alliance approached the problem much more realistically and attempted to work with, not against, those who wished to grow cotton.

At Cleburne in 1886, attendance at the four-day convention of the Grand State Alliance was larger than at the Decatur meeting the previous year. As a result of developments at Cleburne, the Alliance emerged as an aggressive farmer organization of great power and influence. In attendance were delegates sorely disgusted with the pussyfooting methods employed by the Grange in making requests of the legislature for action on farm measures. In contrast, Macune said of the Cleburne meeting:

It was agreed that there was no use in getting up petitions, because Legislators paid no attention to them. So the request for Legislative action was couched in imperative terms, and each paragraph began with the words "We demand." The sovereigns commanded their service. That was the first set of Alliance demands ever made, but it was a precedent that was ever-afterward followed by all Alliance meetings, subordinate, State and National. They made their political wants known by demands, not by petitions. But the custom of making demands instead of petitions was not inaugurated without trouble that came very near disrupting the movement.[23]

It seems that trouble developed in the convention because a few members who were non-Democrats undertook at every opportunity to inject politics into the movement. The majority of members, however, were sincere Democrats who had no intention of permitting the Alliance to become a secret political organization for undermining their party. Many convention delegates approved the substance of the "demands" but were opposed to their adoption on the grounds that they were political questions. Only in the wake of a very heated debate, and then by the narrowest of margins, were the "demands" adopted by the convention. When it became apparent that they would be approved, a select few who were determined to preserve the Grand State Alliance as a nonpolitical farmer organization held in secret a strategy meeting. The tenacity with which proponents and opponents of the "demands" clung to their views because of principles involved created a serious conflict which showed no tendency to abate even after the convention had officially endorsed the "demands."

Within a week after the Cleburne meeting adjourned, the few who had participated in the secret meeting announced the organization of a second Alliance bearing the identical name and dedicated to the same purposes as the older order. Some officers of the Grand State Alliance were elected to corresponding offices in the rump Alliance. It appeared that a rift had developed of so serious a nature that it would lead to disintegration of the order. Trying to forestall such a possibility, Andrew Dunlap, president of the old Alliance, invited all officers and committeemen of both factions to meet at Waco in the fall of 1886 to see what steps might be taken to reconcile differences. At Waco each faction agreed to forego any further action that might jeopardize the life of the movement until there could be convened representatives chosen by the sub-alliances and delegated with powers to dispose of all differences. As evidence of their sincerity, the president and vice-president of the regular Alliance placed their resignations in the hands of C. W. Macune, chairman of the executive committee, whom both factions requested as the president pro tem to summon the Grand State Alliance to meet in special session. Macune issued a call for sub-alliance delegates to assemble in Waco in the spring, and in response five hundred representatives convened.[24]

Macune, a product of the Midwest and West, was born in Wisconsin. When he was only a year old his father died while en route with the family to California. The mother returned to Illinois, where on reaching the age of ten young Macune quit school to help support the family. For a time he worked as a farm hand. In early manhood he moved to California, and then to Kansas before finally landing in Texas. During the course of a versatile career Macune read law, practiced medicine, and served as chairman of the executive committee of the Grand State Alliance, then as business manager of its State Exchange, also as president of the Southern Alliance, and finally as editor of the *National Economist,* official publication of the Southern Alliance. He is said to have been a man of great personal charm, possessed of a fluent tongue and a facile pen, but of poor business ability and questionable ethical standards. He was in his thirty-sixth year when the Alliance delegates assembled at Waco in response to his call.[25] Perhaps at no other time in his varied career did his magnetic personality undergo a test so acid as when at Waco in 1887 he presided over the convention of five hundred stubborn and angered Alliance delegates. There he charmed, he pacified, he soothed, and he commanded the respect of the torn and discordant groups as he welded them once more into a unified body and sent them home as zealous crusaders for the Farmers' Alliance.

The delegates had poured into Waco instructed by their respective lodges to oppose certain men and to block specified moves. There was every indication that representatives were quite determined to carry out these instructions to the fullest. Under the circumstances, complete destruction of the Grand State Alliance seemed to be a foregone conclusion. When C. W. Macune faced that turbulent gathering as its moderator and presiding officer and called for order, he stood at the threshold of one of those rare opportunities whereby a man may or may not rise to greatness within the hour. It had been his intent to open the meeting by explaining why the convention had been called; but when he pounded his gavel for order, bedlam broke loose. At the opening session Macune spent the day entertaining motions and ruling on involved points of order. When the day ended, it appeared that he had flubbed his chance; but it was a different Macune who called the second session to order. Now he refused to recognize delegates from the floor, he would not rule on points of order, either simple or involved, and he accepted no motions until the convention heard his explanation of why the assemblage had been called.

Eventually the meeting became orderly and listened with growing enthusiasm as Macune, with charm and persuasive eloquence, outlined and expounded two proposals which were fundamentally responsible for soothing the frayed tempers and reuniting the disrupted fraternity. Between the two Waco meetings Macune had written to officers of the Farmers' Union of Louisiana, an organization similar to the Alliance, persuading them to send a delegation to the spring meeting. Thus, in the course of his address, when he proposed that the Farmers' Alliance be expanded into a national organization — the Farmers' Alliance and Co-operative Union of America — presence of the Louisiana delegation on the convention floor gave strength and substance to the suggestion. And for his second proposal, Macune called on the convention to launch a half-million-dollar commercial venture to be known as the Farmers' Alliance Exchange of Texas, farmers alone to own the capital stock.

As Macune spoke, many delegates no doubt envisioned themselves as the pathfinders of a great national agrarian fraternity destined to lead American farmers from the economic wilderness in which they had so long wandered. Undoubtedly, they thought, the united farmers of America could wield sufficient political power to compel the Congress to destroy the money monopoly by depriving national banks of the right of issue, and to enact legislation which would restrain monopolistic practices of railroads and other corporations that grew fat at the expense of farmers. The $500,000 Exchange would be a giant among commercial establishments. Few corporations, other than railroads and land and cattle companies, were so large; and probably no wholesale house then operating in Texas was capitalized at more than one-fourth the amount named by Macune. It stood to reason, he implied, that a wholesale house with half a million in capital would be sufficiently powerful to weaken, if not break completely, the structure of monopoly prices maintained by middlemen. The delegates had gathered at Waco as members of an order without a purpose; Macune transformed them into representatives of an organization of destiny. As he spoke, preconvention differences became inconsequential. His proposals were adopted by a wildly enthusiastic body which then proceeded unanimously to elect him its temporary chairman.

Shortly after the Waco meeting steps were taken to incorporate the Exchange under the laws of Texas, and cities were invited to submit bids for its location. Dallas, Fort Worth, and Waco made offers with the Dallas bid of $100,000 in cash plus real estate accepted as the highest. From the membership of the Grand Alliance, twenty-five men were chosen as a board to direct the State Exchange. The primary function of the commercial house was to buy and sell for suballiances and Alliance members. The board named Macune as business manager of the Exchange at a salary of $1,800 per year and required him to post a $50,000 bond. Late in the summer of 1887 the State Exchange opened for business in the City Exchange building at Dallas.[26]

Shortly thereafter the formation of a national farmer organization, popularly known as the Southern Alliance, carried out the second proposal made by Macune at Waco. At the organizational meeting in Shreveport, delegations attended from the state alliances of Texas, Kentucky, Tennessee, and Mississippi, as well as representatives from the State Wheel of Arkansas and the State Union of Louisiana. The convention considered ways and means by which the movement might be expanded, framed demands for presentation to state and national legislative bodies, and elected officers. The mantle of the presidency fell on the shoulders of Macune, the most widely acclaimed Alliance leader.[27]

The fate of the Grand State Alliance of Texas became closely wedded to the fortunes of its Exchange. The board of directors, no doubt enchanted by Macune's vision of a half-million-dollar wholesale establishment, strayed from the path of business acumen and wisdom. Although Dallas never fulfilled its promise to give $100,000 in cash, it did donate a lot 100 by 150 feet on which the board decided to erect, at a cost of $45,000, a four-story brick building covering the entire lot. A building containing 60,000 square feet of floor space was quite a structure in those days. Macune insists that he protested construction of so large a building on the grounds that the resulting debt would hamper activities of the Exchange and possibly jeopardize its future. He said that in his opinion the structure was too large for anything except a warehouse.[28] But the operation of a $500,000 wholesale house as proposed by Macune would at that time have required considerable warehouse space. Had Dallas made its gift of $100,000 as promised, erection of the Exchange building would in no wise have strained

the finances of the corporation. As it was, the building absorbed
more than one-half the subscribed capital, which left a very small
operating fund. But in the fall of 1887,

The Exchange commenced business by handling cotton, grain and farm
implements. The farmers were sold after the plan of a regular commission
house; the latter procured and furnished at good discounts by centering
the trade to a wholesale dealer, who was nominally the Alliance implement
agent, but in fact was selling on his own account. It was but a short time,
however, until the business was extended to the buying and selling of
dry goods, groceries and general supplies.[29]

The contract made with the dealer instead of the manufacturer
has a familiar Grange-like overtone. The Exchange intended, as
had the Texas Co-operative Association, to operate on a strictly
cash basis; but it soon discovered, as had the Grange agency, that
a farmer exchange operating on a cash basis was of no particular
benefit to the average farmer. Then, as had the Texas Co-operative
Association, the State Exchange discarded the cash policy.

Unlike the Grange, however, the State Exchange did not engage
in a haphazard extension of credit. Instead its board set up a
planned system of credit,[30] based on a mutual signing of joint notes.
In carrying out the plan as instructed by the board, county alliances
assembled members for the purpose of directing each individual
to determine as nearly as possible his needs for the ensuing year
in the way of groceries, dry goods, and equipment. When the
individual had compiled his list, an estimate was made of the cost.
The member then executed a note for a sum equivalent to the estimated cost of his supplies. These instruments were converted into
two-name paper as members signed each other's notes. The notes,
which were due and payable at the close of the harvest season
following, were deposited with the State Exchange, there to be
drawn against as supplies were needed by the members who gave
them.

This system, when explained to the membership through the
suballiances, seems, judging from the quick response, to have been
almost universally accepted. By January, 1888, a steady stream of
the promissory notes was flowing to the Dallas store. Originators
of the scheme did not think it would be necessary for the State
Exchange to finance the notes. They appear to have assumed that

banks followed a general rule of accepting two-name paper; consequently they were certain that banks would readily discount the notes when presented by the wholesale house, thus providing the State Exchange with operating funds until the notes matured. The Exchange soon learned that the number of names appearing on notes did not determine their acceptability by banks. Too late, it discovered that who signed a note was more important than how many. Banks refused to discount the notes. Texas banks might have been able to finance the State Exchange had the notes been dispersed among all of them, but the volume was too large for individual banks to handle. When the credit plan became operative, the Exchange had only $18,000 in capital funds — which meant that it could not possibly have financed the plan.

As the notes continued pouring in, farm orders for groceries, seeds, wagons, harness, implements, and dry goods increased to the extent of compelling the Exchange to purchase goods in large quantities. The business manager later recalled some of the larger orders:

One order was placed with the manufacturer for one thousand wagons to be shipped to various points. These wagons were duly made and delivered and paid for in full. Tobacco was purchased in carload lots; five hundred barrels of molasses was purchased at one time and other things in proportion.[31]

By late spring State Exchange indebtedness to manufacturers and wholesalers aggregated more than $400,000. As collateral against the debt, Macune claimed the wholesale house held more than a million dollars in joint notes. That is to say, when banks refused to discount the joint notes, the State Exchange operated for a time on the funds of manufacturers and wholesalers. Within a short while credit agencies began to include in their reports references to the large indebtedness and small capital of the Exchange. A number of the larger creditors became alarmed and sent accountants to investigate the financial condition of the store. An audit of Exchange books resulted in an unfavorable report, which was followed by a meeting of creditors of the Alliance store at which it was agreed that the manager of the Exchange would call for an additional $2.00 stock subscription from each Alliance member, the receipts to be prorated among the creditors. In July, 1888, sub-alliances met to levy the assessments; meanwhile the Exchange directors had launched an intensive campaign urging that all members respond promptly with their payments. At the end of two months of exhaustive solicitation not more than $58,000 had been raised.[32] When the membership failed to contribute a sufficient amount of money to retire, or at least materially to reduce, the indebtedness of the Exchange, its collapse became a certainty.

In part, failure of the State Exchange came as a result of extravagant claims made by the Farmers' Alliance. As early as the summer of 1887, the Grand State Alliance had boasted of a membership of 300,000. According to this figure, an assessment of $2.00 per member should have raised more than half a million dollars. That is to say, the assessment should have raised enough money to pay off the $400,000 debt and leave a surplus of $200,000 for operating funds. Instead the Exchange found it impossible to raise $60,000; but its enemies easily convinced some members of the Alliance that they had been robbed by a dishonest business manager. Many who paid the levy had friends who they knew had also paid. The more gullible were persuaded that all Alliance men had anted up. Undoubtedly several hundred thousand dollars had been subscribed, so they thought. Then the question posed itself: What had become of the money? At every turn gossip and rumor filled the membership with more doubts and suspicions.

The ugly rumors to the effect that several hundred thousand dollars of Alliance money had been stolen were bad enough. But the Exchange's position became even less secure as makers and endorsers of the joint notes became alarmed over how deeply they might have obligated themselves. Those most perturbed were the ones who had signed notes given by others but had made no purchases against their own notes. Some had already purchased goods to, or in excess of, the amount of their notes. Many undertook to raise funds and pay off the notes even though the maturity date, October, was several months off. Macune labeled as false the accusations that many participants in the note venture suffered heavy financial losses. He contended that in so far as he knew none lost money.[33] When members of the Farmers' Alliance refused to respond with two-dollar assessments, the State Exchange was forced into bankruptcy. In general, the note venture of the Exchange was another type of crop-lien with the farmer writing his ticket instead of the merchant. The failure of the Exchange also wrecked Alliance plans for acquiring and operating cotton and woolen mills, implement and wagon factories, a publishing house, and even an Alliance university.

An auditor who checked the books of the defunct Exchange concluded from its volume of business that successful operation of the concern would have required at least half a million dollars in capital. Had Alliance members subscribed the full $500,000, they would not necessarily have guaranteed the success of the Exchange. The markup on merchandise barely covered costs of handling, and made no allowance for overhead.[34] Since the narrow markup margin gave no consideration to the possibility of bad debts, the life of the Exchange depended on a 100 per cent collection of the notes signed by farmers — and a 100 per cent collection might have served no purpose other than to postpone the date on which Exchange property was sold by the sheriff. While the Exchange of the Grand State Alliance lasted but twenty months, and the Texas Co-operative Association of the Grange remained in business more than twenty years, the ultimate failure of each resulted from the effort to operate with too little capital and overextension of credit.

Macune believed that the State Exchange, even though short-lived, had proved to be of inestimable value to farmers and to consumers. We have his own statement:

From a financial standpoint, it is impossible to estimate the great benefit that it [the State Exchange] was to the farmers of the entire state directly, and more or less indirectly to all other classes. In the sale of commodities in general, it had resulted in a very great reduction in prices, probably equal to an average of 40% and this benefit accrued to all classes of consumers. This change was not spasmodic but permanent; for years these lower prices continued. A great many reforms had been brought about in the handling, sampling, sale and shipment of cotton that rebounded to the benefit of the purchaser, and even the merchants who apparently had been injured by the alliance have been greatly benefitted by these reforms in the handling and selling of cotton.[35]

Macune presented no evidence, other than his own assertion, as proof that the Exchange was responsible for a 40 per cent reduction in consumer prices. Nor do daily market quotations of the *Dallas News* indicate any 40 per cent break in prices during the life of the Exchange. There is, however, evidence supporting the claim that the Farmers' Alliance was responsible for breaking an attempted price fix by the jute bagging trust.

The Alliance tangled with the jute bagging trust while at the peak of its power and influence. Hicks credits the breaking of the monopoly price, which was of considerable benefit to cotton farmers, to the Southern Alliance. Macune said it was the work of the State Exchange of Texas. Hicks said: "When the price of jute bagging soared beyond all reason, supposedly because of the formation of a trust, the farmers of the cotton belt stood together under Alliance leadership, substituted cotton bagging for jute, and brought the monopolist to terms."[36] The price war occurred in 1888. In Texas no bagging made of cotton appears to have been substituted for jute bagging; and by Macune's account of the fight, the State Exchange of Texas pursued a course quite different from the Hicks version. Macune wrote of the farmer versus jute bagging trust fight in Texas:

That was the year in which the jute bagging trust had announced that bagging which had previously been selling at eight cents per yard would not be sold for less than twelve cents. Large stacks of bagging had been shipped to dealers in various parts of the State, with a positive prohibition to sell a yard of it at any price. It was stored in warehouses awaiting release from the trust. Indignation meetings were held by the farmers and feeling ran high as a consequence of this condition. There seemed to be no way of getting any bagging outside of the trust. Dissatisfaction with the manner in which the cotton business was being conducted in the city of Dallas induced the manager of the Exchange to negotiate for the purchase of a cotton compress in that city. As a condition of the purchase of a half interest in the compress from certain men in New Orleans they agreed to supply the manager at once with ten car loads of cotton bagging which they were then unloading from the ship-side in New Orleans. The trade was consummated and half interest in the compress purchased for $37,000, and ten car loads of cotton bagging bought at 7½ cents per yard. This was one of the most satisfactory transactions ever pulled off in favor of the farmers, for it broke the bagging trust and gave not only the Farmers Alliance but all the farmers of Texas eight cent bagging for the year. The ten car loads were ordered shipped at once to ten different strong cotton counties in Texas. As soon as this became known to the trust they released by wire all their holdings in the state, and bagging was sold to the consumer all through the summer and fall from 7¾ to 8¼ cents per yard.³⁷

Even for breaking the jute bagging trust, some farmers criticized the Exchange. When the monopoly price was broken, the trust and its agents immediately dropped prices below the bagging price set by the Exchange. Upon learning that jute bagging could be bought elsewhere cheaper than from the Exchange, many members grumbled, accusing the agency of attempting to make a profit on the bagging at the expense of its customers. It does not appear that farmers "stood together" as closely as Hicks implies.

Certain educational benefits were among lasting contributions of the Farmers' Alliance. Because Alliance leaders knew that carefully prepared produce commanded premium prices, part of the organization's educational program stressed to members the importance of care in processing commodities for the market. Farmers were taught that dirty cotton baled along with trash, sticks, and stones brought producers lower prices than clean cotton. The elementary principles of farm marketing learned in the days of the Alliance endured well beyond its life. Hunt contends that a fear of consumer co-operatives created among farmers by the failure of the State Alliance Exchange was its most lasting contribution. He wrote: "The failure of the Exchange kept a constant cloud over officials of the Farmers' Union during the years afterwards, and made them afraid of any movement that had as its objective the setting up of a central exchange."³⁸ Farmer movements were greatly weakened during the last quarter of the century because of the failure to develop among their leaders men experienced in commerce to manage their co-operatives. They lacked leaders of sound business judgment who could command the confidence of farmers.

Aside from the joint note episode, Alliance forays into business ran closely parallel to those of the Grange. The Alliance established both wholesale and retail stores. It attempted a number of manufacturing ventures, and, like the Grange, made a policy of launching them with too little capital. At a time when the State Exchange was already heavily obligated and striving to do business with an inadequate operating capital of $18,000, it did not hesitate to buy a building and compress carrying an $82,000 mortgage. In 1885 an item from Cisco said that the Farmers' Alliance of Eastland County was preparing to erect a flour mill and have it in readiness for the next crop. The company was said to be capitalized for $50,000, of which a considerable amount had already been subscribed.[39] The Alliance may have built a flour mill at Cisco, but not one costing $50,000. Two years later rumors were thick to the effect that a woolen mill, which had been in successful operation at New Braunfels for a number of years, had been sold to the Southwest Texas division of the Alliance.[40] The operation of any number of warehouses, cotton yards, gins, compresses, flour mills, and grain elevators had been undertaken as Alliance projects. There was probably no appreciable difference in the percentage of failures among Alliance and Grange ventures. For both organizations the percentage ran high.

Since both the Grange and the Farmers' Alliance claimed to be nonpolitical organizations, neither permitted political discussions while lodges were in formal session. Plenty of political talk took place before and after lodge meetings, and probably while lodges stood recessed. At any rate, the Farmers' Alliance soon demonstrated an intent to procure remedial farm legislation through political pressure. The manner in which suballiances circumvented the ban against political discussions may be seen in a newspaper account of a suballiance meeting in Dallas County:

On the outside [of the lodge hall] views were freely interchanged on the political situation, and the opinion was general that before the next election comes off the Dallas County Farmers' Alliance will be able to represent on the floor of the conventions, county and State, the conditions, wants and circumstances of their industry. There was no disposition manifested for the formation of a farmers' class distinctively as such, but the conviction seemed widespread that it is the duty of the farmers to resist class legislation detrimental to their interests, and to bring up the profession of the farmer to the full measure of its legislative possibilities and merits.

One gentleman spoke encouragingly of the growth of the Alliance in Texas, saying that with the support it could draw from the labor movement there was no doubt whatever but they could carry the State within a very few years. There was no disposition shown of an intention to desert the Democratic party, the feeling being that the movement would be strong enough to run the party. What they propose doing if that expectation should not be realized is not very apparent, but a large proportion of the order believes that with no other alternative accessible the individual interests of the agriculturalists will be considered of paramount importance.[41]

This report leaves little doubt that politics was discussed, even to the extent of planning strategy by which conventions could be dominated in the interest of agrarians.

In 1896 Evan Jones, president of the Grand State Alliance of Texas, gave his interpretation of the significance of the Cleburne "demands." Said Jones:

These demands, first enunciated at Cleburne, in 1886, modified at St. Louis, in 1889, perfected at Ocala, in 1890, reindorsed at Indianapolis, and still further modified at Washington in February, 1896, are the embodiment of all the fundamental principles of civilization. They have stood the test of the most merciless criticism, abuse and misrepresentation of the old line politicians, and at last have in a large measure been indorsed by, and recommended in the platform of one of the political parties that denounces them so persistently.[42]

Alliance leadership was unquestionably sincere in its desire to keep the organization clear of politics, but "demands" made upon lawmakers centered attention, and a degree of censure, on the failure of Democratic and Republican parties to enact the farmer legislative program. In the face of repeated failure or refusal by party leaders to give favorable consideration to the "demands," Alliance men became incensed at the procrastination of the old parties and favored a new one built around a farmer-laborer core. From this group, dubbed radicals, came the People's or Populist party.[43] In 1890 members of the Southern Alliance attempted to seize control of the Democratic party. In Texas, failure of the attempt resulted in Alliance members' being driven from the party. Under these circumstances there seemed to be no reason for further delay in forming their own, the People's party, which they did in 1892.[44]

By 1890 the Grand State Alliance of Texas was a spent and broken movement, and from that date until the formation of the Farmers' Union in the twentieth century Texas farmers were unorganized.[45] But to imply that during the twelve-year period farmers did not act in unison is to ignore the People's party. Former

Alliance men constituted the backbone of the Populist movement. Mrs. Lease of Kansas, one of the more able Alliance speakers, was never hesitant in dragging politics into the very middle of the forensic arena of the Alliance. When she exhorted western farmers "to raise less corn and more Hell," heads of Texas agrarians nodded in somber assent. Her speech could scarcely be classed as non-political when she told her farmer audience:

Wall Street owns the country. It is no longer a government of the people, by the people and for the people, but a government of Wall Street, by Wall Street and for Wall Street. The great common people of this country are slaves, and monopoly is the master. The West and South are bound and prostrate before the manufacturing East. Money rules, and our Vice President is a London banker. Our laws are the output of a system which clothes rascals in robes and honesty in rags. The parties lie to us and the political speakers mislead us . . . the politicians said we suffered from overproduction. Overproduction when 10,000 little children, so statistics tell us, starve to death every year in the United States, and over 100,000 shop girls in New York are forced to sell their virtue for the bread their niggardly wages deny them. . . . We want money, land and transportation. We want the abolition of the National Banks, and we want the power to make loans direct from the government.[46]

The speeches of "Sockless" Jerry Simpson were along much the same lines. His preachments against railroads were bitter. And the grain "gamblers" of Chicago, whom he accused of taking advantage of the farmer's penury, buying his grain low and selling it high, Simpson attacked with equal vituperation.[47] Meeting in joint encampment at Sulphur Springs in 1891, members of the Farmers' Alliance and Knights of Labor of Northeast Texas heard, among others, speeches by United States Senator Pfeffer, Populist from Kansas, and a Mr. Powers, president of the State Alliance of Indiana. All speakers at the convention emphasized the need for, and advocated the formation of, a People's party.[48]

When 1,300 delegates met in convention at Omaha in July, 1892, for the purpose of drafting a platform and nominating candidates for President and Vice-President of the United States, populism was launched as a national political party.[49] Many people were convinced that the Populist party came into being because of the manner in which the Democratic and Republican parties had ignored legislative proposals of the Grange and the Alliance. That view is implied by George Tyler, who wrote:

The general discontent among the farmers over falling prices of farm products and mounting debts, and their demands for a greater volume of currency, the regulation of railway rates, the abolition of monopolies and a more uniform tax system were about to usher the people's (or Populist) party into existence.[50]

At Omaha farmers and laborers resolved to join their forces in perpetual union for the salvation of the Republic. The platform adopted by the Populist convention demanded government ownership of railroad, telephone, and telegraph companies, and establishment of postal savings banks. It demanded, under either the Alliance subtreasury proposal or some better plan, a safe, sound, and flexible national currency issued directly to the people without the aid of banks. The convention called for free and unlimited coinage of silver and gold at a ratio of sixteen to one, and declared that the national welfare was dependent on a speedy increase in circulating currency to not less than fifty dollars per capita. It also demanded a graduated income tax.[51] The People's party offered a political arena in which old Grange and Alliance men could meet in unity for a renewal of their fight for higher prices for farm produce and for a reduction in the burden of agricultural debts.

Thomas L. Nugent, twice candidate for governor on the Populist ticket, typifies the close relationship which existed between the party and the Farmers' Alliance. A friend who knew Nugent well wrote:

[He] was a fast friend of the Farmers' Alliance, and proved it by his warmest sympathy for the order and its cherished principles. Often did he meet with them in their annual convocations in his home county, and talk with them on the true principles of reform, in simple speech, but with the matchless logic and classic eloquence peculiar to himself; and this during the time he was District Judge. Frequently prominent lawyers of his district would remonstrate with him and tell him that the part he was taking would injure his political influence. But he held fast to the cause of reform; and his memory is embalmed in the hearts of all true Alliance people throughout the State; for, at that time, it was truly encouraging to see one of the greatest and purest men of the State encouraging their cause, especially since being a lawyer, he was not eligible for membership.[52]

Populist leadership was recruited from among men like Nugent who, through their sympathetic work with the Alliance, had proven themselves trustworthy friends of farmers. At least, farmers assumed them to be trustworthy friends.

When in 1896 the Populist party convention named the Democratic candidate their nominee for the presidency, it virtually destroyed the People's party as a separate identity. In the short run, Alliance and Populist programs, as incorporated in their "Demands," appeared to have failed completely. When the nineteenth century came to a close, none of their major proposals had been turned into law. But for the long run the story is different, as many of their most important proposals have been incorporated into the laws of the land. Early in the twentieth century, provision for a graduated income tax was written into the statute books. At approximately the same time, the Federal Reserve System was created, and through this agency circulating currency has been increased by several times the fifty dollars per capita minimum demanded in the Alliance and subtreasury plan. The national bank note, disliked by Grangers, Alliance men, and Populists, has become an item for collectors. Silver never regained its pre-1873 status at the mint, but today it circulates as coin of the realm, while gold has been returned to the earth from whence it came and plays only a fictional monetary role. Under various parity, commodity credit, and purchase programs, the federal government has adopted the whole, albeit a twentieth-century version, of the Alliance subtreasury price support program.

In Texas, even though the Grange was never able to muster sufficient political power to compel the legislature to set up a railroad commission, it had been able to keep the topic of railroad abuses before the public as a live issue. Agrarians and nonagrarians, uniting behind Alliance demands for action, finally succeeded in destroying the legislative inertia. The result was that Texas secured a railroad commission with broad powers for regulating rates and controlling various abuses.

IX

Farmers Get Their Railroad Commission

T HE first Texas freight train ran over a thirty-two-mile stretch of railroad between Richmond and Houston in 1855, and from then until the close of the century the interest of Texas farmers in railroads was second only to their concern over prices of farm produce. At first they were primarily interested in railroad construction and expansion; but they soon developed considerable anxiety over the control and regulation of objectionable railroad practices. Complaints against monopoly rates, discriminatory practices, and other alleged evils grew with increased rail mileage. In comparison to that of northern and eastern states, railroad development in Texas lagged by a full quarter-century; consequently regulatory measures too came later.

For almost a generation Texans had demanded the creation of a permanent agency to supervise railway companies. Since few other public questions, including the old reliable "opposition to sin," seemed to hold vote-getting appeal comparable to agitation for "railroad regulation," politicians did their bit to keep railroad control a live political issue. Unfair railroad practices were blasted in a speech by U.S. Senator Richard Coke, who charged:

[Products of Texas factories] are outrageously discriminated against by the railroads. Manufactured products from distant states are distributed ... throughout Texas by railroads at rates lower than similar articles of Texas manufacture will be carried by them from one point to another in

210

Texas. Cotton goods from Georgia mills, and iron manufactures of other states are favored in the same way over Texas.[1]

Again in 1889, the Senator enumerated other complaints made against the roads by aggrieved farmers:

[Texas] rates were not based on cost of service but on "what the traffic would bear." When harvests were abundant rates were increased and absorbed most farmers' profits. . . . By granting secret special rates, rebates, drawbacks and concessions they fostered monopoly, enriched favorite shippers and prevented competition in such lines of trade in which the item of transportation constituted an important factor.[2]

Farmers were probably more embittered over the practice of fixing rates at "what the traffic would bear" than they were over any other specific or imagined abuse. After 1875, state political conventions regularly incorporated in party platforms one or more planks demanding redress of alleged railroad abuses. A leading Texas politician of the eighties and nineties, in recalling events of the period, said:

In the last quarter of the nineteenth century the question of railroads became a major issue in politics. . . . The Grange and other groups had been active in mobilizing public support of the farmers' program to remedy what they considered the unduly high rates and discriminatory practices of the railroads. This movement resulted in the passage of legislation creating state railroad commissions. . . . In Texas, the regulation of freight rates was a major political issue in the years 1890-1891.[3]

To be fair to the railroads, it is doubtful whether many instances could be found where the rates they charged were as high, or even half as high, as prerailroad overland freight rates. To farmers, however, this seemed beside the point. To them the important thing was the fact that rates never seemed to fall as low as agrarians thought they should.

The Farmers' Alliance must be recognized as a major force in the ultimate establishment of the commission. When referring to the Alliance, people often used the term Grange in much the same manner in which we today refer to all mechanical refrigerators by the name of one well-known brand. This point is clarified not to detract from the Grange, but merely to give the Farmers' Alliance credit where credit is due. When the Grand State Alliance met in convention at Cleburne, there was before the Congress a bill for federal regulation of railroads. The Alliance included among its "Demands" this one:

14. We demand the passage of an interstate commerce law, that shall secure the same rates of freight to all persons for the same kind of commodities, according to distance of haul, without regard to amount of shipment; to prevent the granting of rebates; to prevent pooling freights to shut off competition; and to secure the people the benefit of railroad transportation at reasonable cost.[4]

Within a year the Congress had enacted the Interstate Commerce Law, and thereafter attention of the Alliance was concentrated on bringing about regulation of railroads at the state level. In 1888, the Grand State Alliance reviewed the case history against railroads and demanded legislative action:

The people paid to the railway companies of the United States in 1887, in gross earnings, $822,181,949. Their net earnings for the same year were $300,602,565.
At this point we beg leave to refer you to an address to his Excellency, Governor L. S. Ross, dated Austin, Texas, April 4, 1888, signed by thirty-two members of the Texas Legislature:
First. For six years or more the people of the State have been demanding legislation to restrain the railroad corporations of this State from violating plain provisions of the constitution, and to restrict the powers of the same to impose upon the products and merchandise of the country burdensome and extortionate charges for the transportation of the same. . . .
We demand of our State government the following legislative reforms: . . .
4. That the State establish maximum freight and passenger rates on railroads, chartered by the State, upon a basis that will allow no more than a reasonable income on the money actually invested in the road and to defray the cost of repairs and operating the roads.[5]

Later in the same year, and because of political pressure from agricultural interests, the Democratic party at its state convention included planks in its platform which read:

8. We favor the enactment of such laws as shall restrict the freight charges of railway and express companies, so that they may only yield a fair interest on the money actually invested in them, and at the same time to prevent discrimination in charges against any points within the State.
Resolutions
Your committee further report and recommend the passage of the following resolutions which have been referred to them:
(9) *Resolved;* that the next legislature shall pass laws defining trusts, pools, and all illegal combinations in restraint of trade, and imposing severe penalties in regard thereto.[6]

Political procrastination alone accounts for the prolonged delay in
the enactment of legislation for effective railroad regulation. When
conventions adjourned, party platforms were soon forgotten. Candidates who had campaigned for regulatory measures failed, as state
officials, to fulfil their commitments.

A member of the legislature and a leader among the advocates
of railroad control in the successful fight for a commission, M. M.
Crane, viewed freight rate regulation as a matter of vital importance
to inland agricultural regions:

The question of freight rates was obviously important as the rich black
lands of middle and North Texas were being cultivated. There was no way
to reach foreign markets except by railroads. We had no navigable streams.
The owners of the railroads were like many other people. Having the
power to charge what they pleased, they were never overly modest in
fixing their compensation. The Texans believed they were being unjustly
discriminated against and thereby their vocation as farmers was made
less and less profitable.[7]

In his "Recollections," Crane repeatedly re-emphasizes his belief
that the continuing demand by farmers for railroad regulation was
fundamentally responsible for the creation of a railroad commission.

Certain articles and sections written into the state constitution
at the insistence of Granger delegates for the purpose of preventing
enumerated railroad abuses had been largely circumvented through
dilatory tactics of legislators. By enacting a few general statutes
outlawing unjust discrimination in freight and passenger tariffs and
by fixing maximum freight rates and passenger fares, lawmakers
partially carried out constitutional mandates, but a detailed regulatory code had never been made part of the statutes. With the
prevailing political crosscurrents, probably no code could have been
drafted that had a chance of becoming law. General regulatory laws
have never proved very successful as railroad and public utilities
controls where enforcement depended on district attorneys. But
sand in the hourglass of legislative procrastination finally ran out.

In an atmosphere charged with antirailroad prejudices, the
Twenty-first Legislature convened in regular session. Once more
Jay Gould sensed danger and ordered his palace-like train readied
for a hurried trip to the Lone Star State; but on this occasion not
even a personal appearance by the great tycoon could stem the

flood of ill will against the roads. As had happened in previous sessions, a bill authorizing establishment of a railroad commission passed the House — the vote being sixty-six to twenty-five — but was killed in the Senate. Upper chamber opponents of the measure, men who Crane says were sincere in their convictions, attacked the measure as unconstitutional.[8]

Earlier, when bills had been killed, the railroad commission had become a dead issue for the remainder of the legislative session. But in the Twenty-first Legislature, death of the House bill did not kill the issue. Instead, proponents of regulation rushed through both houses of the legislature a proposed constitutional amendment which specifically authorized the legislature to establish a railroad commission. To Article X, Section 2, which declared railroads to be public highways and carriers, the proposed amendment appended the phrase: "and to the further accomplishment of these objects and purposes [the Legislature] may provide and establish all requisite means and agencies, invested with such powers as may be adequate and advisable."[9] This phraseology was designed to destroy the rampart of unconstitutionality behind which opponents of regulation had safely withstood all previous attempts to control railroads by commission.

In the interim between submission of the proposed constitutional change and the date set for the electorate to vote on the amendment, vigorous campaigns were conducted by both pro- and anti-amendment groups. The Dallas County Farmers' Alliance held a convention which issued a statement to the effect that since the proposed amendment eliminated all doubts concerning the constitutionality of a railroad commission, it should be supported by the people. Also meeting in Dallas some months later, a state freight rate convention considered the proposed amendment and recommended its adoption. At its state convention on the eve of the election, the Democratic party formally endorsed the proposal.[10] By a decisive majority the electorate ratified the amendment in the fall of 1890.

The following spring, the commission issue was back in the legislative halls where it had so regularly appeared for fifteen long years, but this time there was one major difference — the old barrier of unconstitutionality had been removed. Moreover, Democrat James Stephen Hogg, on the day the people approved the commission amendment, had been chosen governor primarily because of his record as a prosecutor of railroads, and because he campaigned for governor on the need for a commission. The decisive manner in which the voters had spoken in favor of the amendment and the election of the railroad-baiter Hogg to the governorship placed the legislature under tremendous pressure to create a control agency. When the session got down to serious business the House overwhelmingly sanctioned a commission bill, but the route through the Senate was stormy. Some senators favored an appointive commission and were ready to approve the House bill; others violently opposed an appointive agency, advocating an elective body instead, while still others, aided and abetted by a powerful railroad lobby, opposed the creation of any kind of commission. The Senate fight became so bitter that the joint committee which struggled to compromise differences between House and Senate bills worked in closed session.[11] Final passage of the bill by each house gave no evidence of the fight made against it. Politicians who, as long as they could, working in legislative secrecy, had made use of every known ruse to kill the measure, dared not risk their political futures by having the records show that they had voted against the bill. On the roll-call vote, only two members of the House and none in the Senate voted against the statute.[12]

In framing the bill for a Texas railroad commission, the lawmakers had drawn heavily on the experiences of other states and of the federal government. U.S. Senator John H. Reagan, then probably the nation's greatest authority on railroad problems, gave generously of his time and advice. The resulting legislation provided for a powerful state railroad commission. As set forth in the preamble, it was:

An Act to establish a Railroad Commission for the State of Texas, whereby discrimination and extortion in railroad charges may be prevented, and reasonable freight and passenger tariffs may be established; to prescribe and authorize the making of rules and regulations to govern the Commission and the railroads, and afford railroad companies and other parties adequate remedies; to prescribe penalties for the violation of this act and to provide means and rules for its enforcement.[13]

The act provided for a three-member commission to be appointed by the governor, the terms of the commissioners to coincide with his. The regulatory body was vested with broad powers to regulate rates and to eliminate abuses practiced by intrastate roads. In his bid for nomination for governor as the candidate of the Democratic party, Hogg asked for and received the support of the Farmers' Alliance.[14] In return for their support, members of the Alliance had expected the governor to select at least one commissioner from their midst. When Hogg failed to appoint a farmer to serve on the agency, farmer organizations began almost immediately to advocate an elective commission. The legislature responded by making the commission elective, but the general electorate were no more inclined to select farmers as commissioners than the governor had been.

In response to the pleadings of his good friend Hogg, John H. Reagan resigned from the U.S. Senate in 1891 to accept the position of chairman of the newly created Texas Railroad Commission. Reagan had long opposed the railroad practice of charging more for a short haul than for a long haul. As chairman, he proposed a system of rates designed to end this, to him, nefarious policy among Texas railroads. The commission adopted the rate structure as proposed by Reagan. It soon learned, however, that effective rate regulation of any sort would be impossible unless the commission could control the issuance of railroad securities. Commenting on railroad practices common to the period, Eliot Jones wrote, "Stockwatering was customary, and resort to it contributed greatly to the popular hostility against the railroads."[15] A railroad president, speaking in 1891, probably expressed the current views of railroad executives on the matter of capitalization when he said: "The question of capitalization concerns the stockholders, and the stockholders only. A citizen, simply as a citizen, commits an impertinence when he questions the right of any corporation to capitalize its properties at any sum whatever."[16]

There were many impertinent citizens, and Jim Hogg was one of them. In his campaign for re-election as governor, Hogg told the people that the courts had sustained the railroad point of view, and, as a consequence, the people of Texas were forced to pay interest (through exorbitant freight rates) on a huge debt created by railroads in violation of the state constitution. Hogg injected the demand for a railway stock and bond law as a vital issue in the campaign of 1892, in which he was bitterly opposed for re-election by George W. Clark of Waco. Hogg charged that favorable consideration of railroads by tax assessors resulted in heavier tax burdens for farmers. He claimed that railroad companies then had outstanding on their Texas properties stocks and bonds totaling $455,250,744, but that the same properties were assessed for taxes at only $63,000,000. Each farmer was left to draw his own conclusion as to the degree of tax discrimination he suffered. Furthermore, Hogg continued, for seven years construction of additional railroad mileage in the state had been negligible, but during this time railroad obligations showed an average increase of $30,000,000 per annum.[17] He proposed to check stock watering by delegating authority to the railroad commission to approve or reject requests made by railway companies for new security issues.

Governor Hogg and the railroad commission might never have made a political issue of the securities question had it not been thrust into their faces by the group of railroads that challenged the powers and constitutionality of the commission. As soon as the railroad commission promulgated a general system of freight rates, the trustee for the International & Great Northern bondholders initiated proceedings in a federal district court by petitioning that the commission be permanently enjoined from enforcing the rates. In addition the suit challenged the constitutionality of the commission act. The trustee contended that since the rates were not sufficiently high to bring in enough revenue to pay operating costs of the railroad and interest on the bonds, they were confiscatory. Governor Hogg charged publicly that "fictitious bonds are not capital nor the representatives of capital. They are the fruits of crime."[18] In opening his campaign for governor in 1892, Hogg attacked the evils growing out of unrestricted bond issues by Texas railroads, saying:

The news goes abroad, and the declaration is commonly made, that there were no railways built in Texas last year; yet during that period they have increased their bonds and stock to the amount of over $40,000,000. . . . I know of one road that, within a few weeks after it sold out for $8,000 a mile, was mortgaged to secure bonds issued to the amount of $37,000 a mile on it. I know another that sold for $9,500 cash a mile and was immediately mortgaged to secure bonds for $35,000 a mile. Neither of these roads was in the slightest degree improved in equipment or otherwise. There is hardly a road within the state that has not, year by year, increased its bonded indebtedness, until now they nearly all owe quadruple their value.[19]

Throughout the campaign Hogg kept hammering on the need for a bond and stock law to put an end to such stock-watering practices.

George W. Clark of Waco, Hogg's opponent for the Democratic nomination for governor, claimed that the policies of the governor were driving capital from Texas. The regular nominating convention split between Hogg and Clark factions, each withdrawing to hold its own separate convention and each claiming to represent true Texas Democrats. The Car Stable Convention held by Hogg followers adopted a plank for its platform which read:

We demand a law that will effectually prevent the issuance of fictitious and watered bonds and stock by railway companies in the State, believing that these great enterprises should be conducted upon commercial principles, and not as gambling devices.[20]

In a message to the legislature following his re-election, Governor Hogg stressed the need for enlarging the functions of the railroad commission to include regulation of railroad securities issues. On April 8, 1893, the governor affixed his signature to a stock and bond law. Railroads still had friends among the lawmakers, however, and the bill did not pass with majorities sufficient to make it effective immediately as an emergency measure; consequently the law did not become operative until ninety days after the legislature adjourned in May. In the four-month interim railroads went on a stock-watering spree by notifying the secretary of state of their intent to issue $42,825,000 in new securities.[21] In the main, the stock and bond law prohibited the issuance of new securities by railway companies except for additional railroad construction, and the commission enforced the law rigidly.

The act creating the commission gave it

complete control over passenger and freight rates, express rates, interchange of traffic, and divisions on through movements of freight. So from the time of its organization the Texas Commission had far more complete power over freight rates than was enjoyed at the same time by the Interstate Commerce Commission.[22]

Shortly after completing its organization, the commission, under the guidance of its chairman, undertook to enunciate the basic principles of its policy:

The Commission adopted the mileage basis of rate making; that is to say, it fixed a charge per hundred pounds per each shipment, based on distance and service performed. . . . owing to conditions for which the Commission is in no way responsible, it has been applied in every instance where the Commission could apply it without a too violent disturbance of business and trade relations built up under different conditions.[23]

While approving as fundamental a policy designed to eliminate the long-short haul discrimination, the commission was forced to admit that conditions over which it had no control made full realization of its tenet impossible. When the state agency was organized, it found in force a rate structure based on mileage for short distances beyond which blanket or postage rates governed. The system of freight tariffs applicable to Texas was controlled and regulated from the St. Louis headquarters of a traffic association formed by interstate railroads. By setting low freight rates on interstate shipments to and from points in Texas, the traffic association practically fixed rates for Texas railroads.

The Texas Railroad Commission found this framework of freight charges to be so firmly entrenched that it could not be suddenly uprooted or materially altered without creating grave economic injustices. Under these circumstances John Reagan et al. reluctantly abandoned the hope of being able to fabricate a rate system based entirely on distance. Of this decision, C. S. Potts said:

The extent to which the Railroad Commission has abandoned the attempt to build a schedule of rates on mileage or distance a commodity is hauled, may be gathered from an examination of the first general schedule of rates published by the Commission which went into effect in August, 1895. In this schedule the mileage principle was made to apply for all distances of 187 miles and less, but for greater distances the blanket principle was made to apply. The new schedule showed considerable reduction in the rates allowed on some of the distances less than 187 miles when compared with the rates charged before the Commission was organized, but the blanket or common point principle was as clearly recognized in the new schedules as it was in the old. In the Commission's general schedule of rates now [1909] in force, the mileage principle is made to apply on distances of 245 miles and less, while the blanket principle is applied on all greater distances.[24]

While appearing to accept the existing rate structure, the Texas commission incorporated one significant change. Freight rates for intermediate points, i.e., towns served by only one railroad, were ordered reduced to the same low levels that were enjoyed by competitive points, i.e., towns having access to two or more railroads — something the companies had never done while rate setting was in their hands exclusively. Since no traffic association had ever bothered to fix local rates, individual railroads had been free to charge as they pleased on non-competing-point freight; consequently shippers in towns classed as local, or intermediate, paid much higher rates than shippers at competitive points. The economic advantages enjoyed by these "common point" towns were easily apparent; thus in 1900, every inland town of any importance owed its growth primarily to the low freight rates enjoyed as a "common point" shipping center. Rates in the first general schedule approved by the commission were to apply at each and every station throughout the state, except those in the extreme west and in the Panhandle above Amarillo.[25]

The really important issue in the legal action brought against the railroad commission by the trustee for the bondholders of the International & Great Northern involved not interest payments on bonds and the stock and bond law discussed above, but the constitutionality of the Texas Railroad Commission — or so thought the commissioners. To the extent to which they were correct, the outcome of the suit was of importance to all states having regulatory agencies. The constitutionality of commissions and their power to fix intrastate freight rates without perpetual judicial interference hinged on the decision of the Supreme Court of the United States.

When the Texas Railroad Commission applied the mileage principle to local or intrastate rates, many specific tariffs were lowered appreciably. These lowered rates were the reasons for the litigation instigated by the trustee of the Great Northern bondholders in conjunction with five railway companies. In these suits, which remained in the courts for more than eighteen months, only six railroads were involved; but when enjoined from enforcing its rates against the six, the commission found it impracticable to fix rates for any railroad. That is to say, for more than a year and a half the injunction tied the hands of the railroad commission. Finding the commissioners powerless to act, railroads were quick to revive earlier rates and practices. Interstate roads resorted to rate-cutting which left Texas manufacturers and dealers helpless and hopeless as they watched their markets taken over by out-of-state interests who enjoyed the low interstate freight rates. The rate-cutting finally led the interstate railroads into a rate war which drove rates to levels excessively low as compared to those set by the Texas Railroad Commission, which some of the warring roads had condemned as "confiscatory and ruinous."[26] Apparently nothing could be done to end the chaos until the slowly moving wheels of justice disposed of the suits against the commission.

In the conduct of the suit against the commission, styled *Reagan v. Farmers' Loan and Trust Company,* Texas state officials probably committed a tragic error in judgment. They became convinced that the most important issue involved was the constitutionality of the Texas Railroad Commission Act. In its *Second Annual Report* the commission explained why this decision was reached:

It was feared that great delay might occur in getting a final decision on the facts of these cases. . . . On this account it was determined to withdraw the answers as to the facts of these cases, and get the question as to the validity of the Commission law automatically determined as soon as possible.[27]

In previous cases coming before the U.S. Supreme Court for final adjudication, the court had never set aside intrastate rates established under authority of state legislatures; consequently the final outcome of the cases involving the Texas Railroad Commission might have been quite different had the commission chosen to put up a legal fight for retention of the rates it had established. When the decision was made not to challenge the contention of the plaintiffs that the rates were confiscatory, the commission virtually admitted that the rates were confiscatory. By acting otherwise it might have been able to convince the court that the railroad indebtedness was largely fictitious and that the rates as set did provide an adequate return. In writing the opinion of the court for *Reagan v. Farmers' Loan and Trust Company*, Mr. Justice Brewer implied that had the court been in full possession of all the facts its decision could have been different. In one instance the justice commented:

The railroad commission and the attorney general at first filed answers, but, after a certain amount of testimony had been taken, (of the nature and extent of which we are not advised, inasmuch as it is not preserved in the record,) they withdrew their answers and filed demurrers.[28]

Again in the opinion, Mr. Justice Brewer posed a doubt whether the absence of profit was, per se, conclusive evidence that rates were confiscatory:

It is unnecessary to decide and we do not wish to be understood as laying down an absolute rule that in every case a failure to produce some profit to those who have invested their money in the building of a road is conclusive that the tariff is unjust and unreasonable.[29]

From this statement, it would appear that a clear presentation of the fictitious nature of a large percentage of the railroad securities would have had a sympathetic hearing, and that with such a presentation the Supreme Court might possibly have ruled that the Texas rates were lawful. Before concluding his opinion the justice expressed a doubt as to the justness of the decision:

It may not be just to take this as an allegation of mere matter of fact, the truthfulness of which is admitted by the demurrer, and which, as thus admitted, eliminates from consideration all questions as to the true character and effect of the rates, yet it is not to be ignored.[30]

Finally, Mr. Justice Brewer summarized the decision of the court in these words:

It follows from these considerations that the decree as entered must be reversed in as far as it restrains the railroad commission from discharging the duties imposed on it by this act, and from proceeding to establish reasonable rates and regulations; but must be affirmed so far as it restrains the defendants from enforcing the rates already established.[31]

The court had ruled; and, for the first time in its history, it had set aside as unlawful rates established under legislative authority. In the future, and on the basis of *stare decisis*, it would presumably follow precedent and nullify others. It did. But the commission had gotten what it considered to be most important, a ruling to the effect that it was legally constituted.

After almost two years of paralysis imposed by the federal judiciary, the railroad commission was again free to fix rates and carry out other provisions of the commission law. In its first annual report the commission claimed to possess information which proved that many Texas railway companies were practicing discriminations of one sort or another. Since it lacked funds necessary for conducting investigations which would prove the wrongdoing, the commission for a number of years could do nothing other than repeat its charges that discriminations were being practiced. Finally the legislature of 1897 saw fit to appropriate $5,000 to be used by the commission for procuring evidence that railroad companies were violating the law. With these funds the commission employed three accountants to examine the books of Texas railroad companies. The accountants uncovered sufficient evidence to justify the filing of suits against a number of companies.[32]

The granting of rebates and other types of discrimination between shippers appear to have been the violations most commonly practiced. Through 1898, the enforcement agencies had settled 135 violation cases, in which railroad companies paid $67,500 in fines.[33] In spite of the commission's contention that there were many more violations, the legislature allocated no additional funds for further investigations. The investigations and prosecutions seem, however, to have had a salutary effect in deterring further malpractice on the part of railroads. An act of the legislature of 1899 which made granting of rebates and practicing of discriminations by railroad officials a felony also helped in stopping these abuses. As a result of remedial legislation which held railroad officials criminally liable for violations of rate laws, and of the investigations and prosecutions, law violations by intrastate railroads soon became relatively few.[34]

The granting of free passes to public officials and selected persons of influence had been a form of discrimination dating from early railroad history, but the practice was not outlawed in Texas until early in the twentieth century. Speaking in 1901, former

Governor Hogg reviewed the evils resulting from free pass discriminations:

Free passes were used to maintain a privileged class at the expense of those who paid. The railways have issued free passes to nearly every tax assessor and county commissioner in the state, who must adjust the values of their property. They have issued them to sheriffs, who serve the process of the law. They have issued them to collectors, who enforce the payment of taxes. They have issued them to justices of the peace and to county judges, and to most all other judges along the line of their railways, who try their cases.[35]

To have made his list of pass holders more complete, Hogg should have included legislators, editors, clergymen, doctors, and lawyers. Almost any person of influence might, if he chose to do so, carry a railroad pass. In case a recipient acted contrary to railroad wishes or interests, however, his name was stricken from the favored list. In 1901 railroads issued 271,285 passes to Texans. It appears that every third or fourth adult male carried a free pass. The "dead-heading" passenger traffic was heavy, and farmers grumbled that they paid the fares of the deadheads. The railroad commission repeatedly called to the attention of the legislature the need for anti-free-pass legislation. The commission was concerned not only with elimination of the pass as a bribe, but also with the loss of revenue suffered by railroads which in turn thwarted efforts further to reduce freight tariffs.[36]

After a struggle lasting more than fifteen years, agricultural interests won their fight for a railroad commission empowered to fix freight tariffs. But to what extent did the commission succeed in effecting the reduction of rates? The Texas Co-operative Association evidently did not think rates had been materially lowered. It criticized the commission rather harshly for accepting the basic rate structure which had been set up by the companies:

That system of blanket rates adopted by this Commission is simply a return to the pernicious system formerly pursued by the Railroad Traffic Association, to defeat which was one leading object of the people in demanding control of railroads through the medium of a commission.[37]

Nor was the T.C.A. pleased that the commission permitted the old Houston-Galveston differential to continue unchanged. Furthermore, the co-operative became highly incensed over a commission order to the effect that cotton, when shipped by rail, should be compressed at the press nearest the point of origin of the shipment. The farmer organization insisted that the rule as applied often necessitated recompressing, that it deprived farmers of the privilege of choosing their own compresses, and that producers who abided by the rule suffered severe losses. At the same time the co-operative requested the commission to set lower freight rates on cotton, claiming that over the years the volume of cotton traffic had increased as the price of cotton had declined, and that under the circumstances railroads by charging lower rates would still make a fair profit because of the increase in tonnage.[38]

It was only natural that the railroad commission should claim full credit for any reduction in freight tariffs. Actually rates seem to have declined for a number of reasons. Enforcement of the stock and bond law gave the commission a more powerful lever for forcing tariffs downward. According to Raines, within seven years after the law became effective railroad securities were reduced more than $5,000 per mile:

Texas Railroad Mileage and Indebtedness 1894-1901[39]

Year ending 30 June	Miles of Railway in operation	Outstanding per mile Stocks	Bonds	Aggregate stock and bonds per mile
1894	9,154	$15,076	$25,726	$40,802
1895	9,291	14,874	25,420	40,294
1896	9,437	14,647	25,302	39,949
1897	9,484	14,320	24,793	39,113
1898	9,540	14,205	24,036	38,241
1899	9,702	13,997	23,562	37,559
1900	9,867	13,724	23,202	36,926
1901	10,154	12,922	22,649	35,571

Assuming 4 per cent as the rate of interest on the bonds (actually most of them bore a higher rate), the $3,000 per mile reduction in bonded indebtedness reduced interest payments by $120 per mile per year, or a total of approximately $1,200,000. If the roads had paid dividends on stock as low as 2 per cent, the shrinkage of $2,000 per mile in capital stock lowered dividend payments by $40.00 per mile, the over-all result being a saving of $1,600,000 on interest and dividends. It might be argued that there was no saving in interest and dividend payments because 1,000 miles of new railroad had been added between 1894 and 1901. In that case, revenue mileage had been increased by 11 per cent, thus increasing the revenue. Under either condition the railroad commission should have been able to reduce freight rates without disturbing normal payments on current indebtedness.

Evidence collected some seventeen years after the railroad commission began to function left no doubt that there had been sizable reductions in freight rates. In 1891, Texas freight tariffs averaged 1.403 cents per ton-mile, but they had gradually declined until by 1907 they averaged 1.039 cents. For the period the decrease amounted to 25 per cent.[40] But during these years freight rates had declined throughout the United States and national per ton-mile averages for 1891 and 1907 were below the Texas averages. It is possible that the interstate traffic association, through its control of interstate rates, exercised a greater influence on Texas intrastate rates than did the railroad commission. As late as 1897 the State Grange had assailed the regulatory agency as being a lawyer commission, no doubt intending to imply that lawyers had looked after interests other than those of the farmers. In answer to the charge, Chairman Reagan claimed that the commission had reduced rates on all commodities and commerce generally and that in two years alone lowered rates on cotton had saved farmers $800,000.[41]

Often the question has been raised as to whether state railroad commissions regulate railroads, or whether railroads regulate the commissions. The law which created the Texas commission and prescribed its powers ordered it to classify all freight. When it began to function, the commission found that Texas railroads were operating under the "Western" classification. Under this system most goods were divided into ten groups or classes. The highest rate prevailed for goods grouped as first class; then from class to class the freight rate was lowered until the tenth class was reached. In addition there were many cheap, bulky, or exceptionally heavy items that were not classified but were given very low individual or "commodity" rates. The commission left the "Western" classification in effect with very slight modification until it established the "Texas" classification in 1906. Even the "Texas" classification followed the general features of the "Western" classification to the extent of providing ten classified rates and a large number of commodity rates. Nor did the Texas commission do too much shifting of goods from their classification under the "Western" system. Perhaps the inclusion of a smaller number of commodities, forty-three, was the major feature of the "Texas" classification. The commodity list included cotton, cattle, coal, hides, lignite, grain, and grain products,[42] but they were not unique in that they had commodity status in all freight classifications throughout the nation. After all, the railroad commission no doubt learned that the transportation system of Texas was part of an integrated structure, and that Texas as a segment had to live with the whole. This discovery caused the agency to proceed with caution when engaged in classifying commodities and fixing rates. Furthermore, if it did not tamper unduly with existing classifications and rate structures the commission was less likely to become involved in lengthy litigation. After the *Reagan v. Farmers' Loan and Trust Company* suit, the Texas commission moved more cautiously with rate changes. Its accomplishments were probably not in keeping with what the agency would have liked to do, but they represented feasible compromises.

X

Hired Hands—Then the Labor Union

THE idea that Texas suffered an acute labor shortage during the last quarter of the nineteenth century, even though largely erroneous, has been widely accepted as true. Those who adhere to the belief that labor was scarce offer a number of plausible explanations in defense of their position. They insist that even though immigration was large, the immigrants gave no relief since most of them, entering Texas from other southern states, came in search of farms of their own. If they were broke when reaching their destinations, the newcomers for a short time placed themselves on the labor market, but as soon as possible they obtained farms of their own and removed themselves from the market. In fact, many were soon in the market to hire labor. It is also claimed that persons coming to Texas from foreign countries were likewise available for hire only temporarily, and for the same reason as the southerners.[1] Mexican labor was not then available except in close proximity to the border. Often the practice of leasing convict labor from the state has been cited as evidence of a labor shortage. However, the petitions which appeared pleading with state authorities to abolish the nefarious practice of leasing convicts imply an oversupply instead of a scarcity of labor. This viewpoint is expressed in a petition Cass County citizens directed to the governor in 1878 requesting that he

cause to be revoked and annulled the laws permitting convict labor to be leased, thus destroying the means of earning an honest livelihood, placing families on the verge of starvation, making tramps of the heads of families, and thus causing great confusion, and by bringing said families to poverty causing, we fear, an increase of crime.[2]

From statements in the Cass County petition, one would assume that there was an abundance of most types of labor.

There is other evidence which suggests the possibility of a labor surplus. For example, there is the county poor farm. As early as the seventies a number of counties maintained these institutions. Probably not all the unfortunate souls living on the farms were able to work, but the name "farm" implies that those who had been confined to these institutions were expected to earn their sustenance by tilling the soil. The very existence of such places constitutes prima facie evidence that not all Texans were self-employed on their own farms. The existence of county farms could also indicate a scarcity of jobs, or at least of other than purely seasonal employment.

Furthermore, ranch records seldom reveal complaints of a scarcity of labor. The Spur Ranch books mention only one year between 1885 and 1909 in which there was a shortage of ranch hands. Usually there were more applicants than the company could possibly use. In the one year when the number of applicants fell below the needs, the ranch awarded contracts for fence building and other projects normally done by ranch crews. Spur Ranch wages of $25.00 to $35.00 per month and board were probably average for ranch labor. Spur labor turnover was high, as it was at most ranches, with 64 per cent of the men remaining in the employment of the ranch one season or less.[3] There is no reason to assume that labor problems on the Spur Ranch were other than typical for the large land and cattle companies, and facts tend to prove that there was no shortage of labor through the ranch country.

Moreover, when the Great Southwest Strike of 1886 failed, members of the Knights of Labor and other strikers were discharged in wholesale lots. The number of men fired by railroads ran into hundreds, possibly reaching several thousand, but there is little to indicate that companies found any great difficulty in replacing them, or that railroad operations suffered serious disruption because of an inability to hire replacements. It is, of course, possible that a small percentage of the discharged strikers may have moved to distant towns, assumed new names, and were rehired. Had there been a tight labor market, railway companies would have had no choice but to rehire the former employees, or to curtail rail services.

It would appear that some students of this period of Texas history have taken the recognized need for the great amount of work that had to be done if Texas were to be converted from a wilderness into an empire as the basis for assuming the existence of a labor shortage. The assumption is not valid. The fact that there is much work to be done does not in itself establish the further fact that there is either a demand for, or a shortage of, hired labor. Regardless of the amount of work to be done, in the absence of an effective demand for labor no shortage of workers would exist. In an economy largely self-contained, effective demand for labor is always low. Families who produced mainly for home consumption and had little to market annually other than a few dollars' worth of surplus products could offer no wages except "keep and kind." Moreover, the self-contained family did all the work on the farm, and the only times when there might have been real demand for extra labor were at planting and harvesting seasons, and then only for short periods. Besides, when the agricultural community produces only small surpluses there is little need for industry and less need for industrial labor. But as agricultural methods tend to become more efficient and larger crops are produced with less labor, marketable surpluses tend to become greater and the need increases for industries to process these surpluses; and with the growth of industry comes an increase in the demand for labor. More efficient farm methods release men and boys from the farm to take over the new industrial jobs. The economic development of Texas has adhered quite closely to this pattern.

In 1870 the 7,927 persons classed as industrial workers constituted less than 1 per cent of the population of Texas, while for the nation no fewer than 5 per cent of the population were classed as industrial workers. Men composed 94 per cent of the Texas labor force, as compared to 79 per cent for the nation as a whole. In Texas, industry employed twice as many children as women, but for the nation women held a three to one ratio over children. By 1900 the industrial labor force made up 1.6 per cent of the population of the state as compared to 6 per cent for the nation. Texas men still held 92 per cent of all industrial jobs, whereas men filled 77 per cent of such jobs in the nation. For the thirty-year period, the most radical change in the labor pattern for the state came about in the changed ratio between women and children. By 1900 three times as many women as children were employed in Texas industries, while the national ratio was seven to one. For 1870 annual wages in Texas averaged $225, as against $380 for the nation; by 1900 the averages had increased to $427 and $457 respectively.[4] In thirty years the ratio of laborers to population in Texas had doubled, while on the national level it had increased only 20 per cent. If we use the average annual wage as a measure of efficiency, we see that both in 1870 and in 1900 the worker in Texas was less efficient than the national worker; but in the interim the efficiency of the Texas worker had increased 90 per cent, whereas the average for the nation had increased only 20 per cent. On the basis of these data, Texas was developing industrially at a relatively faster rate than the nation as a whole. However, Texas labor returns were below the national average, and remained so.

Most writers would probably explain the relatively small percentage of women in industry in Texas as being a characteristic of the frontier state. It seems that there is a more plausible explanation. Since Texas was a predominantly agricultural state, most of the state's industry was restricted to the rough processing of bulky raw products. Timbering and lumbering were important industries, along with cotton ginning and compressing, flour milling, wagon and harness making, and wood planing. In all of these, the work was heavy and of a nature usually open only to men. By 1900 lighter industries had become more important and the number of women workers had increased.

To judge from the amount of publicity given the subject, contemporary Texans were not greatly interested in or concerned about the problem of child labor. Now and then a news item made casual mention of the fact that children constituted part of the labor force. A report on the lumber industry reads:

Jefferson County.

FRONTIERSMAN [Beaumont]: The mills give constant employment to two hundred and fifty hands. This includes the shingle bunchers, most of whom are children. About six hundred and fifty people derive their sole means of living from the labor of these mills. A careful estimate of the number of men engaged in getting out pine and cypress timber, gives one hundred, most of whom have families. The number who live by this means is about three hundred, making in all about nine hundred persons connected with the lumber interests.[5]

The lumber industry undoubtedly employed, as shingle bunchers, a relatively high percentage of the 157 children enumerated by the census of 1870 as industrial workers. The decline in the percentage of children classed as industrial workers in the census of 1900 may be explained by the great decrease in the daily output of cypress shingles in the thirty years. The drop in the output of shingles plus the increase in the use of machinery released children formerly employed as bunchers.

Wage rates varied greatly from industry to industry, from geographic region to geographic region, and from decade to decade. In 1876, the *Galveston Daily News* reported that the International Railroad was paying construction laborers at rates varying from $1.50 to $1.75 per day, with a $4.00 daily rental for horse and mule teams and $3.00 for a yoke of oxen. Each worker had $3.50 deducted from his weekly earnings for board.[6] A year later a story in the *News* said that Mount Pleasant brickyard laborers were drawing monthly wages of $25.00 and boarding themselves.[7] Shortly after the opening of the eighties Dallas bricklayers held a meeting at which they resolved to demand a daily wage of $3.50 and a nine and one-half hour day on Saturday. The contractors were reported as not being disposed to grant the demands.[8] The workers apparently continued working at the old rate and for the full ten hours on Saturday. As 1880 drew to a close, Dallas stonecutters were on strike because of a wage reduction from $2.50 to $2.25 per day.[9] Evidently the reduced rate prevailed and was, over the next few years, lowered still more, because in 1885 stonecutters, working for a contractor who was erecting a government building, struck for a wage increase. They demanded that wages be raised from $1.75 to $2.75 per day.[10]

Further information on wage rates and working conditions comes from an account of a cottonseed oil mill labor dispute in Sherman. The reporter wrote:

> This morning at 8 o'clock the day press force at the cottonseed oil mills of Tassey, McCullock & Co., on North Willow street, walked out on a strike, their demand for a raise of wages from $1.25 to $1.50 having been refused by Mr. Tassey, manager of the establishment. The strikers informed a [Dallas] *News* man that until about two weeks ago they had been receiving $1.50 per day of twelve hours, and state they were not allowed time in which to eat at dinner hour, but are forced to snatch a bite between runs.[11]

Data on Dallas bricklayers, cottonseed oil mill workers in Sherman, and other similar groups show that the average work day approximated twelve hours for all hired labor, and no industry considered a labor week to be less than six days, while some operated on a seven-day schedule.

The last quarter of the century was punctuated by labor disturbances, but, while some of them were important and of major proportions, most of them appear to have been nothing more than manifestations of fits of temper between a worker, or workers, and foremen. When tempers flared the men walked off the job, but the next day usually found them all back at work as though nothing had happened. Newspapers generally gave fair treatment to labor stories. Some Dallas dailies printed seemingly more of the workers' story than of management's, but more often they dealt with both about the same. Personal bias obviously crept into some writing. One correspondent, describing conditions during the railroad strike of 1886, said, "There are men at Fort Worth, Baird and other points who were getting from $90 to $100 when they struck."[12] This writer left the impression that all railroad employees drew wages in that bracket. He did not indicate that any were paid less than "$90 to $100," nor did he show what percentage of workers were in his arbitrary wage bracket. Available material indicates that wages over the state varied from around $12.00 per month for unskilled labor to around $100.00 for certain skills and crafts.

Newspapers almost invariably reported walkouts as strikes whether they deserved to be so designated or not. Unorganized workers instigated many work stoppages, or labor disputes, but most of the major strikes were union-sponsored. The average strike or dispute ended in failure of the workers to achieve any part of their demands. The strike at the Sherman cottonseed oil mill previously mentioned failed completely. A representative of the company claimed that the strike did not interrupt operations at the plant for more than thirty minutes. The company closed down its gin, transferred employees to the press room, and kept the oil mill running at capacity. On the day the strike started, a company spokesman said that a number of applications had already been received for the jobs vacated by the walkout.[13] Within three days the striking employees had given up hopes of closing the plant and the strike deteriorated completely, with the company reinstating a number of the men.[14] As a rule, when these strikes failed the men were re-employed at old rates and hours — that is, all except those who were believed to have been the leaders of the strike. The strike leaders were not often rehired.

As a rule an employee who was not pleased with his wages or the conditions under which he worked had a choice of one of two possible courses: either he could continue to work under terms fixed by the employer, or he could quit. In the spring of 1877, Col. Pierce reduced the wages of nearly every employee on the Texas & Pacific Railway. Furthermore, he began to discharge conductors with several years of seniority in order that they might be replaced with new men at lower wages.[15] Wages were low before Col. Pierce ordered them reduced; and what was even worse, the company was several months in arrears with payments to the men. In the minds of the workers, insult had been added to injury when the company continued to pay substantial dividends to stockholders through the early summer of 1877. When in the latter part of July employees of the road struck, they were careful to keep mail trains moving but stopped all other trains. The strikers were unorganized, but at a meeting held in Marshall for the purpose of preparing a statement of grievances to present to company officials, employees from every department of the railroad sent representatives. These delegates addressed to the general superintendent a most courteous petition in which they asked for redress of certain grievances. In part, the petition read:

To Col. Geo. Noble, general superintendent Texas and Pacific railroad: We the employees of this road, beg leave respectfully to present for your consideration our grievances as herein set forth, to wit: Regarding the wages as now paid us inadequate to the services rendered, we would ask that our wages be restored to the same basis as prevailed prior to April 1, 1877. Would also ask that all money due us up to July 1 be paid by August 15, and for July by September 1, and each month following be paid by the 15th of the succeeding month in which our services are rendered. . . .

Sir, not wishing to be considered hasty in this matter and disclaiming any intention whatever of violence to the company's property and with kindest feelings personally towards yourself, we would beg to ask that you give this your earliest attention and return us an answer within the next 48 hours after this petition comes into your possession; and we furthermore demand that no employee shall be dismissed for any action he may have taken in this matter on account of the same.[16]

Only in one instance did the employees secure a promise from Noble in which he met fully a request of the petition. Perhaps company officials felt that their pursuing any other course would have been viewed by the men as a sign of weakness on the part of the company. The general superintendent returned his answer in ninety-six hours, not forty-eight as requested by the men. He assured the workers that wages earned prior to June would be paid by August 25, and that wages earned prior to August would be in their hands before October. He pledged the men that he would personally urge restoration of the wages prevailing prior to April and assured them that he was confident the company would revoke the cuts. Noble also promised that no participant in the strike would be discharged. He then admonished the men to get back to work, telling them that many had been idle who could not afford the loss of pay. The representatives of the employees accepted the terms offered by Noble, gave him three cheers, and adjourned the meeting.[17] Throughout the state a sense of uncertainty, a nervous tension, permeated all groups of railroad employees — a condition which, the *Galveston News* suggested, prevailed because the men were unorganized and not acting in unison.[18]

Many labor disputes during the period involved workmen of the building crafts, and most of them followed a pattern closely resembling this account of an 1876 disagreement in Galveston: "Work on the bakery in Mechanic, near Center, is proceeding without interruption. The facts about the strike of the bricklayers are: They

were employed for $3.50 per day but wanted $4 after commencing
work, which desire was not complied with."[19] Disturbances between
printers and their employers often tended to move in much the
same manner, as pictured in the story of a Houston strike of 1880:

> Houston, September 30.—The Post's printers struck tonight, demanding
> 40 cents per thousand. They have been receiving 35 cents, which is more
> than has been paid for some time past by any other paper in Houston. The
> strike is said to be instigated by outside influence, but will not interfere
> with tomorrow's issue of the paper.[20]

Two days later the News ran a brief summary of the outcome of
the stoppage: "Houston, October 2. — The Post's striking printers
came back to work tonight, signing an agreement with the proprie-
tor to work at former rates — 35 cents per 1000 ems. The leaders of
the strike were not taken back."[21] The outcome of a large number
of disputes so nearly coincided with the above examples that newspapers could almost have kept the stories set up, running them
again and again by changing only names, places, and dates.

Not even the livestock country entirely escaped the epidemic of
labor disturbances. In 1883, cow hands met near Tascosa, drew up a
list of grievances, and announced that henceforth they would not
work for less than $50.00 per month as hands or $75.00 as bosses
of an outfit. Their protests were directed primarily at wage policies
and working conditions of large cattle companies. Before "fizzling"
out, the strike dragged on for more than a year and attracted an
estimated 325 participants.[22] A couple of years later journeymen
tailors at Fort Worth were more successful than the cow hands. The
tailors struck for a 10 per cent raise and within twenty-four hours
all tailoring establishments in town save one had agreed to meet
the demand.[23]

In 1883, because the Mallory Line at its wharf in New York was
discharging white union laborers and replacing them with nonunion
colored labor, the Knights of Labor called a general strike at Galveston. Before the strike the company had been requested to desist
in its discriminations against union labor and to reinstate the
workers it had discharged. After the company rejected the union's
request some 1,500 to 2,000 Galveston longshoremen and other
members of the Knights of Labor walked off their jobs.[24] After four

days the strike had spread to Houston, where the Knights boy-cotted all shipments waybilled to Galveston. Before the strike ended the union had threatened to spread the work stoppage throughout the state.[25]

The fact that straitened financial circumstances of city govern-ments made it impossible for them to meet their pay rolls sometimes caused public employees to walk off their jobs en masse. The Hous-ton treasury was worse than empty in 1878 when its street commis-sioner paid his workers in scrip and then excused them from their jobs for two hours in order to permit them to try to find someone who would buy the paper. At the end of the recess period they returned to notify the commissioner that thirty cents on the dollar was the best offer they had received for the vouchers and that under those circumstances they were no longer willing to work for the city. At the request of the commissioner they did remove their tools from the street, and one of the aldermen promised to present their case to the city council.[26] At the end of two years, the financial condition of the city of Houston evidently had not improved. This time the citizens of Houston had advanced sufficient funds to pay policemen a month's salary to provide the men with some Christ-mas money, but when the council refused to honor the loan, the next payday for the patrolmen was again payless.[27]

While some workers suffered because of empty tills on paydays, others faced years of unemployment because they had been black-listed. How widespread was the practice of blacklisting it is difficult to say, but it was used by railroads. In a damage suit for $10,000 filed in 1885 by A. F. Richmond against the Missouri Pacific, the plaintiff alleged that he had been discharged by the railroad. The company had given as the reason for his discharge careless per-formance of duties as a conductor. Although Richmond did not question the right of the railroad to release him, he denied that he had been negligent in the discharge of his duties. Cause for legal action arose because the Missouri Pacific had placed the name of its former employee on the company "black list." Richmond claimed that he had been railroading for fourteen years and that he had never encountered any difficulty in securing employment with rail-roads until after his name appeared on the company list. During the two years his name had been on the list he had been unable to secure any kind of railroad employment.[28] In reality the term "black list" did not appear in the suit. Instead Richmond accused the company of libeling him by circulating his name among its officials who were authorized to hire and fire, which, of course, is what the term "blacklisting" today implies. The district court of McLennan County awarded Richmond $250 actual and $1,750 exemplary damages. The company appealed, and after four years the Supreme Court of Texas reversed the action of the lower court, ruling that a corporation might be held civilly responsible for libel, but that a pamphlet with names and reasons for discharging employees placed by the corporation in the hands of persons whose duty it was to hire was a privileged communication.[29] That is to say, the Supreme Court of Texas ruled that blacklisting was legal in the state. Not until 1901 when the legislature made it a misdemeanor did the practice of blacklisting become unlawful in Texas.[30]

During this last quarter of the nineteenth century, only one major construction project in Texas seems to have been materially slowed down because of a labor shortage. Because the stone being used in building the new state capitol was quarried by convict labor, a subcontractor encountered difficulty in attracting needed granite cutters. The local stonecutters' union held a meeting to consider whether or not it was permissible for them to work with the stone that had been quarried by convicts.[31] Evidently the answer was negative, for the National Granite Cutters' Union very shortly thereafter issued warnings to its locals throughout the nation to boycott the Austin job.[32] In a poll of the national membership this boycott was sustained by a five hundred to one vote. In an effort to circumvent the boycott, the subcontractor sent an agent to Scotland for the purpose of recruiting Scotch stonecutters. The agent signed contracts with sixty-two men who were shipped to the United States, an action which violated the federal statute prohibiting the importation of contract labor. National labor organizations quickly demanded that the subcontractor be prosecuted for violating the law, and launched campaigns for raising funds to aid in the prosecution. The contractor was found guilty of violating the law and fined $62,000 and costs. On his last day in office, and for reasons never explained, President Harrison reduced the fine to $8,000.[33]

In the closing decades of the century, many Texans seemed to think that industrial development could be achieved without the concomitant labor union. As industry sprang up in Texas, so also did organized labor. In 1878, the *Frontier Echo* informed its public that the Knights of Labor, a labor movement with "dangerous objectives," was moving south — who knew, perhaps toward Texas:

> A new secret society, called the Knights of Labor, has been organized in the leading northern cities and is extending south. The objective of the order is to control elections and cause laws to be enacted favorable to socialism and communism. A part of the ritual of the order is published in the Volkszeitung, a leading German paper North, as follows:
> "The entire overthrow of the present social system; the abolition of all personal property in the land and other means of production, and their cession to the state; the introduction of the cooperative plan in labor, so every laborer may be a partner in every factory and workshop; the compulsory limitation of hours of labor to eight hours a day or less according to the requirements of the unemployed workmen; the regulation of the prices of labor by arbitration between the employer and the employed until the cooperative system is introduced; compulsory education and the opening of all colleges and universities free to all classes; the abolition of savings banks; the abolition of direct taxation and the institution of a scaled income tax, and the taxation of all church property."[34]

Within the next two or three years the Knights had reached Texas and had established local unions all over the state. Had Texans retained their self-sufficient agricultural economy, the rise of organized labor could have been prevented; but with the transition to a commercialized dependent economy and the rise of industry, labor unions came along, too, as a part of the trappings of the industrialized-commercialized state.

When we attempt to "back-track" to the origin of things, the trail always grows dim. Locating the first signs of organized labor in Texas is no exception to the rule. Railroad employees appear not to have been organized during the period of labor difficulties in the late seventies:

> Hempstead, July 26, 1877.— . . . The men on Texas roads are unorganized and have acted cautiously, evidently determined to embarrass but one road at a time.
> Resolutions adopted insist only upon a restoration of former wages.

They particularly declare that no property shall be damaged. No passenger trains have been delayed.[35]

In 1878 a Workingmen's Benevolent and Beneficial Association meeting at Houston claimed to speak for all laborers throughout the state. By resolution it proposed that the "depressed, betrayed, and enslaved" laborer "demand an equal protection with the capitalist and the bloated bond-holder," and that candidates for governor be queried as to their views on "the passage of new laws for the protection of the workingman and the laborer, and a liberal administration of the government in his behalf." The president of the association said that he considered the resolution an endorsement of the principles of the Paris commune, and resigned in protest, declaring the usefulness of the association to be at an end.[36]

The typographical union was probably among the first to be organized in the state. A brief news paragraph of 1880 read: "Dallas, June 1. — The printers of the city have organized a typographical union."[37] Four months later, because the paper hired a nonunion foreman, compositors of the *Dallas Herald* struck.[38] The typographical union had functioned in Galveston since a much earlier date, presumably as early as the fifties. Some of the building trades claimed to have maintained continuous organization since the sixties. As early as 1880 coal was being mined at Coalville, and very shortly the miners had joined a local of the National Trades Association No. 135, an affiliate of the Knights of Labor.[39] The Coalville local may or may not have marked the entrance of the Knights into Texas. However, the order did not become a formidable body until after organized labor, in March, 1885, emerged victorious from a strike against the Gould railroads.[40] In the same year, the Knights of Labor boycotted the Stetson Hat Company of Philadelphia, and several months later, because Sanger Bros. of Dallas continued to market the Stetson hat, the union instigated a secondary boycott against the Texas firm.[41]

Under the auspices of the Knights of Labor, probably a larger percentage of nonfarm labor was organized in Texas than has been recruited by unions before or since. Within three years after the formation of the first local assembly in 1882, the Knights of Labor membership had grown to such an extent that the state of Texas was designated as District Assembly 78. At its peak the Knights of Labor had no fewer than 30,000 members in Texas.[42] Even though membership in the "One Big Union" was open to farmers, and granting that newspaper reporters sometimes overestimate membership figures, it is entirely possible that for a short period of time the Knights of Labor had as members approximately 50 per cent of the nonfarm workers of Texas. Membership in the union was open to Negroes, and one newspaper reported that more than 500 of them had been admitted to the Waco local.[43]

Although officially opposed to the use of the strike, the Knights of Labor became involved in some of the bitterest strikes in American labor history — among them the Great Southwest Strike of 1886. Labor relations appear never to have been very satisfactory on any railroad dominated by Jay Gould — a condition which, on the eve of the Great Southwest Strike, undoubtedly contributed to a rapid increase in the ranks of the Knights of Labor in the Southwest. In March, 1885, a reduction in the wages of employees of the Texas & Pacific Railway provoked a strike which ended with the workers apparently the victors. But as the year dragged on, Gould showed no evidence whatever that he intended to abide by the agreement which back in the spring had ended the work stoppage. Late in the year Gould issued a statement elaborating his views on how all present and future difficulties between the railroad system and its employees could be satisfactorily settled. He said:

I should be glad to know that every employee of the Missouri Pacific system was owner of more or less shares of the company's stock. If they did, every man would have a personal interest in the property and every man would do his very best to increase its earning power and opportunity. Then the road would be managed and operated by its owners. There would be no labor problem to unravel.[44]

Gould's proposal sounded very much like one of the radical objectives of the Knights of Labor quoted above from the Echo, namely, "the introduction of the cooperative plan in labor, so every laborer may be a partner in every factory and workshop." Gould amended the statement by adding "and railroad." After the railroad strike had been settled in the spring of 1885, new grievances began to accumulate almost immediately, and the representatives of the employees, who sought to work out the differences in an amicable manner, were unable to secure a hearing from either Mr. Gould or his general manager.

Action which finally precipitated the walkout by railroad employees in 1886 was the release of one C. A. Hall from the Marshall shops of the Texas & Pacific Railway. Hall was discharged by the Gould management because of his activities on behalf of the union. The firing of Hall quickly resolved into a test of strength between the Knights of Labor and the company. The union requested the railroad officials to rescind the action and permit Hall to resume his duties. When the company refused to reinstate the discharged employee, a work stoppage began (March 10, 1886), which, with the exception of trainmen who were not affiliated with the Knights, involved the employees of all Gould railroads in the Southwest.[45]

At an earlier date, and through a separate labor organization, trainmen had, with sympathetic aid from the Knights, been awarded wage increases; but in 1886 trainmen did not concern themselves with the fate of other employees. At the beginning of the strike the union posted guards at strategic points in order to prevent property damage by more hotheaded union members, or by nonunion vandals; but the peaceful manner in which the walkout began later gave way to violence, and men were killed on both sides. Since the Texas & Pacific was in receivership, a federal judge deputized company officials, thereby placing in contempt of court striking workers who interfered with the new deputies in the performance of their duties. In addition, Governor Ireland called out the Texas Rangers and the state militia to preserve law and order.

To most of the strikers their objectives were better working conditions and the setting of regular paydays. The basic struggle, however, lay much deeper: it was a battle against corporate control of a way of life. It was a protest by the individual, who hoped to maintain his identity as an individual and not be overwhelmed and overcome by the corporation. It was a losing fight because either the individual must give up a part of his independence to live with the corporation, or the corporation must go. And the corporation was here to stay. Furthermore, the fact that top union leadership gave the strike only halfhearted support doomed it to an early failure. Ruth A. Allen has described the manner in which the strike officially ended:

On May 4 the General Executive Board at the request of the Committee declared the strike ended. There was no counteraction by the railroads. No protection for the strikers was arranged; no consideration of grievances was asked. The surrender was unconditional. For this there seems little excuse. The members of the Board were experienced in the field of labor organization, and could not have believed that, with no demand on their part, the Federal Government would step in and insist that Gould and Hoxie recognize the rights of the strikers in returning to their jobs. Aggressive action by the National Board might have saved something on which the future might build. Whatever their motive, if there was a defined motive, they made a serious error destructive of their leadership and detrimental to the future of the Order — not because it was a single great mistake but because it was a continuation into a climactic situation of ignoring all implications of a struggle. Abandonment by their leaders the workers in the Southwest felt to be a betrayal. Though no charges were made publicly, rumors were persistent that there were matters that needed explanation in the sudden ending of the strike.[46]

However, there were some signs of disintegration before the general executive board declared the strike ended; at least, striking members had begun to drift away from the more isolated railroad towns before May. Toward the latter part of April a Baird correspondent for an Abilene paper wrote, "The strikers are scattered, but half a dozen are yet here and they have families."[47] In the summer following the collapse of the strike, the Knights of Labor held Fourth of July celebrations in Marshall and other Texas towns. Late in July delegations from local Knights assemblies convened in San Antonio, and in conjunction with representatives of other groups considered possible ways of electing to the legislature candidates who were sympathetic to labor.[48] But the organization, which a few months earlier had had anywhere from a few to several hundred members in every railroad town, was dead. A labor leader, who not many years after the strike traveled the state extensively, said he never in all of his moving about met more than two or three who had participated in the Great Southwest Strike of 1886, or who would admit they had taken part in it.[49]

The press of the state was divided in its sympathy toward the two parties to the dispute. The fact that a newspaper was located in a strong labor town did not necessarily mean it was sympathetic toward the workers, nor was the opposite true. However, papers in towns where the Knights had few members were usually more hostile to labor than papers in strong labor communities. The Sulphur Springs *Enterprise* spoke out strongly against onesided law enforcement, saying:

> The strong arm of the law should be applied to all railroads for violations of the law as promptly as it is being administered to those engaged in the strike. The railroads and express companies violate the law daily in their business relations with the people.[50]

The *Taylor County News* agreed with the *Enterprise* but insisted that it gave only one phase of the picture. The *News* then expounded its views on the other phase:

> This is good enough logic as far as it goes, but it only goes half far enough. While the law is used for the purpose of "scorching" the railroad fellows for their shortcomings and misdemeanors, it should also be able to protect them in their lawful rights. Oh, yes; punish the railroad companies by all means when they violate the law, but don't allow the commerce of the country to be clogged.[51]

At that late date the laws of Texas were not "scorching" the railroad fellows very much. Nevertheless, there were laws that made certain railroad practices unlawful, whereas there were no laws against strikes as such. In commenting further on the strike a fortnight later, the *News* denounced the participating laborers as thieves, vandals, and murderers:

> There is a spirit communistic in its character pervading this move that seeks to rule or ruin. There were some few good citizens here who at first sympathized with the strikers but when it was known that the elements controlling the destiny of strikers favored burning bridges, wrecking trains, stealing parts of machinery and above all committing willful murder, the last spark of sympathy died out and the strikers are left alone in their glory — that is, if there be any glory in slaying the hand that has fed them.[52]

In condemning the striking Knights so thoroughly and so viciously, the *News*, no doubt, expressed the sentiments of many Texans.

Out of the wreckage of the Knights of Labor sprang its successor, the American Federation of Labor. Since 1883 certain elements among the Knights had been perfecting plans for organizing a loose federation of craft unions, and after the debacle of 1886 they made a clean break from the Knights of Labor. Not until 1891 was a Texas group represented at the annual national convention of the American Federation of Labor. During the eighties the AF of L may or may not have had affiliates in the state, but it took cognizance of certain labor practices in Texas. The young federation denounced the use of convict labor for quarrying stone for the state capitol as being in competition with free labor, and it protested the importation of the Scotch stonecutters and helped raise funds to prosecute the subcontractor.[53]

In its report for 1890, the year before the first Texas delegate attended the national convention, the American Federation of Labor mentions the fact that two Texas groups had been chartered by the organization. However, not until 1898 was the State Federation of Labor organized in Texas. As early as 1895 some AF of L city trades councils had been formed. At the turn of the century trades councils were functioning in Austin, Corsicana, Dallas, Gainesville, Hillsboro, and Sherman. Early in 1900 twenty-three delegates from seven cities, representing 8,475 workers, met at Corsicana in a trades council convention. This body of delegates denounced the use of convict labor in any capacity where the fruits of labor would enter the market in competition with free labor. It also passed a resolution disapproving the construction of a cotton mill at Corsicana if it was the intent of the promoters to recruit any part of the labor force for the mill from the children of the State Orphans Home located in that city.[54]

In Texas, the American Federation of Labor probably never built up its membership to include as high a percentage of nonfarm workers as did the Knights of Labor; and its crafts never caused a state-wide labor disturbance comparable to the Great Southwest Strike. In the eighties labor, along with the farmer, had engaged the corporation in a desperate struggle for power, for the right to determine a way of life. Both lost. The American Federation of Labor, a leading exponent of business unionism, came not to destroy but to live with the corporation, abiding by business methods and making use of the tools of business to gain economic advantages for its members.

XI

Migratory Industry Settles Down

IN 1870, Texas industry consisted of small shops or plants serving primarily to complete the economic independence of self-contained communities. The scant lightweight equipment which characterized a majority of the establishments could have been loaded on an ox-wagon, leaving plenty of room for the household effects of the owner. Texas industry was highly mobile. If a shop had been located in a village which proved to be too small to furnish the volume of business anticipated by the owner, or if it failed to grow as rapidly as he had expected, he forthwith loaded up his gear and moved on to what appeared to be a greener pasture. From town to town the types of establishments were much the same. Gainesville, in 1876, was described as having

one bank, eight carpenter shops, four wagon makers, six blacksmiths, a gunsmith, three saddlers, two hotels, seven dry goods stores, six groceries, one watchmaker, two drug stores, two hardware stores, two furniture stores, one bakery, seventeen lawyers, four land agents, eight physicians, four schools, two barber shops, two shoemakers, two flouring mills, and various other trades.[1]

Lawyers and land agents always found it relatively easy to move from one part of the country to another. A list of business establishments in Boerne for the late seventies was probably typical of those in frontier county seats. The catalogue read:

There is one saw, grist and flouring mill run by the waters of the Cibolo, running at full capacity; one steam planing mill and factory for wooden ware, two saddlery, one gun and lock smith establishment, a cotton press and gin, an extensive brewery, a tin and copper smithery, and two blacksmiths, besides a number of dry goods and produce stores. The town has three hotels and several private boarding houses.[2]

Sulphur Springs in 1876 marked an exception to the average run-of-the-mill town. Some of its industries were evidently designed to supply a market extending well beyond the confines of the community. A writer for the *Galveston News* said: "That place [Sulphur Springs] now has three planing mills, three furniture shops, three steam gins, two first-class flouring mills with a prospect of another soon, one wool carder, and a foundry in which plows, machinery, etc., are manufactured."[3] From the multiple number of planing mills, flouring mills, and furniture shops, one may be certain that their products were marketed over a trade territory much larger than the Sulphur Springs community. The output of plows and machinery from the foundry also supplied the needs of a relatively broad market territory. Shops located in small isolated communities served local needs, while many establishments in larger towns of more populous regions tended to concentrate on the production of commodities for broad markets. As the century came to a close, many processors in smaller villages were struggling to maintain a precarious existence in the face of competition from large, efficient establishments of the North or the larger towns.

An early catalogue of shops and establishments in New Braunfels is indicative of the absolute independence of the average German community of Southwest Texas:

New Braunfels in 1847 had one physician, two drug stores, three bakeries, one brewery, four blacksmith shops, one locksmith, one gunsmith, two beer taverns, six carpenters, five stonemasons, three tanners, one upholsterer, two saddlers, eight cabinetmakers, three wagonmakers and one carriage factory, one brick kiln, a jeweler, several tailors, shoemakers, and mechanics of almost every kind.[4]

The complete independence of the average German settlement had changed but little between 1847 and 1870 or 1875. These communities had been colonized, and successful colonizers saw to it that a settlement included every type of craftsman essential to the existence and well-being of the colony. Self-sufficiency among the German towns was also induced by the fact that the German people were isolated from Anglo-American settlements by their foreign tongue and "strange" customs. Then, too, they were non-slaveholders in a slave state and were shunned and held in suspicion by slave owners. Finally, the desire to make homes and villages near replicas of those back in the "old country" necessitated quite an array of skilled craftsmen.

Texas communities did not necessarily develop into self-sufficient settlements by choice. Self-contained villages are a phase of the growth of frontier regions. Until a railroad system was completed the great majority of Texas settlements were isolated, and necessity compelled them to satisfy local wants or do without. During the War Between the States, the Confederate government encouraged Texans to engage in any kind of manufacturing venture that would contribute to military needs. This accounts for the increase in the number of industrial establishments and the value of their products during the war decade which saw the value of farms and agricultural output shrink.

Because of the mobile and migratory nature of shops and business establishments, business centers of towns and villages were in a constant state of flux, and contemporary papers seldom went to press without one or more paragraphs telling of new shops being established in town or of old ones being moved elsewhere. Most editors were possessed of considerable local pride and spoke in glowing terms of the prosperity of their towns, even when the tenor of the stories in their news columns clearly indicated that their communities were dying. Although Fort Griffin had passed its prime as an important frontier outpost and its days were assuredly numbered before Robson moved there with his *Echo*, the editor wrote article after article in which he described the lively business activity of the town — but his news columns included paragraph after paragraph of proof that Griffin was on the decline. When the columns of a paper were filled with items of which the following are typical, they did not describe a prosperous village: "Board reduced to $20 per month on 1st of February, at the Planters Hotel";[5] "John Miller, the blacksmith has packed up bag and baggage and gone to Sweetwater";[6] "Frank Clampitt says he will move his livery outfit to some point on the Rio Grande the first of next month";[7] "Cheap John has withdrawn the light of his bright optics from Fort Griffin and hereafter his smile, childlike and bland, will be bestowed on the fair ones of Sweetwater";[8] and "Workmen are tearing down Mr. Conrad's two-story building preparatory to moving it to Throckmorton where it will be used as a court house and for county offices."[9] Columns of the *Echo* told of no newcomers, and in Griffin's boom days Mr. Conrad had been the big merchant.

Some villages suffered because they were too small to be wholly self-contained. While still at Jacksboro, Mr. Robson wrote, "Again we say a good boot and shoe maker is very much needed in this town. Can't somebody send us one."[10] The volume of trade was undoubtedly too small at Jacksboro to maintain a boot or shoemaker. There were yet other factors that contributed to the appearance and disappearance of business establishments. In the absence of refrigeration and because of competition from the smokehouse at every home, the life of the butcher shop was indeed precarious. Again from Jacksboro Robson reported: "Sam Ingram has closed his butcher shop; he says it does not pay because too much meat spoils on his hands."[11] Nevertheless, only a few weeks passed before Robson was moaning, "If some one would only start a good reliable meat market, one source of complaint would be removed."[12] A week later he announced that two meat markets had been opened and were ready to serve customers first-class meats. Thus the stage was set for two failures instead of one. Incidentally, within a period of eight years Robson moved his *Echo* three times — to Jacksboro, to Fort Griffin, and then to Albany. His second move was probably his worst, because he went to Griffin just at the tail end of the buffalo slaughter and just ahead of the removal of the troops from the post. Rare indeed was the community that could truthfully make Lampasas' boast, "Not a mercantile house has failed in the town of Lampasas for five or six years."[13]

According to data from the U.S. Census Report for 1870 the average Texas industrial establishment or shop represented an investment of $2,200, employed three and one-half workers, and had an annual output valued at $4,800. Labor and material costs averaged $3,360, which left for the owner $1,440. From the latter figure, modern accounting methods would subtract depreciation, taxes, and interest on invested capital, which at that time probably did not exceed $250, leaving a net return of approximately $1,200. At the end of thirty years Texas establishments had greatly increased in size, but in comparison to the national average they were still small. The average plant now represented a capital investment of $7,350, three and one-half times larger than in 1870, and employed four workers; output value had more than doubled. Net return per establishment had increased to $1,820. (See Appendix, Table XIV.) There was some increase in the efficiency of labor, but the doubling of per plant output in thirty years with only a 14 per cent increase in the labor force must be accounted for by a great increase in the use of machinery. If current dollars for 1900 were converted into 1870 dollars, the $9,700 value of output per plant became $16,780, and the net return instead of $1,820 became $3,150. Thus production for the average Texas industrial plant had increased much more than current dollar values indicated. (See Appendix, Tables I and XIV.)

By 1870, manufacturing had become fairly well concentrated geographically; and it tended to remain so throughout the thirty-year period. At the outset the ten leading industrial counties produced 44 per cent of all Texas manufactured goods; in 1900 the top ten manufacturing counties turned out 35 per cent of the finished goods. For each date per plant investment in the ranking counties approximately doubled that of the Texas average, while per plant output more than doubled the state average. Furthermore, net returns calculated for the larger establishments, as found in the foremost industrial counties, were more than twice as great as for the average plant. (See Appendix, Tables XIV and XV.)

At the opening of the period, only one-fourth of the manufacturing concerns of the state were located in the ten most important industrial counties, but these establishments represented 50 per cent of the aggregate capital investment. If from the state totals we subtract the capital investment of the ten leading counties, the average per plant investment for the state is reduced to $1,385, which is 'more than $800 below the 1870 average. Since the $1,385 represents the value of land, buildings, and machinery, $1,000 probably is a fair estimate for the machinery and other movable equipment. With so little machinery in the average village shop, one can readily see that moving from town to town posed no great problem. Average net returns for these small establishments ran well below $900 per annum. If, for 1900, we also subtract from the state aggregate the capital investments of the ten leading industrial counties, the average capital investment drops from $7,350 to $5,340, and the net return per shop falls to $1,200. For both 1870 and 1900 the two foremost manufacturing counties produced 20 per cent of the industrial products of the state. (See Appendix, Tables XIV and XV.)

The extent of the industrial backwardness of Texas is vividly demonstrated by a comparison of certain data on Texas and the nation. In 1870, of the national population one person out of forty-eight lived in Texas, but for every dollar of industrial output produced by Texans the nation turned out three hundred and sixty-seven. After the passage of thirty years, one person out of twenty-five of the nation's population resided in Texas, yet Texans produced only one out of every one hundred and nine dollars' worth of goods turned out by the nation's industrial plants. After three decades it could be noted that industrial progress in Texas had moved at a more rapid pace than for the nation as a whole, but the improvement in its relative position signified little more than that industrially Texas still lagged far behind the national average. Viewed from another standpoint, in 1870 the national value of manufactured goods was twice as great as the value of farm products, and by 1900 manufactured products more than trebled the gross farm income. On the other hand, in the thirty years the value of industrial output for Texas increased from one-fourth to one-half that of the gross farm income. Per capita value of manufactures for the United States averaged $109 in 1870 and $171 in 1900. In Texas for the corresponding dates, per capita value of manufactures averaged $14.00 and $39.00. All comparative data indicate that the industrial position of Texas was slowly improving but that the state was, and remained, predominantly agricultural. (See Appendix, Tables XIV and XVI.)

Many Texans were aware of the industrial backwardness of their state and gave considerable thought and effort to ways and means of correcting the condition. Thrall, who wrote extensively on the dearth of manufacturing, said:

> The great want of Texas is manufacturing industry. With the exception of her flouring mills, cotton seed mills, and the New Braunfels woolen mills, and three or four foundries and workshops — all successful testimonials, however, as to what can be accomplished in this way — the state is altogether deficient in manufactures. Yet there is plenty of opportunity and facility in the state for the establishment and successful operation of such a variety of lines. The demand is ample, and the means are native here, awaiting the touch of enterprise and capital. Texas, as yet, is dependent upon the outer world for, from ax-helves to farm wagons — from the hoe to the steam engine; yet the State abounds in mineral wealth, and the timber of the country is profuse in the best of varieties and boundless in extent. With full achievement of the manufacturing era will come the industrial glory of Texas.[14]

Thrall, as did most other Texans who, in his day, wrote of the industrial possibilities of Texas, overestimated the market demand in Texas for the products of the industries he sought to see developed in the state. He endeavored, however, to devote some thought to an analysis of why industrial development came slowly in Texas. He set down his conclusions as follows:

> It must be acknowledged that Texas does not rank high as a manufacturing State; and the reason is obvious. Other pursuits are more certain in their results, and more profitable. No man will work in a factory for forty or fifty cents a day when he can make seventy-five cents or a dollar working in a cotton field; and no capitalist will put his money in factories to yield an income of ten or twelve per cent. when he can put it in a sheep or cattle ranch and realize 20 or 30 per cent. Still there are some factories, and as the country becomes more densely populated, Texas is destined to become an extensive manufacturing state. We have the timber for furniture; the wool and cotton for cloth; the iron, coal, etc.; the water power in almost unlimited quantities, and in the immediate neighborhood of the largest cotton plantations, and the most numerous flocks of sheep, and where living is as cheap as at any place on the Continent.[15]

Some of Thrall's reasoning was sound, and some of it was nothing more than wishful thinking. For example, at the present writing, though the coal deposits of Texas were mined for a generation, the mines have been closed down for almost thirty years. And in spite of its enormous crops of cotton and wool, the state has never been an important textile manufacturing center. Lack of markets has always been a retarding factor in the development of many of the state's resources. Furthermore, under the existing state of the industrial arts many resources, notably metallic ores, could not be successfully utilized. Often contemporaries of Thrall spoke of a profusion of high-grade mineral deposits in the state, when, in reality, most of them were low-grade ores. Texas coal was also of poor quality.

While Thrall's interests extended to the development of the entire state, most of the communities were primarily concerned with what happened locally. Every county and village had spokesmen who lauded the "salubrious climate" and extolled the many and varied opportunities that made the county or village a potential industrial center. In expounding the potentialities of its town, the Jefferson *Leader* said:

This is the best timber region in the country, and here small factories might be started that would pay handsomely. A furniture manufactory and a furniture store, in the hands of a wide-awake, liberal man, would yield large profits. A tannery, with sufficient capital to give it a fair start and properly managed, would pay a large interest on the investment. Men with energy and capital could profitably embark in the manufacture of wagons. We have within a few miles of Jefferson the best iron in the world; only capital and enterprise are needed to develop it and bring it to market. Jefferson is particularly well adapted for a cotton factory, paper mill or woolen mill.[16]

Fifty-odd years later chemists made the southern pine usable for the manufacture of paper, and the paper mill came to East Texas. Year in and year out, county after county, town after town, and community after community apprised at least its own people, if not the world, of caches rich in resources which, when capital became available, would convert a given locality into a hive of industrial activity.

A state business directory for 1878-79 catalogued 141 different business, occupational, and professional headings. Judging from the number of pages required to list the names and addresses under each, the more important trades and services were those of blacksmiths, boot and shoe manufacturers and makers, harness and saddle makers and dealers, commission merchants, buggy, carriage, and wagon manufacturers, and wheelwrights. The number of flour and grist mills was also large, with most of these establishments confined to the northeastern quarter of the state. With nine mills, Sherman was probably the leading flour mill center. The directory's mention of five cottonseed oil mills indicated the growing commercial importance of cottonseed. Quite evidently ice had not yet become a household necessity, for only nineteen ice dealers or manufacturers were enumerated, and one of them, with apparent pride, advertised that his ice came from northern lakes. To Texans of that day photographs were more important than ice; at least, they supported three times as many photographic studios as they did ice dealers. Nine small tanneries were then operating, and fifty-two cotton factors, forty-two of whom were in Galveston, bought and sold cotton.[17] Since the *Directory of the City of Dallas* for the same years catalogued twenty-three cotton factors, we might assume that the state directory was none too accurate. It does, however, serve to give a general idea of the array of trades, establishments, and professions ministering to Texas' economic wants.

The Dallas directory catalogue of businesses, trades, services, and professions restricted its listings to residents of the city. At the close of the seventies, Dallas was a leading commercial center and merchandising was by far its most important business or occupation. Among the merchants were seventy-six grocers, fifty-one commission merchants, and nine agricultural implement dealers. There were also many dry goods stores, hat shops, boot and shoe shops, drugstores, and jewelers. The service institutions included five banks (however, two of them failed during the year), thirteen barbershops, seven bakeries, twenty-eight boardinghouses, a coal dealer, twelve blacksmiths, seven dentists, eighteen boot and shoemakers, and sixty-one attorneys. Serving the building and construction needs of the community were architects, civil engineers, artificial stone plants, brick manufacturers, cistern builders, cabinet makers, carpenters, contractors, and builders. Establishments falling within the category of manufacturing included breweries, cigar shops, candy makers, carriage works, spice and coffee mills, broom factories, and a cooperage. Among the facilities for marketing and harvesting which would attract farmers from the surrounding agricultural trade territory were threshing machines, cotton compresses, cottonseed oil mills, grain elevators, and flour mills.[18] These examples from Dallas give some idea of the business structure of the larger Texas towns of the seventies and eighties.

In the preparation of his *Texas Almanac* for 1880, Thrall discovered that in only twenty-one counties did the value of machinery, tools, and other manufacturing equipment exceed $50,000. All twenty-one were in the eastern half of the state, with Tarrant, Travis, and McLennan the most westerly. But Thrall cautioned his readers not to assume that the machinery represented industrial equipment:

An inspection of the above figures shows that a large proportion of the "Machinery" reported consists of agricultural implements. We have no report on the actual value of manufactured products in our State; but as this industry is developed, probably we shall be furnished with more accurate information.[19]

Thrall was actually saying that census data were neither very accurate nor very reliable catalogues of industrial activity.

At the close of the seventies a major portion of Texas industries do not appear to have been far removed from the handicraft stage. Items which are today accepted as commonplace even among the poor were then rare and luxurious among the wealthy. "Lemonade with sure enough ice, at the Cattle Exchange [a saloon]," gave a frontier settlement a conversational topic for a week, one that could only be surpassed by this announcement: "Ice Cream at Uncle Billy's restaurant, at 2 p. m. tomorrow, Sunday."[20] Editor Robson, author of the two items, followed with a gratis plug, "That was delicious ice cream, Uncle Billy Wilson served up last Sunday. We had one fault to find with it, however — it was too awful cold."[21] When ice-cold lemonade and ice cream could show up in saloons and cafés of Fort Griffin in 1880, one may take it for granted that transportation and technological development were giving the frontier an injection of civilization.

In the early seventies Texas had practically no transportation system, and there was very little industrial machinery in the state. Consequently, the more important undertakings were largely confined to the rough processing of raw materials. There were certain fairly important industries, flour milling among others, in which a single operation converted a raw material into a finished product, and such industries were adaptable to frontier regions. Either the small plants were located in areas rich in raw products, or they were moved when their markets shifted. In the mid-seventies someone brought a portable sawmill to Dallas County, where it served as a custom mill until worn out. The owner would locate the mill in a well-timbered site where it remained until the timber was cleared; then the mill would be moved to a new site.[22]

Flour milling was the state's number one nonagricultural industry in the seventies. The Census Report for 1870 enumerated 533 flour mills, and the aggregate value of their product topped second-place lumber by half a million dollars (see Appendix, Table XVII). By 1877 Dallas County alone milled flour valued at $2,750,000, which exceeded the value of the state output of seven years earlier by more than $300,000.[23] The market area for Dallas County flour was fairly extensive, ranging from Shreveport and Jefferson in the east to Austin and San Antonio in the southwest, and also including many towns along the Houston & Texas Central and International railroads.

By analyzing the data in Table XVII (Appendix), one discovers that in the course of the last three decades of the century the flour milling industry of Texas underwent considerable change. In thirty years the number of mills decreased approximately 50 per cent, but their aggregate capital investment quadrupled. During the seventies the average mill represented an investment of $2,000 and produced a per annum product valued at $4,500; but by 1900 no less than $14,800 was invested in the average mill, which produced $42,700 worth of flour annually. The small flour mill, operating as an essential part of a self-contained community, had been replaced by the large commercial establishment which marketed its products over wide areas. At the opening of the twentieth century, as far as bread was concerned, the average Texas community was no longer self-sufficient. This metamorphosis of the milling industry of the state was in strict conformity with George Tyler's description of the Bell County transition from wheat to cotton and the decline of the local flour mills.

As a system of railroads spread over the state, the production of lumber and timber replaced flour milling as the number one industry. It was estimated that the merchantable pine area of the state covered approximately 68,000 square miles, an area roughly the size of either Oklahoma or Missouri, or a little larger than the six New England states. C. W. Raines quoted a Texas authority on timber who appraised the potential yield of the forests at 347,160,-000,000 board feet for an average of 8,000 feet per acre.[24] The United States Bureau of Forestry, however, estimated the stand of marketable yellow pine at 67,508,000,000 feet,[25] only one-fifth as large as the estimate made by the state authority. Although it is true that the Raines estimate included both pine and hardwoods and the Bureau of Forestry estimated pine only, there would still have been a discrepancy of nearly a quarter-billion board feet in the two estimates had they both encompassed pine and hardwoods. Probably an in-between figure, not a great deal larger than the one set by the Bureau of Forestry, would have been correct.

At one time the state had boasted of its possession of large quantities of cypress. Since this wood was light in weight, had a long life when exposed to the elements, and was easily handled, the demand for it was great in the prerailroad era. The cypress regions were attacked with fury and the supply was quickly exhausted. Even by 1870 cypress was so scarce that practically the entire commercial output went into shingles, and from 1875 to 1901 the daily production of cypress shingles at Orange decreased from 900,000 to 50,000.[26] It has been estimated that during the last twenty years of the century the volume of milled cypress decreased by fully 98 per cent. In the same period sharp increases characterized the production of all other types of lumber.

The lack of cheap transportation which served to retard the spread of cotton also tended to stifle the development of the lumber industry. Lumbering in 1870 centered around Orange and Beaumont, with Houston on the western periphery, and yearly production slightly topped 100,000,000 board feet.[27] In the three towns, all of which were on or adjacent to navigable water, were located the large commercial mills, while small inland mills tended to meet the needs of the communities in which they were located. Some lumber and other timber products had been freighted to western settlements by ox-wagons, but the quantity moved was limited. Bull-wagon freight charges for a haul of four or five hundred miles increased the cost of lumber to ten or twenty times the mill price. But as the system of railroads spread over the state and freight rates declined, the lumber industry boomed with an expanding market. Since railroads used wood for about everything except rails, wheels, and locomotives, their construction and maintenance required vast quantities of wood products; but the growing and sustaining demand for lumber came from the building industry in treeless West Texas. As an example of what the railroads meant to the lumber industry, the *Galveston News* in 1880 named twenty sawmill towns located along the Texas & Pacific east of Dallas. These mills had a combined capacity for sawing 595,000 board feet of lumber daily. Ten years before, only a few very small mills operated in the area, and then only on intermittent schedules. Thrall says that as late as 1880 the state still consumed its total sawmill output and that Texas lumber was scarcely known to the outside world.[28]

From 1875 through the remainder of the century, lumber ranked first in tonnage moved annually by Texas railroads. During the nineties, yearly carloadings of lumber at Orange ranged between 5,404 and 9,220, and the output of forest products was exceptionally high at mills on the Texas & Pacific between Marshall and Texarkana.[29] For the fiscal year ending June 30, 1893, Texas railroads moved 2,996,706 tons of lumber, which, by volume, constituted 37 per cent of the aggregate freighted tonnage of twelve leading commodities.[30] In 1900, the lumber industry of Texas shipped 210,000 cars, or 5,995,000 tons, placing lumber far ahead of any other commodity in both tonnage and revenue for railroads;[31] and part of the mill output was then being shipped to many states throughout the Union and to numerous foreign countries.

The importance of lumbering as a Texas industry tended to increase at an accelerated pace as the nineteenth century drew to a close. During the last two or three years of the nineties 243 new sawmills began operations, bringing the 1900 total to 637. Sawmill employees made up 16.5 per cent of the industrial wage earners, and lumber products accounted for 13.6 per cent of the value of all industrial output. Fully 85 per cent of the output of lumber for the state at the end of the century was coming from 215 mills which were located within the triangle formed by Bowie, Jefferson, and Harris counties.[32]

As further evidence of the industrial importance of lumber, the Kirby Lumber Company, chartered by the state in 1901, became its first multimillion-dollar industrial concern. The firm was capitalized at $10,000,000 with the stock divided into 100,000 shares, half of them preferred and half common.[33] Conditions leading to the formation of the Kirby company have been described by Jerome Swinford, onetime secretary of the Texas Lumbermen's Association:

Three large mills at Beaumont . . . built up an enormous trade: The Beaumont Lumber Company, The Texas Tram and Lumber Company and the Reliance Lumber Company. All of these are among the mills . . . purchased by the Kirby Lumber Company, of Houston, Texas. The organization of this company, with a capital of $10,000,000 was due to the fact, that heretofore large business could not be handled in Texas without bringing together a large number of manufacturers, a thing difficult of achievement, if not under Texas statutes unlawful. Hardly a bill can come now of such magnitude that it cannot be taken care of by the Kirby Lumber Company. They will go after the foreign trade harder than ever, when they have a surplus of stock and they expect to bring to Texas for the enrichment of this section and especially of the toilers who seek their fortunes in this business, the trade and the cash of other countries and peoples.

One of the first orders secured by Mr. Kirby was for 350,000,000 feet of lumber for domestic consumption, and he refused an order for 100,-000,000 feet for export because the price was not up to standard. Previous to the advent of the Kirby Lumber Company there was no concern in Texas large enough to handle such an order, which fact operated injuriously to our manufacturers. It is the expectation of the Kirby Lumber Company to increase their capacity by erecting new mills to 1,000,000 feet or 100 carloads a day. They intend to inaugurate such economies of management, manufacture and distribution as to materially reduce the cost of the product and enable them to compete in nearly every market in the world.

The annual capacity of the Kirby Lumber Company is 400,000,000 feet.[34]

The Kirby mills were capable of producing half as much lumber as all other sawmills in the state combined. In 1901, Texas lumbermen sawed 881,000,000 feet of lumber, shipped 958,000,000 feet, and had 165,000,000 feet on hand at the end of the year.[35] From the formation of the Kirby Lumber Company on, large lumber concerns dominated the Texas industry. Swinford makes clear the two main reasons for the chartering of the Kirby company; first, to avoid prosecution under the antitrust laws which might have resulted from working agreements between lumber companies; and, second, to rip lumber out of the East Texas forest in the shortest time possible. The hardwood reserves were left intact for the time being. Through the nineteenth century Texans did not seem particularly interested in the extraction of turpentine, resins, pitch, or other by-products of pine.

Many Texans who lived outside the pine belt were intrigued by the industrial possibilities of the mesquite. Its great durability, when exposed to the elements, made it quite valuable as posts, pickets, or rails for fences. Mesquite enthusiasts described its gum as being almost identical with gum arabic; they praised its bean as an ideal livestock food; and they declared that its wood possessed the excellent qualities required in the manufacture of furniture and certain wagon and carriage parts. Dr. J. Park of Seguin, who conducted extensive experiments with mesquite bark as a possible source of tannic acid, claimed that the acid from the mesquite embalmed hides much faster than acids from oak barks. According to Dr. Park, this quality alone made mesquite tannin the ideal preservative for Texas tanneries. Park pointed out that the prevailing hot weather in Texas caused hides to begin decomposing if a quick-acting preservative were not used.[36]

In spite of its many admirers, the mesquite never became the raw material for a great Texas industry. But for generations it served many Texans as their barometer and long-range weather forecaster. Old-timers still watch for the appearance of the mesquite leaf before admitting that spring has officially arrived. And the writer can recall old cattlemen predicting the outlook for the coming winter from the mesquite bean crop — a heavy crop meant a hard winter, but a light crop heralded a mild winter.

In Texas during the last quarter of the century the number of secondary and tertiary industries remained relatively small. The great volume of freight supplied to railroads constituted a major secondary contribution of lumber. For 1902 lumber made up 25 per cent of all railroad freight tonnage, and its volume exceeded the aggregate of wheat, cotton, and livestock.[37] And planing mills formed another important secondary lumber industry. For both

1870 and 1900 planing mills were included among the ten major industries of the state (see Appendix, Table XVII). However, carpentering and building (classed as a single industry), while it was the fourth ranking industry at the beginning of the period, did not appear among the leaders at the close of the century. During the whole of the three decades, small wagon and carriage shops were located here and there over the state. But these shops probably did not consume more than a few hundred thousand board feet of lumber annually. In addition, numerous small furniture factories operated in East Texas communities. It was an era in which most furniture was fashioned from wood, but the industry consumed only a relatively small percentage of the yearly output of lumber.

Some secondary industries stemmed from flour milling; for example, Dallas as a milling center in 1885 was considered as a site for a future cracker factory,[38] and the factory came. Most of the larger towns had one or more bake shops whose products were mostly bread. The beef packing industry, too, gave rise to numerous other industries. The editor of an almanac for 1870 mentioned some of them operating in South Texas:

Soap, Glue and Neats Foot Oil. — Soap factories are in operation in Victoria, Gonzales, and we believe, in many other places, in connection with beef packeries. Glue is also made at several places in the State, and Neats Foot Oil is another of the Texas products, naturally growing out of our slaughtering establishments.[39]

In 1870 the product value of secondary industries was considerably less than $3,000,000, but by the close of the century the output of secondary industries probably exceeded $50,000,000 in value.

When the Galveston, Houston & Henderson Railroad converted from wood to coal in 1879, the displacement of wood as the fuel for Texas locomotives had begun. Within another year the Texas & Pacific began to burn coal on its western division — the portion of the road extending westward from Fort Worth. Mines adjacent to the railroad right of way had been opened in Palo Pinto County and coal had been piled parallel to the embankment before rails were laid. Within a few years all major railroads in the state were burning coal, but a few small companies continued to burn wood until about 1905.[40] As a Texas industry, coal mining owed its existence exclusively to the railroad; and, as an industry, it died when the railroad switched to oil-burning locomotives. The rise of the Texas oil industry killed the Texas coal industry. But for very nearly half a century coal constituted an important item of freight for the railroads of the state.

Coal deposits were discovered in many places over the state either from outcroppings or as the result of the digging of water wells. A new discovery usually attracted some attention and often created a little flurry of excitement. As a rule, a newspaper in reporting a coal vein included a catalogue of potential industries which might be developed when coal production reached commercial quantities. Of a coal vein located near Eagle Pass, a reporter wrote as follows:

The vein is 7½ feet thick, is good bituminous coal, and quite as good as the coal of Marietta, Ohio, or Wheeling, Virginia, and better than the coal of Indiana, Illinois or Iowa. The vein will yield two clear tons of coal to the square yard, or 8,680 tons per acre. The vein probably runs eastward to the Nueces. The vein runs 75 miles, and will contain 5,000 square miles. The coal is pure bituminous, contains very little sulphur, and could be used by blacksmiths; also for heating steam-engines, gas-works, and similar purposes. It could be brought to Indianola, where a coaling station for steamships could be established.[41]

Practically all discoveries were described as rich veins of superior coal, whereas, in reality, most of them were thin veins of inferior coal. The high sulphur and slate content of Texas coals rendered them unfit for coking; but since deposits could be mined at relatively low costs, they made available a cheap and fairly satisfactory fuel for railroad locomotives.

As early as 1879 a little coal which had been mined in Stephens County appeared on the Fort Worth market. Freighters who had hauled manufactured goods to the western counties ballasted their wagons on the return trip with Stephens County coal which they offered to buyers in Fort Worth at $11.00 per ton, $2.00 per ton below the prevailing market price for eastern coal.[42] As railroads extended into the territory where coal was mined, the lower transportation costs caused the price of coal to fall in Fort Worth and other eastern Texas towns. In his Fort Griffin paper, G. W. Robson wrote an item about coal taken from an outcropping. He said, "Yesterday we saw three wagons on the avenue loaded with coal, which was taken from the bed of the Clear Fork about one mile above the mouth of King's Creek."[43] Twenty-five bushels of coal were removed from an excavation by workers digging a water well at Bridgeport. Some of the coal had been burned, and those who experimented with it as a fuel reported it to be superior in every respect to coal taken from the McAlester mines of the Indian Territory. According to the reporter who wrote the story, a shaft was to be sunk to test commercial possibilities of the vein.[44] As a result of the discovery by well-diggers, Bridgeport became a coal mining center.

Mining operations were started at Coalville, two or three miles north of Gordon in Palo Pinto County, in the fall of 1880. The Coalville vein was an outcropping on a hillside, and thus was easily accessible to miners who removed coal from the mine in wheelbarrows, then loaded it on wagons and hauled it to the new Texas & Pacific railroad town of Gordon. Within four months the mine had been developed sufficiently to supply fuel for all T. & P. locomotives operating west of Dallas.[45] Since experienced coal miners were scarce on the frontier, the mine operators attempted to recruit seventy-five veterans from the coal fields of Pennsylvania.[46] Within five years the Coalville mine closed down because of a labor dispute; then for a brief period it reopened, with the miners also the operators, before shutting down permanently.

Shortly after the Coalville mine ceased to operate, W. W. Johnson sank a shaft a few miles away at Thurber, and within a few months the former Coalville employees had moved en masse to the Johnson mine. The workers appear to have brought their Knights of Labor local to Thurber with them. After two years Johnson became involved with the union and sold his coal properties to the Texas and Pacific Coal Company,[47] which operated them until the 1920's, when they were abandoned and the company town was scrapped.

There had been no perceptible "rushes" to the Texas coal fields, but the value of the state's coal output at the close of the nineteenth century exceeded the combined value of all other mineral products.

In 1893, Texas railroads moved 1,880,025 tons of coal, which gave coal a position second in tonnage only to lumber.[48] The development of coal fields was of considerable benefit to industries with heavy fuel costs. Largely because cheap coal had become available, the brick and clay products industry ranked number nine in value of products for 1900. As the supply of coal became more plentiful and the price lower, the number of artificial gas plants increased and gas prices decreased.[49] When a railroad switched from wood to coal, the number of stops required for fueling locomotives became fewer. That is to say, the use of coal as locomotive fuel tended to increase the average running speed of both freight and passenger trains.

Not until the late eighties, when coal production began to hit its stride, did the value of the annual production of minerals rise above $1,000,000. But by 1890 the value of mineral output had risen to $2,000,000, and it soared on to $5,300,000 at the close of the century. Throughout the period a rumor of a silver or gold discovery was always good for a newspaper story, and some papers seem to have encouraged the bonanza stories. A number of reported "strikes" created minor flurries of excitement. In the summer of 1880 a rumor spread about a gold find in Mitchell County with ore so rich it assayed $3,000 per ton. The *Galveston News* said that twenty or thirty men were working the ore and trying to keep the discovery secret.[50] Early in the nineties a rumor flew through the state to the effect that the fabulously rich "lost mine" of the Spaniards had at long last been found somewhere in Llano County.[51] But the rich mines and veins never seemed to "pan out."

Of all the minerals found in Texas, salt has enjoyed the longest history of continuous production, commercial or otherwise. In the prerailroad era small salt works or mines dotted the state and produced to meet local or community needs. Most of the works depended on solar evaporation for crystallization, though some employed a crude boiling process. One of the more elaborate plants, equipped at a cost of $5,000 with large vats and copper coils which evaporated water from the brine with steam, had a daily capacity of 500 pounds of salt.[52] A small solar evaporation works erected in Callahan County at a cost of $2,500 and operated at a cost of $600 per year claimed an annual capacity of 450,000 pounds. At that time salt sold for $1.75 per 100 pounds.[53] For a number of years the Colorado Salt Company of Colorado City exploited a salt well by means of solar evaporation.[54] In 1892, however, the company, then near bankruptcy, gained a temporary respite when the Railroad Commission of Texas granted it an exceptionally low freight rate on salt.[55] Ultimately, Grand Saline came to be the center of the salt mining industry of Texas. There, in 1889, a drilling operation penetrated a solid rock of salt to a depth of 125 feet without passing through the deposit.[56] The rock salt could be so cheaply mined that evaporation systems were not able to compete with the Grand Saline plant. Gradually evaporation plants ceased operations.

In the late seventies and early eighties, interest became widespread in the copper deposits of Baylor County. Visitors to the region included a few mining engineers from foreign countries. Some of those interested in promoting the development of copper mining claimed that ore specimens from a vein only eleven feet below the surface assayed 90 per cent copper with a trace of silver. Owners of the mineral rights were said to have been offered 11 cents per pound for the ore at the mine.[57] An item in the *Galveston News* said that experienced miners had pronounced the deposit to be the richest copper ore ever found in America, and that Wichita, Archer, and Baylor counties, all blessed with mineral wealth, could anticipate a stampede of miners and prospectors.[58] And the editor of the *Echo* printed a résumé of his visit with two men from Paris, France, who, according to their own admission, were engineers with extensive mining experience. The Frenchmen had just visited the ore beds and told Robson they were convinced that the copper mines of Northwest Texas, when developed, would prove to be a source of great wealth.[59] To date, the copper ores remain undeveloped; consequently the accuracy of the judgment of the gentlemen from Paris remains unchallenged. *Quién sabe?*

Early Texas enthusiasts always became somewhat excited over the possibilities of the state's iron ores, but no great development ensued. A few small foundries made use of the ores in the manufacture of stoves and plows, and they turned out some military equipment for the Confederacy during the Civil War; but these were not large-scale developments. The lack of coke hampered development of the iron deposits. Texas coal was not suitable for coking and the freight charges on long distance shipments of coke made smelting unprofitable. By using charcoal as a fuel, the state prison at Rusk smelted $10,000 worth of iron for the contractors who erected the capitol building.[60] George A. Kelly, who had offered to make a Grange co-operative of his foundry near Jefferson, had probably been one of the more successful consumers of Texas iron ore.

Quarrying became a relatively profitable, if small, industry during the closing decades of the century. Both limestone and granite were quarried in considerable quantities. For construction of the new state capitol, some 300,000,000 pounds of granite were removed from the Burnet quarries. In addition, almost 1,500,000 tons of granite and limestone went into the building of the Galveston jetties.[61]

During the seventies, eighties, and nineties, the appearance of utilities and service establishments heralded a further movement of the economy away from the era in which the sole concern of man had been food, shelter, and raiment. In 1872, the telegraph placed Dallas in instant communication with the eastern half of the country.[62] Before the decade closed the military had thrown telegraph lines across the state to El Paso and to points in New Mexico and Arizona.[63] Because wooden telegraph poles across the western plains were constant targets for vandals, both red and white, they had to be replaced with iron pipes. In Bell County a group of citizens organized the Belton Telegraph Company for the purpose of keeping Central Texas communities posted with up-to-the-minute information on the cotton market. This service became available not only to Belton, but also to Salado, Corn Hill, Georgetown, Round Rock, Lampasas, and Gatesville.[64]

A newspaper advertisement outlining the 1879 Texas itinerary of the London Circus emphasized a major event of the decade. The advertisement announced wild animal acts, daring trapeze aerialists, and other performances common to circuses; but the feature attraction, the amazing spectacle, said the circus ad, was "Our

Own Mighty Electric Light." The circus carried a mobile power unit which furnished electricity for illuminating the grounds and tents with carbon filament lights. Those who prepared advertising copy briefly described certain amazing characteristics of the "new marvel." Among the advertisement's more intriguing lines about light were: "IT MELTS STEEL WITHOUT APPARENT HEAT." "The Sun, Moon, and Stars pale into insignificance in comparison. It brings to the soul of man a realizing sense of the glory and splendor of eternal, glorious, Heaven." "IT IS REALLY A MIRACLE, A WONDER." "Thousands of people who never attended a Circus visited these shows expressly to see the effect of this Heaven-born light. It is worth traveling FIVE HUNDRED MILES to witness. NOTHING IN THE WORLD'S HISTORY CAN COMPARE WITH IT."[65] As the London Circus toured the state in the fall of 1879, many Texans blinked and stared in open-mouthed awe at the "glorious, Heaven-born light." But the circus just barely got under the wire in capitalizing on the electric light, because shortly after its visit to Texas, Galveston installed a generator and Galvestonians began discarding their coal oil lamps. And within six years local power companies had been organized in Temple, Belton, and Fort Worth. Moreover, Houston was in the process of electrifying its street railways.[66]

However, Texans seemed to take to the telephone much quicker than they did to the electric light; consequently telephone systems were installed at a much faster pace than were electric generating plants. Within four years after Bell exhibited and demonstrated his telephone at the Philadelphia Centennial, Galveston had installed 150 telephones, and 45 more were in use at Houston.[67] Sometime during the fall of 1882, long distance telephone service became available between Fort Worth and Palo Pinto,[68] and within a few months a number of other communities had been included in the service. These early telephones proved to be expensive gadgets. By the mid-eighties some towns were dispensing with their systems because so many subscribers were unable to pay the rental.[69] Also before the close of the seventies, the street railway had become a commonplace. In fact, one in Palestine had been in operation long enough to go broke and sell its equipment to San Antonio.[70]

Before 1880 a number of ice plants were in operation, and

artificial ice was no longer a novelty to residents of towns. But the manufacture of ice was not so commonplace that a description of the process had lost its news value. The *News* carried a story saying:

> An Ice machine in Dallas produces ice cakes 30 feet long and six feet wide, weighing from 10,000 to 12,000 pounds each. They are formed by freezing fine rain or spray after the manner of an icicle. When the operation is completed, the bottom and sides of the cake are thawed loose from the inclined plane, and the cake slides out on a platform where it is cut into chunks six feet square. Four cakes a day are frozen. The works cost $30,000.[71]

In 1879, two ice companies operating in Austin engaged in a price war, driving the price to the then extremely low level of one cent per pound. A newspaper wag could not resist the quip, "I infer they are trying to freeze each other out."[72] On the other hand, the people of Belton, served by a small plant of 1,000 pounds daily capacity, paid ten cents per pound for delivered ice. Machinery for the Belton plant had been removed there from the Rio Grande where in ante-bellum days it had equipped the state's first artificial ice plant.[73]

The advent of artificial ice and refrigeration revolutionized the livestock and beef slaughtering industries. About 1870 a letter widely publicized in Texas and written by General D. A. Maury of New Orleans described a visit by the General to a New Orleans warehouse. The writer said the building was filled with beef slaughtered near Indianola, Texas, some nine days previously but still free of evident taint or sourness. The meat, continued the General, who evidently expected many readers to doubt his attestation as to its excellence, was as fresh and sweet as if it had been butchered less than nine hours. Maury had visited a refrigerated warehouse at which the inside temperature remained a constant thirty-five degrees in spite of an outside temperature which registered a blistering ninety degrees. The writer avowed these facts to be conclusive proof that refrigeration had been proved a success. General Maury visualized the menus of the world freed of salt dishes. Instead, great refrigerated ships would move the sweet fresh beef from slaughterhouses in Indianola to New Orleans, Liverpool, Ceylon, Guinea, and to all parts of the world, retaining in the shipping all the freshness, sweetness, juices, and flavor of the meat. The General even imagined sailors breakfasting daily on juicy tenderloin steaks, forever freed from the ill effects of scurvy.[74]

In the subsequent history of meat processing, not Indianola, as visualized by Maury, but the great inland packeries prepared fresh beef for the world markets. In the late seventies the *Echo* reprinted an item from the New York *Express* which described the conversion of a leviathan steamer, the *Great Eastern*, into a refrigerated ship. Because of its titanic size the *Great Eastern* had been unprofitable as a passenger ship. As a refrigerated ship it would be able to carry a cargo of 2,200 beeves and 3,600 muttons from Texas to London.[75] Beginning about 1876, the exportation of frozen beef increased sharply.

Following the perfecting of the refrigerated car, the dressed beef industry tended to shift from South to North Texas. Those striving to build a satisfactory refrigerated car consistently failed until they discovered that the car had to be ventilated. Once that discovery was made, a proper method of ventilation had to be developed. A Denison company which began to ship beef by rail in 1875 failed because the cars were not ventilated and the meat spoiled.[76] But within two years Fort Worth had successfully shipped fifty frozen beeves to St. Louis in a ventilated Tiffany car, and the slaughterhouse and cold storage buildings of the bankrupt Denison company were being renovated for a resumption of operations.[77] By 1885 the American Refrigerated Transit Company alone moved four hundred cars of fresh frozen beef from Texas annually.[78]

Business leaders of Fort Worth dreamed of developing their city into a meat packing center, but encountered great difficulty in making those dreams realities. Not local businessmen but Swift and Armour ultimately established Fort Worth permanently as a packing center. In 1877 the city fathers looked forward to a visit from John Jones of Louisville, who was inspecting desirable sites for locating a large packing concern.[79] Either Jones did not pay the expected visit, or the men of Fort Worth failed to sell him on their city, because he did not select Fort Worth for the plant. After six years a company acquired a site on which it planned to erect a meat refrigerating works of sufficient size to process 250 head of cattle daily and equipped to utilize all by-products of the animal including the hides, for which a tannery was to be built.[80] From the beginning the company encountered financial difficulties, and two years after it had bought the site its officers were pleading with Fort Worth residents to raise $40,000 to purchase the plant. Since the community had already donated $75,000 to the company, the request for additional funds did not strike a very responsive chord — even though the plant was to be sold at auction to foreign (Chicago) interests if the $40,000 could not be raised.[81] While the dickering went on as to the possible fate of the meat plant, I. Dahlman, of Fort Worth, announced that he had closed a five-year contract with an English firm in which he agreed to deliver 3,000 dressed beeves every two weeks on dock at Galveston.[82] On the eve of the collapse of the cattle boom, and, no doubt, largely because of the news of his big contract, Dahlman succeeded in soliciting enough money to buy the plant from the Chicago group.[83] At the close of the eighties, the meat processing establishment was not in operation.

In the nineties a group of local businessmen incorporated the Fort Worth Dressed Meat and Packing Company with a capital of $500,000.[84] Before all of the funds could be raised and the plant wholly completed, the depression of the nineties hit the country.[85] In spite of the adverse economic conditions under which the company began, it managed to operate for a number of years, supplying meat products to a limited local market. By the turn of the century, however, the Fort Worth Dressed Meat and Packing Company had closed down. Fort Worth's role as an important meat processing center still lay in the future.

At one time or another small meat packeries had operated in various towns over the state, the earlier ones usually in proximity to the coast. In 1876, a cannery operating at Lavaca was "putting up from sixty-five to seventy-five beeves per day in six and two pound cans."[86] Another plant reported that it had completed processing 2,000,000 two-pound cans from 15,000 beeves.[87] Communities either obtained fresh beef from local slaughterhouses or relied on beef packeries for canned or salt beef. The bulk of meat consumed by Texans was home-processed and came from the family smokehouse.

But when scientists and engineers perfected refrigerated transportation, fresh meat could be shipped the world over.[88] The dressed beef industry then became centralized in large concerns to the detriment of small slaughterhouses and canneries. Local butchers, abattoirs, and canneries put up a vigorous fight to forestall the encroachment on their domain by the frozen beef industry. Community processors were given full support by railroads, since the roads preferred to move the live animal, which weighed almost twice as much as a frozen beef carcass. In the battle against frozen meat, railroads refused to furnish refrigerator cars and raised dressed beef freight rates until they were almost double the rates on live animals. Not to be deterred, large packing houses supplied their own cars, ultimately forcing the roads to give up the fight.[89] When the refrigerated car appeared, many stockmen were of the opinion that slaughterhouses would be moved to the range country, but the men of the cattle country were unable to finance the projects.[90] Other obstacles on the range helped keep packing houses in cities.

Since the day De Soto's men made use of a gummy ooze from Sabine Bay to calk their weather-beaten ships, white men had known of the presence of petroleum in Texas.[91] But other than for calking and medicinal purposes no use had been made of the oil until the mid-nineteenth century. Development of the state's first producing oil field followed the discovery of oil at Nacogdoches some two or three years before the famous Drake discovery in Pennsylvania. Periodically, in one section of the state or another, small gas pockets or oil pools had been discovered, often by accident when water wells were being dug or drilled. Early in 1880, three wells in Brown County, varying in depth from fifty to one hundred feet, produced about one hundred barrels of oil daily.[92] The petroleum was marketed locally, by the bottle for medicinal purposes, or by the gallon as a lubricant. By the gallon the price was much cheaper than by the bottle. In December, 1891, a crew, while in the process of drilling a water well near Hicks, in Shackelford County, accidentally discovered a "bountiful flow of oil" at a depth of 148 feet.[93] Twenty years later an oil field had been developed around the discovery which the local chamber of commerce advertised as "The Greatest Shallow Oil Field in the World."

Development of petroleum on a commercial basis of any significance dates from 1894, when an artesian company, while drilling
for water at Corsicana, struck an oil sand at 1,030 feet. Since the
company had a contract for a water well, it quickly sealed off the
oil and proceeded to drill deeper in search of a water stream. In
the meantime, a local real estate firm, after deciding that oil production might prove profitable, negotiated mineral leases on a block
of 30,000 acres in the neighborhood of the discovery. Members of
the firm persuaded Guffey & Galey of Pittsburgh, who also held
oil interests in Kansas, to participate in the venture. Drilling contracts were awarded and the firm went into the risky business of
wildcatting for oil. The first two wells were virtual failures, but a
third, completed in the spring of 1896, came in a producer at twenty-two barrels daily. Within two years, visitors to Corsicana described the area as a forest of derricks. In its first year of production,
output from five wells making up the Corsicana field totaled 1,450
barrels of oil,[94] with production jumping to 66,000 barrels in the
second year, and then, for 1900, leaping to 836,000 barrels.[95] Corsicana oil became a glut on the market. In exhaustive efforts to
dispose of the petroleum flowing from the wells, producers poured
it on the ground, spilled it, wasted it, stored it, and even sold some
of it as fuel to consumers in Corsicana, Dallas, Austin, and San
Antonio; but sales fell far behind production. Wasteful practices
in the oil fields of Navarro County led to the passage, in March,
1899, of a regulatory law governing drilling and other oil field
practices. The measure prescribed specific procedures to be followed in casing wells, and spelled out rules designed to prevent
the wastage of gas.[96]

By 1897, conditions in the Corsicana field had indeed become
chaotic. As a move toward bringing some order out of chaos, J. S.
Cullinan, of Pennsylvania, agreed to lay pipelines, construct storage tanks, and install a refinery.[97] Cullinan created the embryo
from which grew the giant Magnolia Petroleum Company. It was
also Cullinan who organized the predecessor to the even larger
Texas Company. Modern oil refining in Texas dates from the
completion of the million-dollar Cullinan refinery, which by 1901
was refining 1,500 barrels of crude oil daily. As drilling crews

brought in producing well after producing well in the Navarro field, the price of petroleum fell steadily, ultimately sinking to fifty cents per barrel or less; but after the Cullinan refinery began operations the price quickly climbed back to ninety-eight cents. As a possible means for broadening the crude oil market, the Cullinan interests, in co-operation with the Cotton Belt Railroad, undertook to develop an oil-burning mechanism for railroad locomotives. The experiments proved successful when, in 1898, a Cotton Belt passenger locomotive made a run on steam generated by an oil burner in its firebox.[98]

Nothing is subtracted from the importance of Navarro County in the development of oil in Texas when we say that, significant as Corsicana was, it served primarily as a forerunner of the Beaumont field. Development of the Navarro County fields came from the efforts of imaginative men after an accidental discovery of oil. The discovery of Spindletop at Beaumont came from use of the accumulated technological knowledge of a mining engineer, which added up to the conviction that petroleum should accumulate around a salt dome. The discovery of oil at Spindletop resulted from drilling done with the deliberate intent to find an oil pool.

Patillo Higgins, in 1892, had attempted the first Beaumont oil well, but inability to drill through quicksand caused him to abandon the test at 300 feet. Nine years later Captain A. F. Lucas, an Austrian immigrant who had been operating for some years as a mining engineer, successfully completed the work begun by Higgins. For a number of years, Lucas had worked with salt domes in Louisiana, and his work there was responsible for his success at Spindletop. The Louisiana experiences convinced him that oil should be present in the vicinity of the great salt dome popularly known as Spindletop. Furthermore, Lucas had had plenty of experience with the hazards of drilling in quicksand, an experience which became an invaluable asset at Spindletop. Virtually every foremost geologist in the country, with one exception, pronounced Lucas a fool. A top official of Standard Oil had previously boasted that he could drink all the oil found west of the Mississippi. In the face of such formidable opposition, Captain Lucas met with great difficulty in raising the necessary funds for drilling the well. Eventually he sought financial backing in Pennsylvania, where he perfected a working agreement with the prospecting, or wildcatting, firm of Guffey & Galey.[99] Actually, Guffey & Galey were a front for the Mellon interests, who put up the money after assurance from the Rockefellers that they were not interested in Texas. The Pennsylvania firm contracted with Hammill Brothers, pioneer rotary drillers, to sink the well. The rotary drilling process had been developed about 1892 in the territory of the Dakotas,[100] and in subsequent years had proved very effective in drilling through troublesome formations such as quicksand.[101] The know-how of Lucas and the Hammill Brothers plus the gambling instinct of Guffey & Galey insured success at Spindletop.

Wildcat drilling began on the Lucas lease in the fall of 1900, and at midmorning of January 10, 1901, very unexpectedly Spindletop "blew in":

At exactly 10:30 a.m., the well that made Beaumont famous burst upon the astonished view of those engaged in boring it, with a volume of water, sand, rocks, gas and oil that sped upward with such tremendous force as to tear the crossbars of the derrick to pieces, and scattered the mixed properties from its bowels, together with timbers, pieces of well casing, etc., for hundreds of feet in all directions.

For nine days the phenomenon was the wonder and puzzle of the world. It flowed unceasingly and with ever increasing force and volume until when it was finally controlled it was shooting upward a tower of pure crude oil, of the first quality, quite two hundred feet, and spouting in wanton waste 70,000 barrels of oil per day.[102]

For nine wild days, Spindletop sprayed the surrounding countryside with an estimated 70,000 to 100,000 barrels daily. Precise quantity of the flow seems immaterial, since the largest daily flow from any previous well in the United States had been rated at 6,000 barrels.[103] The Beaumont well was, up to that time, the world's largest producing oil well outside the Baku field of Russia. Insofar as single events are concerned, nothing else in the first half of the twentieth century gave such a stimulus to the industrial development of Texas as did Spindletop. Nonetheless, editorial staffs of one or two North Texas dailies did not deem the discovery of sufficient importance to merit a front-page story. In the hectic and exciting days which followed completion of the well, a page-two story in a

Dallas paper gave the flow as 16,000 barrels daily, probably the lowest contemporary estimate of the discovery well's production.

Except for these skeptics in North Texas, Spindletop electrified the whole nation, especially members of the oil fraternity. Leaders of the industry, those motivated by curiosity, many in search of fortunes, and others looking for jobs stormed Beaumont. Spindletop probably did more to preserve competition within the industry than all of the Supreme Court's trust-busting orders. Fantastic prices were bid and paid for land, royalties, and leases as far as 150 miles from the new field. Immediately after the well came in, one near-by tract of forty acres went to a group of speculators for $40,000. They drilled a well and sold it for $1,250,000, but retained the original forty acres with the exception of the spot on which the derrick stood.[104] In the year 1901, the state of Texas chartered 491 oil companies authorized to issue $239,639,999 in capital stock. In that year the Houston Oil Company, chartered for $30,000,000, became the largest industrial corporation created in the state to that time.[105] For a number of years Texas had been authorizing corporate capital, exclusive of railroads, of $20,000,000 to $30,000,-000 annually. The Spindletop year sent the capital authorizations skyrocketing to $300,000,000.

With Spindletop, Captain Lucas, Guffey & Galey, and the Hammill Brothers initiated a new industrial revolution, or a new phase of the old revolution. The impact of the flood of oil was instantaneous. Four railroad companies serving Beaumont and its vicinity immediately began converting locomotives to oil burners. Schumpeter called this "creative destruction," creating a new fuel and destroying or making a sick industry of coal. With the development of the Corsicana field, oil and petroleum products were shipped in tins and drums; but these were too small and bothersome to handle the flood of oil at Spindletop. By 1904, at least 1,500 tank cars had been built to move Texas oil. Fleets of tankers were being fabricated and port facilities dredged and readied to provide accommodations to move oil by sea. In and around the Beaumont area, foundations had been laid for refineries, some of them ultimately to be classed among the largest in the world. A beginning had been made in burying in the bosom of Texas prairies a veinlike network of pipelines through which would flow hundreds of millions of barrels of "liquid gold," or its refined products. Foundries and machine shops began to discard wagon axles, stoves, and plows in order that they might manufacture drilling tools and other oil field equipment. Some of these concerns, Hughes Tools for one, grew large, ultimately providing fortunes which built airplane plants and motion picture studios. Temporary oil field camps, small towns, large towns, medium-sized cities, and the South's metropolis became realities because of oil and its secondary and tertiary industries. Counties impoverished by arid and semiarid conditions and leached land became fabulously wealthy. Cotton farmers at the pauper level became overnight millionaires. Texas became the land of the "new rich." And because of oil, the drought of the mid-twentieth century did not prove so disastrous to Central and West Texas as had the dry period back in 1885-87.

Oil brought into existence an entire new field of law — law built around mineral rights, oil, and gas. It opened vast new frontiers in the field of chemistry. Petroleum geology became a profession, and petroleum engineering developed as a separate specialized field. Production and processing of oil demanded great quantities of lumber and timber, mighty hempen ropes, endless miles and innumerable sizes of steel cable, mountains of pipe and casing varying from less than an inch to as much as three feet in diameter, and vast warehouses filled with a host of other supplies. As the productive process became more extended, the list of industries connected directly or indirectly with petroleum grew longer and longer. Before Spindletop, Texas industries had depended on easily exploited resources of farm, ranch, and forest — raw materials which could be moved directly from their sources for relatively simple processing into finished products. After Spindletop, the industrial structure became involved as a part of the long, indirect, roundabout process of production, through feeder plants, subassemblies, and the secondary and tertiary industries which characterize the complex industrial state.

XII

The Big Change

THE cutting edges of family farms hew through wildernesses leaving in their wake successions of agricultural empires. Texas was no exception. In the short generation which followed 1870, a Texas wilderness of 100,000,000 acres became an empire under the influence of western civilization. The three-decade sweep of farmers, sheepmen, and cattlemen across the plains and prairies so thoroughly branded Texas as a great agricultural state that other phases and aspects of development tend to be obscured by the enormous increase in agricultural output. To be sure, agricultural interests had dominated, and for a time continued to dominate, both the political and economic life of the state. But by the turn of the century a complex and growing superstructure of industry had firmly attached itself to the agricultural base. The census for 1870 classed 95 per cent of the population of Texas as rural, practically the same ratio as the 1790 census gave for the nation. After thirty years census enumerators found only 83 per cent of the population in rural areas, which is to say that the urban percentage had more than tripled.[1] Furthermore, the population density of three to the square mile in 1870, by a Bureau of the Census definition, placed Texas in the category of frontier states; but a 1900 density of eleven persons to the square mile removed Texas from the frontier classification.[2]

Of more significance than the great expansion in agricultural production was the functional revolution on the family farm. That is to say, at the beginning of the period the farmer's bank account was in his smokehouse; but for thirty years the farmer had been slowly transferring his smokehouse to his bank account. The process had not been completed, but there would be no counterrevolution. In 1870, cotton as the wholly commercial farm crop stood isolated and alone bearing the brunt of vituperation, damnation, and hatred. The farm family consumed virtually everything else it raised. An occasional surplus of wheat or corn went to market, but the primary intent of the farmer had been to produce a year's supply of grains, hay, vegetables, fruits, and meats for consumption by his household and barnyard. Only in West Texas did cattle supplement cotton as a strictly commercial product. In the eastern part of the state, both beef and milch cattle served to round out the requirements of the self-contained home. Raw products constituted the bulk of all commodities either consumed or marketed by Texans. Texans of 1870 ate home-butchered meats with home-baked bread, made of home-rendered lard, and meal or flour from home-grown corn or wheat, along with a variety of fruits and vegetables either home-canned or picked fresh from orchards and gardens, and home-grown poultry and eggs. Most beef sold on the hoof, and cotton went to market after being ginned. Much of the surplus wheat found its way to a custom mill, the farmer often marketing his own flour. Most marketable timber sold either as lumber or as shingles. Since raw materials constitute cheap products in contrast to finished goods, the annual value of the output per Texan was not large.

After thirty years many discernible changes had appeared in the economy. Cotton, as a commercial crop, no longer occupied a lonely, isolated position. A number of newcomers now shared the market place with the woolly plant. The status of wheat had changed; it had become almost a full hundred per cent market crop, a position it shared with rice and sugar cane. Most of the hay produced on irrigated farms went to market. Poultry and egg sales had greatly increased. In East Texas both beef and milch cattle were being extended into the commercial field. The state's leading industry, lumbering, turned out only a semifinished product;

but two other industries among the top nine, namely, railroad car shops and planing mills, converted some lumber into finished goods. The products of lumber, in one form or another, accounted for approximately one-fourth of all industrial output in 1900. In the thirty years production of liquors and malts became one of the nine major industries, supplementing flour milling as a processor of grain.[3] But even in 1900 two-thirds of the value of Texas manufactured products still came from industries producing raw materials; consequently the per capita value of output remained at a low level.

The rapid spread of commercial agriculture had been accompanied by a sharp increase in the volume of all agricultural produce, which resulted in serious maladjustments. These disturbances compelled the owners to reallocate land to more efficient usages. In part, reallocation gradually shifted wheat production from the southern part of the state to the north and west where soil and climate were much more suitable for its growth. And because of its high per acre value, cotton production expanded in every section of the state. Furthermore, the commercial crops of cotton and wheat made serious inroads on livestock ranges in the northwest. This allocation of larger acreages to crops best adapted to the land tended to reverse allocation practices of self-contained farms. Regions planted in well-adapted crops exclusively became an important factor in the expansion of agricultural productivity. When countless days of toil and sweat, plus a good season and little damage from pests, resulted in a "bountiful harvest," the self-reliant, independent farmer enjoyed the comforts of plenty; that is, he had an ample supply of meat and bread to last a year. But countless days of toil and sweat plus a good season and few pests often resulted in lower farm prices, which in turn reduced the cash income of the commercial farmer. Under the system of commercial agriculture, the farmer came face to face with the paradox, "poverty in the midst of plenty." This paradox, contrary to his past agrarian experiences, did not make sense and left the farmer puzzled and confused.

As the farmer struggled with his dilemma, first the Grange and then the Alliance appeared as mediums through which concerted efforts might be channeled toward solving the new agrarian problems. Much of the work done by these organizations was futile in that solutions were sought in light of past experience. Seldom are new problems unraveled by this method, but people seem to relish worrying and fretting over their new problems. Among those who proposed old remedies were agrarian and nonagrarian groups. They insisted that the farmer should live at home through diversification and plant a little cotton for clear profit. Followers of this school held that a solution to all agrarian problems lay in perpetuating self-sufficiency. Others argued that the farmer had been sacrificed to the monopoly — or did they mean the corporation? Monopoly paid low prices for farm produce, and kept them low; monopoly charged the farmer high prices for finished goods, and kept them high. Thus, farmer relief depended on the degree to which monopoly and monopoly practices could be regulated or destroyed. Quite naturally farmer-sponsored consumer and producer co-operatives would be proposed as devices for circumventing monopolies, and for narrowing the gap between prices received and prices paid by the farmer. Regardless of a lack of experienced managers or of adequate capital funds, these projects were launched forthwith. Of all proposals directed toward resolving agrarian perplexities, not one touched the fundamental difficulty.

The sudden and permanent increase in agricultural productivity heralded significant changes throughout the whole social and economic structure. Henceforth, smaller and smaller percentages of the population would be needed on the farms. The surplus agricultural population could either remain on the farm, becoming more and more impoverished, or give up the fight and migrate to town. The growing agricultural output became sufficient not only to feed a larger nonfarm population, but also to supply raw materials in quantity for further processing, which resulted in a greater volume of manufactured goods. The conservative nature of man seems always to resist readjustment; here Texans were no exception. Introduction of farm machinery and equipment, enlargement of the family-sized farm, development of an adequate system of agricultural credit, and construction of one or two new systems of transportation worked toward correcting agricultural maladjustments; but the transition required decades for completion. For making necessary readjustments, a generation was too short a period; so from day to day the individual farmer wrestled with seemingly insoluble problems.

Oblivious of the turmoil for which they were largely responsible, cotton and western cattle continued as leaders of the ever increasing number of commercial products of farm and ranch. In terms of value, as has been previously noted, cotton had no really close competitor. However, cotton in practically every section of the state and cattle in the western half exercised a considerable influence over other industries, both agricultural and nonagricultural. It was the prospect of cotton tonnage that lured railroads into and across the state; or, more accurately, it had been the great potential volume of freight in terms of cotton and cattle that gave stimulus to railroad construction. At virtually every railroad town and village had been erected loading pens for cattle and a loading platform for cotton. Moreover, cattle and railroads spelled the major difference between agricultural development in East Texas and that in West Texas. In the east agriculture originated as a self-contained system which gradually evolved into a commercial system, while from the outset cattle launched western agriculture on a commercial basis. During the thirty-year period, commercial crops in general tended to increase in value and quantity by much greater percentages than crops produced strictly for home consumption. The increases in cotton, cattle, and wheat alone had been sufficient to sustain agriculture as the leading industry of the state. Some estimates place the value of cotton produced in 1900 above the total value of all manufactured goods.[4]

Few Texas residents of the last thirty years of the nineteenth century fully appreciated either the magnitude of the economic revolution taking place, or the rapidity with which readjustments were being made. Relatively, urban population grew much faster than rural. In 1870 urban population represented 5 per cent of the whole, but by 1910 fully 25 per cent of the people lived in towns. Furthermore, the growth of urban population tended to accelerate with the passage of time; between 1890 and 1910 urban population increased 170 per cent, while rural growth was only 60 per cent.[5] These significant shifts in population were accompanied by important changes in nonagricultural industries. In the self-contained economy of the seventies, products from 533 flour and grist mills accounted for a third of the value of the goods turned out by the ten leading industries. The next five industries, in descending order of value of output, were: sawed lumber, packed beef, carpentering and building, blacksmithing, and butchering. The value of output for each of the ten leading industries averaged $843,000. By 1900, lumbering had become the leading manufacturing industry in number of employees, value of products, capital invested, and tonnage of freight. At that, lumber products equaled in value only 14 per cent of the cotton crop for the year. At the end of the period, cottonseed oil and cake had become the second most important manufacturing industry in value of output, and flour milling had dropped to third. Moreover, flour mills had ceased to be custom mills, and although their number had been reduced by half, the value of flour produced had risen by approximately 400 per cent. The value of products per industry for the nine leaders in 1900 averaged $7,250,000, representing an 800 per cent increase in thirty years. Over the three decades only lumber and flour managed to retain their positions among the six leading industries.[6]

All the foregoing changes were in keeping with the growth in importance of towns and cities. Rapidly growing towns created a rising demand for lumber, while technology converted cottonseed from refuse, or waste, into a relatively valuable resource, and the shift of wheat production to commercial farms destroyed the small flour mills. The development of inland transportation opened the interior to commercial agriculture and shifted manufacturing centers from the coastal region to the north and west. Within thirty years Galveston County fell from number one manufacturing county to sixth place, while Harris moved from second to first and Dallas rose from ninth to second. El Paso, Bexar, and Tarrant, third, fourth, and fifth ranking industrial counties respectively in 1900, had not been among the top ten at the opening of the period.[7]

For three decades of transition, Texas agricultural and manufacturing industries encountered no sudden or violent economic shocks or revolutionary upheavals. From the standpoint of agriculture, steadily falling commodity prices had perpetuated a depressed atmosphere, but the long downward price trend ended just prior to the close of the nineteenth century. An improvement in the economic status of agricultural interests was evidently at hand. Cotton, cattle, and lumber seemed to be securely entrenched in their roles as agricultural and industrial leaders. But at exactly 10:30 A.M. on January 10, 1901, the eruption of an oil well at Beaumont shook the economy of the state to its core. The blowing-in of the Lucas gusher at Spindletop reshuffled completely the alignment of industries and sounded an ominous challenge to the economic leadership of cotton. In fact, the chain reaction touched off by the gushing discovery well of the Beaumont oil field ultimately caused agriculture to relinquish leadership to manufacturing. The earlier twenty-two-barrel discovery well at Corsicana led to the development of an extensive oil field, the laying of pipelines, and the erection of refineries. Exploration in the Corsicana field had been orderly and sedate compared to the chaotic conditions accompanying the fury with which the Beaumont field was ripped open in the wake of its 100,000-barrel discovery well. In 1896 Texas produced an estimated 1,000 barrels of oil; but in 1901 petroleum output leaped to 4,400,000 barrels, while production for the following year was estimated at 21,000,000 barrels.[8]

The ten-million-dollar Kirby Lumber Company, a Texas industrial giant, was quickly relegated to second place by the formation of the thirty-million-dollar Houston Oil Company. In May, 1901, alone, authorized capital for oil companies chartered in the state exceeded the previous year's total for such corporations by 500 per cent. The $240,000,000 in authorized capital for oil companies chartered by the state during 1901 was roughly six times greater than for all companies chartered in the preceding biennium.[9] As we have seen, S. G. Reed gave cotton credit for inspiring the building of the first Texas railroad and lending encouragement to the construction of many others; but cotton shared these roads with passengers and innumerable other commodities of freight. Not so with oil. Petroleum commanded its own exclusive transportation system, a network of pipelines from oil fields to refineries, and from refineries to major distribution centers. Moreover, oil tonnage moved by rail quickly replaced lumber as the number one item of railroad freight.

For many years petroleum and petroleum products constituted fully 10 per cent of all freight handled by Texas railroads.[10] If the movement of pipe and of oil field and refinery equipment had also been credited to petroleum tonnage, its percentage of freight would have been even higher. For 1944 the personnel engaged in petroleum refining and in lumbering numbered 23,000 and 15,000 respectively, but the value of refinery products exceeded those of lumbering twenty times.[11]

Even though Spindletop gave the oil industry a great boost toward eventually replacing cotton as the dominant element in the economy of Texas, probably more Texans still rely on cotton for a livelihood than on any other single industry. It has been a number of years, however, since the cotton crop exceeded in value the annual production of petroleum. The Lucas well not only converted petroleum from an illuminating oil to a fuel oil industry, but also generated a momentum which accelerated all industrial development within the state. Twenty years after Spindletop the industrial output of the state exceeded the value of its agricultural produce, and for 1944 the value of manufactured goods was five times greater than the aggregate produce of farm and ranch.[12]

The development of Texas during the last quarter of the nineteenth century may well epitomize growth in any dynamic economy. Texans borrowed freely and did some innovating on their own. Neither cotton nor cattle were native to the state, but her soils were rich in food elements required for cotton culture, and with the coming of cheap inland transportation Texas assumed the position of leader among cotton producing states. Texas longhorns had come from Spain, but Texans spread them over the states of the western plains and mountain regions to seed the great cattle ranches. Texas cattlemen in turn found it necessary to improve the quality of their herds, and for improved breeds they turned again to Europe and to the eastern half of the United States. Timber was native to the region, but its uses and processing techniques had been learned centuries earlier. Likewise oil, even though indigenous to the region, had been of no great commercial importance until scientists in eastern universities discovered that crude oil refined easily and produced an excellent illuminating oil. Finally, the drilling machinery which brought in the first wells had been developed outside the state, but, beginning with Spindletop, Texas oil field workers made their contributions to the techniques and know-how of the petroleum industry and introduced new tools necessary to future exploratory operations. In addition to touching off an industrial upheaval in Texas, Spindletop oil burning in fireboxes and exploding in combustion chambers revitalized the industrial world, revolutionized the whole technique of agriculture, and stepped up the tempo of life for man everywhere.

In 1870, less than half the state of Texas had been settled, and that by self-contained farmers, while the other half remained a wilderness. By 1900 the entire state had been transformed into an empire with commercial agriculture the prevailing industry. The transition had been fraught with hardships, and readjustments had met with stubborn resistance. Throughout the period the economic importance of industry steadily and persistently gained on that of agriculture. But not even the phenomenal increase in cotton production and commercialized farming disturbed the existing economic structure or changed the old order as did the Lucas gusher. Beginning at 10:30 in the morning of January 10, 1901, Texas veered sharply toward an industrial economy. The doom of agricultural leadership in Texas was sealed at Spindletop.

Appendix

TABLE I

Wholesale Prices of Farm and Nonagricultural Products 1860-1901.
Excerpted from "Wholesale Prices of Farm and Nonagricultural
Products, United States, 1798-1949." Index Numbers
(1910-1914 = 100) *

Year	Farm products	Nonfarm products	Year	Farm products	Nonfarm products
1860	77	101	1881	89	109
1861	75	98	1882	99	110
1862	86	113	1883	87	107
1863	113	150	1884	82	99
1864	162	214	1885	72	92
1865	148	210	1886	68	91
1866	140	197	1887	71	92
1867	133	176	1888	75	92
1868	138	163	1889	67	89
1869	128	163	1890	71	86
1870	112	146	1891	76	84
1871	102	146	1892	69	78
1872	108	160	1893	72	78
1873	103	156	1894	63	71
1874	102	139	1895	62	74
1875	99	127	1896	56	74
1876	89	120	1897	60	70
1877	89	111	1898	63	74
1878	72	100	1899	64	85
1879	72	100	1900	71	89
1880	80	113	1901	74	86

Compiled from Warren and Pearson, 1798-1889; Bureau of Labor
Statistics, 1890 to date.

* 1950 *Agricultural Outlook Charts*, Bureau of Agricultural Economics, October, 1949,
U.S. Department of Agriculture, Washington, D.C., p. 10.

TABLE II

Texas Farm Averages, Acres, Improved Acres, Farm Values, Per Acre Values, and Implement Values, 1870-1900 °

Year	Average area of farms in acres †	Average number improved acres per farm	Average value per farm	Average value per acre of farm land	Average value per farm of implements †
1870	301.0	48.5	$1,322	$ 5.49	$44
1880	208.4	72.6	1,470	7.06	52
1890	225.3	91.0	2,420	10.74	60
1900	357.2	55.6	2,733	7.65	85

° *United States Census, 1900*, Vol. V: *Agriculture*, pp. 688-709.
† *U.S. Census 1910: Abstract of the Census with Supplement for Texas*, p. 667.

TABLE III

Texas Averages: Per Acre Yields, Per Bushel Farm Prices for December 1, and Per Acre Values of Produce of Wheat, Oats, and Corn 1866-1901

Year	Average Per Acre Yield in Bushels			Average Farm Price Per Bushel in Cents			Average Per Acre Value in Dollars		
	Oats*	Corn†	Wheat‡	Oats*	Corn†	Wheat‡	Oats*	Corn†	Wheat‡
1866-75	26.5	23.7	12.8	71	67	138	18.82	15.88	17.66
1876-85	27.7	19.8	10.8	49	62	103	13.57	12.28	11.12
1886-95	23.1	19.0	10.4	40	50	78	9.24	9.50	8.11
1891	24.5	19.5	12.0	47	55	87	11.52	10.73	10.44
1892	24.5	21.4	12.3	38	45	75	9.31	9.63	9.23
1893	25.1	17.6	10.5	42	54	58	10.54	9.50	6.09
1894	32.7	19.0	15.1	39	56	54	12.75	10.64	8.15
1895	20.7	26.4	5.7	26	31	66	5.38	8.18	3.76
1896	20.0	9.5	11.7	34	41	75	6.80	3.90	8.78
1897	25.0	18.5	15.8	27	41	89	6.75	7.58	14.06
1898	29.7	25.0	14.8	28	34	68	8.32	8.50	10.06
1899	25.0	18.0	11.1	30	36	68	7.50	6.48	7.55
1900	38.0	18.0	18.4	30	47	64	11.40	8.46	11.78
1901	16.3	11.6	8.9	60	80	78	9.78	9.28	6.94

* U. S. Department of Agriculture Yearbook, 1900, pp. 528-30.
  U.S.D.A. Yearbook, 1910, pp. 776-78.
† U.S.D.A. Yearbook, 1910, pp. 503-5.
  U.S.D.A. Yearbook, 1900, pp. 757-59.
‡ U.S.D.A. Yearbook, 1910, pp. 516-18.
  U.S.D.A. Yearbook, 1900, pp. 768-70.

TABLE IV

Computed Values of Texas Farm Products, 1870-1900

Year	Total value of farm products	Per farm value computations from Census and Agriculture Yearbook data	
		All farm products	Cotton
1870 °	$ 49,185,170	$805	$331
1880 †	65,204,329	374	217
1890 ‡	111,699,430	490	265
1900 §	209,346,434	594	267

° *U. S. Census, 1870: A Compendium of the Census,* pp. 688-709.
† *U. S. Census, 1880: Statistics of Agriculture,* pp. 133-36.
‡ *U. S. Census, 1890: Statistics of Agriculture,* pp. 228-31.
§ *U. S. Census, 1900,* Vol. V: *Agriculture,* pp. 298-301.

TABLE V

Texas Population, Number of Farms, Acres in Farms, Acres of Improved Land, and Value of Farms, 1870-1900

Year	Total population *	Number of farms †	Total number of acres in farms †	Total number acres improved land †	Value of farms, equipment and livestock †
1870	818,579	61,125	18,396,523	2,964,836	$ 80,777,550
1880	1,591,749	174,184	36,292,219	12,650,314	256,084,364
1890	2,235,523	228,126	51,406,937	20,746,215	552,127,104
1900	3,048,710	352,190	125,807,017	19,576,076	962,476,273

*U. S. Census, 1900, Vol. VIII: *Manufactures*, p. 862.
†U. S. Census, 1900, Vol. V: *Agriculture*, pp. 688-709.

TABLE VI

Data on Texas Farm Mortgages, 1890-1910

Class	1890	1900	1910
Total	126,314	171,975	195,863
Free from mortgage	119,093	125,504	128,082
Mortgaged	7,221	38,408	64,008
Unknown	....	8,063	3,773

Owned Homes or Farm Homes Mortgaged

	1890	1910
Number	7,221	48,024
Value — Land and buildings	$15,583,093	$297,880,832
Amount of mortgage debt	6,494,633	76,089,272
Per cent of debt to value	41.7	25.5
Average value per farm	$2,158	$6,203
Average debt per farm	$ 899	$1,584

U.S. Census, 1910: Abstract of the Census with Supplement for Texas, pp. 669-70.

TABLE VII

Texas Farms Operated by Owners and by Tenants, 1880-1900

	Farms operated by owners and managers			Farms operated by tenants		
	Number	Per Cent		Number		Per Cent
1880	108,716	62.4		65,468		37.6
			Share tenants		53,379	
			Cash tenants		12,089	
1890	132,616	58.1		95,510		41.9
			Share tenants		75,429	
			Cash tenants		20,081	
1900	177,199	50.3		174,991		49.7
			Share tenants		149,181	
			Cash tenants		25,810	

U.S. Census, 1910: Abstract of the Census with Supplement for Texas, p. 668.

TABLE VIII

Acreage Harvested and Yields of Selected Farm Crops in Texas, 1870-1900

	1870 †	1880 ‡	1890 §	1900 ¶
Wheat —				
Bushels				
produced	415,112	2,567,737	4,283,344	12,266,320
Acres				
harvested°	94,000°°	373,570	352,477	1,027,947
Corn —				
Bushels				
produced	20,554,538	29,065,172	69,112,150	109,970,350
Acres				
harvested°	1,000,000°°	2,468,587	3,079,907	5,017,690
Oats —				
Bushels				
produced	762,663	4,893,359	12,581,360	24,190,668
Acres				
harvested°	....	238,010	528,924	847,225
Cotton —				
Bales ginned	350,628	805,284	1,471,242	2,506,212
Acres				
harvested°	922,000°°	2,178,435	3,934,525	6,960,367

° *U. S. Census, 1910: Abstract of the Census with Supplement for Texas,* p. 676.

† *U. S. Census, 1890: Statistics of Agriculture,* pp. 103-4.

‡ *U. S. Census, 1880: Statistics of Agriculture,* pp. 177, 212.

§ *U. S. Census, 1890: Statistics of Agriculture,* pp. 74-83.

¶ *U. S. Census, 1900,* Vol. VI: *Agriculture,* pp. 322-25.

°° *Fluctuations in Crops and Weather, 1866-1948,* U.S. Department of Agriculture, Statistical Bulletin 101, June, 1951, pp. 80-81.

TABLE IX

Values of Wheat, Corn, Oats, and Cotton for Texas, 1870-1900[*]

Crop	1870	1880	1890	1900
Wheat	$ 391,866	$ 2,441,918	$ 3,589,442	$ 7,592,852
Corn	10,153,941	11,509,808	34,970,748	39,259,415
Oats	297,439	1,761,609	5,334,496	6,241,192
Total value for grain	$10,843,246	$15,713,335	$43,894,686	$ 53,093,459
Cotton	$21,212,994	$39,458,916	$63,263,406	$107,510,010 [†]
Excess of cotton value over grain	$10,369,748	$23,745,581	$19,368,720	$ 54,416,551

[*] Compiled from production data in Table VIII, and price data from *U.S.D.A. Yearbook, 1910*, pp. 501 (corn); 512 (wheat); 526 (oats); 574 (cotton).

[†] The 1900 price for cotton estimated at 8.5 cents per pound from cotton market reports of the *Dallas Morning News* for 1900. The *U.S.D.A. Yearbook* quoted no cotton price for 1900.

Values of Wheat, Corn, Oats, and Cotton as Quoted in the *Texas Almanac*

	1870	1880	1890	1900
Wheat	$ 2,119,000	$ 3,158,000	$ 3,396,000	$ 14,973,000
Corn	22,260,000	36,702,000	36,590,000	45,402,000
Oats	884,000	3,312,000	5,665,000	10,488,000
Total value for grain	$25,263,000	$43,172,000	$45,651,000	$ 70,863,000
Cotton	$36,176,000 [§]	$54,782,000	$67,864,000	$139,641,000
Excess of cotton value over grain	$10,913,000	$11,610,000	$22,213,000	$ 68,778,000

[‡] *Texas Almanac and State Industrial Guide, 1945-1946*, pp. 190-91; 196-97.

[§] *Ibid.*, computed from data on pp. 190-91.

TABLE X

Texas Cotton, Average Per Acre Lint, Average Price Per Pound, Computed Per Acre Value, 1869-1900

Year	Average Yield Per Acre of Lint in Pounds °	Year	Average Farm Price Per Pound, Dec. 1 Cents †	Computed Per Acre Value in Dollars
		1869	16.5	38.94
		1870	12.1	28.56
		1871	17.9	42.24
		1872	16.5	38.94
		1873	14.1	33.28
		1874	13.0	30.69
1866-75	236	1875	11.1	26.20
		1876	9.9	19.01
		1877	10.5	20.16
		1878	8.2	15.74
		1879	10.2	19.58
1876-85	192	1880	9.8	18.82
		1881	10.0	19.20
		1882	9.9	19.01
		1883	9.0	17.28
		1884	9.2	17.66
		1885	8.5	16.32
1886-95	198	1886	8.1	16.04
		1887	8.5	16.83
		1888	8.5	16.83
		1889	8.3	16.43
		1890	8.6	17.03
	In Fraction Bales			
1891	----		7.3	15.18 ‡
1892	----		8.4	18.31 ‡
1893	----		7.0	13.02 ‡
1894	.48		4.6	11.04
1895	.45		7.6	17.10
1896	.33		6.6	10.89
1897	.31		6.6	10.23
1898	.39		5.7	11.12
1899	.48		7.4	17.76
1900	.37		8.5 §	14.87 §

° U.S.D.A. Yearbook, 1910, p. 574; U.S.D.A. Yearbook, 1900, p. 812.

† U.S.D.A. Yearbook, 1910, pp. 580-81.

‡ Texas per acre yield figures were not given for these years; hence national averages were used in computing per acre values.

§ U.S.D.A. Yearbooks gave no prices for 1900 and 1901. The per pound price was computed from cotton market reports of the Dallas Morning News for 1900.

TABLE XI

Average Farm Value for the United States of Cattle, Milch Cows, Horses, and Mules, 1867 to 1901°

Year	CATTLE Price per head	MILCH COWS Price per head	HORSES Price per head	MULES Price per head
1867	$15.79	$28.74	$59.05	$66.94
1868	15.06	26.56	54.27	56.04
1869	18.73	29.15	62.57	79.23
1870	18.87	32.70	67.43	90.42
1871	20.78	33.89	71.14	91.98
1872	18.12	29.45	67.41	87.14
1873	18.06	26.72	66.39	85.15
1874	17.55	25.63	65.15	81.35
1875	16.91	25.74	61.10	71.89
1876	17.00	25.61	57.29	66.46
1877	15.99	25.47	55.83	64.07
1878	16.72	25.74	56.63	62.03
1879	15.38	21.71	52.36	56.00
1880	16.10	23.27	54.75	61.26
1881	17.33	23.95	58.44	69.79
1882	19.89	25.89	58.53	71.35
1883	21.81	30.21	70.59	79.49
1884	23.52	31.37	74.64	84.22
1885	23.25	29.70	73.70	82.38
1886	21.17	27.40	71.27	79.60
1887	19.79	26.08	72.15	78.91
1888	17.79	24.65	71.82	79.78
1889	17.05	23.94	71.89	79.49
1890	15.21	22.14	68.84	78.25
1891	14.76	21.62	67.00	77.88
1892	15.16	21.40	65.01	75.55
1893	15.24	21.75	61.22	70.68
1894	14.66	21.77	47.83	62.17
1895	14.06	21.97	36.29	47.55
1896	15.86	22.55	33.07	45.29
1897	16.65	23.16	31.51	41.66
1898	20.92	27.45	34.26	43.88
1899	22.79	29.66	37.40	44.96
1900	24.97	31.60	44.61	53.55
1901	19.93	30.00	52.86	63.97

° U.S.D.A. *Yearbook, 1910,* pp. 630 (cattle and milch cows); 628 (horses and mules).

TABLE XII

Average Farm Value for the United States of Sheep and Swine, 1867-1901°

Year	SHEEP Price per head	SWINE Price per head
1867	$2.50	$4.03
1868	1.82	3.29
1869	1.64	4.65
1870	1.96	5.80
1871	2.14	5.61
1872	2.61	4.01
1873	2.71	3.67
1874	2.43	3.98
1875	2.55	4.80
1876	2.37	6.00
1877	2.13	5.66
1878	2.21	4.85
1879	2.07	3.18
1880	2.21	4.28
1881	2.39	4.70
1882	2.37	5.97
1883	2.53	6.75
1884	2.37	5.57
1885	2.14	5.02
1886	1.91	4.26
1887	2.01	4.48
1888	2.05	4.98
1889	2.13	5.79
1890	2.27	4.72
1891	2.50	4.15
1892	2.58	4.60
1893	2.66	6.41
1894	1.98	5.98
1895	1.58	4.97
1896	1.70	4.35
1897	1.82	4.10
1898	2.46	4.39
1899	2.75	4.40
1900	2.93	5.00
1901	2.98	6.20

° *U.S.D.A. Yearbook, 1910*, pp. 635 (sheep); 641 (swine).

TABLE XIII

Number and Value of Texas Livestock, 1870-1900

	1870	1880	1890	1900
Horses, No. of *	424,504	805,606	1,125,840	1,174,003
Value of †	$23,344,000	$26,866,000	$ 44,527,000	$ 23,507,000
Asses and mules, No. of *	61,322	132,447	229,405	507,281
Value of †	$ 4,164,000	$ 9,042,000	$ 11,334,000	$ 9,166,000
Milch cows, No. of *	428,048	606,176	1,003,439	861,023
Value of †	$ 6,562,000	$ 8,013,000	$ 11,933,000	$ 17,518,000
Other cattle, No. of *	3,065,995	4,288,522	7,540,196	6,418,912
Value of †	$21,350,000	$41,333,000	$ 63,294,000	$ 77,736,000
Total No. cattle	3,494,043	4,894,698	8,543,635	7,279,935
Sheep, No. of *	714,351	3,651,633	4,264,187	1,439,940
Value of †	$ 2,079,000	$12,048,000	$ 7,128,000	$ 4,590,000
Swine, No. of *	1,202,445	2,449,623	2,255,220	2,665,614
Value of †	$ 2,681,000	$ 6,372,000	$ 8,073,000	$ 10,612,000
Value of all livestock including types not named in the above *	$37,425,194	$76,563,987	$138,409,274	$240,576,955

* U. S. Census, 1900, Vol. V: Agriculture, pp. 386-87; 700-708.

† Texas Almanac and State Industrial Guide, 1945-1946, pp. 214-17.

Values in the Almanac are based on prices as of January 1 of the given years, whereas the total values of all livestock were compiled by census enumerators in the course of census taking. This, in part, accounts for the apparent differences between census figures and Almanac figures. The Almanac totals run higher than census totals for 1870, 1880, and 1890, but lower than the census total for 1900.

The Almanac data also show the peak of the sheep population to be in 1880 instead of 1890 as shown by the census report. The Almanac data on sheep seem to be more in keeping with materials gathered from other sources than do the census figures.

TABLE XIV

Comparative Summary of the Manufacturing and Mechanical
Industries for the State of Texas, 1870-1900[*]

	1900	1890	1880	1870
Number of establishments	12,289	5,268	2,996	2,399
Capital	$ 90,433,882	$46,815,181	$ 9,245,561	$ 5,284,110
Wage earners, average number	48,153	34,794	12,159	7,927
Total Wages	$ 20,552,355	$15,148,495	$ 3,343,087	$ 1,787,835
Cost of material used	$ 67,102,769	$36,152,308	$12,956,269	$ 6,273,193
Value of products including custom work and repairing	$119,414,982	$70,433,551	$20,719,928	$11,517,302
Population	3,048,710	2,235,523	1,591,749	818,579

[*] *U. S. Census, 1900,* Vol. VIII: *Manufactures,* p. 862.

TABLE XV

Ten Leading Manufacturing Counties; Number of Establishments,
Capital Invested, and Value of Products, 1870 and 1900

County	Number of establishments	Capital invested	Value of products
1870: °			
Galveston	91	$ 710,950	$ 1,214,814
Marion	33	338,962	756,250
Harris	64	723,890	578,707
Refugio	13	101,700	556,900
Travis	91	178,825	464,626
McLennan	43	118,000	344,525
Walker	13	160,700	323,570
Wood	36	89,620	312,855
Dallas	44	106,322	279,983
Grayson	53	97,483	210,325
Totals	481	$ 2,626,452	$ 5,042,555
1900: †			
Harris	550	$ 8,069,482	$13,035,491
Dallas	489	7,178,301	11,789,053
El Paso	143	4,604,231	8,910,506
Bexar	333	4,388,318	6,897,629
Tarrant	290	2,922,090	5,669,886
Galveston	305	6,089,840	5,041,932
McLennan	302	2,493,524	3,128,554
Navarro	224	1,244,280	2,578,180
Travis	369	1,034,165	2,175,391
Jefferson	60	3,151,971	2,104,367
Totals	3,065	$41,176,202	$61,330,989

°*U. S. Census, 1870: Industry and Wealth*, pp. 572-73.
† *U. S. Census, 1900*, Vol. VIII: *Manufactures*, pp. 868-72.

TABLE XVI

Comparative Summary of the Manufacturing and Mechanical
Industries for the United States, 1870-1900°

	1900	1890
Number of establishments	512,286	355,405
Capital	$ 9,831,486,500	$6,525,050,759
Wage earners, average number	5,314,539	4,251,535
Total wages	$ 2,327,295,545	$1,891,209,696
Cost of materials used	$ 7,346,358,979	$5,162,013,878
Value of products, including custom work and repairing	$13,010,036,514	$9,372,378,843
Population †	75,994,575	62,622,250

	1880	1870
Number of establishments	253,852	252,148
Capital	$ 2,790,272,606	$2,118,208,769
Wage earners, average number	2,732,595	2,053,996
Total wages	$ 947,953,795	$ 775,584,343
Cost of materials used	$ 3,396,823,549	$2,488,427,242
Value of products, including custom work and repairing	$ 5,369,579,191	$4,232,325,442
Population †	50,155,783	38,558,371

° U. S. Census, 1900: Abstract, pp. 300-301.
† U. S. Census, 1910: Abstract of the Census with Supplement for Texas, p. 259.

TABLE XVII

Leading Industries in Texas; Number of Establishments, Capital Invested, and Value of Products, 1870 and 1900

Industry	Number of establishments	Capital invested	Value of products
1870: °			
Flouring and grist mill products	533	$ 1,066,893	$ 2,421,047
Lumber, sawed	324	870,491	1,960,851
Meat, packed beef	15	200,500	1,052,106
Carpentering and building	147	154,065	652,067
Blacksmithing	380	177,238	534,550
Butchering	7	79,150	484,775
Cotton goods	4	496,000	374,598
Saddlery and harness	138	153,590	348,307
Tin, copper, and sheet-iron ware	71	154,136	334,665
Sash, doors, and blinds	10	140,000	266,400
Totals	1,629	$ 3,492,063	$ 8,429,366
1900: †			
Lumber and timber products	637	$19,161,265	$16,296,473
Oil, cottonseed and cake	103	7,986,932	14,005,324
Flouring and grist mill products	289	4,273,490	12,333,730
Cars and general shop construction and repairs — railroads	56	3,730,792	8,314,691
Cotton ginning	3,222	9,282,101	5,886,923
Liquors and malt	9	4,439,012	2,689,606
Foundry and machine shop products	99	2,809,524	2,682,426
Planing mill — including sash, doors, and blinds	76	932,860	1,605,297
Clay products	171	1,496,666	1,212,266
Totals	4,662	$54,112,642	$65,026,736

° U. S. Census, 1870: Industry and Wealth, pp. 573-74.
† U. S. Census, 1900, Vol. VIII: Manufactures, p. 863.

Notes

CHAPTER I

1. Computed from *United States Census, 1910: Abstract of the Census with Supplement for Texas,* p. 666, and *United States Census, 1910,* Vol. VII: *Agriculture,* pp. 617-19.

2. October 13, 1876.

3. Reprint from the *Galveston Daily News,* October 15, 1878.

4. A. W. Neville, *The Red River Valley Then and Now* (Paris, Texas: North Texas Printing Co., 1948), pp. 184-85.

5. B. B. Paddock (ed.), *A Twentieth Century History and Biographical Record of North and West Texas* (Chicago: Lewis Publishing Co., 1906), I, 205.

6. *Galveston Daily News,* March 31, 1877.

7. *Ibid.,* October 2, 1878. A reprint.

8. George W. Tyler, *The History of Bell County* (San Antonio: Naylor, 1936), pp. 296-97.

9. *Frontier Echo* (Jacksboro), July 27, 1877.

10. William Curry Holden, *Alkali Trails or Social and Economic Movements of the Texas Frontier, 1846-1900* (Dallas: Southwest Press, 1930), p. 227.

11. Charles S. Potts, *Railroad Transportation in Texas* (Bulletin of the University of Texas, No. 119 [Austin, 1909]), pp. 42-43.

12. Paddock, *op. cit.,* pp. 180-81.

13. *Ibid.,* p. 194.

14. *United States Census, 1910: Abstract of the Census with Supplement for Texas,* p. 667.

15. *Ibid.,* p. 281.

16. *Ibid.,* p. 667.

17. *United States Census, 1910,* Vol. VIII: *Manufactures,* p. 862.

18. *Galveston Daily News,* September 1, 1880.

19. Edmund Thornton Miller, *A Financial History of Texas* (Bulletin of the University of Texas, No. 37 [Austin, 1916]), p. 158.

20. Seth S. McKay, "Texas During the Regime of E. J. Davis" (Master's thesis, University of Texas, 1919), p. 147.

21. The twenty counties are: Anderson, Bexar, Bowie, Brazoria, Cameron, Dallas, Galveston, Grayson, Harris, Harrison, Jefferson, Lamar, Lavaca, Marion, McLennan, Nueces, Tarrant, Travis, Trinity, Washington. Hereafter they are referred to as the eastern counties.

22. *United States Census, 1860: Agriculture of the United States in 1860,* pp. 140-48. Data for 1860 in this and the two succeeding paragraphs are taken from the reference here cited.

23. *United States Census, 1870, Industry and Wealth,* pp. 250-61. Data for 1870 in this and the two succeeding paragraphs are taken from the reference here cited.

24. The twenty counties are: Brewster, Childress, Coleman, Dallam, Ector, El Paso, Erath, Garza, Gillespie, Knox, Lamb, Lampasas, Potter, Reeves, Stephens, Taylor, Tom Green, Val Verde, Webb, Wichita. Hereafter they are referred to as the western counties.

25. Seth S. McKay, *Making the Constitution of Texas of 1876* (University of Pennsylvania Bulletin [Philadelphia, 1924]), pp. 45-56.

26. *Ibid.*, p. 74.

27. Ralph A. Smith, "The Grange Movement in Texas, 1873 - 1900," *Southwestern Historical Quarterly*, XLII (1939), 310.

28. *The Texas Almanac for 1870, and Emigrant's Guide to Texas* (Galveston: Richardson & Co.), p. 193.

29. Walter Prescott Webb, *The Great Plains* (Boston: Ginn and Company, 1931), p. 291.

30. Paddock, *op. cit.*, pp. 303-4.

31. *Galveston Daily News*, April 20, 1877.

32. Paddock, *op. cit.*, p. 112.

33. Holden, *op. cit.*, pp. 18-19. (A reprint from: Cook, *The Border and the Buffalo*, p. 113).

CHAPTER II

1. Paddock, *op. cit.*, p. 175.

2. *Texas Almanac for 1870*, p. 171.

3. T. C. Richardson, *East Texas Its History and Its Makers* (New York: Lewis Historical Publishing Company, 1940), II, 865.

4. Samuel B. McAlister, "The Building of the Texas and Pacific Railway" (Master's thesis, University of Texas, 1926), p. 78.

5. Paddock, *op. cit.*, p. 254.

6. *Taylor County News* (Abilene), August 17, 1888.

7. *Frontier Echo* (Jacksboro), March 31, 1876.

8. April 7, 1876.

9. Carl Coke Rister, *The Southwestern Frontier 1865-1881* (Cleveland: Arthur H. Clark, 1928), p. 242.

10. *Fort Griffin Echo*, April 26, 1879.

11. Potts, *op. cit.*, p. 15.

12. *Fort Griffin Echo*, August 14, 1880.

13. *Ibid.*, January 24, 1880. The underscoring is mine.

14. *Ibid.*, September 17, 1881.

15. *Galveston Daily News*, June 4, 1877.

16. *Ibid.*

17. Harley True Burton, "A History of the J. A. Ranch," *Southwestern Historical Quarterly*, XXXI (1928), 357.

18. Paddock, *op. cit.*, p. 221.

19. *Galveston Daily News*, January 15, 1878.

20. *Ibid.*, November 27, 1877.

21. *Albany Echo*, October 13, 1883.

22. Tyler, *op. cit.*, pp. 305-6.

23. *Taylor County News* (Abilene), October 16, 1885. Reprinted from the *Chronicle*.

24. Potts, *op. cit.*, p. 43.

25. Neville, *op. cit.*, p. 199.

26. S. G. Reed, *A History of the Texas Railroads* (Houston: St. Clair Publishing Company, 1941), pp. 212-13.

27. *Galveston Daily News*, May 3, 1876.

28. *Frontier Echo* (Jacksboro), February 16, 1877.

29. *Ibid.*, November 2, 1877.

30. Holden, *op cit.*, pp. 14-15.

31. *Frontier Echo* (Jacksboro), November 3, 1876.

32. *Galveston Daily News*, June 19, 1877.

33. *Ibid.*, September 10, 1876.

34. *Ibid.*, November 7, 1876. A reprint from the Mexia *Ledger*.

35. *Ibid.*, November 22, 1876. A reprint from the Palestine *Advocate*.

36. *Ibid.*, May 28, 1878. A reprint from the Beaumont *Lumberman*.

37. *Ibid.*, July 16, 1880.

38. Potts, *op. cit.*, p. 97.

39. S. G. Reed, "Land Grants and Other Aids to Texas Railroads," *Southwestern Historical Quarterly*, XLIX (1946), 521.

40. Reed, *History of Texas Railroads*, p. 160.

41. *Ibid.*, pp. 155-56.

42. Potts, *op. cit.*, p. 101.
43. Reed, *History of Texas Rail-roads*, p. 134.
44. Tyler, *op. cit.*, pp. 314-16.
45. Paddock, *op. cit.*, p. 187.
46. *Frontier Echo* (Jacksboro), November 9, 1877.
47. *Galveston Daily News*, April 4, 1878.
48. Paddock, *op. cit.*, p. 187.
49. *Galveston Daily News*, September 1, 1877.
50. *Ibid.*, September 5, 1878.
51. Reed, *History of Texas Rail-roads*, p. 154.
52. Potts. *op. cit.*, p. 43.
53. *Burke's Texas Almanac and Immigrant's Handbook for 1882* (Houston: J. Burke, Jr.), pp. 215-16.
54. Potts, *op. cit.*, p. 43.
55. F. W. Johnson, *History of Texas and Texans, 1799-1884* (Chicago and New York: American Historical Society, 1914), I, 589.
56. *Galveston Daily News*, February 25, 1880.
57. *Ibid.*, January 22, 1880.
58. *Ibid.*, June 22, 1880.
59. *Fort Griffin Echo*, August 21, 1880.
60. *Burke's Texas Almanac*, pp. 157-59.
61. Paddock, *op. cit.*, pp. 254-55.
62. *Burke's Texas Almanac*, pp. 126-27.
63. Johnson, *op. cit.*, I, 589.
64. Reed, *History of Texas Rail-roads*, p. 549.
65. *Ibid.*, pp. 544-46.
66. Potts, *op. cit.*, pp. 73-77.
67. Reed, *History of Texas Rail-roads*, pp. 551-52.
68. *Dallas Morning News*, October 6, 1885, p. 5.
69. Reed, *History of Texas Rail-roads*, pp. 565-67.
70. *Ibid.*, pp. 589-90.

CHAPTER III

1. Southwestern Immigration Company, *The State of Texas* (Archives, University of Texas), p. 97.
2. Tyler, *op. cit.*, p. 296.
3. Paddock, *op. cit.*, p. 253.
4. Southwestern, *State of Texas*, pp. 99-142.
5. *Texas Almanac and State Industrial Guide, 1904* (Galveston: A. H. Belo & Co.), pp. 203-391.
6. John D. Hicks, *The Populist Revolt* (Minneapolis: University of Minnesota Press, 1931), pp. 55-56.
7. Southwestern, *State of Texas*, p. 98.
8. *Frontier Echo* (Jacksboro), September 28, 1877.
9. *Galveston Daily News*, December 12, 1877. Reprinted from the Mason County *News-Item*.
10. *Taylor County News* (Abilene), January 22, 1886. Reprinted from the Albany *News*.
11. *Ibid.*, December 25, 1891. Reprinted from the *Texas Farm and Ranch*.
12. *Ibid.*, July 26, 1895.
13. Holden, *op. cit.*, pp. 242-43.
14. *Frontier Echo* (Jacksboro), June 30, 1875.
15. *Taylor County News* (Abilene), February 5, 1886. Reprinted from the New Orleans *Picayune*.
16. *Fort Griffin Echo*, January 25, 1879.
17. *Ibid.*, February 21, 1880.
18. *Dallas Morning News*, November 5, 1885.
19. *Taylor County News* (Abilene), May 11, 1888.
20. *Dallas Morning News*, November 5, 1885.
21. *Ibid.*, October 10, 1885.
22. Burton, *op. cit.*, pp. 357-58.
23. *United States Census, 1910: Abstract of the Census with Supplement for Texas*, p. 667.
24. *United States Census, 1900*, Vol. V: *Agriculture*, p. xxvi.
25. Tyler, *op. cit.*, p. 296.
26. Homer S. Thrall, *The People's Illustrated Almanac, Texas Hand-Book and Immigrants' Guide, for 1880* (St. Louis: N. D. Thompson & Co.), p. 32.
27. *Galveston Daily News*, May 31, 1878.

28. *Taylor County News* (Abilene), June 25, 1885.
29. *Galveston Daily News,* March 14, 1878.
30. *Ibid.,* May 30, 1877.
31. *Frontier Echo* (Jacksboro), October 26, 1877.
32. Holden, *op. cit.,* p. 244.
33. *Ibid.*
34. *Texas Almanac for 1870,* pp. 141-42.
35. *United States Census, 1880,* Vol. I: *Population,* pp. 78-91; *United States Census, 1910,* Vol. VII: *Agriculture,* pp. 632-50.
36. In making these comparisons of economic development between East and West Texas counties, data for 1870 are from *United States Census, 1870, Industry and Wealth,* pp. 250-61. Data on farm values at the turn of the century (1900) are from *United States Census, 1900,* Vol. V: *Agriculture,* pp. 298-301. With reference to the series of comparisons, further citations will be for 1900 data only.
37. *United States Census, 1900,* Vol. V: *Agriculture,* pp. 480-85.
38. *Ibid.*
39. *Ibid.,* Vol. VI: *Agriculture,* p. 193.
40. Reed, *History of Texas Railroads,* p. 739.
41. C. W. Raines, *Year Book for Texas, 1901* (Austin: Gammel Book Company, 1902), p. 353.
42. Thrall, *op. cit.,* pp. 53-54.
43. *Taylor County News* (Abilene), April 12, 1895.
44. *United States Census, 1900,* Vol VI: *Agriculture,* pp. 292 and 299.
45. *Ibid.,* p. 682.
46. *Ibid.,* p. 483.
47. Edwin P. Arneson, "Early Irrigation in Texas." *Southwestern Historical Quarterly,* XXV (1922), 121-22.
48. C. W. Raines, *Year Book for Texas, II* (Austin: Gammel-Statesman Publishing Co., 1903), p. 380.
49. *Dallas Morning News,* October 16, 1885, p. 2.
50. *Galveston Daily News,* April 15, 1876.

CHAPTER IV

1. James A. B. Scherer, *Cotton as a World Power* (New York: Frederick A. Stokes, 1916), p. 3.
2. Reed, *History of Texas Railroads,* p. 733.
3. Potts, *op. cit.,* p. 27.
4. McAlister, *op. cit.,* pp. 87-88.
5. Potts, *op. cit.,* p. 17.
6. Reed, *History of Texas Railroads,* p. 574.
7. Potts, *op cit.,* p. 17.
8. *Galveston Daily News,* October 11, 1879.
9. M. B. Hammond, *The Cotton Industry; An Essay in American Economic History* (New York: Macmillan Co., 1897), p. 171.
10. Tyler, *op. cit.,* pp. 296-97.
11. *Frontier Echo* (Jacksboro), October 20, 1876.
12. *Galveston Daily News,* September 30, 1880.
13. *U. S. Department of Agriculture Yearbook, 1910,* p. 580.
14. *Frontier Echo* (Jacksboro), November 10, 1876; September 7, 28, 1877.
15. *United States Census, 1870: Industry and Wealth,* pp. 250-61; *United States Census, 1900,* Vol. VI: *Agriculture,* pp. 434-35.
16. *Galveston Daily News,* September 28, 1876.
17. Thrall, *op. cit.,* p. 25.
18. *Ibid.,* p. 31.
19. *Texas Almanac, 1941-42* (Dallas: A. H. Belo Corp.), p. 204.
20. *Minutes of the Texas State Grange, 1873 and 1874,* p. 8.
21. Robert L. Hunt, *A History of Farmer Movements in the Southwest, 1873-1925* (College Station: A. & M. Press, 1935), p. 9.
22. Herbert Bock Edwards, "The Grange" (Unfinished doctoral dissertation, University of Texas), p. 142.
23. *Minutes of the Texas State Grange, 1874,* p. 16.
24. Hicks, *op. cit.,* p. 47.

25. John S. Spratt, "The Cotton Miner, 1865-1910," *American Quarterly*, IV (1952), 219.
26. *Ibid.*, p. 220.
27. *Texas Almanac, 1904*, p. 93.
28. Tyler, *op. cit.*, p. 298.
29. *Taylor County News* (Abilene), May 21, 1886.
30. *Ibid.*, May 17, 1889.
31. Hammond, *op. cit.*, p. 79.
32. W. H. Johnson, *Cotton and Its Production* (London: Macmillan Co., 1926), p. 380.
33. Gilbert H. Collings, *The Production of Cotton* (New York: John Wiley & Sons, 1926), p. 89.
34. Hammond, *op. cit.*, pp. 145-46, 149, 224-25.
35. *Proceedings of the Third Annual Session of the Texas State Grange, 1877*, p. 9.
36. September 23, 1879.
37. *Minutes of the Eighth Annual Meeting of the Texas Co-operative Association, Patrons of Husbandry, 1886*, p. 6.
38. Hammond, *op. cit.*, p. 171.
39. Thrall, *op. cit.*, p. 49.
40. Raines, *Year Book for Texas, 1901*, pp. 78-80.
41. Thrall, *op. cit.*, p. 29.
42. U. S. Department of Agriculture, *The Cotton Plant* (Washington: Government Printing Office, 1896), p. 367.
43. *Texas Almanac, 1904*, p. 142.
44. *Texas Almanac for 1870*, p. 105.
45. *United States Census, 1900*, Vol. VIII: *Manufactures*, p. 863.
46. *Galveston Daily News*, November 18, 1877.
47. Reed, *History of Texas Railroads*, p. 730.
48. U. S. Department of Agriculture, *The Cotton Plant*, p. 372.
49. *United States Census, 1900*, Vol. VIII: *Manufactures*, p. 863.
50. Thrall, *op. cit.*, p. 49.
51. Tyler, *op. cit.*, p. 311.
52. Neville, *op. cit.*, p. 216.
53. *Galveston Daily News*, September 1, 1880.

54. *United States Census, 1900*, Vol. VIII: *Manufactures*, p. 872.
55. Thrall, *op. cit.*, p. 49.
56. *Galveston Daily News*, September 19, 1879.
57. *Texas Almanac for 1870*, p. 174.
58. April 23, 1879.
59. *Proc. 7th Ann. Sess. T. S. G., 1881*, pp. 22-23.
60. *United States Census, 1900*, Vol. VIII: *Manufactures*, p. 862.
61. Scherer, *op. cit.*, pp. 305-6.
62. U. S. Department of Agriculture, *The Cotton Plant*, p. 335.
63. *Texas Almanac, 1904*, p. 113.

CHAPTER V

1. *Taylor County News* (Abilene), July 2, 1886.
2. Clara M. Love, "History of the Cattle Industry in the Southwest," *Southwestern Historical Quarterly*, XIX (1916), 371-72.
3. *United States Census, 1900*, Vol. V: *Agriculture*, pp. 700-708.
4. *Ibid.*, pp. 480-85; *United States Census, 1870: Industry and Wealth*, pp. 250-61.
5. *Galveston Daily News*, January 21, 1879.
6. *Frontier Echo* (Jacksboro), June 22, 1877.
7. March 1, 1879.
8. *Galveston Daily News*, September 29, 1876.
9. *Ibid.*, April 18, 1877.
10. Paddock, *op. cit.*, p. 225.
11. Edward Everett Dale, *Cow Country* (Norman: University of Oklahoma Press, 1942), p. 13.
12. Burton, *op. cit.*, pp. 89-90.
13. Rudolf A. Clemen, *The American Livestock and Meat Industry* (New York: Ronald Press Co., 1923), p. 182.
14. Southwestern, *State of Texas*, pp. 118-19.
15. *Ibid.*
16. *Ibid.*, p. 120.
17. Rupert N. Richardson and Carl C. Rister, *The Greater Southwest* (Glendale, Calif.: Arthur H. Clark, 1935), p. 356.

18. Osgood, *op. cit.*, pp. 199-200.
19. Thrall, *op. cit.*, p. 26.
20. Osgood, *op. cit.*, pp. 31-32.
21. *Frontier Echo* (Jacksboro), January 25, 1878.
22. February 2, 1884.
23. Richardson and Rister, *op. cit.*, p. 356.
24. *Taylor County News* (Abilene), July 3, 1885.
25. Clemen, *op. cit.*, pp. 185-86.
26. *Fort Griffin Echo*, July 2, 1881.
27. Paddock, *op. cit.*, pp. 158-59.
28. Osgood, *op. cit.*, p. 105.
29. Holden, *op. cit.*, p. 45.
30. *Taylor County News* (Abilene), February 18, 1887. Reprinted from *Drovers' Journal.*
31. *Ibid.*, July 29, 1887.
32. *Ibid.*, May 15, 1885.
33. *Ibid.*, May 22, 1885.
34. *Ibid.*, May 7, 1886.
35. Burton, *op. cit.*, p. 335.
36. *Taylor County News* (Abilene), July 29, 1887. Reprinted from the Anson *Voice.*
37. Dale, *op. cit.*, p. 83.
38. *Taylor County News* (Abilene), October 16, 1885. Reprinted from the *Planter & Stockman.*
39. *Ibid.*, June 8, 1894.
40. Paddock, *op. cit.*, p. 159.
41. *Ibid.*
42. *Frontier Echo* (Jacksboro), September 22, 1876.
43. *Fort Griffin Echo*, November 19, 1881.
44. *Taylor County News* (Abilene), December 21, 1888.
45. Burton, *op. cit.*, pp. 256-57.
46. *Ibid.*, p. 90.
47. *Albany Echo*, June 2, 1883.
48. *Taylor County News* (Abilene), February 25, 1887.
49. *The Texas Almanac, 1904*, p. 125.
50. Reed, *History of Texas Railroads*, p. 744.
51. *Galveston Daily News*, August 28, 1879. Reprinted from the Fort Worth *Democrat.*
52. *Ibid.*, April 18, 1877.
53. *Ibid.*, July 30, 1879.
54. Paddock, *op. cit.*, p. 305.
55. *Texas Almanac for 1870*, pp. 119-20. Reprinted from the *Texas Almanac for 1859.*
56. *Ibid.*, p. 152.
57. *Galveston Daily News*, November 16, 1877.
58. *Ibid.*, May 12, 1876.
59. *Fort Griffin Echo*, November 5, 1881.
60. *Galveston Daily News*, May 23, 1878.
61. Paul S. Taylor, "Historical Note on Dimmit County, Texas," *Southwestern Historical Quarterly*, XXXIV (1931), 84.
62. *Fort Griffin Echo*, April 24, 1880.
63. *Taylor County News* (Abilene), June 25, 1885.
64. *Fort Griffin Echo*, October 2, 1880.
65. *Dallas Morning News*, November 9, 1885.
66. *Fort Griffin Echo*, January 18, 1879.

CHAPTER VI

1. Roscoe C. Martin, *The People's Party in Texas* (University of Texas Bulletin [Austin, 1933]), pp. 18-19.
2. *Frontier Echo* (Jacksboro), July 19, 1878. Reprinted from the Fort Worth *Democrat.*
3. Ernest W. Winkler (ed.), *Platforms of Political Parties in Texas* (University of Texas Bulletin, No. 53 [Austin, 1916]), p. 181.
4. *Ibid.*, p. 194.
5. *Ibid.*, pp. 180-85.
6. *Ibid.*, p. 222.
7. *Ibid.*, pp. 235-36.
8. Marcus Lee Hansen, *The Immigrant in American History* (Cambridge: Harvard University Press, 1940), pp. 85-86.
9. Reuben McKitrick, *The Public Land System of Texas, 1823-1910* (University of Wisconsin Bulletin, No. 905 [Madison, 1918]), p. 9.
10. Raines, *Year Book for Texas, 1901*, p. 102.
11. Burton, *op. cit.*, p. 246.
12. *Ibid.*

13. *Galveston Daily News,* May 3, 1879.
14. *Taylor County News* (Abilene), April 16, 1886.
15. McKitrick, *op. cit.,* p. 5.
16. Miller, *op. cit.,* pp. 329-34.
17. *Frontier Echo* (Jacksboro), October 25, 1878.
18. *Fort Griffin Echo,* March 1, 1879. The underscoring in mine.
19. *Galveston Daily News,* October 14, 1879.
20. *Taylor County News* (Abilene), May 14, 1886.
21. *Albany Echo,* September 22, 1883.
22. *Ibid.,* August 18, 1883.
23. *Ibid.,* August 25, 1883.
24. *Ibid.,* September 1, 1883.
25. William C. Holden, "The Problem of Maintaining the Solid Range on the Spur Ranch," *Southwestern Historical Quarterly,* XXXIV (1931), 18.
26. *Texas Business Directory for 1878-9,* pp. 357-61.
27. Miller, *op. cit.,* p. 293.
28. Hicks, *op. cit.,* pp. 91-92.
29. Hunt, *op. cit.,* p. 18.
30. Hicks, *op. cit.,* p. 430.
31. *Proc. 8th Ann. Sess. T. S. G., 1882,* p. 11.
32. *Galveston Daily News,* September 4, 1879.
33. *Taylor County News* (Abilene), May 22, 1891.
34. Winkler, *op. cit.,* p. 319.
35. *Taylor County News* (Abilene), January 25, 1889.
36. *Ibid.,* August 15, 1889.
37. *Ibid.,* March 16, 1888.
38. *Frontier Echo* (Jacksboro), May 4, 1877.
39. Miller, *op. cit.,* p. 281.
40. *Ibid.,* pp. 399, 409; *United States Census, 1900,* Vol. VIII: *Manufactures,* p. 862; also see Appendix, Table IV.
41. Raines, *Year Book for Texas, 1901,* p. 51.
42. Miller, *op. cit.,* p. 281.
43. *Fort Griffin Echo,* August 30, 1879.

44. *Ibid.,* June 8, 1879.
45. Paddock, *op. cit.,* p. 180.
46. *Ibid.,* p. 198.
47. *Ibid.,* p. 199.
48. Tyler, *op. cit.,* p. 334.
49. *Taylor County News* (Abilene), October 19, 1894. Reprinted from the *Texas Stockman.*
50. Catherine Nugent (ed.), *Life Work of Thomas L. Nugent* (Stephenville, Texas: Catherine Nugent, 1896), pp. 251-52.
51. *Taylor County News* (Abilene), January 5, 1894.
52. *Ibid.,* April 20, 1894.
53. *Ibid.,* June 15, 1894.
54. Tyler, *op. cit.,* p. 329.
55. *Galveston Daily News,* September 9 and October 30, 1880; *Texas Almanac for 1870,* pp. 132, 152; *Proc. 3rd Ann. Sess. T. S. G., 1877,* p. 34.
56. *Galveston Daily News,* February 25, 1880.
57. *Ibid.,* January 1, 1880.
58. Thrall, *op. cit.,* p. 47.
59. *Galveston Daily News,* September 2, 1879.
60. *Ibid.,* July 30, 1879.
61. *Ibid.,* July 31, 1879.
62. *Weekly Herald* (Dallas), June 11, 1885.
63. Carrie J. Crouch, *Young County History and Biography* (Dallas: Dealey and Lowe, 1937), pp. 101-2.
64. *Dallas Morning News,* July 18, 1886.
65. *Taylor County News* (Abilene), May 25, 1888.
66. *Ibid.,* September 28, 1888.
67. *Ibid.,* August 27, 1886.
68. *Daily Herald* (Dallas), February 17, 1887.
69. *Dallas Morning News,* July 5, 1886.
70. *Taylor County News* (Abilene), July 29, 1887. Reprinted from the Anson *Voice.*
71. *Ibid.,* July 23, 1886. Reprinted from the *Cultivator.*
72. Holden, *Alkali Trails,* p. 131.
73. *Taylor County News* (Abilene), July 30, 1886. Reprinted from the Cisco *Round-up.*

74. *Dallas Morning News,* April 25, 1887.
75. *Taylor County News* (Abilene), July 16, 1886.
76. *Ibid.,* July 1, 1887. Reprinted from the Cisco *Round-up.*
77. *Ibid.,* May 13, 1887. The underscoring is mine.
78. *Ibid.,* August 6, 1886.
79. *Ibid.,* August 13, 1886.
80. *Ibid.,* January 7, 1887.
81. *Ibid.,* February 25 and March 11, 1887.
82. *Ibid.,* September 17, 1886.
83. *Ibid.,* July 16, 1886.
84. *Ibid.,* August 20, 1886.
85. *Ibid.,* July 16, 1886.
86. *Ibid.,* July 1, 1887.
87. *Frontier Echo* (Jacksboro), April 13, 1877.
88. *Taylor County News* (Abilene), January 27, 1893.
89. *Fort Griffin Echo,* November 29, 1879.
90. Paddock, *op. cit.,* p. 162.
91. T. R. Havins, "Texas Fever," *Southwestern Historical Quarterly,* LII (1949), 158-62.
92. *Taylor County News* (Abilene), September 3, 1897.

CHAPTER VII

1. Hunt, *op. cit.,* p. 7.
2. Solon J. Buck, *The Granger Movement, 1870-1880* (Cambridge: Harvard University Press, 1933), p. 27.
3. Edwards, *op. cit.,* pp. 22-23.
4. *Minutes of the Texas State Grange, 1873,* pp. 1-2.
5. *Weekly Herald* (Dallas), October 11, 1873.
6. *Minutes of the Texas State Grange, 1874,* p. 16.
7. Edwards, *op. cit.,* pp. 3-7; 10-12.
8. Ralph A. Smith, "A. J. Rose, Agrarian Crusader of Texas" (Doctoral dissertation, University of Texas, 1938), p. 328.
9. *Proc. 4th Ann. Sess. T. S. G., 1878,* p. 6.
10. *Proc. 5th Ann. Sess. T. S. G., 1879,* p. 19.

11. *Proc. 3rd Ann. Sess. T. S. G., 1877,* pp. 54-56.
12. Smith, "A. J. Rose," p. 49.
13. *Minutes of the Texas State Grange, 1874,* pp. 7-8.
14. *Ibid.,* p. 10.
15. *Proc. 3rd Ann. Sess. T. S. G., 1877,* p. 22.
16. H. P. N. Gammel, *The Laws of Texas, 1822-1897* (Austin: Gammel Book Company, 1898), VIII, 1417-18.
17. Reed, *History of Texas Railroads,* p. 575. Reprinted from *Galveston News.*
18. Gammel, *op. cit.,* IX, 263.
19. *Proc. 8th Ann. Sess. T. S. G., 1882,* pp. 9-10.
20. Reed, *History of Texas Railroads,* p. 571.
21. Gammel, *op. cit.,* IX, 373-76.
22. Smith, "Grange Movement in Texas," p. 312.
23. Edwards, *op. cit.,* pp. 189-91.
24. *Proc. 4th Ann. Sess. T. S. G., 1878,* pp. 14-15.
25. *Proc. 5th Ann. Sess. T. S. G., 1879,* p. 7.
26. *Proc. 8th Ann. Sess. T. S. G., 1883,* p. 33.
27. *Proc. 4th Ann. Sess. T. S. G., 1878,* pp. 24, 51.
28. *Proc. 5th Ann. Sess. T. S. G., 1879,* p. 21.
29. *Proc. 4th Ann. Sess. T. S. G., 1878,* p. 56.
30. *Proc. 3rd Ann. Sess. T. S. G., 1877,* p. 42.
31. *Proc. 5th Ann. Sess. T. S. G., 1879,* p. 21.
32. *Ibid.,* p. 37.
33. *Ibid.,* pp. 36-37.
34. *Proc. 7th Ann. Sess. T. S. G., 1881,* p. 27.
35. *Galveston Daily News,* June 6, 1877.
36. *Proc. 3rd Ann. Sess. T. S. G., 1877,* p. 44.
37. *Proc. 7th Ann. Sess. T. S. G., 1881,* p. 19.
38. Edwards, *op. cit.,* pp. 203-4.
39. *Ibid.,* pp. 200-201.
40. Ralph Smith, "The Cooperative Movement in Texas, 1870 - 1900,"

Southwestern Historical Quarterly, XLIV (1941), 34.
41. Proc. 4th Ann. Sess. T. S. G., 1878, p. 28.
42. Galveston Daily News, May 20, 1876.
43. Ibid., March 10, 1877.
44. Smith, "Cooperative Movement in Texas," pp. 33-34.
45. Proc. 3rd Ann. Sess. T. S. G., 1877, pp. 58-59.
46. Ibid., pp. 10-11.
47. Ibid., p. 48.
48. Ibid., pp. 41-42.
49. Tyler, op. cit., p. 300.
50. Galveston Daily News, June 6, 1877.
51. Edwards, op. cit., pp. 75-76.
52. Minutes of the Third Annual Meeting of the Texas Co-operative Association, 1881, pp. 3-4, 7.
53. Min. 4th Ann. Mtg. T. C. A., 1882, p. 38; Ann. Mtg. T.C.A., 1880, p. 8.
54. Min. 9th Ann. Mtg. T. C. A., 1887, p. 8; Min. 13th and 14th Ann. Mtgs. T.C.A., 1892, pp. 24-25.
55. Min. 5th Ann. Mtg. T. C. A., 1883, p. 31.
56. Min. 6th Ann. Mtg. T. C. A., 1884, p. 18.
57. Min. 5th Ann. Mtg. T. C. A., 1883, p. 34.
58. Min. 7th Ann. Mtg. T. C. A., 1885, p. 18.
59. Min. 10th Ann. Mtg. T. C. A., 1888, p. 8.
60. Min. 19th and 20th Ann. Mtgs. T.C.A., 1897 & 1898, p. 15.
61. Min. 13th and 14th Ann. Mtgs. T.C.A., 1892, pp. 10-11.
62. Min. 6th Ann. Mtg. T. C. A., 1884, p. 17; Min. 7th Ann. Mtg. T.C. A., 1885, p. 17.
63. Min. 13th and 14th Ann. Mtgs. T.C.A., 1892, p. 16.
64. Ibid., pp. 41-44.
65. Min. 15th Ann. Sess. T. C. A., 1893, pp. 8-9.
66. Min. 13th and 14th Ann. Mtgs. T.C.A., 1892, pp. 42-43.
67. Min. 16th Ann. Sess. T. C. A., 1894, p. 11.

68. Smith, "The Cooperative Movement in Texas," p. 48.
69. Min. 3rd Ann. Mtg. T. C. A., 1881, p. 15.
70. Ibid., pp. 39-40.
71. Min. 6th Ann. Mtg. T. C. A., 1884, p. 42.
72. Min. 4th Ann. Mtg. T. C. A., 1882, p. 18.
73. Ibid., pp. 23-24.
74. Min. 6th Ann. Mtg. T. C. A., 1884, p. 38.
75. Min. 7th Ann. Mtg. T. C. A., 1885, p. 13.
76. Min. 4th Ann. Mtg. T. C. A., 1882, p. 25.
77. Min. 6th Ann. Mtg. T. C. A., 1884, p. 41.
78. Min. 13th and 14th Ann. Mtgs. T.C.A., 1892, p. 26.
79. Min. 9th Ann. Mtg. T. C. A., 1887, p. 16.
80. Ibid., pp. 10-11.
81. Min. 7th Ann. Mtg. T. C. A., 1885, p. 13.
82. Ibid., p. 27.
83. Min. 9th Ann. Mtg. T. C. A., 1887, p. 7.
84. Min. 11th Ann. Sess. T. C. A., 1889, p. 13.
85. Ann. Mtg. T. C. A., 1880, pp. 10-11.
86. Min. 6th Ann. Mtg. T. C. A., 1884, p. 27.
87. Ibid., p. 32.
88. Min. 9th Ann. Mtg. T. C. A.; Minutes of Texas Mutual Fire Insurance Co., p. 7.
89. Ibid., pp. 2-3.
90. Min. 15th Ann. Sess. T. C. A., 1893, p. 19.
91. Min. 12th Ann. Sess. T. C. A., 1890, p. 9.
92. Smith, "The Cooperative Movement in Texas," pp. 51-52.
93. Min. 10th Ann. Mtg. T. C. A., 1888, pp. 9-10.
94. Tyler, op. cit., p. 301.
95. Solon J. Buck, Agrarian Crusade (New Haven: Yale University Press, 1920), pp. 75-76.

CHAPTER VIII

1. Buck, *Agrarian Crusade*, pp. 111-12.
2. Ralph Smith, "The Farmers' Alliance in Texas, 1875-1900," *Southwestern Historical Quarterly*, XLVIII (1945), 346-48.
3. Buck, *Agrarian Crusade*, pp. 112-13.
4. Smith, "The Farmers' Alliance," pp. 348-50.
5. C. W. Macune, "The Farmers Alliance" (Unpublished manuscript, Archives, University of Texas, 1920), pp. 3-4.
6. Hicks, *op. cit.*, pp. 104-5.
7. Smith, "Farmers' Alliance in Texas," pp. 353-54.
8. Macune, *op. cit.*, pp. 9-10.
9. Smith, "Farmers' Alliance in Texas," p. 353.
10. Hunt, *op. cit.*, p. 30.
11. Macune, *op. cit.*, pp. 10-13.
12. Smith, "Farmers' Alliance in Texas," pp. 351-52.
13. *Dallas Morning News*, October 3, 1885, p. 2.
14. *Ibid.*, October 6, 1885, p. 2.
15. *Ibid.*, October 5, 1885, p. 2.
16. *Ibid.*, October 10, 1885, p. 3.
17. *Ibid.*, October 11, 1885, p. 2.
18. *Ibid.*, October 18, 1885, p. 2.
19. *Ibid.*, November 4, 1885, p. 2.
20. *Ibid.*, October 18, 1885, p. 2.
21. *Ibid.*, November 6, 1885, p. 2.
22. Macune, *op. cit.*, pp. 20-23.
23. *Ibid.*, p. 14.
24. *Ibid.*, pp. 14-17.
25. Hicks, *op. cit.*, pp. 106-7.
26. Macune, *op. cit.*, pp. 16-19.
27. Hunt, *op. cit.*, p. 34.
28. Macune, *op. cit.*, p. 32.
29. Hunt, *op. cit.*, p. 36; quoted from an article by Clarence Ousley, *Popular Science Quarterly*, April, 1890, pp. 821-28.
30. Hicks, *op. cit.*, pp. 135-36.
31. Macune, *op. cit.*, pp. 24-25.
32. *Ibid.*, pp. 23-26.
33. *Ibid.*, pp. 30-31.
34. Hicks, *op. cit.*, pp. 135-37.
35. Macune, *op. cit.*, pp. 34-35.

36. Hicks, *op. cit.*, p. 140.
37. Macune, *op. cit.*, pp. 26-29.
38. Hunt, *op. cit.*, p. 40.
39. *Dallas Moring News*, November 1, 1885, p. 2.
40. *Taylor County News* (Abilene), October 7, 1887.
41. *Dallas Morning News*, October 18, 1885, p. 8.
42. Winkler, *op. cit.*, pp. 234-35.
43. Tyler, *op. cit.*, p. 328.
44. Hunt, *op. cit.*, p. 35.
45. *Ibid.*, p. 41.
46. Hicks, *op. cit.*, p. 160.
47. *Ibid.*, p. 162.
48. *Taylor County News* (Abilene), July 31, 1891.
49. Buck, *Agrarian Crusade*, p. 142.
50. Tyler, *op. cit.*, p. 326.
51. Edward Stanwood, *History of the Presidency* (Boston and New York: Houghton Mifflin Company, 1916) I, 511-12.
52. Nugent, *op. cit.*, p. 99.

CHAPTER IX

1. Johnson, *Texas and Texans*, I, 589.
2. *Ibid.*, p. 590.
3. M. M. Crane, "Recollections of the Establishment of the Texas Railroad Commission," *Southwestern Historical Quarterly*, L (1947), 478.
4. Winkler, *op. cit.*, p. 236.
5. *Ibid.*, pp. 270-71.
6. *Ibid.*, p. 267.
7. Crane, *op. cit.*, p. 478.
8. *Ibid.*, p. 479.
9. O. M. Roberts, "The Political, Legislative and Judicial History of Texas for Its Fifty Years of Statehood, 1845-1895," in D. C. Wooten (ed.), *A Comprehensive History of Texas, 1685-1897* (Dallas: W. G. Scraff, 1898), II, 275.
10. Winkler, *op. cit.*, pp. 276-79; 282-83; 288.
11. Crane, *op. cit.*, p. 482.
12. Gammel, *op. cit.*, X, 157.
13. *Ibid.*
14. Hicks, *op. cit.*, p. 177.
15. Eliot Jones, *Principles of Rail-*

way Transportation (New York: Macmillan Co., 1931), p. 214.

16. *Ibid.*, p. 309.

17. Johnson, *Texas and Texans*, I, 605-6.

18. Charles S. Potts, "Texas Stock and Bond Law," *Annals of the American Academy of Political and Social Science*, Philadelphia, May 1, 1914, pp. 162-63.

19. *Ibid.*, p. 163.

20. Roberts, *op. cit.*, p. 303.

21. *Second Annual Report of the Railroad Commission of the State of Texas, 1893*, p. 25. ·

22. Theodore A. Fetter, *Southwestern Freight Rates* (Boston: Christopher Publishing House, 1934), p. 48.

23. *First Annual Report of the Railroad Commission of the State of Texas, 1892*, pp. ix-x.

24. Potts, *Railroad Transportation*, pp. 160-61.

25. Fetter, *op. cit.*, p. 52.

26. Potts, *Railroad Transportation*, pp. 133-34.

27. *Second Annual Report of the Railroad Commission of the State of Texas, 1893*, p. 4.

28. Reagan v. Farmers' Loan and Trust Co., 154 U.S. 367 (1894).

29. *Ibid.*, p. 412.

30. *Ibid.*, p. 401.

31. *Ibid.*, p. 413.

32. Potts, *Railroad Transportation*, p. 173.

33. *Seventh Annual Report of the Railroad Commission of the State of Texas, 1898*, pp. 2-3.

34. Potts, *Railroad Transportation*, p. 173.

35. Johnson, *Texas and Texans*, I, 590.

36. *Seventh Annual Report of the Railroad Commission of the State of Texas, 1898*, pp. 2-3.

37. *Min. 17th Ann. Mtg. T.C.A., 1895*, pp. 7-8.

38. *Ibid.*, pp. 8-9.

39. Raines, *Year Book for Texas, 1901*, p. 342.

40. Potts, *Railroad Transportation*, p. 164.

41. *Taylor County News* (Abilene), August 27, 1897.

42. Potts, *Railroad Transportation*, pp. 157-58.

CHAPTER X

1. A. B. Cox, "Economic History of Texas During the Period of Reconstruction" (Master's thesis, University of Texas, 1914), p. 45.

2. *Frontier Echo* (Jacksboro), May 17, 1878.

3. W. C. Holden, "The Problem of Hands on the Spur Ranch," *Southwestern Historical Quarterly*, XXXV (1932), 195-98.

4. State figures are data, or were computed from data, in *United States Census, 1900*, Vol. VIII: *Manufactures*, p. 862. National figures are data, or were computed from data, in *U. S. Census, 1900: Abstract*, pp. 300-301.

5. *Galveston Daily News*, January 8, 1877.

6. *Ibid.*, May 10, 1876.

7. *Ibid.*, July 23, 1877.

8. *Ibid.*, May 2, 1880.

9. *Ibid.*, December 7, 1880.

10. *Dallas Morning News*, October 7, 1885, p. 3.

11. *Ibid.*, October 21, 1885, p. 2.

12. *Taylor County News* (Abilene), April 9, 1886.

13. *Dallas Morning News*, October 21, 1885, p. 2.

14. *Ibid.*, October 25, 1885, p. 2.

15. *Galveston Daily News*, May 8, 1877.

16. *Ibid.*, July 27, 1877.

17. *Ibid.*, July 31, 1877.

18. *Ibid.*, July 27, 1877.

19. *Ibid.*, April 25, 1876.

20. *Ibid.*, October 1, 1880.

21. *Ibid.*, October 2, 1880.

22. Ruth A. Allen, *Chapters in the History of Organized Labor in Texas* (Bureau of Research in the Social Sciences, University of Texas, 1941), pp. 37-39.

23. *Dallas Morning News*, October 29, 1885, p. 3.

24. *Ibid.*, November 4, 1885, p. 3.

25. *Ibid.*, November 8, 1885, p. 1.

26. *Galveston Daily News*, April 9, 1878.
27. *Ibid.*, January 23, 1880.
28. *Dallas Morning News*, October 10, 1885, p. 2.
29. Missouri Pacific Railway Company v. Richmond, XI Southwestern Reporter (Perm. ed.) 355-58 (1889).
30. Raines, *Year Book for Texas, 1901*, p. 206.
31. *Dallas Morning News*, November 19, 1885, p. 5.
32. *Ibid.*, December 10, 1885, p. 2.
33. Allen, *op. cit.*, pp. 46-53.
34. *Frontier Echo* (Jacksboro), May 24, 1878.
35. *Galveston Daily News*, July 27, 1877.
36. *Ibid.*, July 13, 1878.
37. *Ibid.*, June 2, 1880.
38. *Ibid.*, October 12, 1880.
39. Allen, *op. cit.*, p. 91.
40. Johnson, *Texas and Texans*, I, 590-91.
41. *Taylor County News* (Abilene), February 5, 1886.
42. Allen, *op. cit.*, pp. 20-21.
43. *Taylor County News* (Abilene), April 16, 1886.
44. *Dallas Morning News*, October 12, 1885, p. 5.
45. Ruth A. Allen, *The Great Southwest Strike* (Bureau of Research in the Social Sciences, University of Texas, 1942), pp. 44-45.
46. *Ibid.*, pp. 123-24.
47. *Taylor County News* (Abilene), April 23, 1886.
48. *Ibid.*, July 23, 1886.
49. Allen, *Great Southwest Strike*, p. 136.
50. *Taylor County News* (Abilene), March 26, 1886. Reprint from the Sulphur Springs *Enterprise*.
51. *Ibid.*
52. *Ibid.*, April 9, 1886.
53. Allen, *Chapters in the History of Organized Labor in Texas*, p. 123.
54. *Ibid.*, pp. 123-24.

CHAPTER XI

1. *Galveston Daily News*, November 9, 1876.

2. *Ibid.*, June 22, 1877.
3. *Ibid.*, June 1, 1876.
4. Moritz Tiling, *History of the German Element in Texas from 1820-1850, and Historical Sketches of the German Singers' League and Houston Turnverein from 1853-1913* (Houston: Moritz Tiling, 1913), p. 129.
5. *Fort Griffin Echo*, January 25, 1879.
6. *Ibid.*, May 31, 1879.
7. *Ibid.*, July 12, 1879.
8. *Ibid.*
9. *Ibid.*, July 19, 1879.
10. *Frontier Echo* (Jacksboro), November 16, 1877.
11. *Ibid.*, June 7, 1878.
12. *Ibid.*, July 26, 1878.
13. *Galveston Daily News*, May 31, 1877.
14. Thrall, *op. cit.*, pp. 32-33.
15. *Ibid.*, p. 48.
16. *Galveston Daily News*, January 25, 1877.
17. *Texas Business Directory for 1878-79* (The available copy in the library of Southern Methodist University gave no publication data).
18. *Directory of the City of Dallas for 1878-79* (The available copy in the library of Southern Methodist University gave no publication data).
19. Thrall, *op. cit.*, pp. 49-50.
20. *Fort Griffin Echo*, May 8, 1880.
21. *Ibid.*, May 15, 1880.
22. John H. Cochran, *Dallas County: A Record of Its Pioneers and Progress* (Dallas: Arthur S. Mathis, Service Publishing Co., 1928), p. 118.
23. *Galveston Daily News*, September 9, 1877.
24. Raines, *Year Book for Texas*, II, 360-61.
25. *Texas Almanac and State Industrial Guide, 1904*, p. 145.
26. Raines, *Year Book for Texas, 1901*, p. 240.
27. Louis J. Wortham, *A History of Texas from Wilderness to Commonwealth* (Fort Worth: Wortham-Molyneaux Company, 1924), V, 211.
28. Thrall, *op. cit.*, p. 28.

29. Raines, *Year Book for Texas, 1901*, pp. 240-41.

30. Reed, *History of Texas Railroads*, p. 730.

31. Raines, *Year Book for Texas, 1901*, p. 242.

32. *Ibid.*, p. 241.

33. *Ibid.*, p. 390.

34. *Ibid.*, p. 243.

35. *Ibid.*, p. 242.

36. *Texas Almanac for 1870*, pp. 134-36.

37. Raines, *Year Book for Texas, II*, 360.

38. *Taylor County News* (Abilene), June 25, 1885.

39. *Texas Almanac for 1870*, p. 183.

40. Reed, *History of Texas Railroads*, p. 756.

41. *Galveston Daily News*, September 6, 1879.

42. *Ibid.*, January 15, 1879.

43. *Fort Griffin Echo*, June 14, 1879.

44. *Galveston Daily News*, October 30, 1879.

45. *Fort Griffin Echo*, January 8, 1881.

46. *Galveston Daily News*, December 1, 1880.

47. Weldon Hardman, *Boom Town, the Story of Thurber* (Wichita Falls: Johnnie Barley Printing Co., 1930), pp. 21-25.

48. Reed, *History of Texas Railroads*, p. 730.

49. *Galveston Daily News*, March 3, 1877.

50. *Ibid.*, August 19, 1880.

51. *Taylor County News* (Abilene), November 6, 1891.

52. Paddock, *op. cit.*, p. 229.

53. *Fort Griffin Echo*, January 31, 1880.

54. *Taylor County News* (Abilene), April 10, 1885.

55. *Ibid.*, June 17, 1892.

56. *Ibid.*, January 11, 1889.

57. *Galveston Daily News*, October 21, 1879.

58. *Ibid.*, November 4, 1879.

59. *Fort Griffin Echo*, October 16, 1880.

60. *Dallas Morning News*, November 1, 1885, p. 2.

61. Reed, *History of Texas Railroads*, pp. 748-49.

62. Paddock, *op. cit.*, p. 178.

63. *Galveston Daily News*, February 8, 1879.

64. Tyler, *op. cit.*, pp. 308-11.

65. *Galveston Daily News*, October 11, 1879.

66. *Dallas Morning News*, October 13, 1885; Tyler, *op. cit.*, p. 331.

67. *Fort Griffin Echo*, November 22, 1879.

68. *Albany Echo*, November 17, 1882.

69. *Dallas Morning News*, November 11, 1885, p. 2.

70. *Galveston Daily News*, June 23, 1878.

71. *Ibid.*, June 1, 1877.

72. *Ibid.*, July 11, 1879.

73. Tyler, *op. cit.*, p. 309.

74. *Texas Almanac for 1870*, pp. 163-64.

75. *Frontier Echo* (Jacksboro), October 4, 1878.

76. Paddock, *op. cit.*, p. 155.

77. *Galveston Daily News*, August 10, 1878.

78. *Taylor County News* (Abilene), June 12, 1885.

79. *Galveston Daily News*, March 15, 1877.

80. *Albany Echo*, August 25, 1883.

81. *Dallas Morning News*, November 2, 1885, p. 2.

82. *Ibid.*, October 23, 1885, p. 3.

83. *Ibid.*, November 12, 1885, p. 2.

84. Paddock, *op. cit.*, pp. 198-99.

85. *Taylor County News* (Abilene), December 8, 1893.

86. *Galveston Daily News*, December 27, 1876.

87. *Ibid.*, February 5, 1878.

88. Clemen, *op. cit.*, pp. 222-24.

89. Love, *op. cit.*, pp. 298-99.

90. Osgood, *op. cit.*, p. 107.

91. C. A. Warner, "Texas and the Oil Industry," *Southwestern Historical Quarterly*, L (1947), 2.

92. *Galveston Daily News*, February 15, 1880.

93. *Taylor County News* (Abilene), December 11, 1891.

94. Raines, *Year Book for Texas, 1901*, pp. 289-90.

95. Warner, *op. cit.*, p. 23.

96. *Ibid.*, p. 7.

97. *Ibid.*

98. Carl Coke Rister, *Oil! Titan of the Southwest* (Norman: University of Oklahoma Press, 1949), pp. 47-48.

99. Raines, *Year Book for Texas, 1901*, pp. 292, 294.

100. Boyce House, "Spindletop," *Southwestern Historical Quarterly*, L (1947), 39.

101. Warner, *op. cit.*, p. 7.

102. Raines, *Year Book for Texas, 1901*, pp. 293-94.

103. House, *op. cit.*, p. 40.

104. Raines, *Year Book for Texas, 1901*, p. 293.

105. *Ibid.*, p. 390.

CHAPTER XII

1. *United States Census, 1910*, Vol. I: *Population*, pp. 56-57.

2. See Appendix, Table V.

3. See Appendix, Table III.

4. See Appendix, Tables IX and XIV.

5. *United States Census, 1910*, Vol. I: *Population*, p. 772.

6. See Appendix, Table XVII.

7. See Appendix, Table XV.

8. Warner, *op. cit.*, p. 23; Raines, *Year Book for Texas*, II, 366.

9. Raines, *Year Book for Texas, 1901*, pp. 390-91.

10. Reed, *History of Texas Railroads*, p. 730.

11. *Texas Almanac, 1945-1946*, p. 267.

12. *Ibid.*, pp. 180, 264.

Bibliography

This bibliography includes only those sources from which ideas, data, or information have been directly incorporated into the text of this study. A comprehensive bibliography on the history of Texas for the last quarter of the nineteenth century would be far too unwieldy. Furthermore, when writing on a relatively involved historical topic, an author draws from the whole of his past experiences. If this be true, any bibliography, at best, is incomplete.

BOOKS

Allhands, J. L. *Boll Weevil: Recollections of the Trinity & Brazos Valley Railway.* Houston: Anson Jones Press, 1946.

Buck, Solon J. *The Agrarian Crusade. (The Chronicles of America Series,* Vol. XLV.) New Haven: Yale University Press, 1920.

————. *The Granger Movement 1870-1880.* Cambridge: Harvard University Press, 1933.

Clemen, Rudolf Alexander. *The American Livestock and Meat Industry.* New York: Ronald Press, 1923.

Collings, Gilbert H. *The Production of Cotton.* New York: John Wiley & Sons, 1926.

Crouch, Carrie J. *Young County History and Biography.* Dallas: Dealey and Lowe, 1936.

Dale, Edward Everett. *Cow Country.* Norman: University of Oklahoma Press, 1942.

Fetter, Theodore A. *Southwestern Freight Rates.* Boston: Christopher Publishing House, 1934.

Gammel, H. P. N. *The Laws of Texas, 1822-1897.* 10 vols. Austin: Gammel Book Co., 1898.

Hammond, M. B. *The Cotton Industry; An Essay in American Economic History.* New York: Macmillan Co., 1897.

Hansen, Marcus Lee. *The Immigrant in American History,* ed. Arthur M. Schlesinger. Cambridge: Harvard University Press, 1940.

Hicks, John D. *The Populist Revolt.* Minneapolis: University of Minnesota Press, 1931.

Holden, William Curry. *Alkali Trails or Social and Economic Movements of the Texas Frontier, 1846-1900.* Dallas: Southwest Press, 1930.

Johnson, F. W. *History of Texas and Texans, 1799-1884,* edited and brought down to 1914 by E. C. Barker and E. W. Winkler. 5 vols. Chicago and New York: American Historical Society, 1914.

Johnson, W. H. *Cotton and Its Production.* London: Macmillan Co., 1926.

Jones, Eliot. *Principles of Railway Transportation.* New York: Macmillan Co., 1931.

Neville, A. W. *The Red River Valley Then and Now.* Paris, Texas: North Texas Printing Co., 1948.

Nugent, Catherine (ed.). *Life Work of Thomas L. Nugent.* Stephenville, Texas: Catherine Nugent, 1896.

Osgood, Ernest Staple. *The Day of the Cattleman.* Minneapolis: University of Minnesota Press, 1929.

Paddock, B. B. (ed.). *A Twentieth Century Historical and Biographical Record of North and West Texas.* Chicago: Lewis Publishing Co., 1906.

Reed, S. G. *A History of Texas Railroads.* Houston: St. Clair Publishing Co., 1941.

Richardson, Rupert Norval and Rister, Carl Coke. *The Greater Southwest.* Glendale, California: Arthur H. Clark Co., 1935.

Richardson, T. C. *East Texas: Its History and Its Makers,* ed. Dabney White. 4 vols. New York: Lewis Historical Publishing Co., 1940.

Rister, Carl Coke. *Oil! Titan of the Southwest.* Norman: University of Oklahoma Press, 1949.

————. *The Southwestern Frontier, 1865-1881.* Cleveland: Arthur H. Clark Co., 1928.

Roberts, O. M. "The Political, Legislative and Judicial History of Texas for Its Fifty Years of Statehood, 1845-1895," *A Comprehensive History of Texas, 1685-1897,* ed. D. G. Wooten. Vol. II. Dallas: W. G. Scarff, 1898.

Scherer, James A. B. *Cotton as a World Power:* A Study in the Economic Interpretation of History. New York: Frederick A. Stokes Co., 1916.

Stanwood, Edward. *A History of the Presidency.* 2 vols. Boston: Houghton Mifflin Co., 1916.

Tiling, Moritz. *History of the German Element in Texas from 1820-1850, and Historical Sketches of the German Singers' League and Houston Turnverein from 1853-1913.* Houston: Moritz Tiling, 1913.

Tyler, George W. *History of Bell County*, ed. Charles W. Ramsdell. San Antonio: Naylor Co., 1936.

Webb, Walter Prescott. *The Great Plains.* Boston: Ginn and Co., 1931.

Wortham, Louis J. *A History of Texas from Wilderness to Commonwealth.* 5 vols. Fort Worth: Wortham-Molyneaux Co., 1924.

ARTICLES

Arneson, Edwin P. "Early Irrigation in Texas," *Southwestern Historical Quarterly*, XXV (October, 1921), 121-30.

Burton, Harley True. "A History of the J A Ranch," *Southwestern Historical Quarterly*, XXXI (October, 1927), 89-115 (January, 1928), 221-60 (April, 1928), 325-64; XXXII (July, 1928), 29-66.

Crane, M. M. "Recollections of the Establishment of the Texas Railroad Commission," *Southwestern Historical Quarterly*, L (April, 1947), 478-86.

Gard, Wayne. "The Fence-Cutters," *Southwestern Historical Quarterly*, LI (July, 1947), 1-15.

Havins, T. R. "Texas Fever," *Southwestern Historical Quarterly*, LII (October, 1948), 147-62.

Holden, William Curry. "The Problem of Hands on the Spur Ranch," *Southwestern Historical Quarterly*, XXXV (January, 1932), 194-207.

———. "The Problem of Maintaining the Solid Range on the Spur Ranch," *ibid.*, XXXIV (July, 1930), 1-19.

House, Boyce. "Spindletop," *Southwestern Historical Quarterly*, L (July, 1946), 36-43.

Love, Clara M. "History of the Cattle Industry in the Southwest," *Southwestern Historical Quarterly*, XIX (April, 1916), 370-99; XX (July, 1916), 1-18.

Potts, Charles S. "Texas Stock and Bond Law," reprint from the *Annals of the American Academy of Political and Social Science* (Philadelphia), (May 1, 1914).

Reed, S. G. "Land Grants and Other Aids to Texas Railroads," *Southwestern Historical Quarterly*, XLIX (April, 1946), 518-23.

Smith, Ralph. "The Co-operative Movement in Texas, 1870-1900," *Southwestern Historical Quarterly*, XLIV (July, 1940), 35-54.

———. "The Farmers' Alliance in Texas, 1875-1900," *ibid.*, XLVIII (January, 1945), 346-69.

———. "The Grange Movement in Texas, 1873-1900," *ibid.*, XLII (April, 1939), 297-315.

Spratt, John S. "The Cotton Miner, 1865-1910," *American Quarterly*, IV (Fall, 1952), 214-34.

Taylor, Paul S. "Historical Note on Dimmit County, Texas," *Southwestern Historical Quarterly*, XXXIV (October, 1930), 79-90.

Warner, C. A. "Texas and the Oil Industry," *Southwestern Historical Quarterly*, L (July, 1946), 1-24.

MONOGRAPHS, BULLETINS, AND PAMPHLETS

Allen, Ruth. *Chapters in the History of Organized Labor in Texas.* ("University of Texas Publication," No. 4143.) Austin: University of Texas, 1941.

————. *The Great Southwest Strike.* ("University of Texas Publication," No. 4214.) Austin: University of Texas, 1942.

Burke's Texas Almanac and Immigrant's Handbook for 1882. Compiled by J. Burke, Jr. Houston: J. Burke, Jr.

Cochran, John. *Dallas County: A Record of Its Pioneers and Progress.* Dallas: Arthur S. Mathis, Service Publishing Co., 1928.

Directory of the City of Dallas for 1878-79. N.d., n.p.

Hardman, Weldon. *Boom Town, the Story of Thurber.* 52nd Anniversary Souvenir Edition. Wichita Falls, Texas: Johnnie Barley Printing Co., 1930.

Hunt, Robert Lee. *A History of Farmer Movements in the Southwest, 1873-1925.* College Station: A. & M. Press, 1935.

Lang, Aldon Socrates. *Financial History of the Public Lands in Texas.* ("Bulletin of Baylor University," XXXV, No. 3) Waco, 1932.

McKay, Seth Shepard. *Making the Constitution of Texas of 1876.* ("University of Pennsylvania Bulletin") Philadelphia, 1924.

McKitrick, Reuben. *The Public Land System of Texas, 1823-1910.* ("University of Wisconsin Bulletin," No. 905.) Madison, 1918.

Macune, C. W. "The Farmers Alliance." Unpublished manuscript in the archives of the University of Texas, 1920. Copied by the University of Texas Library Archives Collection through the courtesy of Dr. C. W. Ramsdell, 1938.

Martin, Roscoe C. *The People's Party in Texas.* (Bureau of Research in the Social Sciences, Study No. 4.) Austin: University of Texas, 1933.

Miller, Edmund Thornton. *A Financial History of Texas.* ("Bulletin of the University of Texas," No. 37.) Austin, 1916.

Minutes of the Annual Meeting of the Texas Co-operative Association, Patrons of Husbandry. Cotton Gin Grange Hall, Freestone County, Texas, 1880.

Minutes of the Texas State Grange, Patrons of Husbandry. Dallas, Texas, October 7, 1873, and Austin, Texas, April 14-18, 1874.

Minutes of the Third-Twentieth Annual Meetings of the Texas Co-operative Association. 1881-1898.

Potts, Charles S. *Railroad Transportation in Texas.* ("Bulletin of the

University of Texas," No. 119, Humanitarian Series, No. 7.) Austin, 1909.

Proceedings of the Third Annual Session of the Texas State Grange, Patrons of Husbandry. Tyler, Texas, January 9-16, 1877.

Proc. 4th Ann. Sess. T.S.G., P.H. Bryan, Texas, January 9-15, 1878.

Proc. 5th Ann. Sess. T.S.G., P.H. Sherman, Texas, January 14-18, 1879.

Proc. 7th Ann. Sess. T.S.G., P.H. Austin City, Texas, January 11-15, 1881.

Proc. 8th Ann. Sess. T.S.G., P.H. Belton, Texas, August 8-12, 1882.

Proc. 10th Ann. Sess. T.S.G., P.H. Galveston, Texas, August 12-15, 1884.

Raines, C. W. (ed.). *Year Book for Texas, 1901.* Austin: Gammel Book Co., 1902.

————. *Year Book for Texas,* II. Austin: Gammel-Statesman Publishing Co., 1903.

Southwestern Immigration Company. *The State of Texas.* N.d., n.p., *circa* 1880.

Texas Almanac, 1904, 1941-42, 1945-46. Dallas: A. H. Belo.

Texas Almanac for 1870, and Emigrant's Guide to Texas. Galveston: Richardson & Co.

Texas Business Directory for 1878-79. N.d., n.p.

Thrall, Homer S. *The People's Illustrated Almanac, Texas Hand-Book and Immigrant's Guide for 1880.* St. Louis: N. D. Thompson & Co.

Winkler, Ernest W. (ed.). *Platforms of Political Parties in Texas.* ("Bulletin of the University of Texas," No. 53.) Austin, 1916.

UNPUBLISHED MASTER'S THESES AND DOCTORAL DISSERTATIONS

Cox, A. B. "Economic History of Texas During the Period of Reconstruction." Unpublished Master's thesis, University of Texas, 1914.

Edwards, Herbert Rock. "The Grange." Archives of the Texas Collection, University of Texas.

McAlister, Samuel B. "The Building of the Texas and Pacific Railway." Unpublished Master's thesis, University of Texas, 1926.

McKay, Seth Shepard. "Texas During the Regime of E. J. Davis." Unpublished Master's thesis, University of Texas, 1919.

Smith, Ralph Adam. "A. J. Rose, Agrarian Crusader of Texas." Unpublished Ph.D. dissertation, University of Texas, 1938.

GOVERNMENT PUBLICATIONS

Annual Report of the Railroad Commission of the State of Texas, 1892, 1893, 1894, 1895, 1896, 1897, 1898, 1899, 1900, 1901, 1902.

Biennial Report of the Secretary of State of the State of Texas, 1884, 1890, 1892, 1898, 1900, 1904.

Fluctuations in Crops and Weather 1866-1948. ("U. S. Department of Agriculture, Statistical Bulletin," No. 101.) Washington, D. C.: Government Printing Office, 1951.

Missouri Pacific Railway Company v. Richmond, XI *Southwestern Reporter* (Permanent edition). St. Paul: West Publishing Co., 1889.

1950 Agricultural Outlook Charts, U. S. Department of Agriculture, Bureau of Agricultural Economics, Washington, D. C.: Government Printing Office, 1949.

Report of the Secretary of State of the State of Texas, 1881, 1882.

Texas Legislative Manual. (Forty-Fifth Legislature). Austin: Von Boekmann-Jones Co., 1937.

The Cotton Plant. U. S. Department of Agriculture. Washington, D. C.: Government Printing Office, 1896.

United States Census, 1860, Agriculture in the United States in 1860. Washington, D. C.: Government Printing Office, 1864.

United States Census, 1870, Vol. III: *The Wealth and Industry of the United States.* Washington, D. C.: Government Printing Office, 1872.

United States Census, 1870, A Compendium. Washington, D. C.: Government Printing Office, 1872.

United States Census, 1880, Vol. I: *Population;* and Vol. III: *Statistics of Agriculture.* Washington, D. C.: Government Printing Office, 1883.

United States Census, 1890, Statistics of Agriculture. Washington, D. C.: Government Printing Office, 1895.

United States Census, 1900, Vols. V and VI: *Agriculture;* Vol. VIII: *Manufactures;* and *Abstract of the Twelfth Census of the United States.* Washington, D. C.: Government Printing Office, 1902.

United States Census, 1910, Vol. I: *Population;* Vol. VII: *Agriculture;* and *Abstract of the Census with Supplement for Texas.* Washington, D. C.: Government Printing Office, 1913.

United States Department of Agriculture Yearbook, 1900. Washington, D. C.: Government Printing Office, 1901.

U.S.D.A. Yearbook, 1910. Washington, D. C.: Government Printing Office, 1911.

154 *United States Supreme Court Reports,* 362-413, Reagan v. Farmers' Loan and Trust Company (Decided May 26, 1894). Book 38. Rochester, N. Y.: The Lawyers Co-operative Publishing Company, 1901.

TEXAS NEWSPAPERS

Albany Echo.
 1882: November 17.
 1883: June 2; July 28; August 18, 25; September 1, 22; October 13.
 1884: February 2.

Dallas Daily Herald, 1887: February 17.

Dallas Morning News.

 1885: October 1-3; 5-7, 10-13, 16, 18, 21-23, 25, 29; November 1, 2, 4-6, 8, 9, 11, 12, 19; December 10.

 1886: January 1; March 11-May 15; July 1, 5, 18; October 1.

 1887: January 1; April 1, 25; July 1; October 1.

 1888: January 3; April 2; July 3; October 1.

 1889: January 1; April 2; July 2; October 1.

 1890: January 1; April 1; July 1; October 1.

 1891: January 1; April 1; July 1; October 1.

 1892: January 1; April 1; July 1; October 1.

 1893: January 1; April 1; July 1; October 1.

 1894: January 3; April 1; July 1; October 1.

 1895: January 2; April 2; July 2; October 1.

 1896: January 1; April 1; July 1; October 1.

 1897: January 1; April 1; July 1; October 1.

 1898: January 1, 4; April 1; July 1; October 4.

 1899: January 1; April 1; July 1.

 1900: January 3, 4; April 1, 3; July 3; October 2, 3.

 1901: January 1, 3, 11; March 1; April 2,3; July 2, 4; October 1.

 1902: January 1, 5.

Fort Griffin Echo.

 1879: January 18, 25; March 1; April 26; May 31; June 14; August 30; November 22, 29.

 1880: January 24, 31; February 21; April 24; May 8, 15; August 14, 21; October 2, 16.

 1881: January 8; July 2; September 17; November 5, 19.

Frontier Echo (Jacksboro).

 1875: June 30.

 1876: March 31; April 7; September 22; October 13, 20; November 3, 10.

 1877: February 16; March 2; April 13; May 4; June 22; July 27; September 7, 28; October 26; November 2, 9.

 1878: January 25; February 15; May 3, 17, 24; June 7; July 26; October 4, 15, 25.

Galveston Daily News.

 1876: April 15, 25; May 1, 3, 7, 10, 12, 20; June 1; September 10, 19, 28, 29; November 7, 9, 22; December 27.

 1877: January 8, 25; February 14; March 3, 10, 15, 31; April 15, 18, 20; May 8, 30, 31; June 1, 4, 6, 19, 22; July 1, 23, 25, 27, 31; September 1, 9; November 10, 16, 18, 27; December 12.

 1878: January 15; February 5; March 14; April 4, 9; May 23, 28, 31; June 23; July 13; August 10; September 5; October 2.

 1879: January 15, 21; February 8; April 23; May 3; June 8; July

11, 30, 31; August 28; September 2, 4, 6, 19, 23; October
11, 14, 21; November 4.

1880: January 1, 22, 23; February 15, 25; May 2; June 2, 22; July
16; August 19; September 1, 9, 30; October 1-3, 12, 30;
November 17; December 1.

Taylor County News (Abilene).

1885: April 10; May 15, 22; June 12, 25; July 3; October 16.

1886: January 22; February 5; March 26; April 9, 16, 23; May 7,
:   14, 21; July 2, 16, 23, 30; August 6, 13, 20, 27; September 17.

1887: January 7; February 18, 25; March 11; May 13; July 1, 29;
:   October 7.

1888: March 16; May 11, 25; August 17; December 21.

1889: January 11, 25; May 17; August 15.

1891: May 22; July 31; November 6; December 11, 25.

1892: June 17.

1893: January 27; December 8.

1894: January 5; April 20; June 8, 15; October 19.

1895: April 12; July 26.

1897: August 27; September 3.

Weekly Herald (Dallas).

1873: October 11.

1885: June 11.

Index

Abilene, 33, 146
Adair-Goodnight: ranch holdings of, 121
Adamson, Mr.: buys mill equipment, 8
Agrarian organizations: reflect farmer views, 113
Agricultural: education, 50 f.; increase in production, 59 f.; productivity and economic change, 280; state, Texas as an, 277; surpluses, 7
Agricultural and Mechanical College, 163
Agriculture: basic feature of, 5; commercial, development of retarded, 20; commercial, encouraged by farm tenancy, 59; commercial, reasons for, 73 f.; declining prices of 41 f.; eternal problems of, 126 f.; number one industry, 281; price behavior in, 41; rise of commercial, 278, 279; self-contained, 38
Albany, 98
Albany Echo, 92
Alliance; *see* Grand State Farmers' Alliance of Texas
Amarillo, 36, 104, 220
American Federation of Labor: exponent of business unionism, 245; protests importation of stonecutters, 245; protests use of convicts, 245; springs from Knights of Labor, 244; trades councils, 245
American Sewing Machine: State Grange approves, 164
Anson *Voice,* 143; advises more tanks, 98

Archer County, 265
Arizona, 266
Armour, 269
Arneson, Edwin P., 54
Atchison, Topeka, & Santa Fe, 34
Austin, 25, 152, 163, 238, 245, 256, 268, 272

Back-to-the-farm movement, 57
Baggett, Maestro: revival of Alliance, 188
Baird, 33, 98, 233
Baku: Russian oil field, 274
Banks: adequacy of, 10; statistics on, 127 f.
Barbed wire: criticisms of, 16; estimated cost, 124; introduced, 15
Barnes Gin Works, 79
Barter, 3, 5
Baylor County, 265
Beaumont, 15, 257, 273, 275; *Frontiersman,* 232; *Lumberman,* 28
Beds: homemade, 6
Bee County, 107
Beef: cannery output, 270; packing by-products, 261; pork substitute, 7
Bell County, 25, 38, 48, 64, 65, 66, 71, 79, 137, 152, 190, 256, 266
Belton, 30, 79, 266, 267, 268
Bexar County, 282
Big Spring, 33
Bison; *see* Buffalo
Blacklisting: declared legal, 238
Blanco County, 189
Boerne: industries in, 246 f.
Boer War: horses and mules for, 103